CHURCHILL AND WAR

Churchill and War

Geoffrey Best

Hambledon and London

London and New York

Hambledon and London

102 Gloucester Avenue, London N W 1 8H X

175 Fifth Avenue
New York, N Y 10010
USA

First Published 2005

ISBN 1 85285 464 2

A description of this book is available from the
British Library and from the Library of Congress.

Typeset by Carnegie Publishing Ltd, Lancaster
and printed in Great Britain by Cambridge University Press.

Distributed in the United States and Canada
exclusively by Palgrave Macmillan,
a division of St Martin's Press.

Contents

Illustrations

Illustration Acknowledgements

The author and publishers are grateful to the following for their per-
mission to rep[roduce illustrations: Jack Darrah, plates 3 and 4; the
Hulton/Getty Picture Library, plates 5 and 20; the Imperial War
Museum, plates 1, 2, 6–19.

Preface

War was central to Churchill's life. He was a soldier before he was a politician. As an MP he was soon recognised as knowing more about war than anyone else in the House of Commons. He twice held high office in the First World War, and he became world famous as Britain's leader throughout the Second. He also wrote extensively about war. His first three books were based on his personal experience of campaigning on the edges of the British Empire. He wrote a five-volume memoir-history of the First World War, a four-volume biography of his famous soldier ancestor the first Duke of Marlborough, and then, after bringing the Second World War to a successful close, a six-volume memoir-history of that. Wars and warriors are prominent in both the most personal and the least personal of his books: *My Early Life* and the four-volume *History of the English-Speaking Peoples*.

Churchill's mixture of interests, talents and achievements made him a unique figure in the modern history of war. He knew active service in three wars, managed major naval and military departments in wartime and out of it, and had more ideas about how to fight war than any other politician and statesman of his time. His books about the two world wars are written with an urgent sense of their world-historical significance that gives them a character and value entirely of their own. He believed that to die in battle for your country was the highest and best form of death. (His favourite film from 1941, when it came out, was *Lady Hamilton*, which included the death of Nelson. Whenever he saw it, he wept.) At the same time, he admitted that he was horrified by war and he was somewhat abashed by his fascination with it. He was not the warmonger he was often alleged to have been by those who disliked or feared him, although by his own admission war excited him. When he was in it he fought to win, but he was statesman and moralist enough to wish that wars could be avoided. He enjoyed living in peace and was a principled and competent peacemaker. His last great international gesture was towards lessening the tensions of the Cold War.

The centrality of war to Churchill's life makes it all the more surprising that there is no previous book specifically on the subject. This is the gap I have set out to fill. The more I thought about his martial attributes and achievements, the more I felt that they deserved fuller attention than I was able to give them in the modest-sized biography I wrote a few years ago: *Churchill: A Study in Greatness* (2001). For example, there is the remarkable fact that he had achieved his eminence in war not as a man of war but as a politician, the result of a decision taken early in his long life. Almost everything he understood about the history of warfare and the conduct of war he picked up from places other than the barracks and the staff college. Professional military men thought him amateurish; and in some ways he was. He thought, however, that he knew more about their business than they did – and sometimes he was right.

Where did his immense understanding of war come from? How good, close up, are his writings about it? What did he learn in earlier years that was useful to him in later ones? What was his style as a commander in wartime? Was he as good a leader in the Second World War as he thought he was, and as his memoirs suggested? These are just some of the questions I have had in mind and have sought to answer.

Churchill was a man of unusual gifts who did many notable things, above all leading his nation and people through the shadows of 1940–41. He deserves his continuing fame in the world, and I am not at all surprised that books continue to be written about him. A much longer book than mine could certainly be written on Churchill and war. I hope to live to see it.

Acknowledgements

Many people have helped me during the writing of this book. Prominent among them have been Paul Addison, Tony Aldgate, Lorna Arnold, Brian Bond, Piers Brendon, Sebastian Cox, Alex Danchev, Jack Darrah, Michael R. D. Foot, Michael Gottesman, Paddy Griffith, Michael Herman, Sir Bryan Hopkin, Sir Michael Howard, Clifford Kinvig, Allen Packwood, David Reynolds, Lady Soames, Hew Strachan and John and Frances Walsh. I have not the pleasure of knowing Sir Martin Gilbert but, like other writers about Churchill, I must express a debt to him for his massive biography of the great man, upon which all of us gratefully draw.

Many libraries and librarians have made my work possible and pleasant. In Oxford, I gratefully salute the Bodleian and Codrington Libraries, the libraries of St Antony's and Balliol Colleges, and the Oxfordshire Central Library; in Cambridge, the Churchill Archives Centre at Churchill College and Trinity College Library; also the AWE Library and Corporate Archive. I am grateful to Curtis Brown Group Ltd for permission to quote from newspaper cuttings in the Churchill Archive; and to the Master and Fellows of Trinity College, Cambridge, for permission to quote from Walter Layton's draft memoirs.

Three people deserve individual thanks. Two of them are Hambledon and London's co-directors. Without Tony Morris's stimulus and encouragement this book would never have been started or, perhaps, finished. Without the benefit of Martin Sheppard's editorial skills the book would bear many more imperfections than those that remain. The third person to whom special thanks are due is, simply, my wife Marigold.

Abbreviations

Churchill's official biography, *Winston S. Churchill*, was begun by his son Randolph and finished by the historian Sir Martin Gilbert. Randolph wrote the first two volumes and Sir Martin the other six. The volumes they respectively wrote are referred to simply by their names: e.g. Randolph Churchill, ii, p. 453, and Gilbert, vii, pp. 120–24. A complication is introduced by the *Companion Volumes* of documents attached to each volume of the biography. These are indicated by the letters *CV*: e.g. Gilbert, iv, *CV*, i, pt 2, p. 433.

The slightly shortened titles of Churchill's own books are easily recognised. References to *The Second World War* are to the volumes and pages of its well-known first British edition (1948–54) and present no problems. The other three books to which frequent reference has been made – *The World Crisis, 1911–1918*; *Marlborough: His Life and Times*; and *My Early Life: A Roving Commission* – have appeared in so many different editions and languages (let alone shortened versions) that is has seemed best to make reference not to pages but to chapters, which are none of them long.

The books containing Churchill's wartime speeches and broadcasts, all compiled by Charles Eade, are referred to under their individual titles: *Into Battle* (1941); *The Unrelenting Struggle* (1942); *The End of the Beginning* (1943); *Onwards to Victory* (1944); *The Dawn of Liberation* (1945); and *Victory* (1946). All of those speeches, in company with thousands more, may also be found in the eight volumes of *Winston S. Churchill: His Complete Speeches*, edited by Robert Rhodes James (1974).

For Marigold

The Light of My Life

1

Blenheim

It is impossible at Blenheim Palace to forget for long the military hero for whom it was built: John Churchill, first Duke of Marlborough. His victory column dominates the grassy vista from the palace front, and visitors with exceptionally good eyesight can read on its plinth the twenty-thousand word eulogy that has, for nearly three centuries, done justice to him and his many battles. His battle of Blenheim (an anglicisation of the Austrian Blindheim) in 1704 was famous above all others and gave its name to the palace as much for its place in political as military history. It symbolised the securing of England's rising position in the world by arresting Louis XIV's bid, through the union of the French and Spanish crowns, for the hegemony of Europe and the domination of Europe's overseas empires. It was a battle that changed the course of history.

What the visitor is allowed to see today is substantially how its residents saw it a century or so ago. The military note so often sounded in the architectural adornments of the façade is repeated in the interior. The house – for it was and is a lived-in house as well as a showplace – is full of family portraits, in which the first Duke is often to be seen. The inner walls of the grand rooms along the southern front display the huge Flemish tapestries he caused to be made to commemorate the most notable events of his campaigns, including the siege of Lille, the assault on the fortress of Schellenberg and, most famous of all, the surrender at Blenheim of the French commander Marshal Tallard. The chapel's giant marble monument to the Duke and his devoted wife Sarah is oppressively huge, very martial also in its bas-relief representing again the surrender of Marshal Tallard. It is difficult not to feel that the widow who ordained it meant worshippers to have in mind her beloved husband at least as much as the Supreme Being, whose altar, architecturally speaking, stands in a very subordinate place.

In that chapel, soon after his birth on 30 November 1874, was chris-
tened Winston Leonard Spencer Churchill, first son of the younger son
of the seventh Duke. (He dropped the Leonard as soon as he became
independent enough to do so.) His parents never lived at Blenheim, and
it is not clear whether he was there much during his boyhood and adolescence; but it is said that he and his cousin 'Sunny', son of the eighth
Duke, played rowdy games of 'French and English' up and down the
palace.[1] However that may be, he loved the place, and he and Sunny (the
ninth Duke from 1892) were closely attached to one another. When at
the age of thirty-four he fell decisively in love, it was at Blenheim that
he chose to stage his proposal. Whatever his feelings about the great
house and heroic ancestry that added interest to his boyhood, they certainly were not the feelings of rejection they conceivably might have
been.

That boyhood had in it at least the normal amount of military fantasy; normal for those days if not for ours. The boy Winston's presents
at Christmas and birthdays included boxes of toy soldiers, of which he
amassed a collection of about 1500. From Versailles, where he had been
sent to improve his French, Winston wrote to his younger brother Jack
in January 1892 that he would get him from Bon Marché 'a few battalions of Russians, for two francs the dozen'.[2] Yet not every boy who plays
with toy soldiers and fights imaginary battles goes on to attain military
distinction. In seeking the sources of Winston's later talents for war it is
unwise to make too much of his boyhood enthusiasms. At least one of
his playmates, however, thought them noteworthy. His cousin Clare
Frewen, nine years his younger, recalled many years later that

> his playroom contained from one end to the other a plank table on trestles,
> upon which were thousands of lead soldiers arranged for battle. He organ-
> ized wars. The lead battalions were manoeuvred into battle, peas and pebbles
> committed great casualties, forts were stormed, cavalry charged, bridges were
> destroyed – real water tanks engulfed the advancing foe. Altogether it was a
> most impressive show, and played with an interest that was no ordinary child
> game.

'One summer', she further recalled, 'the Churchills rented a small house
in the country for the holidays ... Winston and Jack his brother built a
log house with the help of the gardener's children, and dug a ditch

round it which they contrived to fill with water, and made a drawbridge that really could pull up and down. Here again war proceeded. The fort was stormed. I was hurriedly removed from the scene of action as soon as mud and stones began to fly ...'[3] The house was near Newmarket. Winston was sixteen at the time, the assistant builders were probably the gardeners themselves, and the *pièce de résistance* of the defence was a giant catapult firing unripe apples.

At his three schools – St George's, Ascot, the Misses Thomson in Hove, and from April 1888 Harrow – Churchill was the subject of a good deal of complaint, but rarely for quarrelling with other boys or for fighting. He was on the small side, often unwell, and as likely to be the victim of aggression as its agent. His strong subjects were History, Geography and English Literature; the essay topic he chose in one of the Sandhurst entrance exams was 'The American Civil War' and he received higher marks for English History than anyone else.[4] He could learn poetry by the yard ('I am learning 1000 lines of Macaulay for a prize. I know 600 at present') and he effortlessly absorbed the words of songs, hymns and common biblical passages. Outside the classroom, he was good at swimming and very good at fencing. Harold Threlfall, who was at Clifton College through the same years, never forgot a surprising exchange with a slender, ginger-haired Harrow boy on some inter-school athletics occasion: 'My name's Threlfall and I'm going to run in the 220 this afternoon.' 'My name's Churchill and I'm going to win the sabre competition.'[5]

His commitment to the army was decided in September 1889. He had been in the Officers Training Corps since arriving at Harrow. He was a good marksman ('We use the full-sized Martini-Henry Rifle and cartridges, the same as the Army. The rifles kick a good deal, it is awfully jolly') and the accounts he gave his parents of its field exercises suggest an unusual degree of enthusiasm and understanding.[6] Consider, for example, the two letters he wrote to them in March 1889:

We, that is the Corps, went to Aldershot on Monday and had a great sham fight with some 1300 boys of other Public Schools and about 11,000 regulars ... It was great fun. The noise was tremendous. There were four Batteries of Guns on the Field and a Maxim and several Nordenfeldts.

We were defeated because we were inferior in numbers and not from any want of courage. Our army only consisted of 3500 men and two batteries of

guns and Regiment [*sic*] of Cavalry. While the attacking force was considerably over 8000 strong. I furnish a small plan of the fight at its climax as far
as I could see.

I have bought a Book on Drill as I intend going in for the corporal Exami-
nation next term. I went down to the Range on Tuesday and fired away
twenty rounds.[7]

The army appears to have been taken for granted as his natural destination. It was difficult to see what other career would have met the
requirements of his birth and parentage. His father had been to Oxford,
but neither he nor anyone else seems to have thought it appropriate for
Winston to go, although quite modest attainments sufficed for entry at
the time and Churchill himself was later to think he could have done
well enough there. Theirs was not the sort of family that thought of
sending sons into the church. His father thought him not clever enough
for the law. Journalism and the life of letters, at which he was soon and
unexpectedly to shine, was socially out of the question. A military career
beckoned, but it lay on the far side of an obstacle course of written
examinations. The masters in charge of 'the army side' pronounced that
he was not good enough at Mathematics to have any hope of admission
via the engineers and gunners' institution, the Royal Military Academy
at Woolwich. That cannot have worried Lord Randolph, who in any
case wanted the boy to go into the infantry, chiefly because it was
less expensive. Winston therefore submitted to be 'crammed' for the
Sandhurst exams at Captain James's celebrated establishment. It
squeezed him in at the third attempt, unfortunately (from his father's
point of view) with marks so low that he could only be accepted for the
cavalry. On the other hand, according to the colonel of the regiment he
ultimately joined, 'he passed very much higher than any of the candidates for Cavalry'.[8] He entered the Royal Military College when he was
nearly nineteen, in September 1893.

Winston's educational troubles were now more or less over. It is curious that he was so confident about this. He had been there only a couple
of days when he concluded a letter to his father:

Altogether I like the life. I am interested in the drill and in the military
education I shall receive; and now that the army is to be my trade I feel as
keen as I did before I went in for any of the Examinations. At any rate I am

sure that I shall be mentally, morally and physically better for my course here. Hoping you will write to me and send me some money for myself, I remain, ever your loving son, Winston S. Churchill.[9]

He began to enjoy his studies, which of course included a lot of riding and outdoor work, and to gain good marks in them. The transformation was remarkable, all the more so for the fact that it was only right at the end of his time there that he was allowed to change direction from the infantry, which did not excite him, to the cavalry, which did. The recalcitrant, trouble-prone and nervously excitable schoolboy turned into a cadet who passed out of Sandhurst in December 1894 near the top of his class: excellent in Riding, very good in Fortification and Tactics, good in Military Administration, Law and Topography, good also in Conduct, satisfactory in Musketry; the only subjects in which he scored less than 50 per cent were Drill and Gymnastics.[10]

The regiment into which he was commissioned in February 1895 was the 4th Hussars. Its colourful colonel, J. P. Brabazon, was a friend of the family and, to an aspiring young Sandhurst cadet, an awe-inspiring exemplar of everything a British officer should be. Winston, who had several times been a guest at the regiment's splendid mess in Aldershot, longed to share so glamorous an existence, and was mightily relieved when his father, by now near death, agreed to let him do so. There followed eighteen months of parading and exercising based on Aldershot and Hounslow, varied by spells at the Horse Guards (the army headquarters in Whitehall) and Hampton Court, plus a great deal of spare time.[11]

The glamour soon wore off. Whatever had been in his mind when he first put that uniform on, the life of a lieutenant of Hussars proved less than wholly satisfying. He was well accepted in the regiment and he loved the horsy side of its life, the daily rides and the manoeuvres at Aldershot (sometimes eight hours in the saddle), and the glitter and pomp of parades. He also enjoyed the polo after work was over and, in season, the hunting. But, all that aside, he did not like wasting time. He had no relish for the club-lounging, party-going, dancing and womanising that agreeably filled the leisure time of his social peers; he was not averse to gambling, but he could not afford to forget that he had no money to lose. He was by no means immune to female charm, but girls did not preoccupy him and in any case he was not at ease with them.

It is clear from the thoughtful, observant letters he wrote to his mother, and from the watchful, sensible letters she wrote back, that he had enough of a social life to protect him from being thought eccentric, but it is also clear that by the summer of 1895 he was becoming restless, looking for more than the cavalry life could offer and taking more than a merely family interest in politics.

> I find I am getting into a state of mental stagnation – when even letter writing becomes an effort and when any reading but that of monthly magazines is impossible. This is of course quite in accordance with the spirit of the army ... I think really that when I am quartered in London I shall go and study one or two hours a week with one of James's men ... either Economics or Modern History. If you know what I mean – I need someone to direct my reading.[12]

Moreover, he was hard up. So was the mother to whom he had to look for the subsidies that were essential if he was to remain acceptable in the regiment. (In those years you were paid something as an officer, but you had to pay more to be one.) This embarrassing dependence and relative poverty could not go on for ever. 'The more I see of soldiering – the more I like it – but the more I feel convinced that it is not my *métier*. Well, we shall see – my dearest Mamma.' He began consciously to seek activity and public notice, with two illustrious family role models before him. He wanted to be famous like them. But which would prove the stronger: the father who had once been a potential Prime Minister, or the ancestor who had been the most famous soldier of his age?

As thing turned out, neither one proved stronger than the other. The young Winston in due course did become Prime Minister (his son Randolph found evidence that between 1897 and 1900 his father asserted to three very different people his ardent conviction that he would one day be Prime Minister),[13] and when in 1940 he made himself also Minister of Defence he would share with his military chieftains the making of decisions about strategy and major operations. How far these ambitions might be realised all lay in the future; but it was in 1895 that the pursuit began, and he was remarkably realistic about it. He could not leave the army because he had no qualifications for making any other sort of living, and in any case his dawning determination to go into politics had nothing to do with disliking the army; it was simply that to achieve celebrity as a soldier would take a very long time and a lot of luck. He was also more than half a century too late for looking to the Duke of Marlborough or a wealthy relation to ease him into Parliament through a pocket borough. Now he could only hope to find a seat by making himself financially independent and conspicuous enough to become attractive to the Conservative Party managers and a suitable constituency committee. These qualifications he reckoned he might achieve by getting into lively military situations and by writing about them for the newspapers.

His first venture into this unprecedented line came well before his first year as an officer was up. In *My Early Life* the episode appears as little more than a youthful lark, and he does not mention the twenty-five guineas he obtained from the *Daily Graphic* for writing about it; but it resembles in too many particulars the three more serious adventures that were to follow for one to doubt that he was trying his hand. These five newspaper articles constituted his 'prentice pieces' as a journalist. In early October 1895 he astounded his mother, who would have to foot the bill, by announcing that he planned to go with an officer friend to Cuba to see what he could of the Spanish imperial army's campaign against the nationalist insurgents. From a regimental point of view, it was an eccentric thing to do. The near hibernation into which the regiments of the time went during the winter was normally devoted to hunting and house parties. The justification that he offered to his superiors, that his military education would benefit from such an experience, cannot have carried much weight; they would not have believed that an English cavalry officer could learn anything from Spaniards. He did not tell them about the *Daily Graphic*, just as he kept quiet about his contract with the *Morning Post* when he attached himself to Kitchener's army for the Sudan campaign. On this, as on all later occasions, he brazenly used his social connections and his mother's to open doors and influence people.[14] He did this with such success that when he got to Cuba he was taken to be an official British observer, even being awarded a medal for bravery under fire.

His few days *en route* in New York, where he made some useful acquaintances and one valuable friend, turned out to be more important in the long term for his future than the three weeks he spent in Cuba.[15] In Cuba, he was excited to have a first taste of battle, if the stolid tactics of General Juárez Valdes against an insurgent position could be so described, and he escaped injury or worse on several occasions. 'The General', he told his mother, 'is a very brave man – in a white and gold uniform on a grey horse – [he] a great deal of fire on to us and I heard enough bullets whistle and hum past to satisfy me for some time to come ... We stayed by the General all the time and so were in the most dangerous place in the field.'[16]

Here can be seen for the first time that insouciance about death curiously coupled with confidence in his own ability to survive that consistently marked his military adventures. His reports to the *Graphic* fairly summed up the political situation as 'a war, not a rebellion', and the military situation as a stalemate: a traditional-style European army using unimaginative battle-seeking tactics against an intangible guerrilla host sustained by a sympathetic population. It astonished him that the general attempted no hot pursuit of the enemy after dislodging them from their positions. The war could never be concluded that way![17] Within a couple of years a way had appeared that promised to be much more effective: General Weyler's concentration of civilians into militarily controlled places, towns or *campamentos*, depriving the insurgents of their bases of supply, refuge and intelligence. Churchill didn't learn of this until he was far away, in India, but it seemed to him a good idea, 'cruel but sound'.[18]

Unlike the even more adventurous young correspondent Henry Howard, who managed to cross the lines to live with the nationalists for some days and to form a good impression of them, Winston saw the guerrillas only from a distance, and what he did see he didn't understand or like.[19] He judged them to be an undisciplined, rackety lot. The depth to which he was embedded in the traditions of European warfare and statecraft showed when he wrote in his last article:

> a single really hard-fought battle, whether they won or lost, would convince foreign Powers of their sincerity and in all probability procure their recognition from the United States ... The only tactics they pursue are those of incendiaries and brigands – burning canefields, shooting from behind hedges, firing into sleeping camps, destroying property, wrecking trains, and throwing dynamite. These are perfectly legitimate in war, no doubt, but they are not acts on which States are founded.

Churchill had no reason to be displeased with himself after his safe return from Cuba to New York, where, as a minor celebrity, he 'met the press' and apparently handled them as to the manner born.[20] He then sailed home and resumed his military duties, at the same time trying to find something more exciting and profitable to do. He seems to have made no claim to the authorship of the pieces in the *Graphic*, but he must have felt that he had discovered his *métier* because he offered his services to the *Daily Chronicle* to cover the Cretan insurrection as a special correspondent. He also tried to get transferred to a regiment scheduled to go to South Africa, where trouble with the Boer republics was expected. Sudan was another imminent trouble-spot that caught his wandering eye. Whether as war correspondent or cavalry officer, or preferably both, he was desperate for fame and notice. From Hounslow barracks he wrote to his mother:

> Others as young are making the running now and what chance have I of ever catching up ... A few months in South Africa would earn me the S.A. medal and in all probability the Company's Star. Thence hotfoot to Egypt – to return with two more decorations in a year or two – and beat my sword into an iron despatch box ... You can't realise how furiously intolerable this life is to me.[21]

Stuck with the 4th Hussars, he sailed with them to India in September 1896 and found himself stationed at Bangalore. Life there was easy, with little to do other than the early morning cavalry exercises and the evening polo (at which he excelled), and boring. Never one to be idle, he set himself an exacting course of self-education and continued to look for action. He was back in England in the early summer of 1897, and trying himself out as a speech-maker (at a Primrose League meeting), when news came of the formation of a military expedition to chastise troublesome tribes on the North-West Frontier between India and Afghanistan. Commanding the expedition was to be the experienced and heroic General Sir Bindon Blood from whom, at the house of mutual friends, Churchill had recently extracted a promise 'that if ever he commanded another expedition on the Indian frontier, he would let me come with him'.

Cutting short his leave, he went straight back to India and on arrival at Bombay was gratified to receive the general's telegram: 'Very difficult; no vacancies; come up as a correspondent; will try to fit you in. B.B.' The frontier where Sir Bindon awaited Churchill was a great distance to the north of Bombay, and Bangalore where Churchill's regiment was situated was half as far to the south east, but he had to go there first in order to request more leave. His colonel indulgently told him he could 'go and try his luck'. Now began a heroic rail journey: 2028 miles from Bangalore via Rawalpindi to the railhead at Nowshera:

> five days' journey in the worst of the heat. I was alone; but with plenty of books, the time passed not unpleasantly. Those large leather-lined Indian railway carriages, deeply shuttered and blinded from the blistering sun and kept fairly cool by a circular wheel of wet straw which one turned from time to time, were well adapted to the local conditions. I spent five days in a dark padded moving cell, reading mostly by lamplight or by some jealously admitted ray of glare.[22]

Determined as he was to be a war correspondent, he had left home in such a rush that he had to leave it to his mother to fix him up with a contract with a suitable newspaper. He mailed his first letter before he knew what terms she had made on his behalf. Within two weeks he had found his way onto the general's staff, so for the rest of the campaign he was not only a busy serving officer ('working away equal to two ordinary subalterns', wrote Sir Bindon to Colonel Brabazon) but also correspondent for the *Telegraph* and under contract to telegraph three hundred words a day to the *Allahabad Pioneer*. He was a very hardworking young man.[23] He was furious when the *Daily Telegraph* put not his name but his initials in the by-line, which of course negated his design of 'putting [his] personality before the electorate'. He was angry again when the terms his long-suffering mother fixed with the paper on his behalf were only £5 per letter instead of the £10 that he thought the acceptable minimum.[24]

Sir Bindon Blood's expedition did not take long, but it was exciting while it lasted. Churchill arrived at Malakand, about forty miles north of Peshawar, on 5 September 1897. He accompanied the main body of the force to its fortified camp in the Mahmund valley and, a willing substitute for officers *hors de combat*, was several times in action. An extract from a letter to his mother suggests what it was like:

> When the retirement began I remained till the last and here I was perhaps very near my end ... the wounded were left to be cut up horribly by these wild beasts. I was close to both officers when they were hit almost

simultaneously and fired my revolver at a man at 30 yards who tried to cut up poor Hughes's body. He dropped but came on again. A subaltern ... and I carried a wounded Sepoy for some distance and might perhaps, had there been any gallery, have received some notice. My pants are still stained with the man's blood ... Later on I used a rifle which a wounded man had dropped and fired 40 rounds with some effect at close quarters.[25]

The campaign was short and savage. Churchill was on the way back to Bangalore by 12 October. The troublesome tribesmen of the Buner, Swat and Mahmund valleys, the Afridis and Orakzai, the Mohmands and the Bunerwals, had been, he wrote in one of his letters to the *Telegraph*,

reduced to submission ... Their grain and fodder have been requisitioned. The towers and forts from which they carry on their feuds and wars have been blown up by dynamite and are now in ruins. A severe lesson has been given ... But the cost has been heavy. Twenty-three officers and 245 men have been killed or wounded.[26]

Back at Bangalore, he devoted all the time he could to preparing his newspaper reports for publication as a book. By working six to eight hours a day at reshaping and expanding the *Telegraph* letters, and by intensive use of his efficient mother and her idly inefficient brother-in-law Morton Frewen, he had the satisfaction of learning that Longmans would publish his book *The Story of the Malakand Field Force* as early as February 1898.

The book goes beyond the letters in containing more historical background, more matters of professional military interest, and a few pompous and sententious passages that are quite unlike the easy, familiar and perspicuous prose of the original. They may to some extent reflect Frewen's bungled proof-reading. Churchill's aim, he had written in his letters, was to give his readers 'in safe and comfortable England' a good idea of the realities of military action on the North-West Frontier. In this aim he succeeded admirably. He began with a sketch of the various accompaniments of a foray into mountainous territory peopled by hostile tribes: a force made up of roughly two-thirds Indian and one-third British soldiers, field hospitals set up in preparation for casualties, supplies accumulated at base, hundreds of mules and camels to carry the baggage and the dismantleable mountain artillery, the heat of the midday sun and the cold at night, the heliographs flashing all day long down the valleys with news for 'the tape-machines at the London clubs', the early morning marches of ten miles or so reaching the next night's camp site by the early afternoon, the long slow processions of transport animals arriving several hours after the soldiers (Churchill used this breathing space for writing), the miscellany of camp followers that customarily tagged along behind them. 'The fine deeds and the thrilling moments of a war are but the highlights on a picture of which the background is routine, hard work and discomfort.'

When he came to those deeds and moments, Churchill made very clear how hugely this sort of campaigning differed from the set-piece battles that dominated the history books and popular military literature. The Malakand Field Force's purpose was to punish tribes that had been involved in a recent rising against imperial rule and to overawe other tribes that were tempted to join the rising. Punishment consisted of destroying the tribesmen's villages and possessions; Churchill admitted this sounded draconian but agreed with the imperial authority that there was no other way to deal with the problem. He stoutly justified it against the strictures of ignorant British sentimentalists: the villages, far from being placidly grouped round village greens as his compatriots might imagine, were fortified places where all prosperous inhabitants built towers for self-protection. The tribal warriors themselves were for most of the time invisible and elusive but also ubiquitous; not lines and columns or trenches of uniformed soldiers firing and standing fire in disciplined order, but strong and wiry hill-dwellers in dirty white linen sniping with modern rifles from behind rocks and hidden gulleys, emerging only when the soldiers began to withdraw and then firing at them with unpleasant accuracy. Formed attacks were uncommon but could happen with surprising speed when incautious troop movements made an opening. Night attacks rarely happened; but every night the camps were fired into, causing casualties (surprisingly light in the circumstances) to the soldiers and animals and spoiling everyone's sleep.[27]

Regular features of Churchill's war writing in these early years included objective appraisal of the enemy's quality and frank discussion as to whether the war was worthwhile. The tribes subdued (if only temporarily) by the Malakand campaign, he instructed his public, inhabited the valleys and slopes on the Indian side of the mountains between India and Afghanistan: 'a numerous population in a state of warlike leisure, except at times of sowing and of harvest [in] a perpetual state of feud and strife', happy to fight the British Raj when not fighting among themselves.[28] Simply to leave them to their own savage devices had become impossible since the Indian government had decided, some fifteen or so years previously, that the only security against Russian pressure and Afghan incitement from the other side was to assert control of the mountain passes and to hold the line running from Gilgit via Chitral and Jellalabad to Kandahar.

If today's reader recognises some of these names, his sense of *déja vu* will be completed when he learns that the normal passions of these peoples had just been superheated by a wave of agitation across the whole Muslim world, excited by news of Muslim Turkey's recent victory over Christian Greece (a quarrel about possession of Crete) and, more locally, the preaching of a jihad against the Raj by an inflammatory 'mad' mullah promising paradise to fallen heroes. Churchill did not like what he saw and heard of the local form of Islam. A rationalist and nonbeliever himself, he disliked all superstitions, and this Mahommedanism (as he called it) was clearly as bad as you could get. It locked the tribesmen inside their barbarism. It taught them how to die but not how to live. They were fanatics and barbarians – he instanced particularly their horrible treatment of women and their rituals of torturing wounded opponents and mutilating the dead – living lives ignoble in themselves and dangerous to everyone else. After recording one worse than usual atrocity, he was driven to opine that the world would be none the worse for their extermination.[29]

The trouble, however, was that they were excellent fighters, skilful and courageous. 'To the ferocity of the Zulu are added the craft of the Redskin and the marksmanship of the Boer.'[30] Given also their religious beliefs and their mountain habitat, they were virtually undefeatable; and only campaigns on the largest scale could hope to make even a temporary impression on them. The question then had to be asked whether such campaigns were worth it. On this point, Churchill was more frank and pessimistic with his mother than he dared be in print. The Empire, he told her, was stuck with the 'Forward Policy' initiated by Lansdowne and Roberts (who was acclaimed in the early 1880s for 'pacifying Afghanistan'). 'The force of circumstances on the Indian frontier is beyond human control', he wrote. 'We can't go back and must go on. Financially it is ruinous. Morally it is wicked. Militarily it is an open question, and politically it is a blunder. Annexation is the work which the BP [British Public] will have ultimately to swallow, and the sooner they do it, the sooner things will begin to mend.'[31] His prediction was correct. Annexation followed within four years.

Churchill didn't think much of the political authorities in Delhi or the military ones in Simla, but his admiration of the troops he had been with was genuine and infectious. Nevertheless, he did not hesitate to offer comments as to how such forces could be better constituted; comments which were constructive and not immodestly advanced, but which stuffy seniors thought improper from a lieutenant so junior and footloose. The best troops, he not surprisingly reported, were the British. Their experience of active service on the Frontier was 'of the greatest value' to British regiments.* Watching a column winding its way up a valley, he enthusiastically burst out: 'and then came what is after all the peg on which all the others hang – a British infantry battalion ... as fine a picture in the pages of history as the legions of Caesar, the Janissaries of the Sultans or the Old Guard of Napoleon'. He was able to report many incidents of soldierly expertise and bravery; only in his private correspondence did he admit that there had been some panics too.[32]

Another thing he only admitted in his letters home was the part he actually took in the fighting. He could not resist it whenever he got the chance. His state of mind at this time was truly extraordinary. He wanted to leave the army, to become a public figure and to make a success of politics, yet he relished dangerous situations and liked defying death. 'I am more ambitious for a reputation for personal courage than [for] anything else in the world', he told his mother.[33] In another of his frequent letters to her, he reported that casualties among the officers had led to his being appointed to a command in the 31st Punjab Infantry. Rather a come-down for a cavalry man! 'Still it means the medal ... and possibly that I may bring off some *coup*. Besides I shall have some other motive for taking chances than merely love of adventure.' A few days

---

* Just as regular spells of service in Northern Ireland have been thought valuable to British soldiers through the past thirty years.

earlier, this was how he finished an account of some very fierce fighting: 'I rode my grey pony all along the skirmish line where everyone else was lying down in cover. Foolish perhaps but I play for high stakes and given an audience there is no act too daring or too noble. Without the gallery things are different.'[34] Here, he showed some naivety. There always was a gallery, and always there was someone in it: Winston himself.

He commented on infantry and cavalry with equal confidence. Of the infantry he wrote that, if there was a weakness, it was that many of the soldiers were too young; youngsters coming into the army under the new Short Service system, not there long enough to become hardened veterans and physically not tough enough to tackle muscular adult tribesmen in the hand-to-hand combat that was part of the job. On the other hand, the infantry rifle, the Lee-Metford, was a better weapon than the tribesman's usual Martini-Henry; especially when it was firing the newly-introduced 'dum-dum' bullet. Aware of the growing body of complaint in Europe that this bullet was excessively damaging, he justified it as necessary, inasmuch as nothing less would stop a tribesman at full speed, and as 'not causing any more pain ... than the ordinary lead variety'.[35] This was a fib for public consumption. The truth appeared in a letter he wrote after his return to Bangalore to 'My dear Grandmamma', Duchess Fanny. There, he described the dum-dum's 'shattering effects' as 'simply appalling. Indeed I believe no such bullet has ever been used on human beings before but only on game – stags, tigers etc. The picture is a terrible one, and naturally it has a side to which one does not allude in print'.[36]

It was not surprising that he had much to say about his own arm, the cavalry. The cavalry had been 'extraordinarily valuable' – the tribesmen (differing from the Dervishes whom he found himself charging within a year) seemed peculiarly terrified of being stuck by a lance – and it was regrettable that the Indian government banned British cavalry from crossing the Frontier. The reason was economy. Native cavalry were cheaper and at least as good. But, said Churchill, it was 'professionally disheartening' to the young officer never to have a chance to achieve his proper ambition, to lead his men in action. '"Stables" will no longer be dull when he realises that on the fitness of his horse his life and honour may one day depend ... But when he realises that all is empty display, and that his regiment is a sword too costly to be drawn he naturally loses keenness, and betakes himself to polo as a consolation.'[37]

He had all arms in mind when he penned this moving passage apropos of a private in the Buffs (the East Kent Regiment) whose arm had been amputated at the shoulder; probably on one of those 'large operating tables, made of medical boxes and covered with waterproof sheets' he saw being got ready. Reflections like this did not often grace reports from the front:

> He came of a fighting stock, but I could not help speculating on the possible future which awaited him. Discharge from the service as medically unfit, some miserable pension insufficient to command any pleasures in life except those of drink, a loafer's life and a pauper's death. Perhaps 'the regiment' – the officers, that is – would succeed in getting him work, and would, from their own resources, supplement his pension. But what a poor system it is by which the richest people in the world neglect the soldiers who have served it well, and which leaves to newspaper philanthropy, to local institutions, and to private charity a burden which ought to be proudly borne by the nation.[38]

Doing all that he did on the Frontier and writing his book about it directly afterwards (not to mention his novel *Savrola*) might be thought enough to have occupied the whole of Churchill's mind through the autumn and winter of 1897–88; but far from it. The question, where next to find action and fame, was regularly discussed in his correspondence with his mother and, after a plan to join another Frontier expedition in the spring of 1898 fell through, it became clear that the only opportunity – but a splendid one – was in Egypt and the Sudan.

2

The Sudan and South Africa

The Sudan had been in and out of Churchill's thoughts ever since he went to India. The commander or 'Sirdar' of the Anglo-Egyptian army, General Sir Herbert Kitchener, had long been preparing with extreme thoroughness an expeditionary force to recover the control over the Sudan that had been lost to the Mahdi and his Islamic fundamentalists in the 1880s. It was due to set out in mid-1898 and Churchill longed to join it. The principal difficulties in the way were that Kitchener didnot like war correspondents in general, he didn't like young officers who doubled as war correspondents, and he didn't like anything he heard of young Winston Churchill.

Churchill, however, would not be thwarted. Every string that he, his mother and his relations could pull was vigorously pulled. They engaged the help of Sir Evelyn Wood the Adjutant-General, the Prince of Wales and the Prime Minister. At last the Sirdar, wearied by such importunities and short of officers, allowed the irrepressible young man to join the 21st Lancers, provided he did so at his own expense, at his own risk, and on the promise that he wouldn't write about it – a promise that was given on Churchill's behalf by the influential London hostess, his friend and patroness Lady Jeune. One must doubt whether she believed him any more than Kitchener can have done. His grandmother, who always told him exactly what she thought, later said that it had laid him open to the charge of breaking his word.[1] The nearest Churchill got to honouring that promise was to camouflage his reports as letters to a friend in England, and to maintain an elaborate fiction that it was the friend, not himself, who conveyed them to the editor of the *Morning Post*, the paper with which Churchill had arranged very satisfactory terms. Of course the secret, such as it was, soon leaked out. He would have been very disappointed if it hadn't.

Churchill's trip to the Sudan was secured by another bit of sharp

practice. The highest authorities in Britain had given him their blessing; the Indian military authorities hadn't. He duly applied for another
period of special leave and, lest they should reply in the negative, made
sure he was on his way by an unusual route before their reply could
come through.[2] He went via Marseille to Alexandria instead of the usual
Brindisi, arriving at Cairo on 2 August 1898 and quickly catching up
with the Sirdar's expedition as it moved slowly up the Nile. On the
rugged border between India and Afghanistan, Churchill had been
almost the only newspaper correspondent present.[3] Things were now
quite different. For all his dislike of newspaper correspondents, Kitchener was unable to prevent around thirty of them accompanying his
expedition. All the top men were there, some of them with a subsequent book in mind. It is much to his credit that Churchill, who had
only done this sort of thing once before and was now doubling as a
cavalry officer, wrote reports as good as the best of them and, in *The
River War*, a book probably better than any.[4] As always, Churchill
wrote with concentration and speed. Hubert Howard, who was one of
the thirty, second-stringing for *The Times*, noted admiringly: 'There is
Winston writing early and often ... [He] sits down and in a couple of
hours turns out a letter, neat and ready, a hundred times better than
mine.'[5]

Churchill's account of the campaign and its climactic battle outside
the city of Omdurman on 2 September 1898 is elaborate and comprehensive. There are many pages on the Anglo-Egyptian army's
well-prepared advance up the west bank of the Nile, 'moving so slowly
and with such terrible deliberation, but always moving', while trains on
the newly-laid military railway shuttled to and fro and gunboats on the
river provided accurate mobile artillery support, silencing the batteries
by the city's walls. The Mahdi's army came out of the city of Omdurman onto the plain the day before the battle and settled there for the
night, its separate contingents identified by their plain green, black, red
and white flags. In the British encampment the atmosphere through the
night was tense, reminiscent of Henry V's night before Agincourt. The
Dervishes began their advance shortly before six o'clock in the morning;
their courageous charges were met by the controlled rifle fire of the
imperial infantry and of the 'scientific' weaponry, the artillery and the
Maxim guns, that had come safely up the Nile with them. A hot, noisy,

dangerous and hectic morning of firing and manoeuvring came to an end when, about eleven o'clock, the Dervishes' last desperate assault failed and Kitchener's army began to advance 'in a line of bayonets and artillery nearly two miles long', the Sirdar remarking, as he 'shut up his glasses' at half-past eleven, that he thought the enemy had been given 'a good dusting'. Upon which he ordered a cease-fire and a general advance on the city.[6]

The celebrated charge of the 21st Lancers took place between eight and nine in the morning. Whether it really was, as is often claimed, the last traditional cavalry charge in British history is unclear. Perhaps what is meant is that it was the last such charge with lances; there were charges with rifles and carbines in South Africa.[7] It was certainly gallant and spectacular, and, since one of the troop commanders was Lieutenant Winston Churchill, it was destined to become well known, first through *The River War* and then, thirty years later, through his more analytical version in *My Early Life*. 'As with the charge of the light brigade at Balaclava forty-four years before the most futile and inefficient part of the battle was the most extravagantly praised.'[8] Churchill did not pretend that the charge contributed much towards the victory – indeed, the premier war correspondent G. W. Steevens reckoned that it diminished the extent of the victory, by losing so large a proportion of the cavalry needed to harry the Mahdists' withdrawal – but he rightly judged that it was a dramatic and instructive event. Like so many events in war (and in Churchill's career), there was a lot of chance in what happened.

With their backs to the river on the far left of Kitchener's camp, the Lancers were awaiting orders. The battle so far seemed to be going well. Kitchener began to fear lest the Dervishes, despairing of victory in the field, might withdraw into the city. The Lancers were ordered to clear the ground in front of them and to block the enemy retreat. Their patrols reported the way clear except for a line, or so they thought, of perhaps a thousand Dervishes formed up in a shallow depression. Such a body seemed positively inviting to a cavalry regiment that had little *raison d'être* beyond the charge and had never trained for anything else. The colonel led his men past the Dervish line with a view to taking them from the flank. The Dervishes, however, opening fire on them to some effect, he gave the order 'Right wheel into Line!' and the trumpeter sounded the call they had all longed for: 'Charge!' Then came the first mischance:

> Two hundred and fifty yards away, the dark-blue men were firing madly in a thin film of light-blue smoke ... The pace was fast and the distance short. Yet, before it was half covered, the whole aspect of the affair changed. A deep crease in the ground – a dry water-course, a *khor* – appeared where all had seemed smooth, level plain; and from it there sprang, with the suddenness of a pantomime effect and a high-pitched yell, a dense white mass of men nearly as long as our front *and about twelve deep.* [My italics][9]

The enemy commander, the Khalifa, had anticipated this advance and made ready for it. The prospect the Lancers now faced was appalling but, already going fast and only one hundred yards off, there was nothing to do but to put on more speed and hope for the best. Now came the second mischance. 'It is very rarely that stubborn and unshaken infantry meet equally stubborn and unshaken cavalry.'[10] The theory of a cavalry charge against a line of infantry was that either those infantry would keep their heads and fire their muskets accurately (in which case the cavalry were done for) or, more commonly, they would break in terror and run. On this occasion the musketeers had shot their bolt ineffectively, but the thick-packed Dervish foot soldiers, armed with several sorts of sharp weapons, did not run away. Far from it. 'They stood their ground manfully.' Churchill used a striking phrase to describe what happened. 'The two living walls crashed together with a mighty collision.' Churchill's mount, 'a handy, sure-footed, grey Arab polo pony', landed cleverly in a gap and he got through unharmed, using his Mauser pistol to defend himself against the men who then swarmed round him. (Because of the notorious fragility of his right shoulder he had decided to rely on a pistol if it came to hand-to-hand combat.) Others were not so lucky. 'Brought to an actual standstill in the enemy mass, clutched at from every side, stabbed at and hacked at by spear and sword, they were dragged from their horses and cut to pieces by an infuriated foe.' Of the majority who got through, most were more or less wounded. 'I myself saw Sergeant Freeman trying to collect his troops ... His face was cut to pieces ... the whole of his nose, cheeks and lips flapped amid red bubbles.' 'Men, clinging to their saddles, lurched helplessly about, covered with blood from perhaps a dozen wounds. Horses, streaming with

blood from tremendous gashes, limped and staggered with their riders.'
The casualties were heavy: out of the four hundred who took part, five
officers, sixty-five men and 119 horses killed or wounded.[11]

After the battle, when he had swapped stories with the other survivors, Churchill was able to enrich *The River War* with gory details of
what individual lancers actually had done and had had done to them in
those 120 seconds (as he reckoned) of life or death hand-to-hand combat. It was a singular episode. Over the rest of the field the cavalry's role
was mostly reconnaissance and the harrying of broken formations.
Churchill's lucid description of the battle as a whole shows that most of
the action was conducted at more of a distance, albeit a distance that
was sometimes uncomfortably close. The received image of Omdurman
is of a flat plain with waves of primitive Dervishes advancing on a British
position and being systematically mown down by Maxim guns.[12] The
mowing down is not inaccurate because the Maxim guns, artillery and
rifle fire of the British regiments (and, when they were respectively not
too excited or frightened, the Sudanese and Egyptians) did have that
effect; but some Dervishes had rifles and knew how to use them, there
were enough hillocks and dips to permit surprises, there was much
manoeuvring, and there were many tense episodes. The Khalifa was a
capable general. He made good use of his resources and gave Kitchener
some anxious moments. The comparative figures of casualties compiled
after the battle made it look much easier than it was. It did not feel easy
to participants while it was still going on.[13]

On this occasion, as throughout his life, Churchill paid tribute to the
good qualities of his opponents, while not concealing their bad ones. He
had no hesitation in defining the war as one of civilisation against barbarism, entirely justified by international law; the savagery that these
tribes showed in their conflicts with one another was loathsome and he
understood how the British soldiers, confronted with ghastly and sometimes still stinking remains of massacres as they marched south, and
with the patriotic slogan of 'Avenge Gordon!' in their heads, were
primed to hate their antagonists. Churchill was not a good hater. Here
in the Sudan he might have written, as he did write in Europe forty-
seven years later, 'my hate died with their surrender'.[14] Courage in the
face of danger always fascinated Churchill and in *The River War* he gave
many illustrations of it; also of its companion virtue, fortitude despite

pain. Moving passages of his newspaper reports and the first edition of his subsequent book tell of his walk around the battlefield three days later. 'Occasionally there were double layers of dead bodies ... Can you imagine the postures in which man, once created in the image of his Maker, had been twisted? Do not try, for were you to succeed you would ask yourself, with me: Can I ever forget?' He contrasted the honours done to the British dead with what happened to the others strewn and heaped where they had come into 'the zones of fire'. 'There was nothing *dulce et decorum* about the Dervish dead ... All was filthy corruption. Yet these were as brave men as ever walked the earth.'[15] He denied that the charge of the Baggara cavalry to their certain deaths, the last major incident of the battle, could be discounted as 'mad fanaticism', and there was sombre prescience in his meditation upon them:

> Why should we regard as madness in the savage what would be sublime in civilised men? For I hope that if evil days should come upon our own country, and the last army which a collapsing Empire could interpose between London and the invader were dissolving in rout and ruin, that there would be some – even in these modern days – who would not care to accustom themselves to a new order of things and tamely survive the disaster.[16]

He also found some good things to say both about Mohammed Ahmed, the Mahdi, who had expelled the Egyptians (effectively, the British), and about his successor, the Khalifa Abdullah, whom the Anglo-Egyptians now expelled in turn.[17] Not least he appreciated how these strong religious men had given their countrymen stability and purity of governance and the sort of collective self-respect that we, well over a century later, would identify as proto-nationalism. He personally did not like the religious creed enjoining that purity but he understood how it had given meaning to and dignified the lives of its believers. It was chiefly on this ground that he deplored the destruction of their shrine, the Mahdi's tomb: 'a gloomy augury for the future of the Sudan that the first action of its civilised conquerors and present ruler should have been to level the one pinnacle which rose above the mud homes'. On similar grounds, though also from principles of public decency, he deplored Kitchener's exhumation of the Mahdi's body, followed by removal of the head, which he sent to Cairo, and the despatch of the dismembered parts into the Nile.[18]

He ventured other criticisms of the Sirdar. Kitchener did not like him and he did not like Kitchener. There were stories in the press that Kitchener had actually authorised the killing of the Dervish wounded. Churchill knew that was untrue, but, in view of the 'very general impression that the fewer the prisoners, the greater would be the satisfaction of the commander', he regretted that Kitchener had not reissued an earlier order that the wounded should *not* be killed. That native contingents normally killed wounded enemies and took no prisoners Churchill frankly admitted, though this was an aspect of imperial campaigning that prudent reporters preferred to overlook; more shockingly, he admitted that some of the more brutal types in the British ranks were likely to have done the same.[19]

The River War in its first edition (1899) was an expensive, handsome two-volume book with lots of maps and many attractive little pen drawings by Churchill's Harrow contemporary Captain Angus Mac-Neill.[20] The *Morning Post* material formed only part of the whole. The bibliography and acknowledgments testify to the diligence with which Churchill had collected material for the historical background, absorbed the diplomatic hinterland (competition with France) and, of course, learned about the parts of battle he hadn't seen himself. One of his principal suppliers was Cecil Rhodes's elder brother, the retired Colonel Francis Rhodes, *The Times*'s senior correspondent; he is billed on the title-page as the book's 'editor' – presumably nursing it while the author was in South Africa – and an unusually independent-minded 'editor' he was, adding footnotes here and there to amplify or to express disagreement with what Churchill wrote.

Churchill's open censure of the nation's chief military hero and exposure of his army's minor defects was the subject of much comment when it appeared. For many people it perfected their image of a bumptious and improper young man, much too big for his cavalry lieutenant's boots. Its disappearance from the second edition of the book (1902) has been read as moral cowardice, but it was not necessarily so. Those passages and others critical of various aspects of the conduct of the war indeed disappeared, but they did so as parts of whole chapters of the first edition that disappeared in order to produce an economical, low-priced single volume. The text of the second edition was cut by one third, jettisoning 'personal impressions and opinions, often controversial in character' which he judged inessential to its value as 'a permanent record'. It had become less of a personal testimony and more of an orthodox history book.

Although there were two more military adventures still to come, Churchill's life by now was moving ever faster away from the army and towards politics. The months between leaving the Sudan in September 1898 and entering the House of Commons in February 1901 were packed with action of both kinds. Back in England by early October, he devoted the next two months to working on *The River War* and networking among the Conservatives. At the beginning of December he set off for India for what was to be his last and shortest period of service with the 4th Hussars. Back in Britain by the middle of April 1899, his principal occupation was finding a constituency, and, having found Oldham in Lancashire, contesting a by-election there unsuccessfully in July. The mounting tension between the Boers and the British in South Africa was by then catching his eye. War broke out on 12 October 1899, and he was on the way there by the 14th, sailing on the same ship as the Commander-in-Chief Sir Redvers Buller and his staff.

This time there was no need to camouflage his journalistic status. His services being sought by more than one newspaper, he was able to wring from the *Morning Post*, the most prestigious Conservative paper of the period, the splendid and almost unprecedented remuneration of £250 a month plus expenses. The baggage he took with him included, besides the most up-to-date telescopes and binoculars, thirty bottles of fine wine, six of light port, eighteen of ten-year-old whisky and six of 1866 brandy; he never believed that war should be needlessly uncomfortable.[21] His plan of action was the same as it had been on both previous occasions: to send such reports to his newspaper as could be rapidly made the basis of a book. In the event, two books came out of his South African adventure, both of them in print before 1900 was out. The story of his capture by the Boers and his sensational escape from their prison camp, the most celebrated episode of his early life, followed by his campaigning as a lieutenant in the South Africa Light Horse under Buller, filled the pages of *London to Ladysmith via Pretoria* – Pretoria having been where he was initially imprisoned. His other book, *Ian Hamilton's March*, told the story of his accompanying one column of Lord Roberts's march from Bloemfontein in the Orange Free State through Johannesburg to Pretoria. The books were hastily written and as hastily published. A general election being called in September of that year, Churchill stood for Oldham again, this time successfully. October and November were given over to a hectic, well publicised and very remunerative British lecture tour about his adventures and December and January to a less remunerative repeat performance in North America. Home again in early February 1901, and by now a rich young man and a celebrity, he made his maiden speech in the House of Commons on the 14th, and was to see no more military action until 1914.

The two South Africa books are very like one another and are, together, very unlike the two books that preceded them; so much unlike that one wonders why. The journalist has deposed the historian. He was in such a hurry to make an impression, and to get his books onto the market before any others, that he arranged for his letters to the *Morning Post*, as soon as they had been used for the newspaper, to go straight on to Longmans to be set in type for the book. Their style is chatty and familiar, saved from being ordinary only by the energy that informs them and the drama of their substance. They have little of the gravitas that distinguished the earlier books; their emotional content is commonplace imperial patriotism.[22] The echoes of Gibbon and Macaulay that graced the earlier books are no longer heard, nor is there any trace of the literary conceits that he had put into *The River War* (and that the *Morning Post's* editor had removed); these books come closer to Henty and Buchan. For example:

> I went back for machine-guns, and about half an hour later they were brought into action at the edge of the wood. Boers on the sky-line at two thousand yards – tat-tat-tat-tat-tat half a dozen times repeated; Boers galloping to cover; one—yes, by Jupiter! – one on his back on the grass ... All of a sudden there was a furious rush and roar overhead ... What on earth could this be? ... It was our old friend the gun to the westward who, irritated by the noisy Maxims, had resolved to put his foot down. Whizz! Bang! Came a third shot ...[23]

Another marked characteristic of these books is that they have little of the refreshingly frank criticisms of defects and failures, personal as well as material, that enlivened the earlier ones and marked him out as a morally courageous young man – or a reckless one. One may surmise that he had been taken aback by the *Army and Navy Gazette's* criticisms of his freelancing activities. If his real opinion at the time of

Sir Redvers Buller was the one given in *My Early Life* (1930), the sympathetic picture painted in *London to Ladysmith* must be judged disingenuous. Such criticism as he does venture is general and not particular. The book indeed ends with an allusion to 'some mistakes and many misfortunes' along the hard road to Ladysmith, but in this, rather as in his speeches about mistakes and misfortunes in the Second World War, he also finds cause for congratulations all round:

> Indeed it seems to me very likely that in future times our countrymen will think that we were most fortunate to find after a prolonged peace leaders of quality and courage who were moreover honourable gentlemen, to carry our military affairs through all kinds of difficulties to a prosperous issue; and whatever may be said of the generals it is certain that all will praise the enduring courage of the regimental officer and the private soldier.[24]

Both books also disclose more prominently than the earlier ones Churchill's very singular behaviour in these military operations to which he had attached himself. He was now openly what he had been only covertly in the Sudan, a war correspondent *and* a serving officer at one and the same time: 'a hybrid combination ... not unnaturally obnoxious to the military mind'.[25] After Churchill's escape from the Pretoria prisoner of war camp, Buller magnanimously connived at Churchill's rule-breaking pluralism by giving him a commission in the South African Light Horse. From then on, he was openly both things, a unique state of affairs that no subsequent commander in South Africa seems to have questioned. If he had not fulfilled his military duties satisfactorily, presumably they would have done so. But the fact was that he did fulfil them, taking part in a series of hard-fought actions and skirmishes with gallantry.

One of these actions, at the oddly named Acton Homes, was close by ill-fated Spion Kop, where his insatiable curiosity and drive to be at the heart of events found him a part in the tragedy's dénouement. Spion Kop, he later wrote, 'is a rocky hill – almost a mountain – rising 1400 feet above the [Tugela] river with a flat top about as large as Trafalgar Square. Into this confined area 2000 British infantry were packed.' There was little point in them being there, and no point at all in them staying there once the Boer riflemen were within range and the cleverly-hidden Boer gunners were spraying them with shrapnel. Stay there, however, they did, no orders having been given to the contrary. Churchill, being curious to know what was going on, went with a companion up the back of the Kop, found a scene of bloodshed and havoc, and thought it proper to report his findings to the divisional HQ of General Sir Charles Warren, another of Churchill's old fogey *bêtes noires*. His credentials apparently unquestioned, Churchill was given a message to take to the colonel at the top, promising reinforcements. 'So I climbed the mountain again, this time in pitch darkness ... The firing had died away and only occasional bullets sang through the air.' By that time, however, the colonel had decided that enough was enough and had ordered 'a general retirement'. Churchill went down with him and at last they found Warren's HQ. 'The General was asleep. I put my hand on his shoulder and woke him up. "Colonel Thorneycroft is here, sir." He took it all very calmly. He was a charming old gentleman. I was genuinely sorry for him. I was also sorry for the army.' The next day was spent picking up the dead and wounded under a flag of truce, and by the end of the day after that the whole of Buller's force had withdrawn to where it had started from. 'That', concluded Churchill's lucid later account of the Spion Kop story, 'was all there was to show for the operations of a whole army corps for sixteen days at a cost of about eighteen hundred casualties.'[26]

Churchill managed to remain conspicuous to the end. It was courageous as well as adventurous to ride on a borrowed bicycle through Johannesburg while it was still a Boer city; it was characteristic that he should manage to enter Pretoria in front of the other officers, and to end the day dining at headquarters with Lord Roberts and his staff.* No other correspondent got into – indeed, was in a position to get into – such situations. Churchill was being more than generous to his professional brethren when he wrote: '"All the danger of war and one half per cent of the glory"; such is our motto, and that is the reason why we expect large salaries.'[27]

His accounts of the movements and actions he observed or took part in are clear and dramatic, inevitably simplified for their journalistic purpose, and in some obvious respects subjective. It scarcely diminished their value that, when the war was over and its far from glorious conduct was subjected to anguished scrutiny, faults were alleged in some

* Note the similarity to Sir Max Hastings's adventures in the Falklands War.

of the detail of his stories.[28] On the army's performance in general, his observations were cautiously mixed. He was amazed at the weight and consequent slowness of the baggage trains and the degree of comfort the army sought for itself in camp. He much admired the free-running tactics of the colonial cavalry, and when he got home contributed to the magazine his mother was editing a forceful article urging that the British cavalry, currently trained for formal manoeuvres and the charge, should prepare to be equally flexible.[29]

He could not help but admire the Boers' skill in war and, like most of his imperial kind, admitted looking forward to a peace that would bring them into (or back into, according to one's point of view) the Empire. He frequently commented on the accuracy of the Boer artillerymen, sometimes explicitly to the disadvantage of their British counterparts. For example, on the way to Ladysmith a certain British contingent was 'a tiny target, only a moving speck across the plain. But the Boer gunners threw a shell within a yard of the first troop leader. All this at seven thousand yards! English artillery experts, please note and if possible copy.'[30] Boer use of expanding bullets was occasionally deplored but not made much of; possibly because the imperial forces used them too, partly no doubt because the relevant Hague Declaration against their use had not yet become obligatory. That they had become a controversial topic is, however, clear:

> A field officer of the East Surreys ... showed me an expansive bullet of a particularly cruel pattern. The tip had been cut off, exposing the soft core, and four slits were scored down the side. Whole boxes of this ammunition had been found ... I have a specimen of this particular kind by me as I write, and I am informed by people who shoot big game that it is the most severe bullet of its kind yet invented. Five other sorts have been collected by the medical officers who have also tried to classify the wounds they respectively produce.[31]

The best-known episode of his South African months happened very soon after he landed: the ambush of the armoured train he had insisted on joining, his being taken prisoner, and his escape not many days later from the camp at Pretoria. To this episode he later devoted four chapters and about one-sixth of the pages of *My Early Life*. The enterprise, courage and fortitude he showed are indisputable but it is difficult to find the episode as entirely creditable to him as he himself portrayed it.

Of the armoured train incident on 15 November 1899 that began it, his is only one of several accounts. The simple facts common to all of them were that the train, carrying two companies of soldiers, some sailors with a six-pounder and a breakdown gang, coming under fire and reversing at speed, ran into a neatly-contrived ambush that derailed some of the trucks. While the soldiers returned fire, Churchill took charge of the attempt to remove the derailed trucks impeding the engine's way from the track; under continuous fire he succeeded, and the engine escaped – but he didn't. First of all, it must be noted that the accounts of the affair given by Churchill in *My Early Life* thirty years later and by Aylmer Haldane in his official report several days later are misleading and even, in the latter case, untruthful.[32] The armoured train's pointless and suicidal routine foray (exactly like the Royal Navy's 'live bait squadron' in 1914) was made even more suicidal by Churchill's assumption of its leadership, irresponsibly permitted by its official commander Captain Haldane. If Haldane, known to Churchill since his Indian days, had retained control, and had awaited instructions from headquarters as he probably should have done, the disaster would not have happened. Churchill's depiction of it as a dashing adventure from which he emerged with credit should not be allowed to obscure what a disaster it was for the six men killed, the twenty or so wounded and the rest taken prisoner.

Secondly, there was the question of his status. He had been behaving like a soldier before capture. If he had not luckily left his pistol on the locomotive, and if he had not discreetly emptied his pockets of the bullets in them, those possessions would have committed him. The argument he repeatedly put to the Boer officials at Pretoria, that he was a non-combatant and therefore *ipso facto* ought to be released, was nonsense, and his captors reasonably took no notice of it. They would have taken still less had they known that he was writing at the same time to the War Office asking to be classified as a soldier, so that he might have a chance of being included in a contemplated exchange of military prisoners.

Thirdly, there is the question of parole. This was a gentleman's war, in which the traditional laws and customs of war were generally recognised and parole was both given and observed. One of Churchill's ploys, in the third of his appeals to his captors, was to offer 'to give any parole that may be required not to serve against the Republican forces or to give any information affecting the military situation'.[33] There was some inclination in the Boer high command to let him go on those terms but, before the matter could be settled, he had gone over the wall. In the confusion that followed, stories circulated that he was a parole-breaker. This was not true, and he was justified in hotly resenting them; but in view of his deviousness in other episodes during these frantic years, and his passion to see action, it was not surprising that the Boers wondered how he would have interpreted the terms of his parole, if it had been given.

Fourthly, there is the question of the would-be escapers he left behind. He had been planning to escape with two others, Captain Aylmer Haldane and Lieutenant (or Sergeant) Brockie. Brockie was not later an important person but Haldane was. He went on to become a long-lived general and he never ceased to believe, and recurrently to say, that Churchill spoiled the others' chances by going over the fence prematurely. The facts of the matter were argued over again and again, coming to a final flare-up when Churchill published his definitive version in *My Early Life*. One can easily enough understand that 'in an atmosphere so rich in misgivings, bungling and bad temper ... mishaps and misunderstandings were all too likely'.[34] But Haldane perhaps had a point in regretting that Churchill never had 'the moral courage to admit that, in the excitement of the moment, he saw a chance of escape and could not resist the temptation ... not realising that it would compromise the escape of his companions'.[35]

Finally, there is the matter of the man who secured his safety on his railway journey to freedom. The British-born protectors whom he luckily chanced upon fixed him up not uncomfortably among the wool bales of a train going to the coast, but there was a possibility that, amidst all the couplings and uncouplings of wagons *en route*, the wagon with him in it might have got detached and delayed. The consignor of the wool bales, Mr Burnham, therefore took the very considerable trouble and risk of going with the train himself, telling its guards (whom he had to bribe to let him travel in their cabins) that he was anxious for business reasons to make sure his part of the cargo got to Lourenço Marques without delay. Two of Churchill's saviours are thanked by name but not Mr Burnham, which seems strange.

To sum up, Churchill's character had self-regarding, ruthless and inconsiderate streaks in it, all of which were early in evidence. They were integral parts of the whole character, inseparable from his performance as a wielder of power when it came his way. Since that character also contained strong streaks of decency, patriotism, humanity and courage, which were the better able to do their work for the drive given by his egotism and occasional ruthlessness, his admirers have no cause to complain. Great men come in all kinds and colours, and are not the same thing as saints; a Gandhi or a Hammarskjöld would not have saved Britain (and more than Britain) in 1940. The rough has to be taken with the smooth. In Churchill's case, the rough was rather prominent at this stage of his career. 'He was a young man in a hurry who always broke the rules. It was a secret behind his greatness.'[36]

3

Amateur Admiral

For more than ten years after his arrival in the House of Commons, Churchill was best known to the world as a politician and, from 1908, as one of the leading activists in the Liberal government that laid the foundations of the Welfare State. He soon became as much of a civilian celebrity as he had formerly been a military one. When, half a century later, his son Randolph came to write his biography, he neatly summed up the story of these years as 'How a soldier of fortune by diligence and high ambition turned himself while in his thirties into a parliamentarian, statesman and author of the first order'.[1]

That turning was not worked by himself alone. From 1908 Churchill had the love and support of an intelligent and sensible woman who was to be, so far as his temperament permitted, a calming influence and reliable prop throughout the rest of his life: Having proposed at Blenheim, he married Clementine Hozier on 12 September 1908. With a good wife and a home of his own, Churchill worked hard at his new trade. He took pains to become, what he was not by nature, an effective public speaker; he took up serious reading again; and he gave his full attention to whatever business he had in hand, and showed an exceptional talent for mastering detail. His abilities were noted. Ministerial office first came his way at the end of 1905, as Under-Secretary of State at the Colonial Office. Never out of office thereafter, he became successively President of the Board of Trade and Home Secretary. His official connection with military matters resumed only when he was appointed First Lord of the Admiralty in October 1911.

So rapid a progress through some of the major offices of state, in each of which he performed creditably, was startling enough; but what made it more startling still was his switching parties – in parliamentary language 'crossing the floor of the House' – within four years of entering it. The son of a famous Conservative politician who had once been talked of as a potential Prime Minister, Churchill entered the House as a Conservative and was expected to remain one. But he didn't. He offered plausible reasons of principle for changing sides in 1904, but Conservatives suspected he did so because their party looked likely to lose the coming general election (as indeed it did) and Churchill wanted to be on the winning side. Whether there was anything in that suspicion or not, the fact is that, from this time onwards, Conservatives were reluctant to trust him, even after he had returned to their ranks in the 1920s; and their continuing distrust and dislike were to prove damaging to him at times in both world wars.

Notwithstanding his transformation into a rising politician and his family commitments, Churchill's military interests were not in abeyance in these Edwardian years. They showed themselves in a variety of ways. His books and his much publicised adventures in the early part of the Boer War enabled him to speak up and down the country on military matters with some authority; an authority, needless to say, denied and resented by the established military hierarchy. From February 1900 he was able to speak where it mattered most, in the House of Commons, as Conservative Member for Oldham. He made no attempt to conceal his low opinion of the War Office and the way the continuing war in South Africa was being managed. 'Whether it is a matter of ending the war, or of reforming the army, or even of paying the Yeomanry ... it is necessary to stand over the War Office with a stick to get anything done.'[2] Criticisms of the War Office's misuse of the money voted for it and complaints about its unaccountability frequently filled these, his earliest parliamentary performances.[3]

This low estimation of the War Office remained with him through the next half-century; as did his tendency to suppose that career officers were thick-headed. It was not only constitutional principle that caused him to believe that the higher direction of war should be in the hands of civilians, it was impatience with the ineptitude and inarticulateness of many generals. Sir Redvers Buller, whom he was able to observe close up in the course of a fortnight's voyage to South Africa in 1899, was a classic of his kind:

> He looked stolid. He said little, and what he said was obscure. He was not the kind of man who could explain things, and he never tried to do so ...
> He had shown himself a brave and skilful officer in his youth, and for nearly

twenty years he had filled important administrative posts of a sedentary character in Whitehall. [In South Africa] he plodded on from blunder to blunder and from one disaster to another, without losing either the regard of his country or the trust of his troops ... he gave the same sort of impression to the British at this juncture as we afterwards saw effected on the French nation through the personality of General Joffre.[4]

The same inability or refusal to join in debate, which seems to have been characteristic of a certain strong, silent military or naval type (within the professions a respected one, and of course not necessarily connected with ineptitude), tested Churchill's patience on several subsequent occasions. He could never believe that men who didn't say much had much to say.

It was natural that the military subject that touched him most closely was the failure to make effective use of cavalry. His short-lived active military career had been passed among the cavalry and he was honest enough to admit his affection for its traditional glories: the brilliant displays of colourful uniforms on well-groomed horses, the skills of riders and commanders in maintaining order through complicated manoeuvres, the exhilaration of gallops and charges. The British cavalry regiments yielded to none in dash, polish and expertise; but, he had to admit, the skills they learned on the parade grounds of Aldershot and on Salisbury Plain might not be the ones actually needed in future wars, when perhaps cavalry might not be needed at all. Thirty years later, in *My Early Life*, he credited himself with having already entertained such thoughts as early as 1895. He recalled that he himself, when back in barracks after participating in a great cavalry exercise, had wondered: 'What would happen if half a dozen spoil-sports got themselves into a hole with a Maxim gun and kept their heads?'

Just after his return from South Africa, he contributed an essay on 'British Cavalry' to the stylish periodical his mother was then editing.[5] Criticism of the cavalry's failure to shine in the war so far, he wrote, was unfair. They were not trained for such an enemy and such terrain. They had been *drilled*, and what they were drilled for was *charges*. Consequently, they were at a loss in South Africa. 'They have met the Boer at long bowls and at close quarters ... They have met him – a row of dots far off on the glittering glaring veldt – in the open a-horse and a-foot; and for all their efforts, their sacrifices and their pluck, they have taken precious little change out of the Boer, and have earned nothing but abuse and criticism in England.' It was time to face the facts. 'The hour of shock tactics and close formations has struck.' The glittering displays of Aldershot were 'as obsolete as the armour and archery of the Middle Ages'. He concluded by turning the argument to support the isolationist contention that often appeared in his speeches in the early 1900s: 'leaving continental armies to their business, [we must] make our military arrangements in accordance with our own particular needs and resources, and so substitute for our present miniature European army, a British army for the British Empire'.

For all his pessimism about the future usefulness of the British cavalry, Churchill did not have to forgo the aesthetic and sporting pleasures of cavalry life. He became a major in the Queen's Own Oxfordshire Hussars, a Yeomanry regiment with long-standing Blenheim connections. His cousin 'Sunny' was now its commanding officer, his brother Jack its second-in-command, and his friend, the famous barrister F. E. Smith, a second lieutenant. The local newspaper lists him as commanding now the Woodstock squadron, now the Henley one (the Banbury squadron remained under the command of Major the Hon. E. E. Twystleton-Wykeham-Fiennes). A group photograph of the officers at the 1901 annual inspection shows that Churchill's taste for eccentric clothing was already strong in him: a bush hat and a bow tie.[6] Other photographs, however, show him in the regiment's comparatively modest dark blue uniform and peaked cap. These annual camps, always about the beginning of June and in the park either of Blenheim or some other county mansion, merged happily into social events; Clementine, his sister-in-law Gwendeline Bertie and several other huge-hatted ladies beautified the group on the occasion of a visit from the King of Portugal. Clementine was nursing their second child, Randolph, when her husband was having the time of his life at the 1911 camp, at Blenheim. 'Jack and I took our squadrons at the real pace and exacted the spontaneous plaudits of the crowd ... I made the General form the whole Brigade into Brigade Mass and gallop 1200 strong the whole length of the park in one solid square of men and horses. It went awfully well.'[7] Clementine had been too near giving birth to their first child to be able to join in the fun at the 1909 camp. The long letter Churchill wrote to her from 'Camp Goring' shows that the days he spent with his

Yeomanry regiment had more to them than just being an agreeable
extension of his earlier passion for playing at soldiers:

> We had an amusing day. There were lots of soldiers and pseudo-soldiers
> galloping about, & the 8 regiments of Yeomanry made a brave show. But the
> field day was not in my judgment well carried out ... These military men
> very often fail altogether to see the simple truths underlying the relation-
> ships of all armed forces, & how the levers of power can be used upon them.
> Do you know I would greatly like to have some practice in the handling
> of large forces. I have much confidence in my judgment on things, when I
> see clearly, but on nothing do I seem to *feel* the truth more than in tactical
> combinations. It is a vain and foolish thing to say – but *you* will not
> laugh at it. I am sure I have the root of the matter in me – but never I
> fear in this state of existence will it have a chance of flowering – in bright red
> blossom.[8]

Those last words evidently recall Tennyson's disturbing line in *Maud*
about 'The blood-red blossom of war with a heart of fire'. They disclose
that ambivalence of feelings about war which never quite left him,
although it was often hidden beneath the excitement of battle and the
lust for victory. Again to Clementine, a couple of months later – perhaps
because she had been suggesting that he liked war too much – he admitted to thoughts of the same solemn kind: 'Much as war attracts me and
fascinates my mind with its tremendous situations – I feel more deeply
every year – and can measure the feeling here in the midst of arms – what
vile and wicked folly and barbarism it all is.'[9] He was indeed at that
moment in the midst of arms such as Europe had never seen before. He
was in Würzburg, observing for the second time the German army's
annual manoeuvres (he had attended the 1906 ones at Breslau), and he
was again thunderstruck and alarmed by what he saw. 'This army is a terrible engine. It marches sometimes thirty-five miles in a day. It is in
number as the sands of the sea – and with all the modern conveniences.'
'I am very thankful there is a sea between that army and England.'[10]

In his busy life to this time, Churchill had not paid much attention to
matters maritime. As a growing lad and young army officer, he would
have taken for granted the existence and role of the Royal Navy: the
biggest navy in the world, at least as powerful on paper as the two
next largest navies put together (the 'two-power standard'), apparently

guaranteeing protection of the home island against invasion and its imperial properties against predators. Nor did his business in the House of Commons from 1900 onwards bring him into direct contact with the navy. For his first five years, besides moving from the Tory to the Liberal benches, he concerned himself mainly with South African and army affairs, with a special line in criticism of War Office waste and extravagance. From 1906 until well into 1911, he was busy in his three non- military ministerial offices, and he comfortably joined his new political friend David Lloyd George and the majority of the Liberal Cabinet in deprecating increased military expenditure.

That attitude was, however, becoming yearly more difficult to maintain. Early in 1907, in a debate on Imperial Defence, he spoke of 'the great competition in military armaments which marks and darkens the modern era ... that fierce competition, that rivalry of arms in which so many of the polite peoples of the earth are so ready to engage'. 'Polite' was an eighteenth-century synonym for civilised, and his ironic use of it pointed to the Great Powers (and some lesser ones) of the Continent, whose land forces had been pumping themselves up for years to the point where Europe could reasonably be described as becoming one great armed camp. 'We are put to immense charges in this country, in common with other modern Powers, for military and naval armaments ... We all realise what an enormous boon and advantage it would be ... if we could do something to lighten the burden of armaments, which future ages, I venture to think, will indicate as the blackest reproach upon the civilisation, the science, and the Christianity of the twentieth century.'[11]

The trouble was no longer France but Germany. Contrary to every expectation held throughout the whole of the nineteenth century, the German Empire that had been proclaimed in 1871 over the prostrate body of France was now becoming a menace to Britain, not on land – the thought of a British army engaging in continental warfare was still inconceivable to all save a few advanced thinkers in the War Office – but, astonishingly, at sea. Since 1900 the Kaiser's naval chief, Admiral Alfred von Tirpitz, had been building an ocean-going fleet, no other purpose for which was imaginable than to deter Britain from entering into any European war on the anti-German side. Matching the French navy's modernisations in the late nineteenth century had already swollen the costs of the Royal Navy; now, in the early twentieth, a totally modern German navy was growing year by year, driving the Admiralty not only to further costs but also to new thinking. The strategic plans and naval bases that had served for more than a century were rapidly becoming obsolete. Not the English Channel and the Mediterranean but the North Sea and perhaps the Baltic were where the action was going to be; and that would include the use of many new weapons and devices made available by rapidly advancing science and technology; weapons and devices at which Germany would in the event prove itself generally superior.

Whether the Royal Navy was up to this challenge was a question that increasingly came to disturb the government and the thinking public. To some extent the question was forced on them by the all too audible row going on among the admirals themselves. The senior ranks of the navy in the early years of the twentieth century were not at all the 'band of brothers' of Nelsonian legend. Officers, who were in no position to keep their heads down, were enlisted into either one of two raging factions. One was headed by the quick-minded, outspoken and tempestuous 'Jackie' Fisher, who had been busily pushing his ideas for change since the 1880s and who from 1904 to 1910 sat in the most senior professional seat, that of First Sea Lord. The most dramatic innovation of his years was the revolutionary battleship *Dreadnought* in 1906. The other faction centred on the well-connected and politically-minded Admiral Lord Charles Beresford, Commander-in-Chief of the Mediterranean and Channel Fleets from 1905 and 1907 respectively; a reformer like Fisher, but with different ideas. Churchill had very likely come across the latter – Lord Charles was the brother of Lord William Beresford, who had married the widow of the 8th Duke of Marlborough – but it was Fisher who captivated him (as he tells us at some length in *The World Crisis*) when they first met at Biarritz in 1907. What Churchill initially thought of Fisher is obvious enough. What Fisher really thought of Churchill is by no means so clear. Thus began a connection that would bring Churchill both good and ill.

The crisis that brought Churchill to the Admiralty and reactivated the relationship between Churchill and Fisher came in 1911. The costs of the navy were still growing and the Anglo-French *Entente* had become ever closer since its tentative beginnings in 1904. The prospect of war on the side of France against Germany was brought into sharper focus during the summer of 1911 by the diplomatic crisis following the arrival of a small German warship, the *Panther*, at the Moroccan port of Agadir, the implicit purpose of which was to add military muscle to Germany's complaints about French expansionism in North Africa. For many weeks, war felt very close. The Committee of Imperial Defence (since 1904 the central element of Britain's war planning, such as it was) found it necessary to see the war plans of the armed services departments and to make sure that, if an expeditionary force had to cross the Channel, the navy could guarantee to protect it while it did so. Fisher's successor as First Sea Lord, Admiral Sir Arthur Wilson, gave a lamentably unimpressive performance, made to appear all the more so by comparison with the lucid eloquence of the army's spokesman, General Sir Henry Wilson.[12] The army had enjoyed the advantage of a General Staff since 1904; Wilson (like Fisher before him) insisted the navy didn't need one. The navy seemed to have no war plans other than those in the First Sea Lord's head, and they included nothing to help the army. H. H. Asquith, the Prime Minister, was distinctly unimpressed, and R. B. Haldane, the Secretary for War (responsible for the army), said he could not go on in office unless the Admiralty was quickly brought into line. Asquith acted. He sent for Churchill, who by now had established a reputation as a strong man in office with a flair for public relations.

Churchill came late to the navy. He had begun adult life as a soldier and always prided himself on being one. By the time he was in his thirties he had come across many generals – indeed he had made sure that many generals came across him – but until the summer of 1907 he had little if any experience of admirals. Some of the more controversial things that happened at the Admiralty through the next three years have to be considered in the light of the circumstances of his appointment. Reginald McKenna, his predecessor, had not been an effectively reforming First Lord. He had continued the enlargement of the navy but that was not the same thing. The admirals were gratified when McKenna won the political battle for huge expenditure on new battleships in 1909 (Churchill at the time called it 'an admirals' ramp'), but he had not prevailed over them in the argument about the need for a War Staff. The admirals, with the advantage of the monarch's special interest, were resistant to strong civilian leadership and had not met anything like it before. They liked running their show themselves, and non-service interests figured neither in their counsels nor in their professional trained thinking.[13] Churchill admitted to sharing the common wonder as to whether they were trained to think at all.

That was unnecessarily severe. There were plenty of bright younger officers, and some of the senior ones were more flexible than legend has maintained. But there *was* something in the naval style that encouraged the objective civilian to wonder about it. All naval officers at every level in their exacting hierarchy were habituated to receiving and giving orders, orders demanding instant obedience. Curt speech, short tempers and professional pride, even arrogance, were part of their mystique. Fisher had been unusual in his readiness with tongue and pen. Wilson, wrote the admiral whom Churchill appointed to succeed him, was not only 'deadly dull' but 'of clam-like obstinacy and abrasive manner. He spoke rarely and when he did as likely as not it was to offend someone.'[14] The Admiralty was not going to be sorted out by soft soap and sweet reason. Churchill was put there to be tough and to be, so far as was necessary, unpleasant. Although he liked popularity as much as anyone, he was more prepared than most to bear unpopularity in a good cause. The cause was no less than the security of the British Isles. Having accepted the Prime Minister's invitation, he found himself beset by melodramatic thoughts:

> I thought of the peril of Britain, peace-loving, unthinking, little prepared, of her power and virtue, and of her mission of good sense and fairplay. I thought of mighty Germany, towering up in the splendour of her Imperial State and delving down in her profound, cold, patient, ruthless calculations. I thought of the army corps I had watched tramp past, wave after wave of valiant manhood, at the Breslau manoeuvres in 1907 ... I thought of German education and thoroughness and all that their triumphs in science and philosophy implied. I thought of the sudden and successful wars by which her power had been set up.[15]

Determined that the Royal Navy should be in good shape to meet whatever surprises the German navy might throw at it, he set about understanding the workings and the arcana of his new department with his accustomed gusto, and soon appeared – to fellow landsmen, at least – to become remarkably knowledgeable about it. Prepared though he was to be tough, he could not dispense with circumspection in how he went about his work. Apart from resenting the arrival of a brusque and

nosy Liberal politician as their boss, the navy's Conservative upper strata
were highly politicised, leaking readily in the directions of Westminster,
Pall Mall and Buckingham Palace. George V took a more personal interest in the *Royal* Navy than he did in the other armed service. Its officers
were used to being masters in their own houses and to the practice of
promotion by seniority. The first thing Churchill had to do was to
replace Wilson with someone more modern-minded. The man he had
in view was the professionally respected and personally amenable Prince
Louis of Battenberg, but, as it seemed inexpedient to make him First Sea
Lord straightaway, Sir Francis Bridgeman was appointed as an appropriately named stop-gap. When Bridgeman made difficulties about
being ditched after only a year in post, he learned, what many were to
learn later, that when Churchill was thwarted he could be ruthless. Battenberg duly replaced Bridgeman in 1912 and in harmony with Churchill
(or, as some believed, subservient to him) headed the navy through the
next two years and confidently into the war.

   None of Churchill's other senior appointments was bad, while some
were good. Once they were in office, his relations with all of them seem
to have been harmonious; which was not surprising, since he only
appointed men he thought would see things his way. The best appointment was David Beatty, in succession commander of the Battle- Cruiser
Squadron from 1913 and of the Grand Fleet after the battle of Jutland.
The least good was Fisher's protégé Sir John Jellicoe, appointed to succeed Sir George Callaghan in command the Grand Fleet on 2 August
1914, the very eve of war. Perhaps because of subsequent disappointment with Jellicoe, Churchill later went to some length to explain and
excuse the switch. 'The First Sea Lord and I had a conference with Sir
George Callaghan on his way through London to the North [Scapa
Flow] on the 30th [July] ... We were doubtful as to his health and
physical strength being equal to the immense strain that would be cast
upon him; and in the crash of Europe it was no time to consider individuals.'[16] Although the wisdom of this surgical strike seems not to have
been doubted by naval historians, it created a great stir at the time, and
Churchill's always sensible wife begged him somehow to soften the
blow. 'If you give him a position of honour and confidence, the whole
service will feel that he has been as well treated as possible under the
circumstances, and that he has not been humiliated ... Then, don't

underestimate the power of women to do mischief. I don't want Lady Callaghan and Lady Bridgeman to form a league of Retired Officers' Cats to abuse you.'[17] This would not be the last time Clementine urged her husband to be more kindly and considerate; nor was it the first. It was par for the course that he appears not to have followed her suggestion.

The principal achievement of Churchill's First Lordship was, or should have been, the institution of a naval War Staff, which was begun in January 1912. Proper evaluation of it has been made difficult by our lack until very recently of any precise knowledge of what it did within the larger Admiralty establishment.[18] Certainly, it did not make the dramatic difference to war-planning that its proponents hoped, but there is plenty of evidence that planning went better and with more fresh thinking than before. Its preparation of the British Expeditionary Force's transit to France seems to have been wholly successful. But it had existed for less than three years when the war began, it was understaffed, and it had been set up in such a way that there was no working relationship between it and the Board of Admiralty. The opportunity to place the First Sea Lord in its chair was not taken and senior officers found that they could ignore it if they chose to do so. Churchill later said that they disliked it because 'They did not want a special class of officer professing to be more brainy than the rest';[19] but another reason for their dislike was that in practice it boosted the First Lord's authority at the First Sea Lord's expense.

Of course not all of the changes wrought under Churchill's First Lordship were due to him alone. Some were continuations of developments already in prospect when he took office, such as the improved schemes for pay, punishments and promotion which considerably humanised the service and made it for the first time possible for men to ascend from the lower-deck to the quarter-deck; Churchill, no matter that he was in many ways a social snob himself, set his face against officer caste snobbery about the voice of the secondary school and the smell of the engine-room. Engineering in fact interested him. He now discovered in himself that intelligent enthusiasm for military technology that would continue through the rest of his active life – an enthusiasm carried to unexpected lengths, inasmuch as no other First Lord can be imagined as using his position to instigate research into the construction of tanks.

For two other innovations on the maritime side, his responsibility was relatively direct. Thrilled by aeronautics and clearly perceiving the coming military applications of aeroplanes (which he learned to fly) and 'Zeppelins' (a field in which Germany was menacingly advanced), he promoted and protected the Royal Naval Air Service, the embryo of the later Fleet Air Arm. Secondly, having made the necessary strategic and commercial calculations and arrangements, he also fulfilled one of Fisher's best ambitions by initiating the shift from coal to oil that was essential for the improvement of warship performance and crew comfort. It was one of the many strong points of the latest battleships, the *Queen Elizabeth* class with unprecedented 15-inch guns, that their fuel was oil. That the fleet was in some ways not technically as good as it might have been was mainly because of shortcomings already in the system before he took office.

Churchill's most dramatic venture on the scientific side has had little acknowledgement. Recent research has uncovered what Churchill concealed when he wrote *The World Crisis* – that he spent much of his time at the Admiralty promoting research into and development of a submarine fleet, and that he worked closely with those forward-looking officers who reckoned that the submarine was the weapon of the future.[20] This interesting and creditable story was in fact spelled out in the book's first draft but excised from the finished version. His presumed reasons for so doing are instructive. The story would have had to admit that, because of failure to settle on exactly what kind of submarines was wanted, not enough of them were ready by August 1914. It would also have told how, oppressed by the financial constraints imposed by an anxious Cabinet, Churchill had actually planned to divert to the construction of submarines the money that the tax-paying public believed to be earmarked for another battleship; battleships being the conventional and popular measure of naval strength. It was the pictures and names of thundering battleships (such as *Invincible, Lion* and *Iron Duke*) that gratified the public, not pictures or numbers (E 11, for example, or H 1) of stealthy submarines. Churchill himself responded to the call of the battleship; several of the purplest passages in *The World Crisis* are responses to it. (It is significant that no submarine numbers appear in the index to that book, although the names of even the most insignificant warships do.) Yet he knew in some part of his mind that their day would soon be over, just as he had known that the days of cavalry were over already. He was rarely blinded by sentiment to the changes in the ways of making war that were enforced or offered by contemporary advances in science and industry.

With the probable exception of its submarine fleet, the Royal Navy was, Churchill believed, 'ready' in 1914. But what precisely was it ready *for*? There was no problem about its immediate and workaday tasks. The most immediate and all-important task was to see the British Expeditionary Force safely across the water to France. Churchill had been appointed to the Admiralty to make sure it could do that, and he succeeded. The main movement began on 9 August and it was virtually completed by the 19th, a whole week earlier than the Germans had expected. The entire operation was carried out without losing either a ship or a man.[21] In the longer term, the navy was ready for its traditional task of clearing and guarding the shipping-lanes of the world, and for hunting down the enemy's commerce raiders; thanks to Churchill's strategic foresight, a system of national insurance gave British shipping confidence to carry on regardless of all hazards.[22] The navy was also ready for another of its traditional tasks, the inhibition of enemy trade and the prevention of neutrals acting on the enemy's behalf. This meant, what it had meant for the two centuries past, the unglamorous business of blockade; not 'close blockade' as previously envisaged, because mines and torpedo-firing warships now made that too risky, but 'distant blockade' by surveillance along a line from Norway to Shetland: a revision of plans that the War Staff had completed within its first year.

It was those torpedoes, and the submarines and torpedo-boats that launched them, that perplexed and worried Churchill and his naval planners. Like mines, they had a defensive use, as part of a close blockade, and also an offensive one, bringing unseen hazards into home waters. The Royal Navy had no experience of up-to-date warfare involving such devices. The only recent war from which lessons might be learned was that between Russia and Japan in 1904–5; and those lessons were not encouraging. Mines and torpedoes had done great execution. Offensive operations against the German coast and islands were often considered at Churchill's Admiralty, as they had been for years past, with the occasional addition now of the Dutch coast and

islands – Churchill never allowed his strategic first thoughts to be inhibited by respect for small neutrals – but again and again they were
abandoned as impractical and too risky. The visible dangers might have
been braved; the invisible ones were just too much.

Another of the concerns raised by the Russo–Japanese war was
that the enemy might initiate hostilities before a formal declaration of
war or entirely without one. Japan's surprise attack on Russia's eastern
fleet at Port Arthur, coupled with Fisher's dangerous bombast about
'Copenhagening the Germans', led Tirpitz and his admirals to fear
that Britain would catch them unawares. (The Copenhagen reference
was to Nelson's destruction of the Danish fleet on 2 April 1801, when
Denmark was part of a Russian-led coalition hostile to Britain, but war
had not formally been declared.) Churchill and the British admirals
were worried that Germany might do the same. They were also worried lest the opening of hostilities, whether declared or not, should catch
the British Grand Fleet with its most modern battleships in the wrong
place.

All three British battle fleets were assembled at Portland in mid-July
1914 for a test mobilisation. They were still there, though about to disperse, on Friday 24 July, the day before Serbia had to reply to Austria's
provocative ultimatum. The possibility of war had suddenly come
closer. Austria's rejection of Serbia's reply was known by the morning
of Sunday the 26th. War had come closer still. Churchill had gone to
Cromer for the weekend with his family but he kept in specially-
arranged telephonic contact with Battenberg, who stayed all day at the
Admiralty and kept abreast of the steadily worsening news. They discussed what to do – Battenberg no doubt accepted Churchill's idea of
what to do – and so, at about 4 p.m., Battenberg ordered the fleets not
to disperse. The momentous move came three days later. Austria
declared war on Serbia on the 28th. If Britain thereafter were to find
itself at war with Germany while the bulk of the British navy was still in
the English Channel, the German navy would be dominant in the North
Sea and Germany would begin the war with a major strategic advantage.
Churchill therefore decided to order the First Fleet to leave Portland
next day, the 29th, and to sail up the middle of the Channel and 'pass
through the Straits [of Dover] without lights during the night' and to
head north. He later wrote with relish:

We may now picture this great fleet, with its flotillas and cruisers, steaming slowly out of Portland Harbour, squadron by squadron, scores of gigantic castles of steel wending their way across the misty, shining sea, like giants bowed in anxious thought. We may picture them again as darkness fell, eighteen miles of warships running at high speed and in absolute blackness through the narrow Straits, bearing with them into the broad waters of the North Sea the safeguard of considerable affairs.[23]

The majority of the Cabinet – conciliatory until the German invasion of Belgium on 3 August – being very likely to disapprove of what the Germans would (and did) call a provocative act, the only political colleague he consulted was the Prime Minister, Asquith, who approved. Churchill concluded his colourful account of the episode in *The World Crisis* with this happy reflection: 'We were now in a position, whatever happened, to control events, and it was not easy to see how this advantage could be taken from us.'[24]

What Churchill and the admirals would most have liked to have followed was a great old-fashioned battle in the North Sea, fleet against fleet, from which, they had no doubt, the larger British fleet would emerge victorious. But that was precisely what they were not going to get. The Kaiser's admirals also longed for battle, but only if they could engage against some detached or detachable part of the Grand Fleet, over which they might hope to assert local superiority. The war in the North Sea turned therefore into one of hide-and-seek and 'dare', each side tempting the other to come within range of its guns and submarines, and making offensive 'sweeps' (also, on the German part, raids) to challenge their enemy to come out and fight. Churchill was full of offensive spirit and rejoiced when his ships got into action, as occasionally they did. But his instinctive lust for action, very marked and troublesome in the early weeks of the war, was tempered as the months passed by a rational recognition that to enforce *inaction* on the enemy was the supreme good. So long as Britain maintained its battle fleet, and Germany's counterpart declined to close with it, the grand design of Admiral Tirpitz was thwarted. Britain had *not* been deterred from joining France in war against Germany, and its mastery of the waves (the European ones, at least) remained inviolate. Such a maritime war was boring but effective. As Churchill later conceded, apropos of the superficially indecisive battle of Jutland in 1916, Admiral Jellicoe was the one man who could have lost the war in an afternoon, and he was quite right not to have risked doing so.

Churchill's term of office as First Lord of the Admiralty continued until the Cabinet reshuffle of May 1915. The most conspicuous chapters in it were his dash to Antwerp in October 1914 and his promotion of the navy's attempt in early 1915 to force a passage through the Dardanelles.* As to everything else that happened during his time as First Lord, that is to say the whole war at sea with its mixture of setbacks and successes, it is well-nigh impossible to distinguish what was done in consequence of his persuasiveness or bossiness from what was done by the appropriate naval authorities with his participation or what the naval authorities simply got on with on their own.

That he was responsible in the parliamentary sense for everything happening in his department, and that he liked to appear in charge, encouraged the popular impression that he 'ran the navy', but the truth is not so simple. Fisher, whom Churchill imprudently restored to the office of First Sea Lord when a xenophobic witch-hunt caused the German-born Battenberg's resignation, alleged (just as Churchill's critics would allege again in 1941–42) that he went so far as to issue operational orders off his own bat. Fisher may have been referring to the practice thus ingenuously described by Churchill himself: 'seeing what ought to be done and confident of the agreement of the First Sea Lord, I myself drafted the telegrams and decisions in accordance with our policy, and the Chief of the Staff took them personally to the First Sea Lord for his concurrence before dispatch'.[25] The normal thing, however, was for important decisions to be taken by what Churchill called the 'War Staff Group': himself, the First Sea Lord (sometimes also the Second), the chief of the Admiralty War Staff and the Secretary to the Admiralty; and it often happened that Churchill's bright ideas, although the War Staff could not avoid giving time to their consideration, were in the end rejected. When so many people were involved in decision-making and in the wording of instructions to be signalled to distant commanders, it was not easy for critics then or later to pin responsibility on individuals; and it is not easy for historians now.

---

* See below, Chapter 4.

An early example of the kind of row that recurred throughout Churchill's career came when Admiral Sir Christopher Cradock met with disaster off Cape Coronel in mid-October 1914. Cradock's ramshackle squadron in the South Atlantic was supposed to be looking out for Admiral von Spee's squadron, which, after causing much alarm and doing some damage in the Pacific, was believed to be steaming towards the southern coasts of Chile and Argentina. When at last Cradock received information from the Admiralty of von Spee's whereabouts and suggestions as to appropriate action, he gave battle and was destroyed. Was Churchill responsible for the ambiguities and confusions in the signals that helped to send him to the bottom? Churchill argued that it was the admiral's own fault for being imprudent. Others pointed the finger at the First Lord himself; but to the sharp-eyed (and sharp-penned) Assistant Director of Operations, who was ideally situated to know what went on and was normally quick to find fault with Churchill, the man most to blame was Admiral Sturdee, the Chief of the War Staff.[26] For the failings of the War Staff itself, and the operational shortcomings that might have been less marked if it had been established earlier, the finger points less at Churchill, who had established it as soon as he could, than at Fisher, who had held it up for years before that.

Two naval innovations for which Churchill could take some credit ironically had the effect of speeding the onset of unrestricted submarine warfare. One was the arming of merchant ships (*not* passenger ones) with guns of modest calibre, so that they might defend themselves against U-boat attack. This presupposed, as was the almost universal presupposition until the end of 1914, that U-boats would attack their mercantile prey on the surface – as to begin with most in fact did. But of course they weren't going to go on like that if it gave their prey the opportunity to shoot at them. Churchill's other anti-U-boat device made surface-based operations by submarines even more suicidal. This was the Q-ship, looking like an ordinary commercial vessel but cunningly concealing guns which it would unmask when the U-boat had been drawn unsuspectingly close. Over tea at St-Omer in December 1915, Edward Spears heard the former First Lord enthuse about 'dodges to catch submarines, the boat which pretends to surrender, the crew tumbling overboard and then guns unmasking ...'[27] Q-ships had some success – ten U-boats sunk, at the cost of twenty Q-ships – but at the cost also of coarsening the moral sensibilities that alone could check the slide towards unrestricted warfare.[28] Churchill, however, was not to blame for that. The technological imperative was pushing maritime warfare in that direction anyway.

4

Antwerp and Gallipoli

Leading the world's biggest and best navy into war might have been thought enough to satisfy the most martial ambition, but it wasn't enough for Churchill. Apart from cherishing a longing to command large forces on land, his capacious mind took in the war in all its aspects and he had ideas about every one of them. Few of his colleagues in the Cabinet had ever given any thought to the conduct of war. All of them noted his enthusiasm for it, and most were thankful that there was at least one amongst them who seemed to know what to do. Churchill was interestingly observant about his own state of mind. At midnight on 28 July, the day Austria-Hungary declared war on Serbia, he wrote to Clementine from the Admiralty:

> My Darling One and beautiful. Everything trends [*sic*] towards catastrophe and collapse. I am interested, geared-up and happy. Is it not horrible to be built like that? The preparations have a hideous fascination for me. I pray to God to forgive me for such fearful moods of levity. Yet I would do my best for peace, and nothing would induce me wrongfully to strike the blow. I cannot feel that we in this island are in any serious degree responsible for the wave of madness which has swept the mind of Christendom ... Everything is ready as it has never been before. And we are awake to the tips of our fingers. But war is the Unknown and the Unexpected! God guard us and our long accumulated inheritance ...[1]

There was nothing unexpected about the German invasion of Belgium. What was not known to begin with was how much of Belgium it would cover. For the first four weeks, only Brussels and its southern regions were afflicted; the Schlieffen Plan's purpose was not to occupy Belgium but to pass through it *en route* to Paris, and it was no great matter to the German High Command that substantial Belgian forces remained intact around the supposedly impregnable fortress city of Antwerp. The exposed northern flank of the German armies and the

Belgians' modest forays against it could, however, no longer be neglected once it became clear, in early September 1914, that the Schlieffen Plan had failed. By then Churchill was becoming a nuisance to them too. Perceiving a strategic opportunity, he had landed a small force of marines at Ostend with maximum publicity and installed part of his Royal Naval Air Service at Dunkirk. The marines made inland sweeps in armoured cars to tackle the German cavalry detachments that were terrorising the Belgian countryside, while the airmen reported on the movements of the main German forces and bombed the more accessible Zeppelin bases.

For a few weeks Churchill's 'Dunkirk guerrillas' had the good effect of putting heart into the locals and persuading the German generals that they might have to face a British move on the Belgian coast, imperilling their northern flank and potentially denying their navy the use of the Belgian ports. Their predictable response was to advance into the parts of Belgium not yet occupied and to summon their siege train to deal with Antwerp, where the government and most of the Belgian army had found refuge. By 28 September the German army had advanced close enough to the perimeter of the forts to begin bombardment. King Albert, at the head of his soldiers, was desperate for military support, and Kitchener and Churchill were determined to provide what they could. News came to London on 2 October that the Belgian government and army were about to abandon Antwerp; it was incorrect with regard to the army, but the British ministers were not to know that. The Prime Minister being in Wales and inaccessible, Kitchener and Grey summoned Battenberg and Churchill (who happened to be about to go to the front anyway) to a late night conference, the conclusion of which was that Churchill should at once go to Antwerp and try to keep the Belgians' spirits up until the promised British and French contingents could get there. Kitchener undertook to send General Rawlinson with a British division, and Joffre on behalf of the French also offered support. How long it would take for these reinforcements to arrive remained to be seen; they still had not arrived by the time the Belgians decided it was time for what was left of their army to get out.

So far, the story has little of the sensational in it. It was a crisis and it made sense for a senior figure – especially such a martial-minded one as Churchill – to go to Antwerp to represent the British interest there; the Admiralty's particular interest had been attended to since

29 September by Admiral Oliver, who had disabled the big ships in the harbour so as to prevent the enemy making use of them. Churchill of course relished the assignment and went at once, arriving on the afternoon of 3 October. In his wake were scheduled to come, on the 4th, a small detachment of Royal Marines and, he hoped not later than the 5th, his own creation the 'Royal Naval Division', an embodiment of his zeal for amphibious operations but at this date, by his own admission, still 'inexperienced, partially equipped and partially trained'.[2] He had not intended the rawer recruits to be included, but the Admiralty omitted to winnow them out.[3] These novices arrived on the morning of the 6th, a whole day later than he had reckoned on, by which time Rawlinson's division was only disembarking at Ostend and Zeebrugge, the French were even further away, and Antwerp's military situation was becoming unquestionably hopeless. King Albert's Council of War decided that same evening to withdraw the Belgian field army westwards and to leave the city to defend itself as long as it could; which, in the event, was for three days more. Churchill returned to London during the night of the 6th, leaving what Captain Richmond called his 'tuppeny untrained rabble' to fight on as best they could for the next couple of days. Most of them were either taken prisoner or interned in the Netherlands, whose border ran close to Antwerp on the western side of the Scheldt.[4]

The Churchillian sensation had come on the morning of the 5th, when he telegrammed the Prime Minister thus:

> If it is thought by HM Government that I can be of service here, I am willing to resign my office and undertake command of relieving and defensive forces assigned to Antwerp in conjunction with Belgian Army, provided that I am given necessary military rank and authority, and full powers of a commander of a detached force in the field. I feel it my duty to offer my services because I am sure this arrangement will afford the best prospects of a victorious result to an enterprise in which I am deeply involved ...[5]

The Cabinet is said to have burst into laughter when this was read out. It was not just that Churchill's proper post was back in Britain at the Admiralty and that his enemies (many in number, including the whole Conservative Party) were demanding that he return to his desk there, which the Prime Minister instructed him forthwith to do. It also seemed an improbable notion that a suddenly created General Churchill (Kitchener apparently expressed no objection to such a promotion) could improve on what the professional generals and Allied commanders were already doing in a foreign land. Churchill, however, was so exhilarated by his experience in Antwerp that, directly after his return, he begged the Prime Minister to release him from the Admiralty and to let him have one of the 'glittering commands' in the huge volunteer army that Kitchener was planning.[6]

Antwerp's resistance at least gave the Allies a little more time to concentrate forces in front of the German movement towards the Channel coast. So far as the Belgians were concerned, it was a gamble that did not quite come off. Churchill never doubted that it had been a gamble worth taking: 'so sovereign in war are the virtues of positive effort, of refusal to acquiesce in defeat, so baffling to purely military calculation is the influence of amphibious power'.[7] Churchill later stoutly defended his share in it in *The World Crisis*, writing that he felt responsible for having involved his inadequate Naval Division and for encouraging the Belgians to carry on by promising them more than he was able to deliver. 'I felt it my duty to see the matter through.' These were honourable sentiments. It was also true that he had, soon after arrival on 3 October, extracted from the Belgian government an undertaking to continue resistance for at least three more days; an undertaking from which they were released by the Allies' failure to reinforce them within that period.[8] Nevertheless, it was universally felt, not least by his wife, that Churchill had temporarily lost his grip on reality, and the Conservative press was severe on him. Several familiar traits of character help to explain to explain what had happened: they included his thirst for activity, sense of honour, love of limelight, defiance of death, impetuosity, and dreams of high military command. Whether his presence *after* the 3rd had really done much to 'brace the Belgians to their task' (as he put it) is doubtful, but he believed it had done so – and so did those friends and colleagues who gave him a hero's welcome on his return.[9]

Churchill's Antwerp venture finds its proper place as an incident in the vast military drama that was unfolding through the weeks from mid-September to late November: the establishment of the Western Front. That phenomenon, something that no one had expected, no one wanted, and no one knew what to do about, determined the shape of the war for the next four years. Both sides had expected the war to be brought to an end quickly by victory or defeat in big battles. Recalling the war between France and Germany that began in July 1870 and was over within six months, they took insufficient note of the American Civil War's four years. The main feature of the first four weeks was Germany's implementation of the long-matured Schlieffen Plan: five of its seven armies swung into France via southern Belgium in a movement designed to embrace, at its furthest edge, Paris.

By the middle of September, that plan had gone awry; the western-most army had (for reasons sound enough at the time) ended up not west but east of Paris, and the whole German advance had been brought to a standstill at the battle of the Marne. What followed over the course of the next eight weeks became misleadingly known as 'the Race to the Sea'. Neither antagonist had yet abandoned hope of turning the other's flank. 'Each in turn extended his line [northwards] until it touched the coast, because he had been unable to envelop and roll up his adversary. The protection of the water was welcomed only when the destruction of the opposing army by manoeuvre was proved impossible.' By the last days of November military stalemate and winter weather left no option but to 'dig in'. A line of trenches began to be formed 'which until March 1917 never varied by as much as ten miles in either direction'.[10]

By this time the notion of circumventing the unexpected stalemate by attacking Germany from another side was exercising many French and British minds. The idea of military action in that quarter was not Churchill's alone, nor was it new in 1915. Another early expectation that had been dashed (like that of a short war) concerned Russia's military capability, which had been thought immense. So far, it had proved disappointing. The war in the east had begun with crushing defeats of the Russian armies advancing into East Prussia, and although Russia had been more successful in its operations against Germany's ally, Austria-Hungary, Germany was after all the power most to be feared. It therefore seemed desirable in London and Paris to do something in the east to help Russia and perhaps also little Serbia, gallantly harassing Austria-Hungary on its southern side. To begin with, the plans were diplomatic as well as military. Turkey (to give the Ottoman Empire its more familiar alternative name) and the Balkan states in varying combinations had been at war with one another several times within living memory, but in August 1914 they happened to be at peace. Their neighbours and patrons the Great Powers having begun a great war, these smaller states were bound to wonder which side to plump for and what they might get out of it. Turkey, controlling the Straits and by its control of Palestine a menace to British Egypt and the Suez Canal, was the highest prize in the diplomatic game. Germany won it. Britain's lingering hope that Turkey could be kept out of the war was dashed in November, when two German warships, *Goeben* and *Breslau*, reached Constantinople. The other three so far neutral Balkan states (Greece, Rumania and Bulgaria) remained on the sidelines, as did Italy, all waiting to see what might be in it for them. Churchill admired the Greek Prime Minister Venizelos, who was known to be more friendly to the Allies than the monarch. Greece had aspirations to control the Straits and to dominate Constantinople – but so did Russia. Britain was mortified to discover that the mutual suspicion of Greece and Russia was such that to gain the assistance of the one was to forfeit the assistance of the other. By the end of 1914 it was clear that Russian sensibilities were the ones to be attended to: the Russian armies had run short of munitions; a German spring offensive might crush them; and the Turks had opened a front against them in the Caucasus. It was clear also that nothing decisive was going to happen for a long time on what was now called the Western Front.

The idea of forcing the Dardanelles, the sea passage between the Aegean Sea and the Sea of Marmara, and the gateway to Constantinople, had been around for many weeks (indeed, it had been on and off the Admiralty's planning tables for many years) but now it acquired new attractions. Churchill had long hoped to undo the damage done at the very beginning of the war when his Mediterranean admirals failed to stop the German warships getting to Constantinople. The Mediterranean had so far interested the Admiralty less than the northern seas. Churchill and the naval planners never tired of mulling over ambitious plans to distract Germany on its northern borders by seizing islands off the German coasts or, one of Fisher's obsessions, entering the Baltic to land troops (preferably Russian ones) in Pomerania. Churchill too indulged in these fantasies, but the Dardanelles increasingly attracted his attention until it became, at the turn of the year, his obsession.

By this time, the first weeks of 1915, the Turkish high command was busy improving the Dardanelles defences. They had not amounted to much when, on 3 November 1914, war with Turkey having become inevitable, Churchill ordered a naval bombardment of the outer forts. Whether or not the Turks would have made ready for attack without this preliminary notice of British interest is unclear; what is certain is that the defences were soon made formidable: mobile howitzers and field guns were added to the forts, and minefields scientifically laid in the fast-flowing waters. The obvious mode of attack against such a place was by land forces, and this was regularly envisaged whenever operations were mooted in the last months of 1914. The navy's part would be to carry the soldiers there and to help by bombarding enemy positions. The attractive prospect was also entertained that, once the Gallipoli peninsula, on the west bank of Dardanelles, was conquered, the warships could steam through and terrify Constantinople into surrender. Kitchener, whose burdens were immense, sometimes said he could provide troops sufficient for this task; sometimes that he couldn't. His reputation and power being then at their height, and his word being law, nothing could be done to commit him to one course of action or the other; the easygoing Prime Minister Asquith had nothing like the ultimate authority Churchill would insist on possessing twenty-five years later. With the project hanging fire, Churchill made his Admiralty 'War Group' look again at the possibility of a purely naval operation. As he did so, he became more than usually excited.

On 3 January 1915 the naval commander in the Eastern Mediterranean, Vice-Admiral Carden, received this telegram, the peremptory and typically Churchillian tone of which must have caught his attention:

> From First Lord. Do you consider the forcing of the Dardanelles by ships alone a practicable operation? It is assumed older ships fitted with mine-bumpers would be used, preceded by colliers or other merchant craft as mine-bumpers and sweepers. Importance of results would justify severe loss. Let me know your views.[11]

The penultimate sentence about losses was standard Churchillian first thoughts about an exciting new operation. His second thoughts were usually more cautious. The unfortunate Carden, who had been tranquilly superintending the Malta dockyard for the past three years, was put in a difficult spot. Churchill's question was clearly of the kind that expected a positive answer, but no commander likes sending men on missions from which they are unlikely to return, and mines were far from being the only hazards in such an operation. Two days later Carden sent an answer in terms as near as he dared to what Churchill wanted: 'With reference to your telegram of 3rd instant, I do not consider Dardanelles can be rushed. They might be forced by extended operations with large number of ships.'

Churchill took this to mean that the passage of the Dardanelles could probably be 'forced' by the navy alone and that the attempt should be made. Objectively, however, it must mean, as it seems to have meant to Churchill's professional advisers at the Admiralty, that Carden, the man on the spot, was unhappy, doubtful and reluctant. Churchill did not wish to believe that. Whether because his advisers did not speak their minds clearly enough or because he was in such a state that he could not understand them, he was unwilling to be told that the operation was impractical. He became its leading advocate in the War Council and told the council that it had the admirals' blessing. They subsequently said that it hadn't. Historians continue to mull over these clouded events. It is impossible to determine exactly what his naval advisers said or didn't say when he talked it over with them. There are grounds for believing that if he had not pressed so hard for the answers he wanted, or had been less hectoring in debate, he would have discovered that most of them had misgivings about it that grew as the weeks passed. Fisher, the professional who mattered most, began by assuring Churchill of his support but soon lost confidence in the enterprise, astonishing Churchill in the end by saying that he had never believed in it at all. If he had not been the driving, opinionated man he was, Churchill might have earlier realised that the operation enjoyed less support than he liked to believe. Yet even a calmer man might have thought the attempt worthwhile. It seems that the 'lay' members of the War Council continued to think it was, even though some of them must have known what Fisher really thought and might well have known what others thought too.[12]

By the middle of March a senior general, Churchill's friend Sir Ian Hamilton, was on his way to command the British and imperial forces that Kitchener, at last won over to the project, was assembling for the landing on the peninsula. Its immediate purpose was to facilitate the navy's operation by distracting the Turkish forces and silencing at least some of their guns. Churchill could have ordered a stay of naval operations pending the making of a joint army and navy plan; such a plan as was made for the landings five weeks later – or a better one. Fifteen years later, having had plenty of time for the cultivation of second thoughts, and writing a retrospective piece about things he might have done differently, he admitted that 'it would have been prudent to have broken off the naval attack' at an earlier date.[13] For whatever reason he didn't do so, using the argument that he had earlier used when discussing troop movements with Kitchener, that the naval operation had already begun – which meant no more than that Carden's ships were intermittently shelling Turkish gun positions from outside the Straits, a supposed softening-up process. This was unconvincing. One may either suppose that naval *amour propre* by then was too closely engaged or surmise that Churchill didn't like to admit, perhaps not to himself and certainly not to others, that he was having second thoughts.[14]

Second thoughts or not, he did nothing to delay or stop the spectacular assault scheduled for 18 March (by which time the unfortunate Carden had broken down and been superseded by Admiral De Robeck). Churchill gave an accurate account of it in *The World Crisis.*

> Ten battleships were assigned to the attack and six to their relief at four-hour intervals. The attack was to be opened at long range by the four modern ships. When the forts were partially subdued the four ships of the French squadron were to pass through the intervals of the first line and engage the forts at 8000 yards. As soon as the forts were dominated the mine-sweepers were to clear a 900-yards channel through the five lines of mines constituting the Kephez minefield. The sweeping was to continue through the night, covered by two battleships, while the rest of the fleet withdrew. The next morning, if the channel had been cleared, the fleet would advance through it into Sari Siglar Bay and batter the forts at the Narrows at short and decisive range.[15]

It was perhaps as good a plan as the men on the spot could have devised, and it was meticulously put into execution, but it failed because of two miscalculations, both to do with the minefields. Already for some days before the 18th, the minesweepers – civilian-crewed trawlers brought from Britain and roughly adapted to their task – had found it impossible to achieve anything under the twin menaces of the strong currents and the Turkish guns. The plan had therefore been modified to give them a better opportunity after those guns had been silenced. Some of the forts were duly silenced but it proved impossible to silence the mobile guns which the Turks had brought up. The majority of the known minefields remained unswept and one very recently laid minefield was undetected until too late. By five o'clock, when the attack was called off, the battleships *Irresistible*, *Ocean* and *Bouvet* had been sunk or were sinking, and the *Inflexible* and *Gaulois* were severely damaged. British casualties were light but six hundred French sailors went down in the *Bouvet*.

Churchill, on receiving De Robeck's report the next morning, never doubted that this was only the first stage of an operation that would immediately be continued; an assumption confirmed two days later on receipt of De Robeck's plans for a renewed assault. But within another three days the admiral had thought better of it. He had been talking with the generals who had arrived to plan the landings for which Kitchener had now found troops. He explained that success at sea (where the mines haunted him) would be more likely if combined with an assault by land. He proposed to do nothing more until he had concerted arrangements with Sir Ian Hamilton. Churchill was not merely disappointed, he was furious. He drafted a telegram ordering De Robeck to return to his original intention and took it to his War Group of advisers, expecting them to approve it. When, however, he put it to them, he found that the majority of them, with Fisher at their head, no doubt regretting that they had not spoken out more plainly earlier on, took De Robeck's part. There was a terrible row. Churchill contemplated resignation, but 'that would only have made matters worse. Nothing that I could do could overcome the Admirals now they had definitely dug their toes in.'[16]

De Robeck may have misjudged the situation. Some of his officers thought a renewed assault on the following day could have succeeded. It was now known where all the minefields lay, and the Turkish forts had fired off a great deal of ammunition.[17] The Turks were surprised when the assault was not renewed. Churchill never doubted that if the naval assault had succeeded either at its first attempt or its second, being followed by Hamilton's landings very soon thereafter, the course of the of the war and the history of the world would have been changed. He may have been right; but, as things were, he had to make the best of a bad job. Disappointed by De Robeck's prudence, and coming under public criticism for the failure so far, Churchill passed his last four weeks at the Admiralty excitedly ordering reinforcements, both naval and military, for the combined operation now in progress. Fisher having for the time being put himself out of contact, the First Lord's last official minutes, dictated on the very day that the political ground was beginning to crumble under him, issued as from a confident minister in supreme command.[18] From such a height, his fall was to prove very painful.

The Conservative Party and press had long been trying to bring down Churchill. Now they got him. They found their opportunity in the recriminations following the failure of the naval attack on 18 March. Perhaps that might not have mattered too much on its own, had not the anti-Churchill campaign, in the middle of May, coincided with a bizarre combination of events that worked wholly to Churchill's disadvantage. First of all, there was a destabilisation of relations between Churchill and the First Sea Lord, Fisher, coupled with (and partly occasioned by) some extreme and unstable behaviour by the ageing admiral himself. In so far as this worked to precipitate Churchill's undoing, it was his own fault. His infatuation with the capricious admiral was of a piece with his lifelong tendency to take up with colourful and controversial characters who excited him but whom his wife and well-wishers thought dangerous – in short, 'bad influences': the most conspicuous besides Fisher being the buccaneer barrister F. E. Smith (who became Lord Birkenhead), the newspaper proprietor and financier Sir Max Aitken (who became Lord Beaverbrook) and, at the end – though by then Churchill was so old and unwell that it was of no significance – the shady Greek shipowner Aristotle Onassis.

Neither the King nor the Prime Minister had approved Churchill's idea of bringing the seventy-five-year-old Fisher back to the Admiralty when the First Sea Lord Battenberg had to be replaced at the end of October 1914. Churchill, however, was adamant that he would have him, adapting the justification of his choice to his different audiences. To the public at large, he praised Fisher's dynamism and expertise.

To an intimate like Violet Asquith, he said he knew the old man's foibles and was sure he could manage him.[19] They got on famously to begin with, joshing one another like excited schoolboys, but by January 1915 suppressed irritation began to undermine the jocularity as the unstable older man increasingly resented his impetuous junior's interferences in the Sea Lords' realm. Freed after Fisher's death in 1920 from his magnetic attraction, Churchill in due course would describe him as 'harsh, capricious, vindictive, gnawed by hatreds arising often from spite, working secretly or violently as occasion might suggest by methods which the typical English gentleman or public schoolboy are taught to dislike and avoid'.[20]

On 14 May 1915 occurred another of the events that, unfortunately for Churchill, combined to undermine him. *The Times's* military correspondent alarmed the country and shook the government by revealing that the army in France was crippled by a shortage of shells. On the 15th, Fisher resigned; a familiar tactic, but this time he seemed really to mean it. And at the same time the Prime Minister was suffering personal distress because his pretty young confidante, Venetia Stanley, had unexpectedly announced her engagement to be married. With the shell shortage now added to the Dardanelles failure and no good news coming in from Gallipoli, the Conservatives' case for substantial change was irresistible.

Asquith himself by this time was willing to contemplate re-forming his administration as a coalition. The Conservatives' demand for Fisher's return to the Admiralty was scuppered by the admiral himself, who posed impossibly egoistically conditions for doing so.[21] Their demand for Churchill's removal from the Admiralty had to be met. The unwarlike A. J. Balfour was made First Lord, Churchill was moved to the unwarlike, non-executive post of Chancellor of the Duchy of Lancaster, and his days at the centre of power were over for the rest of the war. He continued to have enough of a finger in the pie to qualify for a share of the blame for Gallipoli, but his share in the military decision-making was minimal. He subjected the Dardanelles Committee (as Asquith's pseudo-War Council was now named) to a deluge of memoranda and speeches urging ever more action there and decrying pessimism as to its outcome, but Kitchener, now the unchallenged master of the stage, politely paid no notice. From being at the centre of strategic policy making, Churchill was edged towards its periphery. Increasingly targeted as the prime mover in the Dardanelles failure (an allegation with much truth in it) and the Gallipoli stalemate (an allegation with very little), he became ever more defensive and depressed until the Gallipoli venture came to its disappointing end and the Dardanelles Committee was abolished. At the end of the year 1915, now facing an inquiry into what had gone wrong, he decided to give it all up and to become a soldier again.

5

Mud and Munitions

After Gallipoli, Churchill was never again to enjoy so central and authoritative a position in the direction of the First World War; but he never gave up trying to make his views have an effect on its outcome. It is safe to reckon that the only time he ceased to think about the war were was when he was absorbed in painting, an occupation his sister-in-law persuaded him to take up in the weeks of depression following his departure from the Admiralty. Although he remained in the Cabinet, it was with the non-executive post of Chancellor of the Duchy of Lancaster. He was allowed a seat on the Cabinet's war-directing body, the Dardanelles Committee. He could circulate memoranda and talk as much as he liked – but power had gone from him. In his 1921 essay 'Painting as a Pastime' he recalled:

> In this position I knew everything and could do nothing. The change from the intense executive activities of each day's work at the Admiralty to the narrowly-measured duties of a counsellor left me gasping. Like a sea-beast fished up from the depths, or a diver too suddenly hoisted, my veins threatened to burst from the fall in pressure.

The Dardanelles and Gallipoli continued to excite Churchill's mind until well after the army's evacuation from the peninsula at the end of 1915. Through most of the following year, when the sources and conduct of those campaigns became the subject of an official inquiry, he felt obliged to devote much time to vindicating his role in the initial planning of them, and to arguing that, given better luck and larger resources, they would have worked strategic wonders. He further believed that wonders could still happen, if the large Anglo-French forces tied up in nearby Salonika could be used for a surprise attack on the peninsula now that the Turkish army had withdrawn and gone elsewhere. It was, he argued, what the enemy would least expect, and therefore just what an astute tactician ought to do. But 'no such audacious scheme crossed the minds of our rulers [who] yielded themselves with placid hopefulness to the immense frontal attacks which were being prepared in France'.[1]

Historians will continue to debate whether Churchill's dedication to a south-east Balkans strategy was sensible or not; and military historians will mostly continue to maintain, with Churchill's military contemporaries, that his ideas were overambitious. In a military sense, however, his ideas had much to be said for them, although some of the political aspirations at various times aired to justify them – Bulgaria snatched from the German embrace, Serbia succoured, Romania and Greece secured for the Allies, the Turkish Empire stabbed in its vitals – may have been too imaginative.[2] It was, whatever its merits, an imagination very much to Churchill's liking. His optimistic interest in the Balkans as a way of sapping German power stayed green through the coming years. It was still going strong in 1943 and 1944.

If the members of the War Cabinet (headed by David Lloyd George after his supersession of Asquith in December 1916) paid little attention to Churchill's advice about how to conduct the war, it was not because they did not receive it. Out of office, Churchill made cogent speeches in the Commons and up and down the country; he also wrote copiously in several of the national newspapers. (Having next to no private income, most of his income when out of office had to come from his pen, at this stage of his career as at all others until well after 1945.) Back in office from May 1917 (but never again in the War Cabinet), he was prolific in the circulation of cogent memoranda containing appreciations of the current situation, suggestions about strategy and the organisation of the home front. He annoyed some of his colleagues, especially Conservative ones, by trespassing on what they regarded as their preserves – a regular form of behaviour whenever he was in office – and by gallivanting off more often than they thought proper to be with the army. In May 1918 he even asked Field-Marshal Haig to find him a *pied-à-terre* near GHQ so that he could come and go easily.[3] These visits were not just for being near the front – they seem to have been essential to his mental wellbeing. 'You have always spoken to me of the rest and happiness it gives you to be with the Army in the field', wrote Sir John French to him when he was feeling low; 'A view of the troops and the enemy will change your perspective'.[4] But Churchill also liked to be with the army when he was feeling high. The company of soldiers, preferably generals, was delightful to him (which was paradoxical, his view of generals being that they were usually overrated). It was the nearest he could get to being a general himself.

'War direction', his own striking phrase, was what he yearned for and what he believed he was born for.[5] Unable to do it in high style as a general in the army, he had to be content with doing what he could in Westminster. Considering his reduced circumstances after the débâcle of May 1915, the number and variety of things he managed to do was remarkable and, among his own political kind, unique.

In November 1915 he resigned from his post of 'well-paid inactivity' and announced his intention to join his fellow-soldiers – he was still a major in the Oxfordshire Hussars – at the Front.[6] The brief spell in Flanders that followed was a quixotic episode that highlighted his bravery and eccentricity but did not otherwise add to his wartime usefulness. Its origin was his pique and frustration at being excluded in mid-November 1915 from the small War Council that was to replace the defunct Dardanelles Committee. On 15 November he made his resignation speech in the Commons. By the evening of the 18th he had crossed the Channel. Sir John French intercepted him on arrival, took him to GHQ at St-Omer and said he would like to give him command of a brigade. Churchill gladly accepted the offer but sensibly suggested that, before he did anything else, he should acquire some experience of local conditions. He was fixed up with a ten-day visit to the Grenadier Guards holding the area around Neuve Chapelle. From 1 to 11 December he was back at St-Omer awaiting a posting and enjoying GHQ's social life and political gossip, enlivened by his new friend, the go-getting Canadian Sir Max Aitken. Three more days with the Guards followed, then another comfortable week at GHQ, digesting the news that the Prime Minister had vetoed his elevation to the rank of brigadier-general. He would have to be content with the command of a battalion. Before he could embark on that, the coming of Christmas made possible a week back in London.

On 5 January he took command of the 6th battalion of the Royal Scots Fusiliers, who were soon to return to the front across the Belgian border at Ploegsteert, 'Plug Street' in British military parlance. He served as their

commanding officer for four months, during which time London and
the House of Commons saw him again twice, from 2 to 13 March and 19
to 27 April. When all its interruptions are taken into account, his
Western Front service did not amount to much. It came to an end on
6 May 1916. His wife sought to persuade him that he ought to give it
longer. No other officer can have taken up arms so abruptly and laid
them down so soon again, but, as in the South African war, he was a law
unto himself and the power of his personality made it possible for him
to get away with it.

While he was with the Fusiliers, however, he did his duty energetically
and to good effect, and in a style quite his own. He even managed to
dress oddly; a group photograph taken on 29 December 1915 shows him
looking ill at ease in a uniform belted too tight and too high, and in the
French 'tin hat' he insisted on wearing because it was more comfortable
than the British one.[7] The battalion was not in good shape when he took
over. It had suffered terribly in the battle of Loos and had been in the
mud of Ypres since then. Spirits were low and standards relaxed. His first
days of command were awkward. What the other ranks thought of his
appointment we do not know. We do know what the officers thought,
because several of them later wrote or talked about it. They had not liked
the prospect at all. Churchill's arrival did not reassure them. He never
liked meeting people he did not know, he had a disagreeable way of
scowling or glowering at them before saying anything, and he had no
small talk. The first parade was a shambles and the first mess night frosty.

The atmosphere, however, soon improved. No matter what parts of
his mind lingered in St-Omer and Westminster, Churchill showed no
lack of zeal for his work. He roused the battalion from its depression,
bringing to his role a degree of imagination and enthusiasm beyond the
reach of longer-serving officers to whom it had all become routine. He
showed talent as an instructor, appearing unexpectedly as an expert on
delousing (highly necessary for men who had not taken their clothes off
for weeks) and the science of sandbag-filling. Within the few days available, he planned and put on a sports day and evening concert just before
the return to the front. 'We laughed at lots of things he did', recalled
one of his lieutenants, 'but there were other things we did not laugh at
for we knew they were sound. He had a unique approach which did
wonders to us.' (The convalescent Siegfried Sassoon, when the two men

met in September 1918, felt 'that I should like to have him as my company commander in the front line'.)[8] He showed an uncommon interest
in the welfare of the other ranks, sometimes ignoring the proprieties of
hierarchy and (as had happened in his Admiralty days) thereby annoy-
ing some of his fellow officers. It is unknown whether officers or men
thought ill of him for rewarding himself with the luxuries he ordered
from Clemmie: brandy and cigars, 'large slabs of corned beef: stilton
cheese: cream: ham: sardines: dried fruits: you might almost try a big
beef steak pie but not tinned grouse ...'[9]

Plug Street was held to be a 'quiet' part of the front, but there was
no lack of activity: shells passing over or failing to do so, watch to be
kept day and night in case of attacks, the trenches and wire to be maintained, and the German wire to be nocturnally interfered with. Going at
night into no man's land with Churchill was nerve-racking. He was
clumsy and careless. One narrative of being with him recalls the sudden
loud whisper, 'For God's sake keep still, Sir!'; another, the gruff command 'Put out that bloody light' – which turned out to be Churchill
himself, not realising that he was lying on the control of his own torch.[10]
His courage, even rashness, in the face of danger won his men's respect.
Experiencing at first hand the lives and deaths of infantry in the trench
warfare he had been criticising from a distance since the previous winter, he was confirmed in his conviction that other ways must be found
to defeat the Germans. Edward Spears, who saw a good deal of him during those weeks, recalled: 'Winston had an inquiring mind of rare
quality. He always turned up with some new invention – once it was a
bullet-proof waistcoat. On another occasion a bullet-proof raincoat
which would have sunk anyone wearing it in any sea.'[11] More fruitful
were his thoughts about 'mechanical warfare' and command of the air,
which he lost no time in pressing upon the government as soon as he
returned home.

This extraordinary episode showed that Churchill was brave, which
was already well known. It showed that he was impulsive and eccentric,
fuelling his critics' conviction that, no matter how brilliant and various
his parts, his judgement was unbalanced and unreliable. It fuelled his
contempt for the War Office: 'By God I would make them skip if I had
the power, even for a month.'[12] And it knocked on the head his notion
that he could find fulfilment again as a soldier. He tried to give himself

to the army in the field, but he couldn't do it. Westminster called him, not just when he was among the well-connected at GHQ but also when he was supposedly trying to get away from it all amidst the mud and ruins and shell-bursts of Plug Street. The many letters he wrote to Clementine are full of affection and longing, some of them touching impressively on the themes of love and mortality, but increasingly as the weeks went by they contained questions about what was going on in the political world and requests for her to attend to his interests there. He also began writing to political colleagues, discussing their next moves. In the end – an end that came more quickly than anyone can have expected, and one that Clementine thought too early for the good of his reputation – he was drawn back to Westminster like iron to a magnet. Not actual fighting but war direction was his *métier*, and London was where it had to be done. It was characteristic of the man, however, that his political and administrative commitments there by no means prevented him from returning as often as he could to where the fighting was going on. Once Haig had fixed him up with a small château near Verchocq, which he could reach by a two-hour flight from Hendon, he 'managed to be present at almost every important battle' from May 1918 to the war's end.[13]

There may have been other men in Britain who fired off more good ideas than Churchill about improving the management of the war, but none of them had Churchill's stature or access to the centre of power. It was bad luck for the country, as well as for Churchill himself, that, because of the Dardanelles and Gallipoli millstones hung around his neck, because the Conservatives in the coalition government so much disliked him, and because he was not actually popular in his own party either, not much notice was taken of his constructive criticisms on the direction of the war from the spring of 1916 to his return to office in July 1917: 'wilderness months', not unlike those of the 1930s when again he had important things to say and again said them to little effect. One of his dominant concerns was efficiency in use of manpower: at the front, in the armed forces generally, and in the economy. Most famously, he challenged the claim of the Western Front generals that their blood-letting battles tended to the Allies' advantage, in that more Germans were killed than Britons or Frenchmen.[14] Churchill felt sure they were wrong, worked hard at the evidence, and demolished their case in the most closely-worked chapters of *The World Crisis*, headed 'The Blood Test'.[15] If the Dardanelles campaign had succeeded, things would have been different. But after its failure:

> There was nothing left on land but the war of exhaustion ... No more strategy, very little tactics; only the dull wearing down of the weaker combinations by exchanging lives, only the multiplying of machinery on both sides to exchange them quicker ... Good, plain, straightforward frontal attacks by valiant flesh and blood against wire and machine guns, 'killing Germans' while Germans killed Allies twice as often, calling out the men of forty, fifty and even of fifty-five, and the youths of eighteen, sending the wounded soldiers back three or four times over into the shambles – such were the sole manifestations now reserved for the military art.[16]

Churchill's conviction that there must be other ways to fight the well-entrenched Germans than by frontal infantry attacks began long before the battle of the Somme confirmed it in the summer of 1916. Neither in this great war nor in the next did Churchill ever cease to think longingly of the possibilities of amphibious operations to attack the enemy's flanks or rear. After all, Britannia was supposed to rule the waves: why was not more imaginative use made of its commanding position? One does not know – because Fisher tended to bring out the silly side of him – how seriously to take the birthday letter Churchill wrote to the old admiral in January 1916: 'a descent on the German coast, the bringing in of Denmark and the entry and domination of the Baltic would secure a decisive victory for the Allies'.[17] He had an idea for speeding victory in the Middle East that sounded good but, like so many of his best-sounding ideas, soared ahead of the technically practical. Admiring the fine campaign that took Allenby into Jerusalem in December 1917, Churchill remarked that the Turkish forces in the Gaza region could have been made to retreat northwards much earlier by a well-prepared descent on Haifa or thereabouts to cut their railway lifeline and threaten their rear.[18] But no one in high command had suggested an action so obvious – no doubt because 'the rocky and turbulent coast denied access' and 'Jaffa, a so-called harbour, was merely an open roadstead'.[19]

He maintained a lively interest in naval affairs and found no cause to change his opinion that admirals could be just as unimaginative and pedantic as generals. The admiral to whom he had given charge of the Grand Fleet disappointed him. Even though he had to admit that Jellicoe had been right to enforce the utmost prudence in proximity to enemy mines or torpedoes, Churchill maintained that he had thrown away the battle of Jutland on 31 May 1916, the long-awaited great naval battle that Churchill and everyone else had longed for. He went lovingly over every detail of the battle in fifty-five pages of *The World Crisis*, coming at last to this challenging conclusion: 'Praiseworthy caution had induced a defensive habit of mind and scheme of tactics which hampered the Grand Fleet even when the special conditions enjoining caution did not exist.'[20] He rejoiced when the First Lord of the Admiralty in 1917 replaced Jellicoe with the fresher Sir Rosslyn Wemyss, and when Wemyss promptly appointed Roger Keyes to replace Reginald Bacon in charge of the 'Dover Patrol', the unofficial title of the very important operation to prevent U-boats traversing the Straits of Dover. Keyes at once improved the efficiency of the barrier, about which Bacon had become complacent, and went on to plan and in his own person to command the dashing and nearly successful attack on the U-boat base at Zeebrugge during the night of 22–23 April 1918. Keyes was the sort of navy man Churchill most admired, and they remained good friends for more than twenty years. Churchill's connection with the navy came to an end, however, or had an end put to it, when the hard-headed Scottish businessman Sir Eric Geddes became First Lord of the Admiralty in September 1917. Good at whatever administrative job he undertook, determined to be master in his own house and, although no politician, in alliance with the Conservatives in the government, Geddes resented Churchill's attempts to maintain an interest in naval policy and soon came to blows with him in Cabinet.[21]

Keyes's heroic attempt to put the U-boat base at Zeebrugge out of action answered exactly to one of Churchill's fixed ideas of a worthwhile operation, as De Robeck's attempt to force the Dardanelles would have been if it had worked: risky and bold, expensive in lives and *matériel* but hugely rewarding in the military advantage consequent upon it and subsequently lodged in the national epic by resounding oratory and awards for bravery. Churchill did not mind men being sacrificed in a good cause but hated them being sacrificed in a bad one. It was because the army's assaults on the German Western Front defences were hugely expensive in lives and *matériel* but unrewarding in military advantage that he detested them so much and resourcefully sought alternatives. We have already examined one of those alternatives, the attack round the rear. Now we must approach the other: in his own pioneering phrase, the 'mechanical battle'.[22]

Churchill's criticisms of the British army's repeated attempts to break through the Germans' elaborate defences elicit no sympathy from the school of military historians that continues to maintain that Douglas Haig, Commander-in-Chief from December 1915, and the generals under him did as well as could have been expected; or no worse than could have been avoided, in circumstances which – it is too easy for an islander to forget – included inescapable obligations to demanding allies.[23] Such were the circumstances in July 1915 when the War Committee had to face the fact that the situations in Russia and France made it necessary for the British army to launch the attack that became the battle of Loos. Churchill pointed out that losses would be heavy and gains improbable. 'There is a great deal of truth in what Mr Churchill has said', said Kitchener, 'but unfortunately we have to make war as we must and not as we should like to.'[24]

Historians inclined to do the Western Front generals justice have understandably been stimulated to greater efforts by the campaigns of deprecation and even ridicule initially unleashed against them, and by extension against the war as a whole, by *Oh! What A Lovely War* (the play, 1963; the film, 1969).[25] Much ignorance and prejudice has filtered into popular perceptions of this towering episode in modern history, together with misunderstanding and misinformation about the causes of the war and the justifications for it. Popular perceptions of the battles themselves, however, and the conditions under which front-line soldiers fought and died are not inaccurate. The fact that some survivors did not subsequently moan about them as much as others, or did not moan at all, does not mean that those battles were not terrible.

Churchill gave them their due in the second volume of *The World Crisis*. He knew what he was writing about. Apart from studying the latest news from the front daily, he had his own direct experiences of it and he knew many soldiers who had much more. His purpose in portraying the Western Front battles in all their horror was of course partly to add force to his argument that they should have been stopped sooner, or should not have been undertaken at all, but he was also doing his job as a good historian with a passion for striking prose, giving dramatic events the description they demanded and slapping on the colour for legitimate effect.[26] Churchill loathed useless sacrifices. This above all explains the desperate determination of his search for other ways. That loathing, together with his awed admiration of the soldiers who went through these hells, may be felt in the following fine passage. It concerns the conduct of the war in the autumn of 1917. By that time the Prime Minister and most of his Cabinet had become seriously mistrustful of the judgement of the army's high command, 'the Haig–Robertson strategy', and Lloyd George himself was gearing up to challenge it. Churchill, not in the War Cabinet but acutely concerned about everything that it was doing and plying Lloyd George with advice, had hoped that a decision would be taken for Britain to stay on the defensive in Flanders and to send such troops as were available for offensive operations to Italy. Exactly the opposite happened. In consequence, the Italian front collapsed at Caporetto and the British and imperial armies were committed to the fearful ordeal of Passchendaele. That battle once determined on, Churchill sensibly argued that the generals should at any rate be required to state their objectives and the time by which they expected to attain them. They should not be allowed to continue their offensive indefinitely, regardless of objectives not attained and losses increasingly suffered. But they were allowed to do so, with consequences he pulled out every stop to describe.

> The terrific artillery pulverised the ground, smashing simultaneously the German trenches and the ordinary drainage. By sublime devotion and frightful losses small indentations were made upon the German front. In six weeks at the farthest point we had advanced four miles. Soon the rain descended, and the vast crater fields became a sea of choking fetid mud in which men, animals and tanks floundered and perished hopelessly ...
>
> New divisions continued to replace those that were shattered ... Still the will power of the Commander and the discipline of the Army remained invincible. By measureless sacrifices Passchendaele was won. But beyond, far beyond, still rose intact and unapproachable the fortifications of Klercken. August had passed away; September was gone; October was far spent. The full severity of a Flanders winter gripped the ghastly battlefield. Ceaselessly the Menin gate of Ypres disgorged its streams of manhood. Fast as the cannons fired, the ammunition behind them flowed in faster. Even in October the British Staff were planning and launching offensives and were confident of reaching the goal of decisive results. It was not until the end of November that final failure was accepted ... It cannot be said that

'the soldiers', that is to say, the Staff, did not have their way. They tried their sombre experiment to its conclusion ... They did it in the face of the plainest warnings, and of arguments which they could not answer.[27]

Recognition that the war had to be fought did not mean ceasing to consider how to fight it intelligently. Churchill was one of the earliest promoters of that debate, which historians still continue. Years before the 'pity of war' writers began to swing opinion their way in the early 1930s, he had argued that the methods by which the Germans were being fought on the Western Front were so unpleasant and unproductive – 'vast, futile and disastrous slaughter' – that, besides seeking other places to do the fighting, other ways of doing it should be urgently considered. He used two lines from one of those writers, Siegfried Sassoon, at the head of his 'Somme' chapter: 'Pray God that you may never know / The Hell where youth and laughter go.'[28]

Churchill's preferred other way was the tank. His eager and imaginative interest in military technology – an early chapter in *The World Crisis* was titled 'The Romance of Design' – showed here at its most intense and persistent. In fact he had begun to devise a solution to the trench warfare problem before the problem had fully declared itself. He had begun to look into the tank possibility while he was still at the Admiralty, very early in the war. He was not the only free-thinking warrior to sense the need for armoured fighting vehicles that could cross barbed wire and trenches, using caterpillar-tracks to do so; J. F. C. Fuller, Maurice Hankey and Ernest Swinton were prominent among the others. But Churchill was the only high-placed individual capable of disregarding official proprieties in order to get something done quickly. He set the engineers going in the race to manufacture a viable prototype, to begin with in the workshops of his 'personal fiefdom', the Royal Naval Air Service, and then, early in 1915, under the direction the Director of Naval Construction and with an initial budget of £70,000 – about which he had not consulted the Sea Lords for fear they would veto it.[29]

A really promising prototype was not produced until early 1916. Already by then Churchill, newly arrived on the Western Front, was pressing his vision on the Commanders-in-Chief. Addressed to Sir John French on 3 December, the very eve of French's departure, it went straight into the hands of his successor, Sir Douglas Haig, and aroused some interest, though not nearly as much as Churchill would have liked.[30] In a memorandum strikingly headed 'Variants of the Offensive' he wrote:

> The cutting of the enemy's wire and the general domination of his firing-line can be effected by engines of this character ... They should be disposed secretly along the whole attacking front two or three hundred yards apart. Ten or fifteen minutes before the assault these engines should move forward over the best line of advance open, passing through or across our trenches at prepared points. They are capable of traversing any ordinary obstacle, ditch, breastwork, or trench ... Nothing but a direct hit from a field gun will stop them. On reaching the enemy's wire they turn to the left or right and run down parallel to the enemy's trench, sweeping his parapet with their fire, and crushing and cutting the barbed wire in lanes and in a slightly serpentine course ... [They] are capable of actually crossing the enemy's trench and advancing to cut his communication trenches; but into this aspect it is not necessary to go now. One step at a time ... They can climb any slope. They are, in short, movable machine-gun cupolas as well as wire-smashers.[31]

The enthusiasm and commitment were obvious but they were not infectious. It was at this date more of a vision than a blueprint, understandably beyond the imaginative capabilities of staff officers already burdened with the complexities of organising familiar masses of artillery and infantry in what was becoming a regular style. The tank, moreover, was still very much an untried novelty and a technological challenge. The uncommitted were justified in wondering to what extent such recent inventions – they could truthfully have said such translations from science fiction – could be relied on to perform the promised marvels; the early tanks were not surprisingly prone to accidents and break-downs, and all tanks were poisonous to be in for any length of time. Towards the end of the battle of the Somme there was some tentative use of them, condemned by Churchill as too little and too early. At Cambrai and in the later 1918 offensives they had some successes, but to the end Churchill (and of course his fellow tank enthusiasts) went on lamenting that full advantage was never taken of their capabilities. In the autumn of 1917, with the Passchendaele disaster still unrolling, and with the Munitions Budget for the coming year to prepare, he submitted a searching review of the military situation to the War Cabinet, leading to the conclusion that the only realistic way to break through the German defences broadly and swiftly enough to compel 'a general retirement' in

1918 (or 1919 for that matter) was by the use of 'organized mechanical processes and equipment'; doing at last what the infantry on their own, locked into the footsloggers' slow speed of advance, could never do.[32]

As the performance of tanks improved and the variety of types multiplied, so it became necessary to face up to the means by which they might be destroyed. Churchill never denied that they would be vulnerable to field guns, arguing hopefully that – especially if the operation was a nocturnal one – not more than one tank would be knocked out before its fellows achieved their breakthrough. Early in 1918 Sir Henry Wilson voiced the objection that the enemy would blow them up by land mines. This elicited from Churchill a fine display of ideas which interestingly anticipate some of 'Hobart's funnies' of twenty-five years later: tanks with long hammers in front of them to beat the ground or heavy rollers to press upon it; path-clearing tanks with specially reinforced undercarriages; and robot tanks controlled by wires that would explode the mines before the manned tanks reached them.[33] Nothing dampened his confidence and optimism about their potential. While tanks cleared the way, tracked supply vehicles could follow the infantry with food and ammunition to keep them going. By the end of the year, writing to his cavalry friend Archibald Sinclair, he jauntily declared that 'the cavalry myth is exploded' and that he was working to have the cavalry regiments converted into tank ones. The Germans, reinforced in the west following the Bolshevik withdrawal of Russia from the war, were again in a position to do some attacking, but 'tank led counter attacks on the flanks of hostile salients' were among the tactics that would repel them. 'Let them rejoice in the occasional capture of placeless names and sterile ridges; and let us dart here and there armed with science and surprise.' He concluded on a rhapsodical and breathless note. 'Arm yourself therefore my dear with the panoply modern science of war. Make catsmeat of those foolish animals who have broken your hearts so far. Embark in the chariots of war and slay the malignants with the arms of precision.'[34]

Tanks may have been his favourite vehicle of 'science and surprise', but there was no field of battlefield invention he did not patronise. He rejoiced when the first Minister of Munitions, David Lloyd George, circumvented the War Office quagmire by spending a rich friend's money to bring the (subsequently invaluable) Stokes mortar into production. He had no qualms about the use of chemical weapons, although it is not clear he would ever have wanted to be first user of them; it was a non-toxic form that he insisted on being developed at the outset of the war, when no one else was showing any interest.[35] He was thrilled by the possibilities of mounting big guns on railway wagons, thereby attaining such mobility that the enemy would be unable to target them. His interest in the military use of the air produced, while he was at the Admiralty, the Royal Naval Air Service, which undertook the first ever bombing attacks on military targets in enemy-held territory (the Zeppelin sheds at Cuxhaven, Düsseldorf, Friedrichshaven and Köln), and which had to undertake 'the air defence of Britain' against the Zeppelins, the War Office feeling unable to release any aircraft for that duty.[36]

Air power continued to engage his mind throughout the rest of the war and it figured prominently in his thoughts about the final onslaught. The most extended account of them is to be found in his weighty memorandum for the War Cabinet of 21 November 1917, inquiring whether it had a 'War Plan' for 1918 and putting forward his ideas as to what it should be. There would not, he thought, be much difference in numbers on the Western Front; the Americans who would in due course be arriving would be matched by the release of Germans from the east. (In the event, the German reinforcements got there first and upset Churchill's and everyone else's plans by their Spring Offensive.) But there remained 'the great province of war machinery and the resources of superior generalship operating through war machinery'. He identified six forms of such 'machinery': artillery, tanks, railways, gas, trench mortars and air supremacy. In the course of some far-sighted paragraphs, he anticipated many of the debates and strategies of the Second World War and some of the arguments he himself would use then.[37] City bombing, he considered, was unlikely 'to compel the Government of a great nation to surrender … In our own case we have seen the combative spirit of the people roused, and not quelled, by the German air raids … Therefore our air offensive should consistently be directed at striking at the bases and communications upon whose structure the fighting power of the enemy's armies and his fleets of the sea and of the air depends.' Such an air offensive, planned to coincide with a land offensive and precisely to help it, ought to produce good results.

He acknowledged that this new arm had many critics and that some of their arguments demanded answers. His general answer was just the same as 'Bomber' Harris's would be, twenty-five years later: a proper bombing offensive had never so far been carried out. What was needed was an Air Staff to take war in the air as seriously as war on land and at sea was taken. Critics observed that bombing was notoriously inaccurate. Churchill reasonably answered that it would not continue to be so when it received the same tribute of scientific attention as had been lavished on naval gunnery, and when the present amateurish dropping of bombs gave way to 'specially trained men dropping them in regulated salvos so as to "straddle" the targets properly'. Control of the air once established, 'considerable parties of soldiers could be conveyed to the neighbourhood of bridges or other important points, and, having overwhelmed the local guard, could from the ground effect a regular and permanent demolition'. There was no end of useful mischief that 'flying columns' (literally flying) could do.

These and many more ideas about the conduct of war – war present and war future – flowed so copiously from Churchill's pen (more accurately, his secretary's typewriter, dictation already being his preferred mode of composition) that the unwary reader might suppose he had nothing else to do. In fact he was, from July 1917, head of the huge industrial complex managed by the Ministry of Munitions, and he had again a seat in the Cabinet. Lloyd George, the Prime Minister, valued his counsel and shared his misgivings about the conduct of the war on the Western Front; perhaps he also felt that Churchill would be more trouble outside the administration than inside it. Conservatives generally were affronted by his appointment and made sure that he was not invited to become a regular member of the inner War Cabinet. The business of his department, however, was so relevant to many of the War Cabinet's deliberations that he was often invited to its meetings; besides which he made sure that it knew his mind by sending it memoranda of the kind cited above. One is at times reminded of Hilaire Belloc's character 'Aunt Jane', who

> Provides information without hesitation
> For people unwilling to learn;
> And often bestows good advice upon those
> Who give her small thanks in return.[38]

Smallest thanks came from the First Lord of the Admiralty, Sir Eric

Geddes; upon whom in due course Churchill took an ingenious revenge.[39]

Whether it is more true to say that Churchill ran the Ministry of Munitions effectively or that the Ministry of Munitions ran effectively with Churchill at its head is difficult to judge. The ministry's origin in 1915 lay in the War Office Ordnance Department's inability to produce munitions in the quantities and at the speed required. David Lloyd George was its first minister and from his time onwards it had swollen month by month until, by the time Churchill took it over, it was enormous and unwieldy. One of the many efficient men – businessmen, economists and statisticians for the most part – who helped him to reorganise and to run it (and who was happy to serve him again next time round) summed up his impact thus:

> Winston Churchill's special contribution was to bring discipline and organisation to the Ministry ... His Memoranda, with their wealth of words, bombarded the growing staff of the Ministry (12,000 when he took over, 20,000 two years later), stimulated their minds and kept them on their toes. But while Lloyd George's personality had inspired individuals to throw the rule book overboard in the quest for results, Winston harnessed men into a disciplined team which he then drove. It was his apprenticeship for the great task he was to shoulder twenty years later.[40]

Churchill's reorganisation of the ministry consisted of its division into a group of departments: Finance; Design; Steel and Iron; Materials; Explosives; Projectiles; Guns; Engines; Allies; Labour; and Statistics. Each was headed by an appropriately expert businessman who was left to run his own show. These heads met now and then as a governing council to thrash out problems together, until even that measure of corporate activity was replaced by a small coordinating body curiously known as the 'Clamping Committee'.[41] The result was equally satisfactory for the production of munitions and for the convenience of the minister (not least because such devolvement enabled him to spend time in France, where the ministry had a branch office in Paris). 'Instead of struggling through the jungle on foot I rode comfortably on an elephant whose trunk could pick up a pin or uproot a tree with equal ease, and from whose back a wide scene lay open.'[42]

Lloyd George had summoned businessmen to his aid; Churchill was

happy to follow suit. He obviously learned a lot from them. 'Here were
the finest business brains of the country working with might and main
and with disinterested loyalty for the common good.' One to whom he
grew close was James Stevenson from the Johnny Walker Distillery
Company, 'the most ingenious and compulsive manager and master of
difficulties – material or personal – with whom I have ever served'.
'With [Stevenson], with his close colleague Sir Arthur Duckham [an oil
man], and with the young, profound Professor Layton who assembled
and presented the weekly statistics, I was brought into the closest daily
contact.' Layton, a rising young Cambridge economist, did much more
than just produce statistics, important task though that was. He became
Churchill's right-hand man in the ministry, accompanying him to War
Cabinet committee meetings and to France, drafting his memoranda,
chairing the ministry's 'Clamping Committee' and checking the figures
submitted by the service departments – which, it seems, were often misleading or wrong.[43] It must have been from this cohort of experienced
businessmen and economists, from encountering their points of
view and observing them at work, that Churchill developed the very
businesslike ideas about war direction with which he showered his
Cabinet colleagues through the next eighteen months, and which he
wielded to such good effect when he really was in charge twenty-five
years later.

The munitions business brought him into contact also with two
American millionaires who were to be of importance in his later life.
With one of them, Charles Schwab, his connection had begun while he
was at the Admiralty. Schwab was chairman of Bethlehem Steel. His
company built submarines for the Royal Navy in a third of the time
taken in British shipyards, and he circumvented his country's neutrality laws (which forbade the export of munitions directly to belligerent
states) by having their component parts taken to Montreal for assembly;
such achievements endeared him to the Churchillian heart.[44] The other
was Bernard Baruch, difficult to classify because of his various aspects
as financier, businessman and backroom politician. He was one of the
three powerful men appointed, after the United States's entry into the
war in April 1917, to run the War Industries Board. With this body
Britain's Minister of Munitions naturally had intimate dealings, in
the course of which Churchill and Baruch struck up an epistolary

friendship that ripened into a lasting one when they met in Paris at the end of the war. The benefits of this relationship were by no means one-sided. Britain and the United States had a common interest in Chilean nitrates, necessary for explosives among other things, and Churchill's experienced nitrates department became their common agent. America's munitions industries took time to develop, whereas those of Britain and France had attained an enormous and even surplus capacity by 1917. The American soldiers who were so urgently needed on the Western Front, and who were shipped across the Atlantic with all possible speed, had to be provided with guns, ammunition, aero-engines (a French speciality) and other equipment by Churchill and his French counterpart, Louis Loucheur, another businessman with whom Churchill got on well. It also fell to them to re-equip the Italian army after Caporetto. It is evident from Churchill's pride in his doings at the ministry and in its achievements, as also from his enemies' failure to find fault with this chapter in his career, that he was as effective a Minister of Munitions as he was in all his other ministerial roles. From this particular one, however, we may receive the impression that, had his life run in different channels, he had it in him to become a business tycoon.[45]

His post at the Ministry of Munitions gave Churchill a hand in the actual management of a matter of extreme national importance which had been bothering the government since 1915: the budgeting of manpower in a war of total mobilisation. So long as the war was expected to be only a short one, and the British army was fed by volunteers (which it was until mid-1916), the needs of industry and vital services on the home front were neglected, or left to chance. Skilled men in war-sustaining industries and men skilled or otherwise in such vital industries as coal mining were applauded for their patriotism and bravery when they 'signed up'. If any thought was taken as to the long-term economic consequences of their departure, it was taken by owners and managers who could do nothing to stop it – and who knew how the trade unions would react to the gaps being filled with female and other allegedly 'unskilled' labour.

As the war went on and on, and the army's demands for cannon fodder continued to grow, the Cabinet came to recognise that some civilian occupations were so essential to the war effort that they should

1. Churchill in 1895, a second lieutenant in the 4th Hussars. He liked dressing up. The gorgeousness of this full-dress uniform would not be matched again until he became Lord Warden of the Cinque Ports in 1946. (*Imperial War Museum*)

2. Prisoner of war at Pretoria, 1899. Churchill, understandably down in the mouth, seems to be distancing himself from the soldiers as if to support his claim to be only a civilian. (*Imperial War Museum*)

3. Churchill, First Lord of the Admiralty, 1912–14, in his Privy Councillor's uniform, on a patriotic postcard. The sea-plane is of the kind he had learned to fly. The motto recalls David Garrick's song 'Hearts of Oak' and its refrain, 'We'll fight and we'll conquer again and again'. (*Jack Darrah*)

4. Churchill, commander of the Henley squadron of the Queen's Own Oxford-shire Hussars, at one of the territorial summer camps he regularly attended between 1900 and 1914. His taste for unusual headwear is again in evidence. (*Jack Darrah*)

5. With David Lloyd George, January 1910. Churchill was at this time in the most radical phase of his political life with the Liberals, matching David Lloyd George's invective against the House of Lords: one of the several episodes that faithful Conservatives never forgot. (*Hulton/Getty Picture Library*)

6. Churchill's slouching posture and natural stoop contribute to his looking something of a mess, alongside the French General Fayolle, as he waits for a posting at GHQ France in December 1916. Again, the headwear commands attention: a French tin hat. (*Imperial War Museum*)

7. Lille, 29 October 1918. The city has just been liberated and the war would soon be over. Churchill intently observes a military parade. Standing in front of him, left foreground, is Lieutenant-Colonel Bernard Montgomery, Chief of Staff to the 47th Division. (*Imperial War Museum*)

8. Churchill in his classic civilian outfit. Close to him one got a waft of rich Havana cigars and lavender water. He is at the garden gate of Ten Downing Street for one of the two Cabinet meetings on the morning of 10 May 1940. By nightfall, he was Prime Minister. (*Imperial War Museum*)

be regarded as 'reserved', protected from the War Office's relentless recruiting drives. The Ministry of Munitions made an attempt to 'badge' workers in essential industrial occupations; the visible sign of exemption from military service being necessary to save such men from being abused as cowards. A Ministry of National Service was set up. Its early months were undistinguished, but by the time Churchill returned to the official scene it was in the capable hands of Sir Eric Geddes's less abrasive brother, Auckland Geddes, who worked to reclaim from the War Office some of the ground it had formerly monopolised. This was a momentous development, the germ of the budgeting of manpower resources that would soon be taken much further. GHQ in France would have to understand it must make up its mind what it wanted: *either* endless soldiers *or* endless munitions; Britain could not forever provide both. When GHQ nevertheless persisted in expecting both, the War Cabinet in December 1917 concluded a review of human resources by telling GHQ it could have only 150,000 new men for the following year instead of the 600,000 requested. At the same time the Cabinet made clear its expectation that the army in France would undertake no more grand offensives for the foreseeable future; it looked instead to action on the British army's other fronts, in Salonika, Palestine and Mesopotamia. In this way by the beginning of 1918 the War Cabinet had its hands firmly on the country's combined economic and manpower resources, *and* on strategy; a novel situation which unfortunately did not survive the crisis caused by Ludendorff's March offensive and the consequent desperate scrabble for soldiers wherever they could be found.

Churchill, as may be imagined, was delighted to find himself intermittently involved in many of these discussions, although at the same time frustrated to be kept outside the inner sancta of power: the War Cabinet (which he could only attend when invited) and its War Policy Committee. What is most interesting about this part of Churchill's career is the extent to which his management of the Ministry of Munitions in the First World War displays, fully developed, the interests and attitudes that marked his management of the Admiralty in the early months of the Second World War and then, for the five years of his premiership, the Second World War as a whole. He was already chivvying the dilatory and prying open the hidden by means of urgent inquiries of the kind that later went under the scarlet rubric of 'Action This Day'. An example is a minute of 3 August 1917 to Walter Layton:

> How many tanks and of what patterns are to be ready month by month for the next twelve months? By whom, and to what extent, have these programmes been approved? How much steel do they require? How much do they cost? How much labour skilled and unskilled do they require in these twelve months? ... Let me know the number of people in the Tank Department [and their salaries]. Show particularly any part of Tank production which overlaps aeroplane production, i.e. any transferable margin, whether of skilled mechanics or of ball bearings, etc., in which these two branches of production are clashing competitors.

The answers to all these questions he required, as so much would be required later, 'on a single sheet of paper'.[46] Obvious in the last sentence of the quotation is his pursuit of economy and efficiency in the use of materials and manpower; behind which is barely hidden his hatred of the egoistic departmentalism that obstructed such economy and efficiency. He met that departmentalism at its worst in the Admiralty, in respect of which Churchill was a gamekeeper turned poacher. Through the last two years of the war, the navy seemed to him to be consuming men and materials greatly out of proportion to its share in the essential fighting of the war. Tradition and custom allowed it the right to consume beyond the reach of Churchill's (or any other minister's) control. Always a law unto itself, it now showed no inclination to bow to a common concern.

A great row blew up in August 1917, when their undiminishing distrust of Churchill led the Conservative Ministers for the Navy and Army, Sir Eric Geddes and Lord Derby, to threaten to resign unless Churchill's attempts to bring order and priorities into the handling of national resources were rebuked.[47] Churchill's grasp of the whole war situation was broader than anyone else's and the points he was trying to make were very good ones. He set down his point of view in a long letter to the Prime Minister, the only person who could, if he would – or would, if he could – enforce unity of purpose among dissonant departments of state. Churchill conceded that as Minister of Munitions he had no right to offer views on strategy and tactics unless expressly invited to do so.

> On the other hand in the sphere of *matériel* the Minister of Munitions is entitled to review and examine the whole of our resources and to express his

convictions as to the best use than can be made of them. For instance if the new ship building programme requires a large cut to be made in the quantities of shell steel required for the Army, it is right for the Ministry of Munitions to know what the Admiralty position in shell steel and ammunition is, and to state the facts statistically and comparatively to the War Cabinet. Or again, if long range guns are urgently needed by the army, it is open to the Ministry of Munitions to draw attention to the very large reserves of such guns now being discarded by the Admiralty, and to indicate the use that could be made of them on land. Or again if the Admiralty claim entire control of the oxygen supplies and use oxygen for purposes far less refined and important than some of those under the charge of the Ministry of Munitions with consequent peril to our whole aeronautical supply, it should be open to the Minister to draw attention to the relative merits of the competing services ... At present the Admiralty claim a super priority upon all supplies; not only as respects the most urgent and vital parts of that immense business, but even in regard to comparatively commonplace needs. They assert the doctrine that the least important Admiralty needs should rank before the most urgent claims of the Army or of Aeronautics. In my view there should be a frank and free discussion on the merits in each case and a loyal and friendly effort by departments – even after a little plain-speaking – to do the best they can by the public cause.[48]

This is a powerful expression of what lay at the heart of Churchill's idea of proper 'war direction'. He did not in the end send that letter, presumably because, after letting off steam, he reflected that it wouldn't get him anywhere – it might even result in his losing such opportunities for war-directing usefulness as he actually had. He might well have feared that Lloyd George would not keep him in the Cabinet if his political enemies ganged up against him. As always, he had no band of parliamentary followers to fight his corner. In this matter he knew he was right – and objectively he *was* right, his case was unanswerable – but he expected the Conservative hard men's dislike of him and the prevailing departmental sovereignty ethic to prevail; and his expectation was fulfilled. He was not invited to attend the War Cabinet as often as was his department's due, and the Admiralty and the War Office continued in their old ways to the end.[49] 'The one great blot upon the high economy of the British war effort in the last year of the struggle was the undue and unwarrantable inroads upon the common fund made by the Admiralty.'[50]

A memorandum for the War Cabinet in mid-July 1918 shows him having to go over the same ground again, this time more with reference to the army. The crises on the Western Front and their heavy casualties had caused the government to take as many as 100,000 men out of their 'reserved' occupations and into the army. The iron and steel industries were particularly hard hit and production would inevitably be lowered, just at a time when the much-needed Americans were arriving and had to be armed largely by their European allies. Thanks to Layton and the smooth running of his ministry, Churchill's knowledge of what was happening throughout his industrial domain was extensive and exact. On this occasion he was able to report that the output of aeroplane engines in the previous week was down from the expected 1132 to 688; and that the removal of thirty skilled mechanics from Messrs Barr and Stroud meant failure to deliver their labour-saving 'new anti-aircraft height-finder' which 'would in a few months have made possible the release of thirty men many times over from anti-aircraft batteries in the field'.

'Most remarkable of all', he concluded, 'is the case of the tanks.' The War Office, having for long taken little interest in them, had woken up to their value and was now asking for as many tanks as it could get; besides which the French sought delivery of three hundred large ones this summer. 'The only thing that has been done to assist me in this matter has been to take hundreds of men from the manufacture of tanks, thus dislocating the whole of the Metropolitan Works, with the result that for the sake of getting enough men to make a couple of companies of infantry, the equipment of perhaps four or five battalions of tanks will be lost ... I must avow myself unable to comprehend the processes of thought which are at work.'[51] There were, of course *no* processes of thought at work. Even in a nation as largely mobilised for war as Britain by 1918, and in an economy considerably collectivised, the army and the navy were still selfishly grabbing what they could (or, to place the responsibility where it really belonged, the War Cabinet was doing nothing to stop them grabbing), wrecking the establishment of production priorities in relation to overall strategic demands that had been begun by General Smuts's 'Priorities Committee' towards the end of 1917.[52]

With these and many more experiences of the difficulties of fitting the fighting forces into an efficient national war-fighting machine, it was natural that Churchill should come to believe – if he had not before the war already come to believe – that, to use the convenient but hackneyed expression, war was too important to be left to the generals – or, he would have added, the admirals. (In due course this also applied to the air marshals, when their service had achieved independence.) Civil–military relations – that is, relations between the civilian politicians forming the government and the military organisations nominally serving that government's purposes – went through a succession of awkward phases during the First World War. To begin with, there was the spectacle of Britain's most famous soldier, Field-Marshal Lord Kitchener, as Minister for War. This was unprecedented because, for more than two centuries, it had been an article of constitutional faith that the military should be subordinate to the civilian authority, as Britain's previous most famous soldier, the Duke of Wellington, sedulously had been. The politicians closest to Kitchener (Churchill being one of them until May 1915) found it difficult to argue with so eminent a military figure, even when they felt sure he was wrong, and they found it almost impossible to extract from him and his War Office the facts that might make argument fruitful. His death in mid-1916, however tragic in form – he was drowned when the cruiser on which he was travelling to Russia was torpedoed – was constitutionally a relief to his Cabinet colleagues. The War Office reverted to civilian control in the person of David Lloyd George and remained civilian thereafter.

David Lloyd George's accession to the premiership in December 1916 may be taken as the beginning, the very slow beginning, of the process by which the Cabinet (or War Cabinet) asserted its rights to an equal share with the military high command in the making of strategy and to equal access to military information and Intelligence. At the same time the Prime Minister and some of his Cabinet colleagues (GHQ France did not lose its last representative in the government until late 1917) were asserting a claim easily ignored amidst the public passions of a free country at war: the claim that the king's government, supported by the House of Commons, not the military chieftain promoted by the press, was the authentic representative of the national interest. This claim had Churchill's wholehearted support. He was a principled parliamentarian and it upset him to see the Commons failing in its constitutional duty or being prevented from doing it. Among his many ideas about efficient 'war direction' in a nation with a representative government, none was more important to him than that the people's representatives should be involved in it and that the people themselves should know what was going on. At the heart of his direction of the Second World War, these ideas were already fully fledged in the First.

The fruitful participation of people and Parliament depended on a helpful promotion of their relationship by the press. Churchill loved the press much more than he hated it, but he was acutely aware of how that relationship could become unhelpful. While the press lived off war stories that were often untrue, and while the military chieftains fed the press with the partial stories it wanted them to publicise, ministers could not properly answer questions in the House because to do so would disclose facts useful or heartening to the enemy. For this reason, Churchill advocated the more frequent holding of Secret Sessions from which the press would be excluded. It was not that he wanted needlessly to curtail press freedom – he ridiculed and deplored the government's touchiness when it suppressed a periodical for pointing out that what GHQ presented as an immense Allied victory in Champagne could also be read as a prudent German strategic retreat – it was simply that he did not like ministers being inhibited from plain-speaking in the Commons or speaking to the press instead of to Parliament.[53]

> Hardly any question can be discussed properly and completely if every word is to be made public and to be read forty-eight hours afterwards by the enemy, by our Allies and by our own soldiers in the trenches. Why cannot I or other Honourable Members have the opportunity of speaking to our fellow Members in the House of Commons on some of the great, vital, urgent questions of the hour, without having it all printed in the *Berliner Tageszeitung* and the *Hamburger Nachrichten* two days later?

The House of Commons, he maintained, was letting itself be sidelined so long as it failed to 'exercise a real, vital, earnest, active, vigilant influence upon the conduct of public affairs'. Churchill's belief in the good sense of the House knew no bounds. 'Half of our mistakes and many of our misfortunes could have been avoided if the great issues of war policy and strategy could have been fought out across the floor of the House of Commons in the full light of day.'[54]

> The main difference – let us never forget it when we are discussing these Parliamentary and Constitutional forms and remedies – between the British

and Prussian Constitutions consists in the House of Commons ... We must be very careful that in the processes of war we do not contract the contagion of the disease of those against whom we are striving ... It would indeed be the irony of fate if we liberated Germany and enslaved ourselves, and if at the same time that we were Anglicising Prussia we found that we had Prussianised England.[55]

He feared that his beloved Britain could slide into such a state unless the prerogatives of the House of Commons were stoutly asserted. Some of the most pungent pages of *The World Crisis* are devoted to an analysis of how the nation's war-directing machinery (a phrase he liked to use) had become unbalanced. The House of Commons and the ministers answering to it were, he diagnosed, squeezed between the press on one side and the military chieftains on the other; a squeezing all the more painful because the press and the chieftains played each other's game; the press fastened upon the chieftains either to praise or to blame them, and the chieftains who had it in them to cultivate the press did so. Ministers' authority suffered when the press built generals up as supermen and peddled their opinion that the civilian administration was not giving them the backing and trust they deserved:

A series of absurd conventions became established, perhaps inevitably, in the public mind. The first and most monstrous of these was that the Generals and Admirals were more competent to deal with the broad issues of the war than abler men in other spheres of life. The General no doubt was an expert on how to move his troops, and the Admiral upon how to fight his ships ... But outside this technical aspect they were helpless and misleading arbiters in problems in whose solution the aid of the statesman, the financier, the manufacturer, the inventor, the psychologist, was equally required.

Churchill was so moved by contemplation of military incompetence that he went on to give a sarcastic sketch of the version of civil–military relations that the press (and not just the popular press; the *Morning Post* was just as bad as the *Daily Mail*) palmed off on the gullible public:

The feeble or presumptuous politician is portrayed cowering in his office, intent in the crash of the world on Party intrigues or personal glorification, fearful of responsibility, incapable of aught save shallow phrase-making. To him enters the calm, noble, resolute figure of the great Commander by land or sea, resplendent in uniform, glittering with decorations, irradiated with the lustre of the hero, shod with the science and armed with the panoply of war. This stately figure, devoid of the slightest thought of self, offers his clear far-sighted guidance and counsel for vehement action or artifice or wise delay. But his advice is rejected; his sound plans put aside; his courageous initiative baffled by political chatterboxes and incompetents.[56]

Where was the commoner who could face down this man of Mars? Where was the civilian of national reputation, untrammelled by party, equal with the military chieftains in strategic and professional wisdom, able to gather all the talents into a broad-based government and to speak for England too? Churchill didn't doubt that such a man could be found. Such men had been found before when England needed them; he would duly highlight them when, twenty years later, he wrote his *History of the English-Speaking Peoples*. Now, in the fearful crisis of the 1918 German spring offensive, he urged Lloyd George to assume the mantle: 'Parliament should be called together with the utmost dispatch and on your initiation ... Violent counsels and measures must rule ... Courage and a clear plan will enable you to keep the command of the nation. Lift yourself by an effort of will to the height of circumstances and conquer or succumb fighting.'[57] On second thoughts he didn't send this letter – having earlier pressed on Lloyd George the raising of a *levée en masse*, he perhaps decided the Prime Minister might have had enough of him already that day – but that is what *he* would have done.[58]

And that of course is what he himself did when he got the chance in 1940: presenting to the world the model of a wartime government with a Prime Minister who was also Minister of Defence and who, as if to remind the people of his military credentials, appeared from time to time in the uniforms of air commodore, colonel of Hussars and – the nearest to the navy he could get – the rugged-looking Trinity House outfit of greatcoat, bright-buttoned blazer and peaked cap.

6

From Peace to War

Churchill was in his office in the Ministry of Munitions when the war came to its sudden end. In a vivid passage in the closing chapter of *The World Crisis*, he recalled looking out of the window, up Northumberland Avenue towards Trafalgar Square, waiting for Big Ben to strike the eleventh hour of the eleventh day of the eleventh month of 1918, the fifth year of the war.

At its first stroke,

> I looked again at the broad street beneath me. It was deserted. From the portals of one of the large hotels absorbed by Government Departments darted the slight figure of a girl clerk, distractedly gesticulating while another stroke resounded. Then from all sides men and women came scurrying into the street. Streams of people poured out of all the buildings. The bells of London began to clash ... Around me in our very headquarters in the Hotel Metropole disorder had broken out. Doors banged. Feet clattered down corridors ... All bounds were broken. The tumult grew. It grew like a gale, but from all sides simultaneously ... Almost before the last stroke of the clock had died away, the strict, war-straitened, regulated streets of London had become a triumphant pandemonium.

Of course he rejoiced with the happy crowds, 'the brave people who had borne so much and given all, who had never wavered, who had never lost faith in their country or its destiny', but it was not long before the pessimistic realism that governed his thinking about war and peace reasserted itself. Within only a few weeks, the general election had shown many of those 'brave people' in a different light, the light of vindictive triumphalism egged on by a chauvinistic popular press. Churchill, wedded though he long had been to the principle of magnanimity towards the vanquished, was appalled to hear himself yielding to the demands of his constituents at Dundee that the Kaiser should be tried and, if possible, hanged.[1] The public mood regarding Germany remained fierce and demanding through the months that followed, the months of much publicised peacemaking in Paris and the transformation of President Wilson's rational and conciliatory 'Fourteen Points' peace plan into a treaty, signed at Versailles at the end of June 1919, that was regarded by all but the most internationalist Germans as a *Diktat*, an imposed and unfair settlement.

Churchill did not consider the Treaty of Versailles to be as bad as that, but he was acutely aware that the peacemaking process was so ill-managed that the seeds of future troubles were copiously sown. Churchill's principles of magnanimity and reconciliation had no power to survive in the heated atmospheres of victorious democracies. Reasonableness was overborne by the rage for revenge. The Kaiser escaped being hanged but Germany was to be squeezed till the pips squeaked. Churchill thought the economic clauses of the treaty particularly disastrous: 'malignant and silly to an extent that made them obviously futile. Germany was condemned to pay reparations on a fabulous scale. These dictates gave expression to the anger of the victors, and to the failure of their peoples to understand that no defeated nation or community can ever pay tribute on a scale which would meet the cost of modern war.' Churchill felt sure that these demands would work nothing but woe, and he was only mistaken to the extent that the woe turned out to be worse than expected.

Germany's payment of reparations to France, Belgium and Britain became mixed up with the United States's insistence on total recovery of the money it had lent to Britain and France. 'The fact that these [reparation] payments were made only from far larger American loans reduced the whole process to the absurd. Nothing was reaped except ill-will.'[2] German society from the time of Versailles onwards was consumed with resentment about the way their country had been treated and, as was felt by some outside Germany as well, victimised. Many of those resentments were unreasonable, not least that against the 'war-guilt' clause, the justice of which Churchill seems not to have questioned. In a major foreign policy speech on 13 April 1933, he refuted in some detail the charge that Germany had been subjected to a 'Carthaginian peace'. Some German resentments, however, were unmistakably reasonable, and the net outcome of the whole set of them was exactly what Churchill had anticipated and feared from the start: an indignantly aroused Germany raring to break the chains imposed upon it – chains which moreover its gaolers failed to keep secure – and to assert once more its giant strength at the heart of the Continent. He concluded the 1914–18 parts of *The World Crisis* with an awed tribute to Germany's war-making capability and an anxious wondering about the future: 'Will a new generation in their turn be immolated to square the black account of Teuton and Gaul? Will our children bleed and gasp again in devastated lands?' What Churchill did *not* anticipate was the peculiarly virulent form which that arousal was to take.

Churchill was not himself one of the peacemakers. He was busy at home in his new post of Secretary of State for War and Air. It was a reasonable appointment in view of the military expertise he had displayed through the preceding five years, but he made no great success of it. A combined responsibility for army and air force (the navy, as usual, was a law unto itself) would not have been easy to exercise, even if the Treasury had not been dead set on economies across the board and if Churchill himself, a Liberal cost-cutter at heart, had not been willing to assist the Treasury by backing the 'Ten Year Rule', the Cabinet's injunction to the armed services that their planning should exclude the possibility of major conflict for the next decade.

On the Air side of his responsibilities, he protected the independence of the infant RAF (army and navy equally resenting the new arrival) and brought back to its management its wartime chieftain, Sir Hugh Trenchard, whose stamp upon it now became indelible. Air historians have, however, universally criticised Churchill's lack of interest in the development of civil aviation. He was rightly praised for his management of the demobilisation of the army, a delicate business that had begun to go badly wrong before he could get a decisive grip on it. Reformers nevertheless regretted that he took none of the opportunities lying open for a reforming minister who had long been conspicuous in finding fault in the ministry of which he was now the head. The explanation of his inactivity in this respect, or the excuse for it, may have been that the army (or what was left of it after the mass demobilisation of the recent war's volunteers and conscripts) still had more than enough to do. It had to garrison Ireland, where the popular movement for Irish independence took the island to the verge of anarchy in 1919 and 1920, facing the Cabinet with the unwelcome possibility of military action in support of the beleaguered Royal Irish Constabulary. Churchill's attempt to avert such an extremity, the raising of a 'Special Emergency Gendarmerie' and an 'Auxiliary Division' of ex-servicemen, was not a bad idea, but it turned out to be counter-productive: history has no good words to say about the 'Black and Tans' and the 'Auxis', as the two corps of volunteer toughs respectively became known. Then there was the Middle East, in ferment after the collapse of the Ottoman Empire. British troops were still deployed all the way from the Dardanelles to Baghdad and in Palestine and Egypt, awaiting a political settlement of the region that was not to come until 1921. Finally there was, what weighed most on Churchill's mind, Russia.

Britain had a vested interest in Russia. One purpose of the Gallipoli campaign had been to sustain and reinforce Russia's war effort. After the withdrawal from Gallipoli, Britain and France had been supporting Russia by other means, with the consequence that, by the time the revolutionary government withdrew from the war, there were Allied detachments in Russian ports together with large dumps of arms and munitions. It was natural promptly to reinforce them and to place them at the disposal of the counter-revolutionary generals who proclaimed their continuing loyalty to the Allied cause. What to do when civil war broke out, and the implications of intervention were raised, were questions that tormented other ministers than Churchill. But there is no doubt that he was more profoundly, even disturbingly, affected than other members of the government by Russia's withdrawal from the war, and by what happened to Russia in the process. That withdrawal, in the autumn of 1917, meant that Germany no longer had to fight a war on two fronts and could concentrate all its efforts against the war-worn Allies in the west.

The Bolshevik revolutionaries who were responsible for this betrayal of their country's allies were politically and morally odious to Churchill, who for all his social reformism before the war had always made a point of being anti-socialist. Now he made a point of being anti-Bolshevik. Of course he was not alone in detesting the Russian revolution and fearing its consequences. His view was the general one in the years 1918 and 1919, when the Bolsheviks' achievements were fresh and attractive to the Left all over west and central Europe and America too, and when Soviet foreign policy was at its most cockily aggressive. The 'peacemakers' in Paris might have been persuaded to make war on Bolshevism, if they had not had more than enough trouble in making peace with Germany and its wartime allies and in managing the return to peacetime at home. Churchill had an astonishing shot at persuading them to do so. Lloyd George, unable to make his mind up and with much else to think about, allowed Churchill to go to Paris in mid-February 1919 to try out his scheme of Allied intervention on the all-powerful Council of Ten. The day before its meeting, Churchill explained his plan to President Wilson. Wilson pooh-poohed it, but Churchill was not deterred. When next day he got to the Council, from which not only Lloyd George but also, as it happened, Wilson, Clemenceau and Milner were absent, he put on such a performance that he completely won its other members over – an excessive effect that Wilson and Lloyd George had to go to some pains to reverse.[3]

The most the leaders of the victorious powers found themselves able to do was to give support (mostly moral, some material) to the Soviet Union's newly-independent neighbours and to the Russian counter-revolutionaries. Churchill remained extraordinarily worked up about the Bolsheviks, as he always called them. He tried every political trick he knew to keep British forces in action against them, and went on abusing them long after his political colleagues and public opinion at large had tired of his harangues. He once offered his opinion, as a ground for belief in the existence of Hell, that there must be somewhere for Trotsky to go when he died.

The charge against Churchill that he was a 'warmonger', in most respects unfair, has some merit here. The reason for this was partly because he disliked socialism in any form, and he saw Bolshevism as its worst form; partly because the murder of the Tsar and his family in July 1918 revolted his monarchical and humanitarian principles; and partly also because his principle of honour forbade him to desert the 'White Russians' whom his country had encouraged and assisted to fight the 'Reds' – the same principle that made him ashamed to abandon the Belgians in Antwerp in October 1914. By unilaterally pulling out of the war in 1917, the Bolsheviks had betrayed their country's allies, and had done so on terms so profitable for Germany that Ludendorff was enabled to renew the war for another twelve months. It is instructive to note, however, that these anti-Bolshevik feelings of Churchill's, strong though they remained through the interwar years, were trumped by *Realpolitik* considerations when the Nazi threat declared itself in the 1930s. Churchill then shocked most strait-laced Conservatives by talking of engaging Stalin in an anti-Hitler front; hopeful talk of which nothing came. Significantly enough, the same cycle of recrimination and reconsideration repeated itself in 1939–41. The German-Soviet Non-Aggression Pact, on the eve of Germany's assault on Poland, had the effect of withdrawing from the Franco-British alliance a hoped for ally and giving its enemy much material advantage. Two years later, on the evening of the day of Germany's assault on it, Churchill instantly offered the Soviet Union friendship and aid. Bolshevism was still bad, as he frankly admitted to his British audience, but the threat from Nazism to Britain and to the world was worse.

In February 1921 Lloyd George moved Churchill from the War Office to the Colonial Office, where he remained until the Coalition collapsed in October 1922. Churchill had no special interest or expertise in colonial affairs – India and the white Dominions were the parts of the Empire that had so far commanded his attention – and he did not let his new office take up too much of his time. His anti-Bolshevik passion remained unassuaged despite his having lost the political battle; the Cabinet decided to withdraw support from the counter-revolutionaries in November 1920, and without allies inside it Churchill was powerless to block the road leading to establishment of trade relations with the Soviet Union. Regarding Ireland, however, he underwent something of a change of heart – responding perhaps, after many years, to Clementine's early observation that, if he had been Irish, he would have been a nationalist himself. He found he could muster some understanding of the Irish nationalists' cause and much personal respect for their military leader, Michael Collins. He was one of the group of ministers entrusted with the negotiations that led to the establishment of the Irish Free State in December 1921. In the following year he did its embattled government good service by standing by it in the civil war that erupted, and by not intervening militarily despite provocations such as the assassination of Sir Henry Wilson, the Chief of the Imperial General Staff, which inevitably maddened Conservatives who had opposed the idea of a Dublin government from the start.

Historians of the British Empire have found much to argue about in

Churchill's settlement of the Middle East while he was at the Colonial Office; but it may well be doubted whether he did worse than anyone else could have done, given so much excitable nationalism throughout the Turkish and Arab regions and antagonism between Jews and Palestinians in the former Holy Land. What concerns us here is that he brought to his new post the same readiness to impose economies that marked him in the previous one. Churchill was an imperialist through and through, but that didn't mean he rejected the orthodoxy of trying to run the empire on the cheap. Britain was willing to spend money, if it had to, on armed forces to maintain the security of the Mediterranean and the Suez Canal, which meant garrisoning Egypt and Palestine. It was desperate to reduce costs on everything else in the region. Churchill did what he was expected to do with his usual rapid determination. By September 1922, 'he had reduced Britain's expenditure in the Middle East from £45,000,000 to £11,000,000'.[4] His grand plan included the steady withdrawal of troops from Iraq and Jordan, both countries being set up as quasi–independent kingdoms in training to assume responsibility for their own security. To reduce the costs in Iraq until the British occupation could be phased out, he insisted that troublesome tribesfolk could be disciplined more cheaply by the RAF's light bombers, which might drop non-toxic gas as well as explosives, than by the army's elaborate punitive expeditions on the same pattern as the one he had taken part in – and commented on the cost of – a quarter of a century before.[5] The generals were indignant, but Churchill was not the man to be moved by the indignation of generals. For some years, the aerial method was thought sufficient and satisfactory, both in Iraq and in British Somalia; so much so that retention of the bomber for colonial purposes was Britain's sticking-point whenever the legality of bombing came up in disarmament talks.

Churchill continued to be willing to enforce economy in the armed forces in his next ministerial office, but before he could take that up, at the end of 1924, there ensued a strange two-year interlude. Lloyd George's unstable coalition came to pieces when its Conservative members decided to leave it in October 1922. In the consequent general election, which the Conservatives won, Churchill was galled to find his Dundee seat floating away on the rising tide of Labour. Out of Parliament after twenty-one years, he had plenty of other things to keep him

busy, not least the writing of *The World Crisis* and the journalism he had
to turn to when out of office, but he naturally longed to return to the
corridors of power. An opportunity came when the Prime Minister, by
now Stanley Baldwin, called a general election near the end of 1923.
Churchill contested the seat for Leicester West, but lost to a Labour man
again. What was worse, the Labour Party won enough seats to be able
to take office in alliance with the Liberals.

The prospect of having 'socialists' (as Churchill excitedly perceived
them) as allies joined with other grounds of disgruntlement to turn
Churchill away from the Liberals and back towards the party of his
first allegiance. Conservatives might distrust him and attribute his
return to their fold as shameless opportunism – with the Liberals in
disarray, theirs was clearly the party of the future – but of course a man
of Churchill's stature and talents could not be turned away. After an
exhilarating and nearly successful campaign as an 'Independent Anti-
Socialist' candidate for the prestigious Westminster constituency, he
was adopted as 'Constitutionalist' candidate for Epping and returned to
the House of Commons at the general election of October 1924.[6] Great
was the surprise of the Conservative Party when it learned that the
Prime Minister had asked the returned prodigal to take the office of
Chancellor of the Exchequer.

Churchill had been party to the imposition of the Ten Year Rule and
found no cause now to recommend its abandonment. He had always
believed in restricting the services' expenditure in peaceful times when
no danger threatened; he saw no dangers threatening now, and in the
mid-1920s it was possible to hope that the intermittent naval disarmament talks between Britain, the USA and Japan might culminate in a
'naval holiday', such as he had hoped to interest Germany in in 1912.[7]
The RAF and army were accustomed to put up with financial starvation,
but the Admiralty, annually absorbing by far the largest slice of the
defence cake, was not. Churchill, whose long experience at the Admiralty had familiarised him with its ways and wiles, believed the admirals
were as usual exaggerating their requirements and misreading the world
situation.

In one particular at least he may have been wrong. The admirals had
given more consideration to the Pacific hemisphere than he had.
Churchill either could not or would not take Japan seriously. Although

he sometimes spoke of Japan with admiration, more often he spoke of it as insignificant. The Admiralty and the Chiefs of Staff in the later 1920s found no naval powers to worry them on the European side of the world, but they were worried about Japan (and even the USA) on the other side. It was now that the Admiralty began its long endeavour to make Singapore the invulnerable base it needed to be if the security of Britain's Asiatic and Australasian empire was to be guaranteed. 'Invulnerability' was in fact beyond Britain's means to 'guarantee', but that was the sort of grandiose language that imperial pundits were accustomed to use. Churchill never subsequently admitted to misjudgement in denying the admirals all the cruisers they asked for, but his persistent inattention to the matter of Singapore did in the end draw from him a reluctant confession that he should have known better.[8] Indeed he should. But it might have made no difference in the long run. The simple fact no one wanted to face was that the empire had become too big and gangly to be defended in the old Victorian way, and that it was no good relying for ever on prestige, bluff and good luck – in this case, the good luck of not having to fight Japan at the same time as enemies nearer home.

The year 1929 was the beginning for Churchill of a second, longer and more disturbing interlude in his career. The general election in May resulted in the Labour Party becoming the biggest party in the House. With the support again of the Liberals, it therefore formed the government. Churchill, disgusted with this turn of events, and with the final volume of *The World Crisis* off his hands, decided to have a holiday and make some money in North America, to complete the book about his early life he had already begun and then to set about the more challenging project of a biography of the first Duke of Marlborough. All went well with the holiday and the money-making until just before he was due to return home. He was actually in New York, consorting with his millionaire friends, when the Great Crash began. How much he lost, and why, remains obscure, but it seems certain that he found himself much poorer when he got home than he had been when he set out.[9]

Chartwell, the country house near Westerham in Kent that he had been doing up since 1922, had to go out of commission. Most of it was placed under wraps; only Churchill's study was kept open, so that he could carry on writing without interruption. When not occupying the garden cottage there, the Churchills stayed in hotels or places rented by the month. To make ends meet, so far as they ever did meet, he had to ply his trade as a writer more tirelessly than ever: finishing the memoir *My Early Life* that he had been composing for some time past, churning out pieces for periodicals and newspapers, and beginning the Marlborough biography for which he received a hefty advance. On top of all that, there was his political career to continue, no matter how discouraging the circumstances.

All in all, the 1930s began badly for Churchill. He was not alone. The 1930s began badly for everyone else. The Great Crash on Wall Street turned out to be the detonator of a chain reaction of misfortunes and disasters. Economic depression and political disturbance were everywhere. For the Left, it only proved what the Comintern had been preaching, and what the Soviet Union had supposedly demonstrated, that capitalism was shown up for the fraud it really was; Communist parties everywhere prepared for action. For the Right, it meant holding on tight to whatever could be salvaged from the wreck and backing the anti-socialist parties and movements that promised to restore stability and order; fascism acquired force elsewhere than in Mussolini's Italy. The economic progress and peace-preferring internationalism that had marked the later 1920s yielded before the demands of protectionism and nationalism. In no country was the beginning of the 1930s more angry and ominous than in the country which Churchill had always thought likeliest to disturb the peace of Europe: Germany.

The appearance of Adolf Hitler at the head of the German state and, as he would have thought more important, *Volk* on 30 January 1933 did not alarm Churchill as much as the reappearance of a nationalistic, militaristic and expansionist Germany. For those with eyes to see and ears to hear, that essential Germany had been there since Versailles, under the hopefully liberal cover of the Weimar Republic. Weimar's days were effectively over by 1930, when the National Socialist Party, the Nazis, suddenly leapt to become the second largest party in the Reichstag with the votes of six and a half million Germans behind them. Their Führer, so far known only to specialists in German politics, began to be a figure of international interest. Churchill does not seem to have paid any attention to him until 1932 and, like many others viewing the German

situation from afar, was at first neither surprised nor particularly
alarmed by him. (It was a commonly held idea until well into Hitler's
years as Chancellor that he was more moderate than many behind him,
and might indeed only be their front man.) It was the rise of Nazi mil-
itancy in Germany that brought from Churchill this passage in a
powerful speech of November 1932. As was to happen regularly through
the coming seven years, he was putting an unpopular point of view,
arguing that conceding to Germany some measure of rearmament and
'equality of status' would not necessarily promote the peace of Europe.
We should not be taken in, he said, by the German demand for equal
status.

> That is not what Germany is seeking. All these bands of sturdy Teutonic
> youths, marching through the streets and roads of Germany, with the light
> of desire in their eyes to suffer for their Fatherland, are not looking for sta-
> tus. They are looking for weapons and, when they have the weapons, believe
> me they will then ask for the return of lost territories and lost colonies ...
> [Just look at the state of Europe today.] Fears are greater, rivalries are
> sharper, military plans are more closely concerted, military organisations are
> more carefully and efficiently developed, Britain is weaker ...[10]

Raising public consciousness regarding the German danger became
Churchill's preoccupation and main mission in life in the course of the
year 1933. He had for several years been leading a backbench campaign
against the National Government's Government of India Bill, a moderate measure offering a modicum of self-government to India that was
insufficient to satisfy the demands of the Indian middle class but more
than sufficient to prompt Churchill to see in it the end of the Empire.
That campaign did not end until 1935, and Churchill stayed with it to
the last. By then, however, the German danger had come to command
the greater part of his attention. In speech after speech, article after article and (not that they were yet numerous) broadcast after broadcast, he
called attention to Germany's rearmament and its implications for the
peace of Europe, perhaps the peace of the world. This, for example, is
from a broadcast towards the end of 1934:

> It is startling and fearful to realise that we are no longer safe in our island
> home ... Only a few hours away by air there dwells a nation of nearly sev-
> enty million of the most educated, industrious, scientific, disciplined people
> in the world, who are being taught from childhood to think of war and

conquest as a glorious exercise, and death in battle as the noblest fate for man. There is a nation which has abandoned all its liberties in order to augment its collective might. There is a nation which, with all its strength and virtues, is in the grip of a group of ruthless men preaching a gospel of intolerance and racial pride, unrestrained by law, by parliament or by public opinion.[11]

He was denounced as a trouble-seeking warmonger by Hitler in his speeches, by Goebbels's propaganda machine and by peace-minded people in his own country, but that was a misrepresentation. Churchill was not looking for war if lesser use of force could avert it. He believed in negotiation from strength. Until as late as early 1938 he was willing to believe that a settlement of German grievances might be achieved (especially if some more tractable leader than Hitler appeared) on terms not intolerably unjust to its neighbours; he did not believe that Germany could be brought to such an agreement unless there was credible military muscle behind it. To his mind, a Britain (with France and other allies) strong enough to pose a credible military threat to Germany made reaching such an agreement more likely.

Criticism of Britain's wavering and feeble policy towards Germany went hand in hand with exposure of Britain's military inadequacies. The 'National' governments of Ramsay Macdonald and (from June 1935) Stanley Baldwin were not as supine about rearmament as Churchill alleged. The Ten Year Rule was abandoned in 1932, the Chiefs of Staff turned their attention away from Japan and back toward Europe, and rearmament – admittedly of a measured, Treasury-controlled order – became official policy from early 1935. But Hitler's unilateral revisions of the Treaty of Versailles evoked no strong response from a government unwilling to tell a pacifistic electorate that a small amount of blood spilled now could save a lot of blood spilled later; Churchill was recalling these early years of Hitler's remilitarisation of Germany when he proposed that the first, introductory volume of his *Second World War* should be titled 'The Unnecessary War'.

Showing no interest in the army and not much in the navy, Churchill was fixated on the menace of the Luftwaffe – like everyone else, he had an exaggerated belief in its bombing capability – and he engaged in a series of battles with the government about its size and quality relative to the RAF and about Britain's air defences. His was a unique voice in this unending debate and his position vis-à-vis the government was peculiar. On the one hand, he was universally recognised as a man whose opinion on military matters was worth heeding, and the government actually allowed him to have a hand in the improvement of Britain's air defence system, giving him in June 1935 a place on the Air Defence Research Committee and appointing his scientific adviser to its technical subcommittee.[12] On the other hand, his public stance was one of consistent criticism of the government, and his comments and suggestions were considerably enriched by information confidentially passed to him by officials who shared his concern or who were dissatisfied with what went on in their departments. Sometimes the government could guess where he had got his facts from, sometimes it couldn't. Chartwell in these years became a self-appointed shadow administration in waiting, with Churchill's informants covertly coming and going and his little band of friends and advisers gathering most weekends to discuss how to keep their unpopular flag flying. They needed all the fortitude they could muster when Stanley Baldwin, who half liked Churchill, was replaced as Prime Minister by Neville Chamberlain, who did not like Churchill at all, and who was, moreover, a more determined appeaser.

Hitler's *Anschluss* with Austria in March 1938 had somewhat improved Churchill's standing; this was, after all, exactly the sort of expansion that he and his few allies had been predicting. Hitler's next move, demanding the cession to Germany of Czechoslovakia's German-speaking borderlands, was accompanied by such violence of language as to bring the British people for the first time face to face with what Churchill had been urging since 1934, the necessity of making a stand. For a little while, in September 1938, war seemed possible and the British people appeared ready for it. Historians still differ as to whether Britain should or could have gone to war then. The British and French publics were persuadable to go to war if rousingly enough called to do so. So many were the variables in the military and diplomatic consequences which might have followed that it is impossible to say, with Neville Chamberlain's admirers, that the fortunes of war would surely have favoured Hitler. The bulk of British military advice to the Cabinet was indeed against going to war, but there is significance in the fact that British strategic and military assessments in the later 1930s were always based on the worst case for Britain, while positing the best case for prospective foes.[13] War, however, was avoided. The Prime Minister flew to Munich for his third meeting with Hitler and returned to Britain waving the worthless piece of paper that the Führer had signed, proclaiming that, after all, there was to be 'peace in our time'. The crisis blew over. From the one extremity of tension and emotion, the public swung instantly to the other extreme of relief and happiness. The tide of understanding that had suddenly risen to support Churchill just as suddenly subsided, to leave him temporarily stranded.

Churchill became very unpopular with the Conservative faithful in the autumn of 1938, after Munich. British public opinion by then was in a highly nervous state, a state for which hysterical is scarcely too strong a word. When the Munich agreement was debated in the House of Commons, Churchill was not its only critic, but he was the most eloquent and trenchant one. He dared to say 'the most unpopular and unwelcome thing' that could be said in the circumstances – that, far from having cause to rejoice, 'we have sustained a total and unmitigated defeat'. That alone would have damned him in the eyes of the Conservative faithful. The damnation was sealed by his peroration:

> I do not begrudge our loyal, brave people, who were ready to do their duty no matter what the cost, who never flinched under the strain of last week – I do not grudge them the natural, spontaneous outburst of joy and relief when they learned that the hard ordeal would no longer be required of them at the moment, but they should know the truth. They should know that there has been gross deficiency in our defences, they should know that we have sustained a defeat without a war, the consequences of which will travel far with us along our road; they should know that we have passed an awful milestone in our history, when the whole equilibrium of Europe has been deranged, and that the terrible words have for the time being been pronounced against the Western democracies: 'Thou art weighed in the balance and found wanting.' And do not suppose that this is the end. This is only the beginning of the reckoning. This is only the first sip, the first foretaste of a bitter cup which will be proffered to us year by year unless by a supreme recovery of moral health and martial vision, we arise again and take our stand for freedom as in the olden time.[14]

For a little while, Churchill was the most unpopular politician in the country. Conservatives were confirmed in their belief that he was irredeemable in his capacity for disloyalty, and the timid and fearful had new cause to wonder whether, after all, he was not the warmonger the Nazis liked to allege. That this phase of discredit and unpopularity did not last long was entirely Hitler's work. First came the moral shock of *Kristallnacht*, on 9 November 1938, when Nazi squads burnt synagogues, smashed Jewish shop windows and arrested Jews by the thousand, then in March 1939 the completion of the destruction of Czechoslovakia left no room for doubt that 'peace in our time' had been a fraud. Even the Prime Minister could see that Hitler had been lying all along in his declarations that his territorial ambitions did not go beyond the reincorporation of German-speakers in the Third Reich. Too late to stop him absorbing Czechoslovakia, the government decided to try to prevent him doing the same to Poland, all too obviously the next in line; Britain and France together threw down the gauntlet to Hitler by undertaking to come to its aid (exactly how was not clear) if Germany attacked it. Churchill's star rapidly rose again, but he was politically prudent enough not to gloat about it. It was universally taken for granted that when war came, as soon it must come, he would be back in office. Hitler made war inevitable by sending his forces into Poland early on 1 September. Chamberlain, still clinging to the slender hope that even at this late hour Hitler might be persuaded by the threat of war on two fronts to think again, told Churchill he wanted him in the select War Cabinet he proposed to form. At eleven o'clock on Sunday 3 September the Prime Minister gloomily told the nation that, Hitler having persisted with his assault on Poland, Britain was 'in a state of war with Germany'.

The House of Commons met soon after noon that Sunday. Churchill of course was there, pleased to receive a note asking him to see the Prime Minister when it broke up. He was pleased also to be again at war for a noble cause. He wished the war could have been avoided but now that it had come – just as in 1914 – his feelings about it were quite unlike those of any other Member of the House.

> As I sat in my place, listening to the speeches, a very strong sense of calm came over me, after the intense passions and excitements of the last few days. I felt a serenity of mind and was conscious of a kind of spiritual detachment from human and personal affairs. The glory of Old England, peace-loving and ill-prepared as she was, but instant and fearless at the call of honour,

thrilled my being and seemed to lift our fate to those spheres far removed from earthly facts and physical sensation.[15]

That afternoon, Churchill learned that he was again to be First Lord of the Admiralty. This appointment was the best he could have expected, but it was less than he believed to be his due. He had been given command of part of the nation's war machinery and was confident that he could manage it well, but he knew that other parts would be managed less well and that the Prime Minister in charge of the whole had no heart for the job. This was the war for which he had been preparing over the past five years, a war he believed he was more competent than anyone else to direct; and he was prevented from directing it. That did not keep him from firing off memoranda and letters of good advice to the Prime Minister and to his colleagues, just as he had done from his ministerial offices in the previous war. On the whole no notice was taken of them. The zeal and energy Churchill displayed in the Admiralty should have inspired emulation, but it didn't. Consequently, he continued to feel frustrated. He also knew he was still the object of suspicion and distrust. With such a reputation and a past, he could not suddenly be taken into the bosom of a Cabinet composed entirely of Conservatives. He would have liked the government to become a national one of all parties, but that was not going to happen. The Labour Party made known its unwillingness to join in a coalition under Chamberlain, and the Liberals decided not join it either. The Prime Minister had only invited Churchill to join the government because he had to. Churchill was still an outsider, brought into the Cabinet and its inner war-managing circle of necessity, not choice.

Quite apart from his discomforts in the War Cabinet, Churchill's nine months at the Admiralty were months of considerable impatience and frustration. The war at sea was not as exciting as he wanted it to be or as he thought the British people expected him to make it. The navy was indeed for some weeks caught unprepared by Germany's totally unexpected use of magnetic mines. Before any significant German warships had been sunk, Britain lost one of its few aircraft carriers, the *Courageous*, and the battleship *Royal Oak* – the latter, embarrassingly in Scapa Flow, supposed to be impregnable to submarines. Being First Lord was, however, not Churchill's only public activity. He did more than any other minister to keep the British people informed about the war and aware of the issues, broadcasting no less than six times during these 'Phoney War' months and making the most of the navy's gallant successes – indeed, exaggerating some of them. He got into trouble with the Foreign Secretary for saying rude (and, in truth, unreasonable) things about neutral states, especially Norway and the Netherlands, for not embracing the side of their island champion.[16] The War Cabinet became familiar over the months with his proposals for livening up the war by dropping mines in the River Rhine, laying them in Norwegian waters, bringing Norway and if possible Sweden into the war, and, more surprisingly, by 'the entry and domination of the Baltic'.[17] He was annoyed not to be invited regularly to meetings of the Anglo-French Supreme War Council until February 1940. He was there, however, on 28 March when at last it endorsed a version of his Norwegian scheme; a version that duly began to be implemented on 8 April. What the consequences of its endorsement earlier on would have been it is impossible to say. Churchill assumed that they would have been good. As things turned out, the immediate consequences at this date were bad. He was as surprised as everyone else to discover, in the course of 9 April, that Hitler too had been thinking about Norway and had got there first.

Churchill's months at the Admiralty were also uncomfortable for the Admiralty. Its strategic mission – to protect the trade routes and to enforce blockade – was already properly understood, and it was as well prepared for its worldwide tasks as the inadequacies of some of its equipment and vessels permitted. It did not need Churchill to get it going. The signal 'Winston Is Back', flashed around the fleets on the evening of his arrival, could be read both ways: the navy's memories of him were mixed, and he knew it. He recalled to active service, and placed in high command, several ageing admirals whom he had come to admire during the previous war: Sir Roger Keyes, born in 1872; the Earl of Cork and Orrery, born in 1873; and the relative youngster Sir Edward Evans, born in 1880. He retained as First Sea Lord the agreeable Sir Dudley Pound (born in 1877), who had a useful talent for seeming to go along with the First Lord's bright ideas while discreetly arranging for their difficulties to be subsequently and tactfully exposed.[18]

Another indication that some of Churchill's mind was still stuck in the past was his difficulty in ceasing to believe in the efficacy of 'capital ships', grandly named battleships with big guns reminiscent of those that won the Royal Navy's most famous battles in the centuries before 1914 and ought to have won the battle of Jutland in 1916. The Royal Navy had plenty of them but some were old and overdue for refits. Reviving the idea that had so excited him and Fisher in 1914–15, Churchill thought these elderly battleships could now be done up as, he believed, unsinkable floating batteries and made the centrepiece of a fleet to break into and dominate the Baltic. It took many weeks of Admiralty staff work to convince him that the scheme was impractical. (Suicidal was how it struck everyone else.) That was one of his sillier ideas. But Churchill was far from singular in such attachment to battleships. It was felt throughout the maritime Great Powers. Battleships were still the principal means by which national enthusiasm for navies was maintained and the normal measure by which the strengths of navies were judged. So long as there existed a *Scharnhorst,* a *Gneisenau,* a *Bismarck* and a *Tirpitz,* it was no more than prudent that there should also be a *Prince of Wales,* a *Hood,* a *Nelson* and a *Duke of York.* Yet the battleship's long years of supremacy were nearly over, as some naval experts were beginning to realise. The money spent on them could be spent as well in other ways – on aircraft carriers, perhaps, as the Japanese and Americans had realised – and battleships were more vulnerable to attack by submarine and, more important, by aircraft than their apologists liked to admit. Through the first two years of the war Churchill failed to take in how vulnerable battleships without air protection actually were. He seemed to learn the lesson in respect of smaller ships after the navy's experiences off Norway in 1940 and Crete in 1941, but he clung to the belief of stout-hearted traditionally-minded admirals that modern battleships could defend themselves against aerial attack, and insisted accordingly on the *Prince of Wales* and *Repulse,* under the command on one such admiral, going to Singapore in December 1941. Their fate at last drove the lesson home.[19]

If his received notions about battleships and the Baltic were unhelpful, his notions concerning administrative efficiency and economy, similarly rooted in his experiences during the 1914–18 war, bore brilliant fruit. In that war, with Walter Layton's help, he had instituted a regime of internal inspection and auditing within the Ministry of Munitions and, so far as circumstance allowed, reaching into its associated departments. Now with the help of Professor Frederick Lindemann, one of his Chartwell cronies, he instituted the same within the Admiralty. It was only a small outfit, just a handful of young economists and statisticians reporting to Lindemann, known to the Admiralty and in Whitehall as the First Lord's Statistical Branch or (in Civil Service terms) Department, but its usefulness was great and its significance for the future immeasurable. Its task was twofold. It helped Churchill to understand the whole of the business for which he was responsible to have all its incomings and outgoings and internal movements placed before him weekly in statistical or tabular form: the visual equivalent to the big war maps he liked to look at every day. From them he could see where progress was being made or shortcomings were occurring, where things were going to plan and where they weren't. These facts were no more than any conscientious departmental head should have wanted to know; what was new with Churchill was his determination to override the nuisance of disputed statistics – the inevitable product of departments in competition, each with its own statistical section – and to get the facts from his own independent source and not from the heads of sub-departments who might have an interest in colouring them. There was something here for officials to object to, but not much. More objectionable to officialdom were the Statistical Branch's inquiries into matters that had excited the First Lord's suspicions: materials being hoarded or wasted, resources not being fully used, men or ships in the wrong places, cover-ups and bungles.[20]

The Norway campaign that consumed his attention during his last five weeks at the Admiralty brought out both the best and the worst in him. The best showed in his quickness to respond to unexpected bad news, the characteristic energy and resolution with which he sought to catch up after being wrong-footed, and the readiness to take responsibility. The worst showed in the extent of his interference with the way the professionals went about their work, whether in the Admiralty itself or at their command posts off the Norwegian coast or tenuously on it. Of course there was nothing new in this. Demarcation lines had little reality for him. There was more interference than usual at this juncture because, with a complaisant First Lord beside him and no other strong character to balance him in the wobbly war machinery, he was able to dominate the scene to a degree that was no longer possible once that machinery had received the major overhaul he gave it as soon as he had the chance.

The Norwegian campaign took the shape it did because Churchill and the Admiralty had long been making plans for action on that side of the North Sea and were at last authorised to implement one of them. The Royal Navy mined the waters at Narvik, Norway's northernmost and strategically most important port, on the very same day that the German navy set out to land troops at Narvik and Norway's other major ports. By midday on 10 April, the daring German mission was everywhere accomplished. The Allied response was slow and muddled. Useful hours were lost while the Admiralty adjusted its mind to the reality that the German heavy warships credibly reported as being at sea were not heading for the Atlantic but were doing something totally unexpected. That fact duly taken on board, the navy acted swiftly, finding the German vessels hiding in the fjords and inflicting heavy losses on them; victories which, however, did nothing to disturb German possession of the ports or, what mattered supremely, command of the air. British and French soldiers were hastily embarked, too often without appropriate equipment, and landed near Narvik and Trondheim from 14 April onwards, with a view to seizing those ports when sufficiently reinforced to do so. Churchill conceived a bold naval attack up Trondheim's long fjord. Having apparently persuaded everybody that (despite its similarity to the Dardanelles) it could be done, he was furious to find the Chiefs of Staff belatedly changing their mind and insisting on more prudent measures. Only at Narvik was there any success on land. A mixed force of British, French and Polish troops took it on 28 May. The war meanwhile had taken a dramatic new turn with the German invasion of France on 10 May and rapid collapse of the Allied armies. The little Narvik contingent followed its much larger Dunkirk counterpart back to Britain.

During the Norwegian campaign Churchill was often involved directly in strategic and tactical naval and military decisions.[21] To what extent his activities caused or compounded the confusions and crossed purposes with which the whole unhappy story of the campaign is riddled is impossible to judge. Its historians are at one in affirming that he was at the heart of at least some of them, but who now can tell whether the operations he took a hand in went better or worse than they would have done had they been left to the professionals? It must be noted that confusions and crossed purposes abounded whether Churchill was involved or not: they were bound to occur when actions had to be taken in a rush and the machinery for coordinating them was so unsuitable and defective. The Norway emergency required quick and accurate Intelligence and the planning and execution of Amphibious Operations – or, in the words of Churchill's institution later in the year, Combined Operations. The Intelligence material that came in was not bad but it was misread and mishandled by a naval establishment with *idées fixes* about German intentions. As for Combined Operations, they were far from being prepared for or even wanted. When a force to take Narvik was at last assembled and dispatched, the commanders of the naval and army elements, Admiral the Earl of Cork and General P. J. Mackesy respectively, took their orders from their separate department chiefs, met one another for the first time when they were off the Norwegian coast, and promptly quarrelled. Churchill emerged from the gruelling experience of the Norway campaign with a determination that Combined Operations should never again be such a shambles, and that Intelligence should receive the respect it deserved.

It was ironic that his involvement in such a fiasco, and his personal responsibility for some of it, should have happened just at the moment when he had the opportunity to achieve his lifetime's ambition. He later recognised how lucky he had been.

> Considering the prominent part I played in these events and the impossibility of explaining the difficulties by which we had been overcome, or the defects of our staff and governmental organisation and our methods of conducting war, it was a marvel that I survived and maintained my position in public esteem and Parliamentary confidence.[22]

It was not such a marvel, really. The mistakes he made and the bungles he was involved in during the brief Norwegian campaign counted less against him than the undiminished sense in all parties that he alone in the government, like him or not, was the man who was zealous about war and who, moreover, could fire the people to be zealous too. Neville Chamberlain could not match Churchill in these respects. The House of Commons debated the Norwegian fiasco over two days, 7 and 8 May. The Opposition pressed it to a vote of confidence, which the government won by so reduced a majority that Chamberlain felt obliged to try to enlarge its basis by inviting the other parties to help form a National coalition government (the very thing Churchill had wanted the previous

September). On Thursday 9 May Chamberlain set about discovering which of the only two possible successors, Churchill or (much more popular with the Conservative Party and the Whitehall mandarinate) the Foreign Secretary Lord Halifax, he should recommend to the King in the now inevitable event of his resignation. Halifax ruled himself out, ostensibly on the ground that as a peer he could not do the essential business in the House of Commons, inwardly because he knew he simply could not face it.[23] At 5 p.m. on Friday the 10th, word came from Clement Attlee the Leader of the Labour Party that it would serve under any Conservative Prime Minister so long as it was not Chamberlain. Churchill, by then the only candidate in the running, was Prime Minister an hour later.

In the course of that very same day, German forces crossed Belgium's first line of defences and took its most essential fortress – occupied the duchy of Luxemburg – seized the most important bridges and airfields in the Netherlands – and began their advance through the supposedly impenetrable Ardennes region towards the Meuse and France.

Democratic Warlord

The westward drive of Hitler's armed forces that began early on 10 May 1940 signalled that the 'Phoney War' or, as Churchill later described it, the 'Twilight War', had given way to something more serious, but Churchill 'took it all as it came'. This was what he had been waiting and hoping for. Like almost everybody else, he was confident that the French army would be able to deal with the invader and, although his own country's readiness for war fell far below the ideal, he never doubted that in the long run the combined strength of France, Britain and their respective empires would sooner or later prevail over a Germany unfitted (so the government believed) for a long war and undermined (so he expected) by the resistance of the peoples it oppressed. He later recalled that, by the time he went to bed, at 3 a.m. on the 11th, 'I was 'conscious of a profound sense of relief. At last I had authority to give directions over the whole scene.'[1] He had finally arrived at the centre of things, the place where he wanted to be and where he insisted on staying. Some of his critics complained that, once there, he behaved like a dictator. This was unjust; but no more than many of us was he innocent of dictatorial inclinations, and it is undeniable that he put himself, by British standards, in a position of exceptional authority. Being the man he was, he did more in this position – he covered a wider span of responsibilities – than any other man could have done, and was proud of doing so. He used his supreme position to take on work, not to avoid it; and, indeed, there was plenty of work to do.[2]

The task that most immediately pressed upon him, as disasters and disappointments multiplied through the months of May and June 1940, was to gear Britain and the British people up to the demands of a serious war. Churchill was well prepared for serious war but Britain was not. Neither the armed forces nor the economy behind them were impressive. The army, emaciated by years of financial starvation, in the words of one of its best generals was 'totally unfit to fight a first-class war'.[3] The navy was large and looked impressive but was behind with its building and renovating programmes, woefully short of convoy escort vessels and hard put to it to master the U-boat menace. The air force, on which the bulk of defence expenditure had recently been spent, proved adequate for the defence of Britain but more inadequate than its spokesmen dared admit for taking the war to the enemy.

Nor was the economy well prepared for war. Apart from the aircraft and electronics industries, much of it was old-fashioned, inefficient and inflexible. Nothing had been done to build on the lessons learned in the First World War. Little thought had been given to the fundamental question of the management of resources, both material and human. A Ministry of Supply had existed since August 1939 but it had little authority and, of course, no experience. The other preparatory measures did not amount to much. It had been known since April 1939 that British men would become liable to conscription when they reached the age of twenty, and the government had begun recruiting women into agricultural work. Sugar, butter and meat were rationed, but rationing of almost everything else and intensive exploitation of the land were yet to come. The Treasury had long been warning that Britain could not afford a long or an expensive war. Its calculation would prove to be correct. By the end of 1940, Britain was bankrupt and entering a long period of financial servitude to the United States.

Despite Britain's noble military history and imperial swagger, and notwithstanding the public's phlegmatic acceptance of the inevitability of war in September 1939, British society cannot be said to have been in a high psychological state of war-readiness. What else was to be expected after twenty years of self-conscious recovery from the wounds of the First World War and of earnest pursuance of the rewards of peace? The mood of September 1939 had changed little by April 1940. Nothing had happened since the war began to make it seem more serious or worthwhile.

What, in the earliest days of May 1940, did Britons think they were fighting for? The cause to which Britain was most ostensibly committed, the assistance of Poland, had been virtually forgotten. It had never been as well understood or popular a cause as assistance to Czechoslovakia had been for a short time in the late summer of 1938, and that had disappeared from view too. There remained, of course, the cause of standing up to a militarised, fascistic and would-be hegemonic Germany, the cause Churchill had been preaching since 1933, but it is a question how much that in itself really moved the general public or was understood by it. Nine months of quiet on the Western Front and of freedom from air raids had bred complacency as to Britain's security, and uncertainty as to what the national war policy was other than the traditional one of naval blockade, soothingly supposed to slowly but surely break the German ability and will to fight. Only the previous month the Prime Minister, Neville Chamberlain, had given public expression to that complacency when he opined that 'Hitler has missed the bus'; from which it was comforting to draw the implication that Britain was no longer in danger.[4] Talk about terminating a pointless and economically damaging state of war was not uncommon in Westminster and Whitehall in the spring of 1940. In the country at large the people were confused and uneasy, ready to go wherever the governing elite chose to lead them.

Hitler was not irrational in reckoning that the British, if they were rational, ought to realise that there was nothing to be gained and much to be lost by carrying on with the conflict. Churchill liked to claim, both in his speeches at that time and in his memoir-history written later, that the British in 1940 were the same 'lion-hearted' race (he often used that resonant word 'race' when he meant nation or people) that had faced down Spain in 1588, France in 1805 and the Kaiser's Germany in 1914, and it is true that by about the end of June the nation seemed to be united in a spirit of steadfastness and patriotism; but how much of that spirit had been there already, and how much of it was aroused and fashioned by Churchill himself, defies measurement. In later May and early June the British public was so battered and bewildered by shocks and disasters that if a different leader – Lord Halifax, for example – had told it that there was no point in going on with the war, it would have followed him. The British people were ready to swing either way. Being the leader at the time and persuading the Cabinet to support him – another momentous act of leadership that we shall soon consider closely – Churchill was able to swing the people his way, and by so doing to change the course of history. But it was a near-run thing.

Churchill was inspiring for most of the masses, but the elites of Westminster and Whitehall were reluctant to march to his tune. His position as Prime Minister was precarious to begin with. Almost everyone in politics and power acknowledged that he knew more about war than anyone else in the top rank of politics, and that if there was to be a war he had to be in the government; but not many of his own party or of the Whitehall mandarins wanted him to be in supreme command, because he had given so many grounds for distrust in the past. He was only reluctantly, even only provisionally, accepted as Prime Minister by the great majority of Conservative MPs (who greatly outnumbered all the others in the House of Commons) and it was entirely possible that they might turn against him. The Labour Party accepted him at this juncture more from dislike of Chamberlain than because they liked him. Politically-minded working people in the country at large moreover tended to distrust and dislike him because of what they knew – or thought they knew – about his activities in Britain's never-resting class war, and what they recollected of his boisterous hostility to the Bolshevik revolution.

His anxieties at home were nothing compared to the anxieties that pressed in from abroad. The Netherlands quickly succumbed; its royal family and government fled to London and armed resistance ceased with the terrible bombing of Rotterdam on 14 May. In Belgium, which took longer to subdue, government and monarch went different ways; King Leopold and the army surrendered on 28 May, the government fled to France. The French high command too late became aware that the main German thrust was coming through the Ardennes and across the Meuse between Dinant and Sedan, and failed to repel it. Already by 16 May the situation looked so bad that Churchill flew to Paris (the first of five increasingly agitated visits) to find out what was going on. From that day on, he and every well-informed Briton feared the worst. By 20 May, when the leading Panzers had reached the Channel, plans for evacuating the British Expeditionary Force were set in train; and on the 25th it began to withdraw towards Dunkirk, shedding most of its equipment on the way. By the night of 3 June the Royal Navy had managed the evacuation of an unexpectedly large number of British and French troops; some thousands more would later be rescued from ports much further west. Continued French resistance proved ineffective. Paris was occupied on 14 June and the government, now in Bordeaux and headed by the aged defeatist Marshal Pétain, sued for an armistice.

It was during those catastrophic days at the end of May that Churchill made the most momentous decision of the whole war: the decision to go on with the war in the face of such setbacks and such a gloomy outlook. The decision did not rest with him alone, but it was his will that won the argument. The question, whether to try to get out of the war, was repeatedly debated between 24 and 28 May in the little War Cabinet and at last in the Cabinet proper, and thus the decision was, as constitutionally it should have been, that of His Majesty's Government. If Churchill's will was to prevail, he could not enforce it; he had to win his colleagues round. The colleague least likely to be won round was Lord Halifax, the Foreign Secretary. It is impossible to doubt that if Halifax had become Prime Minister on 10 May, as he could have done and as many people including the monarch wanted him to do, the argument would probably have gone the other way. In the early and midway stages of the War Cabinet's discussions, Neville Chamberlain and Halifax were interested in exploring the possibility of negotiating an acceptable peace deal through the good offices of Mussolini, not yet himself at war. Churchill and the other two members, the Labour Party's leaders Clement Attlee and Arthur Greenwood, either simply would not do that or could not believe that any good would come from doing so.

In his memoir-history of the war Churchill, in what has justly been described as 'the most breathtakingly bland piece of misinformation in all those six volumes', denied that such discussions had ever taken place.[5] It may be presumed that he was embarrassed by the memory. It is not clear that he needed to have been. If he did at first seem reluctantly willing to contemplate the approach to Mussolini, which his friend the French Prime Minister Reynaud also wanted, it would have been because he was playing for time: waiting to see, first, the Chiefs of Staffs' report on Britain's prospects for going it alone, a report delivered on the 26th; and, secondly, how much if any of the army would get home from Dunkirk. The Chiefs were not absolutely discouraging; they thought Britain had a fighting chance, provided the navy could keep the lifeline to North America open and the RAF could keep itself and its supporting factories in being. What would happen at Dunkirk, no one could predict. Churchill's political position, as has already been

explained, was in those early weeks far from assured. The bulk of the
Conservative Party would have gone wherever Chamberlain went, and
it was essential to avert the possible resignation of the esteemed Foreign
Secretary, Halifax. By the 28th, Chamberlain having come round to
Churchill's position, Churchill took the issue to the whole Cabinet and
secured its support, and Halifax accepted the majority decision. The relative success of the Dunkirk evacuation seemed to confirm that it was
the right one. For better or worse, Britain would fight on.[6]

Meanwhile, the sky continued to darken. Hitler was rapidly becoming master of western Europe. Belgium, the Netherlands and
Luxemburg, Denmark and Norway were already under military occupation. An attempted French counter-offensive in early June proved a
failure. So desperate was Churchill to keep France (or at any rate its
overseas empire) in the war that on 16 June, encouraged by a few determined Frenchmen already in London, his War Cabinet put to the
French government, now in Bordeaux, a hastily cooked-up proposal for
an indissoluble union of the two states.[7] The French government, with
Marshal Pétain about to take control, rejected it out of hand and, the
very next day, sued for an armistice. Within a week the seaward regions
of France were also under German occupation, while the inland region
became a vassal regime governed from Vichy. Britain had lost its only
militarily significant ally, while Germany since 10 June had gained the
alliance of Italy, something the Admiralty had particularly hoped would
not happen. To sum up the effect of those disastrous weeks: what had
looked like a reasonably promising situation for Britain to be in at the
start of a major war had suddenly become a very unpromising situation
indeed, and the job description of a British war leader had been hugely
extended.

Churchill was already engaged in the activity that remained one of his
priorities through the rest of the war: rallying the spirits of the people,
maintaining their confidence and hopefulness, and keeping the nation
as united as possible in determination to carry the war on to a victorious end. It should be noted en passant that a huge quantity of revisionist
research and writing has appeared in the past twenty years or so, all of
it devoted to showing that, behind the proclaimed and cultivated
national unity, there were actually many social disaffections and divisions, some of them being continuations from before the war and

some produced by wartime conditions. They were not entirely concealed during the war but they were not much talked or known about, partly because the authorities naturally discouraged the publicising of them and (what younger historians born into a different climate may tend to miss) partly because of the patriotic self-censorship exercised by people who could have publicised them.* Discovery of these 'realities behind the façade' and 'myths' began soon after Churchill's death and reached such a crescendo in the 1990s that it may have become difficult to realise that, notwithstanding so many elements of disunity, the encompassing reality was of remarkable unity.[8] To an extent that can never be measured but that has never been queried even by those who haven't liked the man, Churchill created and maintained this impression of unity, and gave it his peculiar accent.

Churchill did this not only by the rousing speeches he made but also by the eccentric image he projected: an image unique, now impressive and now amusing, eminently caricaturable. His most pronounced sartorial departures from the establishment norm before the war had been his unusual hats (not least, the French tin-hat he had worn in the trenches in 1916) and the boiler-suit outfit he put on for bricklaying at Chartwell. Now he appeared publicly in a variety of service uniforms and, not only when at home, in the one-piece zip-up 'siren suit' that called to mind a baby's rompers. At home and when unwell he might receive visitors in colourful dressing-gown and Chinese dragon-embroidered slippers, or in bed (if it was during the morning) and even while he was in the bath. On tour, unless he was in one of his uniforms or in the Western Desert, where he affected a huge topee, he continued to wear his dandyish pre-war black jacket and pin-stripe trousers, gold watch-chain over buttoned waistcoat, silk handkerchief in breast pocket and spotted bow-tie and unusual flat-topped black hat, halfway between

---

* The degrees and kinds of self-control that could then be imposed by such ancestral considerations as patriotism, loyalty, duty and honour may not be easily understood in a demilitarised and atomised society that has become habituated to publicity-seeking, scandal-mongering, the betrayal of confidences and the disclosure of secrets. Consider for example the way Bletchley Park's secrets were faithfully kept for thirty years by more than ten thousand people.

a bowler and a homburg. He always had a cigar going and he would sometimes wave it; but more often he waved his silver-mounted walking stick, on the point of which he sometimes balanced his hat. He always managed to appear energetic and keen, stepping out briskly ahead of the rest of his party and sometimes making them trot. His 'V-sign' became universally familiar. He was a 'character' and apparently an approachable human being; he was a legend in his own lifetime, about whom good stories were told. He never let himself appear downcast, though privately he often was so. What he said of his performance when he met the collapsing French government on 11 June was true on every such occasion: 'I displayed the smiling countenance and confident air which are thought suitable when things are very bad.'[9] And he was evidently a normal family man who seemed to be 'just like us', with a loving wife and perhaps one or other of his daughters often at his side. Nothing more unlike Adolf Hitler could possibly be imagined.

Another notable difference from the reclusive Führer (who never allowed himself to be seen visiting bomb-damaged German cities, and indeed virtually never saw them at all) was Churchill's visible presence in the heart of the nation. He stayed in London through the Blitz and the invasion scare, as did the royal family and the rest of the government. Nothing did more to maintain popular morale under bombardment and other hardships than the knowledge that the residents of Buckingham Palace and Downing Street were sitting it out like all other Londoners. There had been talk in the summer of 1940 of evacuating the government to somewhere in the provinces, but Churchill (recalling perhaps the French government's bolt via Tours to Bordeaux) forbade it. He also deprecated the evacuation of children to North America – Princesses Elizabeth and Margaret could have gone but didn't – and of course he had no sympathy at all with British adults who fled to America or stayed there. The fact of his staying at his London post was brought home to the nation at large by newspaper photographs of him still walking the streets of Westminster and, once the Blitz had begun, those of the East End that had been bombed, responding to the cheers of the 'bombed-out' by waving with his cigar hand or his stick and making his V-sign.

There is no doubt that such engaging personal attributes helped to make people like him and trust him. But it was his speeches that fired

them to fight. His ability to make speeches more remarkable than those
of any other Member of Parliament or public person had long been his
political power base and the source of his political resilience.[10] As First
Lord of the Admiralty he had broadcast more addresses to the people
than any other minister and he had taken pains to meet head on his
listeners' tendency to wonder what the war was about. For instance,
after a moving passage about 'the hideous agony of Poland' he went on:
'Although the fate of Poland stares them in the face, there are thought-
less dilettanti or purblind worldlings who sometimes ask us, "What is it
that Britain and France are fighting for?" To this I answer, "If we left off
fighting you would soon find out".'[11]

The peculiar muted atmosphere of those opening months and his subordinate position in the government had not been calculated to bring
out the best in him. The month of May changed all that. Having become
the chief man in government and accepted responsibility for committing
the British people to a total war which many establishment insiders considered unwinnable, it was now up to Churchill to persuade the British
people and their potential helpers around the world that, nevertheless,
all would be well. He began it in the Commons on 4 June, in his speech
about Dunkirk, the speech concluding with the memorable:

> We shall go onto the end, we shall fight in France, we shall fight on the seas
> and oceans, we shall fight on the seas and oceans, we shall fight with grow-
> ing confidence and growing strength in the air, we shall defend our island,
> whatever the cost may be, we shall fight on the beaches, we shall fight on the
> landing grounds, we shall fight in the fields and in the streets, we shall fight
> in the hills; we shall never surrender ...

An Independent Member experienced the power of that speech as
millions more must have done, once it had entered into circulation:

> most of us were thinking ... 'How on earth are we going to do it? And what
> happens if France falls, as Mr Churchill clearly fears?' The greatness of that
> speech was that it filled in, with simple vivid strokes, a picture of the impos-
> sible made possible. Every man saw himself in that picture somewhere,
> fighting 'on the beaches, in the streets, in the hills': and we all went out
> refreshed and resolute to do our best. If Churchill saw a way out of this
> mess ... that was good enough for us.[12]

Thus began the series of great speeches that have passed into English literature as well as world history. Fewer of them were actually broad-cast than survivors from that time like to think and seem to recall, but that is easily explained: his voice and style were so distinctive and engag-ingly imitable that persons reading the texts of his other speeches in newspaper and pamphlet heard the speeches in their heads.[13] He explained how the war was going, he gave the bad news (most of it, any-way) as well as the good, of which, of course, he made the most. He told the British people and their kindred in the Dominions they were indomitable, encouraged them to believe in themselves and encouraged the rest of the free world, especially the Americans (at whom this ora-tory was partly aimed) to believe in the British. It was the British people as a whole, not just their armed services, he was summoning to arms in the 'Finest Hour' speech: 'What General Weygand called the Battle of France is over. I expect that the Battle of Britain is about to begin.' In the justly admired words of an American journalist, Churchill 'mobi-lized the English language and sent it into battle'.[14] David Cannadine thus admirably summarises the speeches and their effect:

> The issues seemed appropriately Churchillian in their momentous and noble simplicity: victory or defeat, survival or annihilation, freedom or tyranny, civilisation or barbarism. To such an unprecedented national crisis – actu-ally terrible yet potentially heroic – Churchill's grandiloquent rhetoric, so often out of place and out of date, was for once perfectly attuned ... In 1940 Churchill finally became the hero he had always dreamed of becoming, and his words at last made the historic impact he had always wanted them to make ... At a time when Britain was on the defensive, Churchill's speeches were themselves the best – and sometimes the only – weaponry available.[15]

As Prime Minister he was responsible not only for maintaining the country's morale but also for making Britain's way in the world. Espe-cially in what remained of 1940 and throughout the following year, while Britain and its Empire were still virtually on their own and the odds were stacked against them, it was essential to give the British people and the watching world the impression that Britain was doing all right and would win through in the end. Privately, Churchill knew very well that, unless the United States came wholeheartedly into the war or Hitler made egregious mistakes, Britain's chances of imposing its will on Ger-many were minimal. The 'Give us the tools and we will finish the job' broadcast of 9 February 1941 was no more than rousing bravado.

Meanwhile, he felt it important to show fight, not just to hurt the enemy so far as that could be done but, much more important, to keep the Americans supportive. That 'Britain could take it' was not enough. He had also to prove that Britain could dish it out. Hence the impatience and the fanciful schemes, the exaggerated expectations and the recurrent irritations of 1941 and the first half of 1942, when his hopes again and again were dashed and, instead of glorious victories that he could expatiate on, all he got was disappointments, defeats and unimagined humiliations (above all, Singapore in February and Tobruk in June 1942) one after another. Defending himself and his war machinery in the Commons, Churchill 'won debate after debate while losing battle after battle'.[16] Only in the autumn of 1942 did he at last find a general who could give him a resounding and undeniable victory, enabling him to proclaim that, although it might not be the beginning of the end, it was at any rate the end of the beginning.[17]

The months from May 1940 to November 1942 (after which month the war began at last to go better) were the period when this singular talent of Churchill's was of the most importance. His speeches could no longer have the same concentrated effect once Britain had allies again – and very major allies too: the Soviet Union from June and the United States from December 1941 – and war news came flooding in from new fronts the whole world over, including exotic South-East Asia and the Pacific. Churchill never really liked broadcasting and he was glad to have to do it less often. In 1944, there were no broadcasts at all from 26 March to the end of the year. When he did face the microphone, it was likely to be to address the Americans or one or other of the suffering subject nations of Europe, a series begun early and resoundingly with 'Français! C'est moi, Churchill, qui vous parle' on 21 October 1940.[18]

From his first visit to Washington in late December 1941 to the last of his wartime summits at Potsdam in July 1945 he was recurrently out of Britain, keeping the allies onside and visiting the armed forces. Much publicised (and in the cases of Montgomery and Harris, self-publicising) commanders of those forces joined foreigners such as Timoshenko and Patton in the pantheon of popular heroes, diverting from Churchill some of the publicity and popularity that earlier had all gone to him. That the limelight came to be shared also by President Roosevelt and 'Marshal Stalin', as Churchill ended up calling him (after experimenting with 'Monsieur Stalin' and 'Generalissimo Stalin'), was to some extent Churchill's own doing, praise of them having become a regular feature of his reviews of how the war was going and how sure Britain was to win with such great allies.

The mere passage of time also took its toll. As Britain graduated from the heroic early months to the grinding and dreary hardships of a tough war going on longer than anyone had expected, people became war-weary, more willing to criticise the government, to grumble and to admit that they had had enough. When the V1s and V2s began to fall on London and the Home Counties in 1944, Churchill did not broadcast to the people with brave words of defiance and encouragement, as he had done during the Blitz, but tardily admitted the new weapons' unpleasant existence in matter-of-fact speeches to the House of Commons, in effect classing them as just one more of the burdens that had to be borne until the war came to its ever-delayed end.[19]

In only one major particular was Churchill's understanding of the British people's mood defective, and that was something that came to a point during the winter of 1942–43. The British people, men and women in the armed services as well as on the home front, were by then more and more inquiring what post-war Britain was going to be like. Churchill's 'broad, sunlit uplands' were all very well, but what about employment and housing? These popular concerns were a legitimate extension of Churchill's avowed war aim, 'victory at all costs'. 'Victory' for the people meant more than it did for Churchill. He was so obsessed with winning a victory in military terms that only grudgingly did he turn part of his mind to the people's more comprehensive aim of a victory that would inaugurate the construction of a better Britain, a victory that would justify all wartime's sacrifices and be a 'glory' of its own kind.[20] 'Better', for the Labour Party, of course meant 'socialist'; it was only to be expected that men and women on that side of the wartime party truce would already be thinking constructively about the future. Some Conservatives were doing so too; not of course in any socialist vein but in an openly collectivist one, born of war-time planning experience. Churchill himself well understood the virtues of planning and controls – we have seen how he had been a conspicuous advocate of them in the Great War – but he disliked this kind of talk because it was 'socialistic' and, to his war-fixated mind, a distraction from the main business of the hour. By the time Montgomery's desert victory allowed him to pronounce that Britain had turned the corner and the publication of the Beveridge Report had brought popular interest in post-war possibilities to boiling point, Churchill could ignore the question no longer. In response to growing pressure from his more forward-looking colleagues (including, significantly, Professor Lindemann), Churchill did turn part of his mind to the domestic future. He devoted one of his by now rare broadcasts to the theme, he smiled on the production of social blueprints, and in September 1943 he put Lord Woolton in charge of a newly-created Ministry of Reconstruction.[21]

Notwithstanding his failure to put on a convincing show in this respect, Churchill's personal popularity stayed high, experiencing only short-lived slumps. One of the causes of its staying so was that he in effect enjoyed the advantage that used to be enjoyed by monarchs in earlier centuries: personal immunity from the criticisms of a respectful people while his ministers took all the flak for their discontents. His role changed as the months and years went by. It changed from that of trusted warlord, perceptibly in supreme command of the nation's war effort, to that of distinguished *compère*, reporting inimitably on the progress of a war that had long ceased to be merely a British and imperial affair. By the end of the war two of Churchill's main roles were the important ones of symbol and mascot: the symbol of the nation's pride in having for so many months stood alone against the forces of darkness, and the mascot of its determination to go on to the victorious end. He belonged more to that glorious past and, largely through his own inability to give his mind to any but strategic, military and diplomatic matters, less and less to the popularly longed for future.

No wonder, then, that when the British people had the opportunity in July 1945 to elect a team to take them into that future, they voted for someone else. Churchill at first interpreted this rejection in terms of 'ingratitude', but he was mistaken to do so. The voters who put Labour into office distinguished between the coalition-leading wartime Churchill, for whom they retained respect and even affection, and the Conservative Party leader Churchill, of whose post-war intentions they were understandably wary. The *Daily Mirror's* cartoonist Zec nicely represented the popular mood in his picture of a hopeful young couple who, as they walk into the future, turn to wave to a setting Churchillian sun and to say, 'Thank you for light in the darkest hours'.[22]

Remaining a popular and on the whole trusted leader in a total war was one thing; doing so in a democratic and constitutional way was another. From the start of Churchill's national leadership this was one of his priorities, and it came from the heart. Churchill's dedication to the British constitution and to the freedoms and rights of the individual that it nurtured and protected was unquestionable. The development of the constitution and the crystallisation of those freedoms and rights made the grand theme of the *History of the English-Speaking Peoples* he had in draft by 1939, and it was the chief cause of his enthusiasm for the British Empire's giant offspring, the United States. He was heart and soul a parliamentarian and a House of Commons man. There is no doubt about that. How much of his heart and soul were also democratic is matter for speculation; his social instincts and assumptions had much of the aristocratic, even the feudal in them, and the crowds that cheered his beaming progresses were much mistaken in thinking he was a cuddly 'man of the people'. Of course he insisted he was a democrat and, in the exciting years when he was running with the Liberals and with the radical David Lloyd George, he had uttered very democratic sentiments indeed.[23] What he essentially meant, however, when he spoke of democracy was liberal constitutionalism, which is not the same thing, although in itself it is a very good thing and perhaps more apt for the protection of fundamental rights and freedoms. The most important parts of the constitution, he correctly believed, had all been put in place well before Britain became superficially 'democratic' in the course of the later nineteenth century.

On top of his profound respect for the constitution, and especially for that part of it where he had spent the whole of his political life, the House of Commons, there were two strong sources of his repeatedly-proclaimed determination to direct the war by unbroken democratic means: first, it was a war waged by a free and peace-loving people against dictatorship, tyranny and aggression; and, secondly, it was a war in which the United States must, he believed, be equally concerned.

Churchill's early wartime speeches made much play with the fact that the British people were not as ready for war as the regimented populations of the dictatorships.[24] On 27 January 1940, for example, he said: 'In this peaceful country, governed by public opinion, democracy and Parliament, we were not as thoroughly prepared at the outbreak as this Dictator State whose whole thought was bent upon the preparation for war.' But, he continued, the British were rapidly making up for lost time and Britain's direction of the war would be better than Germany's because it was within a parliamentary system:

> During this time of war great powers are entrusted to the executive government. Nevertheless we exercise them under the constant supervision of Parliament, and with a wide measure of free debate ... In our country public men are proud to be the servants of the people. They would be ashamed to be their masters. Ministers ... feel themselves strengthened by having at their side the House of Commons and the House of Lords sitting with great regularity, and acting as a continual stimulus to their activities. Of course it is quite true that there is often severe criticism of the Government in both Houses. We do not resent the well-meant criticism of any man who wishes to win the war ... Criticism in the body politic is like pain in the human body. It is not pleasant, but where would the body be without it?[25]

There, in a nutshell, is Churchill's philosophy of British democracy at war, and his practice kept pretty close to it. Parliament did continue to sit with regularity throughout the war. Churchill and the other Ministers of the Crown did continue to attend their respective Houses, to encounter criticisms and to answer questions; they acknowledged their responsibility to Parliament. If they did sometimes fob off awkward questions with half-truths and evasions, that was nothing new. Sessions were sometimes held 'in secret', but only when debates would inevitably cheer the enemy: as for instance when Churchill, not normally afraid to admit defeats and reverses, kept very bad news about the Battle of the Atlantic for a secret session; or when there was a matter of extreme diplomatic sensitivity on the agenda, as when he had to explain why Admiral Darlan, so long Vichy's biggest bogeyman, had suddenly appeared as an ally.[26]

A 'wide measure of free debate' fairly described the variety and breadth of debate that continued to flourish within the symbiosis of Parliament and press. There were few of the press excesses that had distressed Churchill in the 1914–18 war. Government departments and publicity agencies naturally harped on the bright side of things and ignored the dark, but they did not often tell lies. (I am not so sure the same could be said of government-promoted films.) Much of what happened in the House of Commons was uncomfortable for Churchill, but he was powerless to stop it. He could not silence critics, some of whom – Aneurin Bevan, Emanuel Shinwell, Richard Stokes and Lord Winterton – gave him and his ministerial colleagues a hard time; the most he could do in self-defence was to deprecate their intemperance, impugn their patriotism and thankfully reflect that they were acknowledged extremists and that, no matter what they said, the majority of Members would remain solidly behind him. He made again the good point he had made in the *World Crisis* about the responsibilities of the Commons and the press not to misuse their freedoms:

> The House must be a steady, stabilising factor in the State, and not an instrument by which the disaffected sections of the Press can attempt to promote one crisis after another. If democracy and Parliamentary institutions are to triumph in this war, it is absolutely necessary that Governments resting upon them shall be able to act and dare, that the servants of the Crown shall not be harassed by nagging and snarling, that enemy propaganda shall not be fed needlessly out of our own hands and our reputation disparaged and undermined throughout the world ... After all, we are still fighting for our lives, and for causes dearer than life itself ... The duty of the House of Commons is to sustain the Government or to change the Government. If it cannot change it, it should sustain it. There is no working middle course in wartime.[27]

That reference to 'disaffected sections of the Press' is a reminder that Churchill had little more success in suppressing the uncongenial outside Parliament than he had in it. The press accepted military censorship of its reports from the theatre of war but remained free to say what it thought proper at home. The Communist *Daily Worker* was suppressed from January 1941 but came back with a bang in July 1942. Churchill's Conservative crony Lord Beaverbrook, proprietor of the *Daily Express*, campaigned along with the Communist Party for a Second Front through months when Churchill's inability to provide it grievously embarrassed his relations with Stalin. The populist *Daily Mirror* got into trouble for its campaign against the War Office, but a modest rectification of its manners sufficed to keep it in business. Churchill got it into his head that the film *The Life and Death of Colonel Blimp* would be bad for morale, but the film was made and exported nonetheless.

He would have liked to limit the use made of psychologists and psychiatrists in the Fighting Services ('it is very wrong to disturb large quantities of healthy, normal men and women by asking the kind of odd questions in which the psychiatrists specialise'), but they went on being used just the same.[28] His powers to stop and to sack within the government's own domain were nothing like as far-reaching as the 'dictator' school of critics has supposed. For example, his fears of 'socialist' influence in the army led him to seek to emasculate the Army Bureau of Current Affairs, but neither the Secretary of State for War, Sir James Grigg, nor the Lord Privy Seal, Sir John Anderson, supported him; nor did he succeed in his endeavour to remove the admirable senior soldier responsible for ABCA, Adjutant-General Sir Ronald Adam. The Democratic Warlord was also a thoroughly constitutional one.

8

The Grand Alliance

Churchill gave little thought to the question of Allies before June 1940. Until then, Britain's only but apparently adequate ally was France. He shared the comfortable majority view through the 1930s that the French army was unbeatable; a view the more comfortable for freeing Britain from the obligation to send more than a tiny military force to fight beside it. Then came Dunkirk: miracle, deliverance or disaster, according to point of view.* Why the French army failed to cope with the German invasion, and whether Britain's withdrawal of its land and air forces had any share in that failure, are still matters for debate. Whatever the explanation, the tragic issue was soon decided. Paris was occupied on 14 June and the French government, removed to Bordeaux and headed by the aged defeatist Marshal Pétain, sued for an armistice on the 22nd. Churchill had tried everything he knew or could dream up to keep France somehow in the war, but to no avail. Britain was now, apart from the Canadian contingent that had arrived in advance of the rest of the Empire's slow-mustering armies, on its own.

There was at once a lot of brave talk about the glory and advantage of being on one's own and freed from an unreliable ally, but the well-informed knew better. Since Britain, even with the Empire, could not now hope to do more than not lose the war, the possibility of actually winning it depended on securing the help of a powerful ally; which could only mean the United States. In this connection Churchill was something of an expert. He had spent several months there, he knew rich and influential Americans, his journalism was syndicated in the American press, and he was a favourite speaker at Anglo-American events in London. He had taken pains in the later 1930s to call American attention

---

* Two of the best books about it bear the titles *Strange Defeat* and *Strange Victory*.[1]

to the clouds gathering over Europe and to remind his readers and listeners how many values and interests the two countries shared. Confident in the strength of the Anglo-French alliance, he had, however, never thought of the United States being more than a friendly neutral. After the fall of France, friendly neutrality would no longer do. What Britain needed, and what Churchill bent himself to secure, was the United States as a co-belligerent. This endeavour filled much of his mind and time through the following eighteen months.

The omens were not unpropitious. President Roosevelt was known to believe that Nazi Germany was a growing threat to world peace and to American national interests. This had become plain in a few diplomatic gestures he made in the later 1930s; gestures plain enough to annoy the Führer. The American press's lively interest in the Spanish Civil War had turned into a critical curiosity about the fascist states that could only work to Britain's benefit. Once war had broken out, Britain received much more sympathy than Germany. Propaganda films showing the ruthlessness of the Blitzkrieg against Poland and the bombing of Warsaw frightened European neutrals but nauseated Americans. But sympathy with Britain did not mean an intention to join in the war. In the run-up to the Presidential election of November 1940 the America First Committee represented one point of view, the Committee to Defend America by Aiding the Allies the other. The latter proved the more influential. Roosevelt was re-elected for a third time. It would now be seen what 'aiding the allies' amounted to.

It may well be asked whether the United States and Great Britain were not destined to become allies in war against Nazi Germany, whether Churchill had been there or not. The answer is that they probably were. The United States and the Americas generally were of such importance to British trade and finance that the security of Atlantic commerce had long been a *sine qua non* of British strategic thinking. British agencies had been quietly cultivating American good opinion for several years, the royal visit in 1939 crowning a successful public relations campaign. Any British Prime Minister at war with Germany was bound to cultivate the best possible relations with the United States, and to settle for whatever alliance might be on offer. But no alliance that might have otherwise have come about could have been as close and, all things considered, as harmonious as the one that Churchill and Roosevelt came to preside over. Their good understanding of one another and their personal friendship – for such, in its way, it was – served to dampen down and minimise the many divisive elements in the alliance: different national economic and financial interests, different imperial interests, different military cultures, and armed forces so given to quarrelling with one another that quarrelling with those of an ally came naturally. That not more troubles sprouted from these fissiparous tendencies was because of example and admonition from the top: the Churchill–Roosevelt relationship, a relationship unique in the histories of national leaders and of Great Power alliances.[2]

The first move towards it was actually made by the President, well before the time when Churchill would doubtless have taken the initiative himself. Rightly reckoning that Churchill would welcome correspondence with him, and somewhat distrustful of the judgement of the American Ambassador in London (Joseph Kennedy, the father of J. F. Kennedy, and no friend to the British), Roosevelt wrote a cautiously-worded note to Churchill in mid-November 1939, the heart of which was the sentence: 'What I want you and the Prime Minister to know is that I shall at all times welcome it, if you will keep me in touch personally with anything you want me to know about.' 'Thus', wrote Churchill, 'began that long and memorable correspondence – covering perhaps a thousand communications on each side, and lasting till his death more than five years later.'[3]

The friendship in due course came to rest on much more than correspondence. They had met once before, if being at the same dinner counts as meeting, in London in 1919. (Churchill had forgotten it, although in his memoir-history he pretended otherwise. Roosevelt had not forgotten how he had then thought Churchill a show-off and 'a stinker'.) The motion for their meeting again came from Roosevelt's side in the spring of 1941. By then he had made great progress with his long-laid design to bring the United States as close to the British cause as Congress and public opinion would permit. Britain's requests had so far on the whole been met, though always with strings attached. Britain being bankrupt by the end of 1940, and its plight being made clear in one of Churchill's most impressive long letters, Roosevelt conceived the 'Lend-Lease' scheme for keeping Britain and its allies supplied with what they needed for continuing the war; a generous scheme indeed but not without strings, one of them being that Britain and her imperial allies were expected to keep on fighting, and enabled to do so, until such time as 'the arsenal of democracy' would make up its mind to do some fighting too.[4] When that might be, however, was up to Hitler. America's support of Britain was by now open and unembarrassed. It remained to be seen how long Hitler would put up with it. (It is tantalising to speculate on how long Hitler and Roosevelt would have waited had not Pearl Harbor precipitated a decision.) The US Navy's protection of 'Lend-Lease' ships was quietly extended from American coastal regions to include Greenland and the Azores, its destroyers were spoiling for a fight, American vessels were attacked and Churchill was longing for a big incident similar to that of the *Lusitania* that would shake the United States off the fence. The President's continuing refusal to be hurried disappointed Churchill, but he was encouraged by the suggestion that it was high time they met. The momentous encounter took place in Placentia Bay, Newfoundland, in August 1941.

The meeting went well. It did not bring the United States much closer to co-belligerence but the budding 'special relationship' was advertised in the so-called Atlantic Charter, a stirring statement of war aims; not something Churchill himself would have thought necessary but predictable from the land of Wilsonian idealism. Soon after his return home, Churchill made on 24 August one of his longest broadcasts about 'the voyage which I made across the ocean to meet 'our great friend, the President of the United States' (note the expression 'our great friend', which he often repeated) and about its importance – an immediate importance far outmatched by the place in world history he chose to give it:

It symbolizes ... the deep underlying unities which stir and at decisive moments rule the English-speaking peoples throughout the world. Would it be presumptuous for me to say that it symbolizes something even more majestic – namely, the marshalling of the good forces of the world against the evil forces which are now so formidable and triumphant and which have cast their cruel spell over the whole of Europe and a great part of Asia? This was a meeting which marks for ever in the pages of history the taking-up by the English-speaking nations ... of the guidance of the fortunes of the broad toiling masses in all the continents; ... the highest honour and the most glorious opportunity which could ever have come to any branch of the human race.[5]

This was Churchill carried away, as so easily happened, by excitement and emotion instinctively channelled into grandiose rhetoric. Differences in the interpretation of the Atlantic Charter were not long in appearing. But the Placentia Bay meeting was immensely important for all that. The two men got on well together, decided they could trust one another (subject to whatever reservations realistic statesmen have to make) and discovered many common interests. They were to be together again eight more times in the course of the next five years; about 120 days altogether.[6] These meetings, set up mainly by Churchill, who believed in the efficacy of personal diplomacy more than the Foreign Office, gave a new phrase to the language: Summit Meetings, or simply, Summits. After the Soviet Union had entered the war, there were Summits of the Big Three, the leaders of Britain, America and Russia at Teheran and Yalta. (Roosevelt to begin with sought to include China as a 'Big Power' too, but Churchill despised its leader Chiang Kai-shek and distrusted his pushy wife; for reasons of his own the President had given him up by 1944.) These Summit meetings that Churchill invented and valued so much were an important innovation in the practice of diplomacy.[7]

A great deal has been written about the Churchill–Roosevelt friendship, not least by Churchill himself, but some aspects of it remain puzzling. There is plenty of evidence that each man was at times disappointed or annoyed with the other – a small book could be made of the letters and telegrams Churchill drafted but never sent – and it is possible to suppose that Churchill's failure to attend the funeral of 'our great friend' in April 1945 was in part because he felt the President had latterly become unsupportive. At the same time it has to be recognised that people do not inevitably cease to be 'friends' because they sometimes have rows, nor are friendships forgotten after their fading. In the heyday of the friendship between Roosevelt and Churchill it was helpful and comforting to them both, and much to the benefit of their respective nations.

Churchill invited himself to Washington directly after the news of Pearl Harbor and arrived again in Placentia Bay on 22 December with his usual entourage after a stormy nine days inside the new battleship *Duke of York*. Roosevelt was rightly impressed with the war plans Churchill brought with him. He had not hitherto encountered the full force of Churchill's strategic intellect and prescience. These plans, thoroughly discussed with the Chiefs of Staff during the voyage, were comprehensive and ambitious. 'There must be a design and theme for bringing the war to a victorious end in a reasonable period.'[8] Churchill already knew that the President and his Chiefs had already decided that, if America were to find itself at war with both Germany and Japan, it would make sense to deal with Germany first; one big potential cause of argument was thus removed. The first part of Churchill's plans, accordingly, was headed 'The Atlantic Front', by which he actually meant the Mediterranean from Turkey at one end to French Morocco at the other. It suggested exactly what, after some vicissitudes, came to pass: a deal with the authorities in Vichy's North African territories and Anglo-American landings therein, to meet from the western side the Anglo-Imperial forces of General Auchinleck expected to sweep in from the east. The third part, 'The Campaign of 1943', looked forward to the Allied forces' landing on the German-occupied Continent no later than 1943 and was detached from realism only in relying on the occupied peoples to rise in 'fury' as soon as their rescuers drew near, thus making the Germans' military situation so much the less viable.

The second part, 'The Pacific Front', was full of interest but of mixed quality. The First Sea Lord, Sir Dudley Pound, cannot have been awake or concentrating when Churchill's draft plan was discussed. Realistically enough it recognised that Japan's conquests would spread further before there was any hope of checking them, but it showed no sense of the geographical and logistical difficulties of 'fighting them at every point . . . so as to keep them burning and extended'.[9] Churchill's mind so far made no room for Japan; indeed it would never make much room. It needed an even bigger shock than the sinking of the *Prince of Wales* and *Repulse* (on 10 December) to disturb his deep-rooted ignorance and complacency; that bigger shock, the fall of Singapore, was still seven weeks away. His over-reaching excitement in the last days of 1941 led him to write of joint naval operations in the Pacific at a time when the Royal Navy was hard pressed to meet the demands of the Atlantic and the Mediterranean; besides which it was fantasy to think that short-range lumbering battleships like the *Nelson* and *Rodney* could be of any use in the vast waters of the Pacific. On the sensible side, he recommended the improvisation of aircraft carriers (a good idea, failing the construction of proper ones), and even proposed that the production of suitable 'seaborne aircraft' should take precedence over the needs of the planned British bombing offensive. This paper showed Churchill's capacity to produce good ideas and bad ideas haphazardly mixed together, but it risked giving offence to Americans in its assumption that they did not already have their own ideas about these matters. If their Anglophobe naval chief Admiral Ernest King saw it – and he probably did – he must have regarded it as patronising and impertinent.[10]

Churchill's North American visit (he also went to Ottawa for a few days) proved to be an unmixed success. His enthusiastic zeal for the success of the alliance was engaging and infectious. He treated Congress to one of his best speeches and he saw plenty of the President. Their friendship flourished through the next twelve months. They learned to keep off topics about which they were sure to disagree – British India, above all. Their good relationship enabled them to anticipate many of the difficulties and problems that dog military alliances, and to sort them out when nevertheless they occurred. By far their most important achievements came in these early days. One was their agreement to sink national distinctions in the common cause. They decided to establish an integrated system of war management, at the operational peak of which would be a Combined Chiefs of Staff Committee. Distinctions were one thing; differences were another. Example and symbolism mattered more than practice. This historically unprecedented committee did not often meet – in its full glory only on Summit occasions – and when it went into 'closed session' people knew that the Chiefs were having a first-class row. According to General Stilwell's diary about a meeting at Cairo in late 1943, *en route* to Teheran: 'Brooke got nasty and King got good and sore. King almost climbed over the table at Brooke. God he was mad.'[11] Such rages cannot have happened often. An ameliorative influence in the opposite direction was the appointment of Field-Marshal Sir John Dill to be the British Chiefs' representative in Washington. He turned out to have exactly the right touch for handling so obviously delicate an assignment.[12]

The even greater achievement was in agreeing that American and British forces should campaign together under a single Supreme Commander, British or American as the case might be, and that the two nationalities should be completely integrated in all associated staff and planning work. Nothing like this had ever been seen in alliance relations before.[13] Tensions, rivalries and jealousies inevitably disturbed the harmony of this enforced brotherhood from time to time. National prejudices and preferences were not always suppressed; Churchill himself, for example, was led into a petty display of them in his correspondence with General Sir 'Jumbo' Maitland Wilson, Supreme Allied Commander in the Mediterranean, even childishly objecting to his HQ's occasional use of American spellings.[14] It is a question how far Roosevelt's and Churchill's magisterial intentions were respected. Many American generals were Anglophobes, many British generals were patronising, and the most senior of them, Sir Alan Brooke, was often overconfident and tactless. Lower down the staff and planning levels, harmony seems to have been much better. There is no doubt that, despite serious differences about strategy, it proved to be a notably successful and complete alliance. Sharing a common language and purpose no doubt helped; but what also helped was the example of the officer given supreme command of the first combined operation, the landings in French North Africa (Operation Torch), and subsequently chosen to command the biggest combined operation of all, Operation Overlord, in June 1944, General Dwight D. Eisenhower. Not a great strategist but a genial, conciliatory, diplomatic man, well able to carry his political as well as military responsibilities, his determination to run a harmoniously integrated operation was summed up in his famous pronouncement that he didn't mind anyone being called a son-of-a-bitch, but he wouldn't stand for them being called an American son-of-a-bitch or an English son-of-a-bitch.

Churchill was with Roosevelt twice more in 1942. Throughout this year and until the summer of the next their friendship was at its warmest, and Churchill's ability to influence the President was at its most considerable. The military alliance began with disagreements between the British and American Chiefs about where to launch their first combined operation: whether to turn the Germans out of North Africa, which was the British preference, or to go straight across the English Channel, which was the American. Roosevelt put an end to the argument by coming down on Churchill's side. He promised full collaboration and sharing of secrets on the atomic bomb project, which, although it was being conducted in the United States, was originally a British idea. He had kind words for Churchill when the shocking news of Tobruk's surrender reached Washington and at once undertook to make available the tanks that Churchill said were the Eighth Army's greatest need. The two leaders were still close through the most exotically sited of all the Summits, that at Casablanca in January 1943. It was only thereafter that differences regarding strategy and diplomacy began, slowly at first, to disturb their good relationship.

The differences regarding strategy were partly, and the differences regarding diplomacy almost wholly, to do with the Soviet Union. Hitler's invasion of Russia on 22 June 1941 gave the war a completely new complexion. Following the principle that 'my enemy's enemy is my friend' Churchill had at once declared, in a speech broadcast that same evening, that Britain would stand by Russia in its fight. The War Cabinet had already looked at the probability of the German action and apparently given Churchill the go-ahead.[15] Whether he would have found such encouragement in the Commons is a moot point. Conservatives generally were astounded to find themselves allied to the state they had long loathed; for Evelyn Waugh's conservative Roman Catholic hero, Guy Crouchback, the war ceased to feel worth fighting.[16] Churchill himself did not pretend that he had suddenly become pro-Communist. He simply distinguished between the regime and the people: 'the cause of any Russian fighting for his hearth and home is the cause of free men and free peoples in every quarter of the globe'.

The costs and embarrassments of such an alliance were not slow to make themselves felt. Churchill himself was feeling the costs badly by the middle of 1944. But what else was Churchill to have done in the middle of 1941? At that time Britain and the Empire were still fighting on their own, invasion was still a possibility, Bomber Command was getting nowhere, the intervention in Greece had proved a costly disaster, U-boats were rampant in the Atlantic and Rommel's star was in the ascendant in North Africa. It was a time for clutching at straws; and all the more so because, if Germany quickly conquered Russia (or as much of Russia as it sought to conquer) as Churchill and most supposed experts thought possible, Britain would find itself facing a Germany of hugely increased strength. The purpose of Churchill's instant befriending of the Soviet Union in June 1941 was not to attach Britain to a known Power that could help win the war but to support an unknown Power that might lose it. The emergency was felt to be such that Britain, itself in painful need of all the supplies and war materials it could get, began shipping as much as it could to Russia's Arctic ports in the convoys whose fearful experiences constituted one of the most gallant campaigns of the war.

Roosevelt took much the same view of the strategic situation, opening Lend-Lease facilities to the Soviet Union and hoping that the pessimists were wrong about the Red Army. By the end of the year it looked as if they were. With the United States's entry into the war, the President began to share the problem that was already bothering the Prime Minister: how to deal with Stalin. Churchill, for his part, thought he could ingratiate himself with Stalin as he had done so successfully with Roosevelt, but flattery got him nowhere; his view of Stalin consequently veered from 'this great rugged war chief' at one end of the gamut to (privately) 'Uncle Joe' and 'the bear in the Kremlin' at the other. Now and then he told himself and his circle that he thought he was beginning to understand Stalin, but of course this was a delusion; he was as incapable of understanding Stalin as Chamberlain had been of understanding Hitler. Roosevelt didn't attempt ingratiation but he had his own reasons for establishing good relations with Stalin and in doing so suffered from a delusion of his own; he thought he could handle Stalin better than Churchill, and actually told him so.[17] The three of them met together only twice, at Teheran in November 1943 and at Yalta in February 1945; Stalin absolutely would not stray far from the Soviet Union and the President was nothing like so ready a traveller as Churchill. Churchill twice felt it advisable to go to Moscow on his own, once on their joint behalf in August 1942 and once off his own bat in October 1944.

As for Stalin, his demands through 1942 and 1943 were clear and insistent: all the munitions and equipment that the Allies could send, a treaty of alliance that would recognise Russia's war aim of moving its frontiers westwards (to enhance security against renewed German aggression), and the immediate opening of a 'Second Front' in western Europe to take pressure off the Red Army in the east. Trying to meet these demands gave Churchill much trouble and distress. He was generous regarding gifts of munitions and equipment, ordering that Russia's immediate needs should precede Britain's. He was also justly indignant that all the sacrifices put into the Arctic Convoys elicited neither sympathy nor gratitude, and his inability to honour for many, many months his promise to start a Second Front was a standing embarrassment. Keeping the relationship sweet involved him in disagreeable pretence and compromise; his government had to discourage as best it could the continued expression of anti-Soviet opinion, Soviet propaganda could not be prevented from flooding Britain, and the 'London Poles' were beseeched not to make a fuss about the Katyn Massacre when the Germans publicised their dreadful discovery in 1943.[18]

Churchill's knowledge of history and his respect for a Great Power's national interest gradually led him to accept Stalin's demands for frontiers more or less on their pre-1914 pattern, but that brought further embarrassments with it. It meant extinguishing the independence of the three little Baltic republics and, worse, meant persuading the 'London Poles', the Polish government in exile in London, that they could not expect to return to the Poland they left – if indeed they could ever return at all. This was a bitter pill for Churchill as well as the Poles to swallow, Poland's territorial integrity having been Britain's ostensible reason for going to war in the first place; all the more bitter, when it meant bowing to the *force majeure* of the Red Army's victories and the prospect of a Soviet sphere of influence all over Eastern Europe.[19] Churchill spent more time on 'the Polish question' than on any other diplomatic issue in the last year of the war, but Stalin, like the London Poles, proved immovable. Churchill's Moscow visit in October 1944 was mostly devoted to wrangling about Poland, but more fruitfully he proposed to Stalin, whose armies were already entering the Balkans, a formula to save them from getting at cross-purposes there: this was the so-called 'percentages agreement' which recognised Britain's right to an interest at least in Greece, the only bit of the Balkans British regular forces would get to.[20] Stalin accordingly withdrew support from the Communist guerrillas in Greece, Churchill spoiled the family Christmas by making a dash to Athens to sort out the troubles there, and ever after congratulated himself and the western world that he had 'saved Greece from Communism', which was probably true.

A 'Second Front' was the Russian demand that most embarrassed Churchill and Roosevelt. They could not deny the reasonableness of Stalin's plea that some of the burden should be taken off his armies in the east by the opening of a second front in the west, presumably in

France. The 'Proposed Plan and Sequence of the War' that Churchill took to Washington with him in December 1941 did not anticipate such an operation until 1943. In early 1942 he toyed for a while with the American Chiefs' ambition to launch it later that year but was relieved when the British Chiefs convinced him that it was impossible at such short notice; he was glad therefore to find the President willing to back instead the North African operation that he had wanted from the start. Stalin having so far been encouraged to think that a Second Front would be launched in 1942, Churchill decided to tell him the bad news in person. He also saw it as an opportunity at last to meet the man of mystery and to win him over; the second of his two chapters about it is titled 'A Relationship Established'. His plane touched down early in the evening of 12 August 1942. He did not look forward to the meeting. 'It was like carrying a large lump of ice to the North Pole.'[21]

The meeting went off better than it might have done. Churchill played his cards cleverly. He got over the difficult bit first, the postponement of the Second Front, offering as a substitute the heavy bombing of Germany that the RAF had begun and the USAAF would soon join. Stalin agreed that bombing was valuable, but it was not the direct engagement with the Wehrmacht that Russia was looking for. Churchill then produced the North African landings plan and showed what was in his mind about its likely development.

> If we could end the year in possession of North Africa we could threaten the belly of Hitler's Europe, and this operation should be considered in conjunction with the 1943 operation ... To illustrate my point I had meanwhile drawn a picture of a crocodile and explained ... how it was our intention to attack the soft belly of the crocodile as we attacked his hard snout. And Stalin, whose interest was now at a high pitch, said 'May God prosper this undertaking'.[22]

Stalin's God, whoever He may have been, did not 'prosper this undertaking'. Churchill as usual underestimated how long things would take. North Africa was not in Allied hands until five months later than hoped. Then, instead of putting all their resources into a northern Second Front, the western Allies were lured into opening an Italian front that had the effect of putting the Second Front off for another year. All the more reason for Churchill to keep Bomber Command going at full blast; it saved him from feeling that he had let the Russians down.

The relationship between Roosevelt, Churchill and Stalin, although successful enough in the military sense of furthering the war against a common enemy, was inevitably more troubled in its political aspects. Suspicions and misgivings abounded on all three sides. Churchill, undoubtedly impressed by the Russians' military performance and, once he had met him, by Stalin himself, managed for most of the time to forget his primordial dislike of Communism; but, whenever things went wrong, it came flooding back. To begin with, he and Roosevelt were worried lest Russia should be defeated or come to terms with Germany, as it had unexpectedly done in 1939 (and, before that, in 1917). Then, as the war progressed and the Red Army showed that it could handle the Wehrmacht, their worry became the opposite one, about the possibility of a Russia-dominated post-war Europe.

Stalin for his part was instructed by his ideology to suspect that Britain and the United States might revert to true capitalist type and do what resistance-minded German generals were hoping the western allies would do – make peace in the west and free the Wehrmacht to move all its strength to the east. There were rabid conservatives in Britain who would have liked Churchill to have done this. In abstract, he could see the point; in practice, it was unthinkable. This was a modern and passionate people's war, not an eighteenth-century calculating dynastic one, and the British people had, with his encouragement, become enthusiastic about their Russian allies. His soldier's heart swelled with admiration for the Red Army's gigantic battles and with sympathy for its huge casualties; he knew, although in *The Second World War* he could scarcely bring himself to admit, that it was the Russians who bore the brunt of the work towards defeating the common enemy.

The Soviet Union's growing preponderance in the Grand Alliance was one explanation why Churchill felt his position in it to be less than grand as the war entered its closing phases. Another was a clouding of his relations with Roosevelt. In its own way the United States was becoming preponderant too. Given its size and industrial capacity, this was sooner or later inevitable. The larger its share of the war in Europe became, the more confident became the President and his advisers in pressing their own ideas about how to conduct it and in withdrawing support from Churchill's 'Mediterranean Strategy'.

What also hurt Churchill was the President's inclination to deal with

Stalin independently. Churchill felt that he and Roosevelt should always present a common front; when *he* had dealings with Stalin, it was (so he said, probably truly) always on the combined Anglo-American behalf. What had Roosevelt to say to Stalin that he thought Churchill needn't know about? Three things in particular. Roosevelt was anxious to secure Russian assistance in the latter stages of the war in the Pacific; his grand conception of a post-war 'world organization' depended on Russian cooperation, and he wanted Stalin to know that their views about the British Empire and what should happen to it after the war were similar. He was also not so interested in what would happen in Europe after the war and became tired of being endlessly badgered by Churchill about it. By the time of the 'Big Three' summit meeting at Yalta in February 1945, Churchill was made to feel that it was more like a meeting of the Big Two-and-a-Half.

With the end of the war in the Pacific, three months after its end in Europe, Churchill's Grand Alliance died a natural death. Churchill, by then out of office, was not surprised. The war had not ended as gloriously for him as it had begun. He had ceased to enjoy it, though he still maintained that confident, cheerful face in public that was his hallmark. If he had begun as an optimist, by the end he was a pessimist. The weighty war memoir he began to write in 1946 mirrored his feelings.[23] The title of its sixth volume is *Triumph and Tragedy* and its theme is: 'How the Great Democracies Triumphed, and so were Able to Resume the Follies which had so nearly Cost them their Life'. This testy return to the theme of volume one (the failure to stand up to Hitler in the 1930s) did himself and his erstwhile partner Stalin less than justice. The Great Democracies could not have triumphed without the Russian alliance and Churchill had done a good job in keeping the alliance going for so long as he was its moving spirit. As for the alleged tragedy, it was not his fault that the Soviet Union's powers of recuperation proved to be so much greater than expected, or that the war aims of the United States should have included the deflation of the British Empire.

Finally, we must consider the two allies who disappeared early in the war but made a come-back later on: France and Poland. The 'Free French', whom Churchill gladly welcomed to Britain in June 1940, quickly became such popular representatives of France that it was difficult for British people to understand that, for their 'great friend' across the Atlantic, Vichy France remained the real thing until October 1942. Until then (when German forces occupied it) 'Vichy' was technically a neutral country with which the United States had no quarrel and which was invaluable to humanitarian organisations as an opening into occupied Europe. It was obvious therefore that the British-backed Free French campaigns against parts of the French colonial empire remaining loyal to Vichy would create diplomatic problems. The good relations between Churchill and Roosevelt prevented those problems from disturbing the alliance; but they did build up in Washington a body of resentment against General de Gaulle that became seriously disturbing when the plan for Operation Torch, the Anglo-American landings in Vichy French Morocco and Algeria, had to include reliance on 'turning' the French authorities there to the Allied side.

It needed one of Churchill's most carefully composed speeches, and a Secret Session, to explain to the Commons why yesterday's enemies (for so the Vichy French were understandably regarded) were today's collaborators, with every prospect of becoming tomorrow's allies. Where would de Gaulle fit in? The General was much more popular with the British people than with the Prime Minister.[24] Churchill's patience with the cussed General wore thinner at this time than at any other, but an absolute break was avoided – de Gaulle and the ex-Vichy general in command in Algeria, Giraud, were made to shake hands in a famous photograph – and the way was cleared for the gradual amalgamation of 'Free' with 'Vichy' forces as welcome extra strength in the Grand Alliance for the remainder of the war. General Juin's French corps performed splendidly in the long-drawn-out Italian campaign through 1944–45. American attempts to oust de Gaulle from the French political leadership failed, and Eisenhower allowed the French General Leclerc to be the first Allied commander to enter Paris on 24 August 1944. Churchill showed both his usual magnanimity and his political good sense in arguing that France should be allocated one of the zones of occupation of Germany and a seat at the top table at the United Nations, then constituting itself in San Francisco.

Poland, the ally by treaty for whose sake Britain entered the war in the first place, largely disappeared from public consciousness after Germany and the Soviet Union gobbled it up in September 1939. Then, in the summer of 1940, the British public came to realise that a Poland-in-Exile existed with a government in London (like the refugee governments of the Netherlands, Norway and Czechoslovakia), that Polish airmen were helping the RAF to win the Battle of Britain, and that a few Polish warships had escaped to join the Royal Navy. Polish soldiers began to be heard of; first within the British army and from 1943 as an army of their own, when many thousands who had survived being taken prisoner by the Russians in 1939 were returned to Britain via Persia and the Middle East. To none of the governments in exile was Churchill more attentive and helpful than to the Polish government; to none of the foreign forces fighting with the Allies did he more often or more sincerely give praise. Questions of honour touched him to the core and he could never forget how the Poles, allies beyond reach of help, had suffered and how they were suffering still.

No matter how hard he tried, however, it became very difficult to get on with the Polish government. They naturally felt revolted by the alliance with the Russians, their national enemies both ancient and modern. Churchill found himself in the uncomfortable position of a go-between sympathetic to both sides, on the one hand trying to reconcile the 'London Poles' to the facts of Alliance life, on the other trying to persuade Stalin – who had his own interim Polish government waiting to move back to Poland – that the London Poles deserved some respect. When the Katyn massacre became known about, Churchill was pained to feel obliged to advise 'his' Poles not to make too much fuss about it. They rejected his advice, with the result that Stalin refused to have any more to do with them.

As for Stalin's insistence that the post-war order should include a westwards shift of Russia's frontiers at Poland's expense, Churchill had too much understanding of history and *Realpolitik* to contest it. The most he could do was to try to get Stalin's agreement that the new Poland's form of government would be democratic and that the London Poles would be part of it. Working on Poland's behalf filled more of his time than any other non-military issue through 1944 and the first half of 1945. Its dramatic high-point came in the summer of 1944, when the Russian forces were nearing Warsaw and the Polish Home Army, an underground organisation loosely commanded from London, rose in Warsaw in rebellion against the Germans in the expectation of help from both west and east. What Stalin gave was little and late; he also obstructed what little help could expensively be flown to them from the west (in reality from southern Italy, by now in Allied hands). Churchill and SOE had not thought the rising prudent in the first place, but once it had happened Churchill did everything he could to succour it and sought to persuade Roosevelt to join him in a powerful appeal to Stalin to support the rising. The President declined to do so; another of those rifts in the Special Relationship to which Churchill was by then becoming accustomed.

9

Strategy

The aspect of Churchill's warlordship that has been most written about, not least by Churchill himself, is that of strategy. His memoir-history of the *Second World War*, once it gets beyond the summer of 1940, is dominated by it, and understandably so. Apart from defending the British Isles against the threat of invasion, the major task for the rest of the war was to orchestrate the military power of the British Empire and its allies against Germany and its allies. Thwarted in his dearest desire, to command great armies in the field, the next best thing for Churchill was to plan the strategy within which the great armies of his Grand Alliance operated; and he thought he was good at it.[1]

Churchill's government inherited from Chamberlain's two hopeful ideas about how to encompass the downfall of Germany. The first was that Germany's economic strength would slowly but surely be ground down by the British naval blockade. This idea soon lost its power to persuade. Germany's seizure of economically profitable territories all over Europe reduced the blockade's power to hurt, while a dispassionate observer could have concluded in 1941 that the tables were turned, inasmuch as the belligerent now more threatened with economic constriction was Britain. The second idea, that the Nazi regime would be sapped from within, by an officers' revolt or by a collapse of civilian morale, lasted much longer. There are indications that Churchill would not absolutely have declined to consider a negotiated peace with a non-Nazi German government for many months after the crisis of May 1940 was over.[2] He had given up hope regarding the officers well before a valiant few did at last attempt a coup in July 1944, but the belief that civilian morale was collapsible (a belief repeatedly fortified by the Joint Intelligence Committee, which was as misguided in this respect as the Air Ministry) remained attractive to the end and partly explained Churchill's endorsement of the bombing of German cities.

For the rest, everything began to change in May 1940. Even while the smoke still hovered over the beaches of Dunkirk and some of the French army was still fighting, Churchill's mind turned to the means of counter-attack.[3] 'The completely defensive habit of mind which has ruined the French must not be allowed to ruin all our initiative ... An effort must be made to shake off the mental and moral prostration to the will of the enemy from which we suffer.' He rapidly produced a series of papers and instructions containing, between them, the seeds of four novel organisations: the Special Operations Executive to 'set Europe aflame'; Commandos (he thought Australians would be ideal for this dashing work and characteristically took it for granted that Australians would be ready to do it); Paratroops; and a Directorate of Combined Operations (that is, the three services planning together). Amphibious landings on enemy islands and coastlines had always fascinated him; now they were the only way the enemy could be got at and the invaded nations stirred up to resistance. These were enterprising and promising ideas; the only thing amiss with them was that Britain in June 1940 had hardly any army, even less equipment, and no immediate possibility of producing the sort of landing-craft he had first projected in the Kaiser's time and now pursued with new enthusiasm.

It was thoroughly in character for Churchill to wish to turn at once to the counter-offensive and to conceive of striking operations without reference to their logistical props. Characteristic also was the notion that these imagined mobile Striking Companies should be ready to land here or there on the continental coastline, wherever opportunity offered: Norway, Brittany, the Channel coasts, the islands off the German coast, even perhaps in the Baltic. Implicit here was one of the principles (which those who disliked him thought no principles at all, simply opportunism) that would soon materialise at the heart of Churchill's strategic thinking: the principle that hard and fast plans for particular operations in particular places were to be avoided because they could get in the way of exploiting opportunities as they turned up. By the middle of 1942, this had become a mantra in his arguments about operations in the Mediterranean theatre, to the increasing annoyance of his American allies who had one big idea and wanted to stick to it. As of 1940, this *idée fixe* of Churchill's was still in the bud and, given Britain's parlous situation, it represented the best that Britain could do. It offered little room for disagreement.

There was a second strategic principle implicit here too; perhaps more of a preference than a principle. Churchill shied off massive full-frontal assaults and preferred piecemeal peripheral operations, as opportunities offered, whose cumulative effect in the long run would be, so he liked to think, demoralising and attritional.[4] His strategic thinking in both world wars shows this. In the First, he sought other places to fight than the Western Front and was appalled that soldiers had to 'chew barbed wire' there; like so many of his generals, he never forgot the Somme and Passchendaele. In the Second, these early designs of his for really substantial raids on enemy territory – much larger than any that were ever found practicable except at Dieppe, which was scarcely practicable and entirely disastrous – were consistent with the general tenor of his strategic thinking when the recovery of British military capability in 1941 made such thinking profitable; he preferred to force the windows at the back of the house to breaking in the front door. Operation Overlord in June 1944 was a front-door assault, about which he was very uneasy until it had succeeded. The strategic bombing campaign was a front-door assault, too, about which he was never entirely happy although he never interfered with it. He would have been unhappier still had he known that historians, considering its commander's attitude and the casualties he was prepared for his men to take, would say that it was the Second World War's Somme.

By the time the summer of 1940 yielded to autumn, Churchill's circumstances had changed again. An island nation that had rejected the towering enemy's peace proposals, and was consequently threatened with invasion and subjected to aerial bombardment, could not afford to indulge exclusively in offensive thoughts. Invasion remained a possibility until it had become clear that Hitler was too entangled on the *Ostfront* to have enough resources for so major an operation in the west. Naturally concerned that Britain should be well prepared to repel invaders, Churchill stimulated the recruitment of the Home Guard (his own good title for what had been started as the Local Defence Volunteers) and was reassuringly pictured inspecting coastal defences and anti-aircraft batteries. But he would not make national defence the all-absorbing priority that his military advisers wished. Offensive operations still lured him, partly no doubt in order to sustain the national mood of cocky defiance, and a quick succession of events in later 1940 meant that they could begin to be conceived as elements of a grand strategic plan.

The biggest of these events was Italy's declaration of war on 10 June. So long as France had been still in the war, its allotted place in Allied strategy was to secure the Mediterranean for British passage to and from its possessions and properties (not least oil) in the Middle East and beyond. Now Mussolini looked set to make good his promise to the Italian people that the Mediterranean Sea would become an 'Italian lake'. He had brought into being an up-to-date navy and an impressive-looking air force. In Africa he presided over an empire – Libya, Eritrea, Italian Somaliland and Abyssinia – that threatened the security of Britain's vassal Egypt, Sudan, the Suez Canal and the Red Sea approach to it. Middle East Command at once had to deal with these threats. A substantial share of the British army was in Egypt and Palestine already and Egypt was the obvious destination for the imperial military contri-butions that were coming from India, Australia, New Zealand and South Africa. Expulsion of the Italians from their East African possessions began at once (it involved the temporary abandonment of British Soma-liland, which infuriated Churchill – unconsciously acknowledging the importance of 'prestige' in the imperial mind) and was complete by May 1941. Dealing with Italy on its Mediterranean side, however, took much longer and became a messy business.

The Mediterranean was not just a theatre of war that Churchill had to think about; it was in fact one he had often thought about before and now relished thinking about again. Mastery of the Mediterranean was essential to his stirring image of the British Empire; India and the profit-able possessions in South-East Asia, accessible only via the Middle East (as Britons called the Levant) with its oil and its Suez Canal. His 1914–15 project for seizing control of the Dardanelles, knocking Turkey out of the war and creating an alliance of Balkan states against Germany came to life again in grand ideas, generally backed by the Foreign Office, of creating another such alliance (a different group of states this time) and bringing Turkey into the war on the Allied side. After the Soviet Union became involved, another of the earlier purposes was revived: a friendly Turkey would facilitate assistance to the Russians. Changing circumstances enforced changes in the scenario – German control of the whole of the Balkans by mid-1941 was the biggest one – but Churchill's focus on the strategic centrality and opportunities of the Mediterranean and Balkan theatre remained constant, and he resolutely refused to let problems in other areas, for example Singapore, distract him from it. This was the master notion at the heart of his strategic thinking, and he never gave it up. Because it came to include a vision of British forces entering the northern Balkans and marching on Vienna, and because by the end of the war Churchill was lamenting that Allied forces had not reached Vienna, Prague and Berlin before the Russians, early Cold War historians slipped into thinking that he had foreseen the Russian danger from the start. That was not so. His Balkan ambitions until 1944 were primarily anti-German and in no way anti-Russian.[5]

This strategy of opportunism (using the word in no pejorative sense) was a good notion in itself, but turning it to military advantage required shrewd judgement of situations as well as logistical mastery. The first test of it came early in 1941. General Wavell's Western Desert Force, commanded by the dashing General O'Connor, was in process of winning a lightning campaign against the much larger Italian army in Libya, and its advance party was poised to race on towards Libya's capital city and principal port, Tripoli; few Germans had yet arrived to support the Italians and the prospects of gaining control of the whole of Italian North Africa were good. Had Tripoli been taken and British authority been imposed on those territories, there would presumably have been – one can only offer reasonable conjectures – no 'Desert Fox', less agony for Malta, and an earlier rapprochement with the Vichy French in Tunisia and places westwards. But such possibilities, briefly sighted in February, vanished almost at once. O'Connor's best soldiers, his New Zealanders and Australians, were taken away to go to the Balkans.

The Balkans had been luring Churchill since the previous autumn. Mussolini, whose armies were already in Albania, had launched an attack on Greece at the end of October 1940. Britain in 1939 had guaranteed the independence of Greece (and of Romania, even more inaccessible than Poland), part of the process by which the dictatorships and the democracies squared up to each other. Churchill now sent five RAF squadrons to the Greeks' aid. While Italy was its only enemy, and for so long as Yugoslavia remained at least neutral, the Greek army appeared to be well able to defend its homeland on its own.* British Intelligence (including 'Ultra') disclosed early in 1941, however, that German forces were beginning to arrive in Bulgaria and Romania and that they would be on their way south in the spring. Churchill, the War Cabinet, the Chiefs of Staff and the Commander-in-Chief Middle East (whose theatre of responsibility included the Balkans) now began to discuss with anguish and urgency whether they should move troops to the aid of their ally apparent. The only troops they could quickly move would have to be taken from the British and Commonwealth forces in North Africa.

The story of these discussions and the making of the disastrous decision that came out of them is complicated and painful.[6] Apologists for Churchill are able to point out that mixed feelings about the venture had replaced his initial enthusiasm by the time 'the men on the spot', Eden, Wavell and Dill, made the decision delegated to them. Churchill must nevertheless take the greater share of responsibility for it, having promoted the idea so energetically in the first place. He failed to balance certain loss (the near certainty of eliminating the Italians from Libya before the Germans could arrive in strength) against such speculative gains as a Greek redoubt or leverage on Turkey. All this in an atmosphere of misunderstandings and illusions regarding the reliability of the Greek army and the military potential of Yugoslavia. This ill-considered venture was soon over. General 'Jumbo' Maitland Wilson's expeditionary force had only been in Greece for a few weeks when they found the Germans pouring into Greece through Yugoslavia, the Greek army evaporating, and the Luftwaffe everywhere. An orderly retreat began on 21 April and the force had quitted Greek soil by the 25th. But the disaster was not yet complete. Most of the troops were taken not to Alexandria but, through shortage of shipping, to Crete. The Germans pursued them, seized the crucial airfield, and compelled a second evacuation. No less than 11,000 British and Anzac troops were taken prisoner and the Royal Navy suffered grievous losses in heroically

* Greeks are as well entitled as Australians, New Zealanders, Canadians and other peoples of the British Empire to remind Britons that the UK did not stand entirely on its own against Fascism in 1940–41.

evacuating the rest. (By now, naval humorists were referring to the army as 'the evacuees'.)

Churchill's account in his memoir-history of the Greek expedition and its Cretan aftermath are elaborate and defensive; even including a kind of testimonial, given by British troops to their German captors, that they still had, 'generally, absolute confidence in Churchill'![7] His embarrassment, however, did nothing to lessen his enthusiasm for the Mediterranean as a principal theatre of operations. Wavell, having been deprived of all his early advantages and furthermore driven back to the Egyptian frontier by the newly-arrived Rommel, was pushed and prodded to resume the offensive and was sent great quantities of *matériel* (the military term for the hardware needed for fighting) to enable him to do so. The Chiefs of Staff urged that Egypt could be defended quite economically and that where such *matériel* was more pressingly needed was in the Far East, for the defence of Malaya and Singapore against the Japanese attack that seemed sooner or later inevitable, but they urged in vain. Restlessly impatient for British victories on land in the only area where they were possible, in July Churchill replaced Wavell (perhaps unfairly regarded as a failure) by the well-reputed General Auchinleck, whom he was soon prodding to get on with it in the same way that he had prodded Wavell. Nearer home, in December he replaced the uncongenial CIGS Sir John Dill with General Sir Alan Brooke, who was more difficult to get on with but was at least more interested in the Mediterranean.

The year 1941 ended without the land victories Churchill longed for, and the first half of 1942 was to prove militarily even more disappointing, but long-term pessimism was henceforth impossible, now that Britain at last had the ally he had been hoping and playing for, the United States. (How useful the unexpected ally, the Soviet Union, was going to be was still, at the turn of 1942, unclear.) Churchill had a strategy ready for the American army: to land in Morocco and Algeria by arrangement with the Vichy French authorities there, and to form one side of the pincers of which the other would be Auchinleck's army (in the event it was Montgomery's) advancing from the east. This plan was in due course adopted and implemented; but not before it had been rubbed into Churchill and the British Chiefs that what their new allies were really interested in was a straightforward assault on the German-dominated

Continent at the earliest opportunity. They accepted the Mediterranean option only because Roosevelt insisted they had to do something aggressive before 1942 was out, and because their British counterparts succeeded in persuading them that a cross-Channel landing at such short notice was technically impossible. Churchill had initially been ready to attempt one but he too had to face facts. Not for the first time, Stalin's hopes of a Second Front were disappointed.

There was not to be one in 1943 either. To Churchill's great satisfaction, the Mediterranean continued to be the principal theatre of Allied land operations, but this was not because of his persuasion alone. The French authorities took longer than expected to accommodate themselves to the Allied cause, Montgomery's army did not cross the Tunisian border until late March, by which time the Luftwaffe and Wehrmacht had been in Tunisia for four months. It was early May before the Allies finished clearing the country of Axis remnants; by then, even if there had been any plan for a cross-Channel operation later that summer, it was far too late to organise one. But such planning, although still dear to American hearts, had in fact been abandoned back in January at the Casablanca Summit and Staff Conference. A group under General Sir Frederick Morgan had begun planning for Operation Overlord some time in 1944, but that was far in the future. Churchill and the British Chiefs at the Casablanca Conference meanwhile won assent to their argument that the obvious thing to do in the European theatre in the coming year, after clearing North Africa, was to seize Sicily; after which, who could tell what opportunities might present themselves in the direction of Italy.

Allied strategy continued to unroll along the lines of Churchill's aspirations, although at every turn more slowly than he expected. Sicily was in Allied hands by the middle of August 1943, Mussolini's regime was done for, and the surrender of Italy was imminent. Twelve months had passed since Churchill regaled Stalin with his image of the Nazi crocodile's vulnerable underbelly. Now his dream was coming true, and not just because the British Chiefs had done better homework before Casablanca than the Americans; it was also because an opportunity, a Churchillian opportunity, seemed to be opening in Italy that it would be folly to neglect. But an opportunity *for what?* The Allies could not achieve happy agreement about this. For Churchill, once the

Wehrmacht had arrived (as it did almost instantly upon Italy's surrender on 8 September), the purpose of the Italian campaign was, first, to form a surrogate Second Front, engaging German divisions that might otherwise be fighting the Red Army; secondly, to facilitate assistance to the guerrilla armies engaging many German divisions in the Balkans; and, thirdly, less explicit but coming into clearer focus with every passing month, to drive on in due course from the north Italian plain towards Vienna. None of this had much appeal for the Americans. They went along with the Italian campaign because in the spring of 1943 it seemed an opportunity too good to miss, and in any case there was nowhere else for their army to go (except the Pacific), but their commitment was strictly limited. Even before they had finished in Sicily they insisted on an implementation of Operation Overlord in May 1944, plus the transfer of seven good divisions from the Italian to the Channel front. Eisenhower was transferred from the Mediterranean to be the Allied forces' Supreme Commander in northern Europe early in 1944.

Meanwhile, Churchill was losing his magic touch with the President. Roosevelt was no more interested in Churchill's Mediterranean and Balkan visions than were his military and diplomatic advisers. The President became exclusively intent on making a success of Overlord and so finishing the European half of America's war as soon as possible. (The British kept forgetting that the Americans had another very different war on their hands.) Roosevelt turned a deaf ear to the arguments and pleas with which Churchill peppered him, and after Italy's surrender absolutely refused to sanction any diversion of forces or *matériel* to support the attempt to seize the Italian Dodecanese islands (Rhodes, Leros, Samos and Cos) that Churchill forced on a reluctant Maitland Wilson: another of the 'opportunities' that was insufficiently thought through, precipitately begun and ended in disaster.

From this time on, Churchill's strategic fixation on Italy and, to a lesser degree, the Balkans was accompanied by a persistent uneasiness concerning Overlord, an uneasiness obvious enough to cause Stalin to confront Churchill with it at the Teheran Summit at the end of November 1943. Churchill had to reply that he *was* wholeheartedly behind the Overlord plan, and when he came to write *The Second World War* he testily denied that he had ever nurtured misgivings about it, but the fact is that he continued to voice them right up to the eve of the

landings on 6 June. He was furious when Roosevelt refused to allow any
diversion of forces from the long-planned American landing in the
south of France to strengthen General Alexander's offensive northwards
from Rome. Alexander held out radiant hopes of a brisk advance up the
peninsula and from the plains of Lombardy through the mountains –
the 'Ljubljana Gap' sounded easy enough – into Austria; Churchill's
Balkan vision realised. To Churchill and his favourite general (who
understood exactly in what terms to correspond with him) this was a
much better employment of forces than a soft landing on the French
Riviera, Operation Anvil, planned to ease the task of the forces in
Normandy and to speed the conveyance of supplies to them.

Was Churchill right? It is possible that the Allied armies in Italy (by
now not just Anglo-American but Commonwealth, Polish and French
as well), if not reduced by subtractions for the Riviera landing, might
well have cleared Italy of the German invaders in 1944 before winter
made further campaigning impossible; which would have been agreeable for the Italian people, and advantageous for the Allies in providing
airfields nearer Germany and easier assistance to Tito's partisans. But
how much harm would that really have done to Germany? Churchill
and Alexander surely underestimated the problems of forcing a passage
through such defensible territory as the Alps and allowed themselves to
be hypnotised by repeated incantations about the 'Ljubljana Gap'.
Whether the clearing of Italy would have done more good to the Allied
cause than was done by the opening of the ports of Marseille and
Toulon by the Franco-American forces' drive into the French interior is
a question that will continue to be debated.[8]

Grand strategy in the European theatre moved away from Churchill's
grasp after the Normandy beachhead had been secured by the end of
June 1944. (He still had more freedom regarding South-East Asia, and
had a fearful row with the Chiefs of Staff about it in the summer of 1944.)
The liberation of Western Europe and the invasion of Germany had been
the dominant aim of the Grand Alliance for more than two years, and at
last it was under way. All now depended on the Allied armies – British,
American, Canadian, Polish and French – and on the chain of command
between them and the Supreme Commander of the Allied Expeditionary
Force, General Eisenhower. It was no part of American military doctrine
that the political authorities should interfere with a commander in the

field once he was in post, and President Roosevelt had no wish to do so, even though he was titular Commander-in-Chief of his nation's armed forces. British military doctrine similarly deprecated such interference, and Churchill's constitutional position was less dominant than the President's. No matter how much he would have liked to go on handling grand strategic matters, the situation had changed. It was symbolic that, although the primary theatre of operations was now nearby, he was not free to visit it at will. Cabinet, Military Chiefs and ultimately King George VI himself stopped him from risking his life in the invasion fleet on 6 June, and Montgomery made it clear that he had little time to devote to visitors. Churchill was not able to visit the front as often as he had done throughout the 1914–18 war, but he did get there on several occasions, the most photographed of them showing him present when the Siegfried Line and the Rhine were crossed in March; the photographers were not allowed to be present when he led a ceremonial urination on the former German fortifications.[9] Whatever his thoughts about the conduct of the campaign, his disappointments at its deceleration through the autumn of 1944 and its setbacks in the winter that followed, Churchill could not treat Eisenhower (Supreme Commander of a host now predominantly American) as he had earlier been accustomed to treat his British commanders. Being politically astute, he did not normally attempt to do so. He had plenty of other matters to engage his attention: the Italian campaign, all the more dear to him now that it had become mainly a British affair, the reassertion in Burma of imperial power in South-East Asia, and his darkening premonitions about the Soviet Union's intentions towards Poland and the Balkans – indeed, towards wherever its mighty armies might end up. These premonitions were made all the darker by his disappointment and anger at Stalin's refusal to assist, or to help the RAF to assist, the Warsaw Rising in August and September 1944.[10]

It was this latter concern and nothing less that prompted his one attempt to interfere with Eisenhower, at the end of March 1945. Churchill and the British Chiefs, who shared his political concerns, had come to suppose that Eisenhower would try to get to Berlin before the Russians. They were angered when they learned that he had no such intention, and Churchill ventured to remonstrate with Eisenhower and the President. Eisenhower patiently stood his ground, pointing out that

the borders of the zones of military occupation had been agreed with
the Soviet Union months before, that Berlin was well inside the zone
allocated to the Russians, and that getting there first (if it could be done,
which was by no means sure) would be of less military advantage than
deploying his forces elsewhere. That there might be some political
advantage (which was also by no means sure) was, he said, not his concern. Washington of course backed its man; Churchill was driven to give
in and did so gracefully.[11] But the thought, that 'we could have got to
Berlin first if only Roosevelt and Eisenhower had listened', rankled and
it became a standard item of Cold War polemics.

At the same time, the strategic air offensive against Germany had gathered pace.[12] The strategy of aerial bombardment was not established
simply because Churchill ordered it to be so. It would have begun anyway – this was what the RAF had been preparing to do since 1919 and it
was part of the received national strategy of damaging the enemy economy and morale from a distance – but it acquired singular importance
for Churchill for two different reasons. First, after Dunkirk, the fall of
France and the beginning of the Blitz in 1940, it was one of the few ways
that Britain could show fight and hit back. Churchill naturally had no
hesitation in endorsing and encouraging it. Being in those early months
almost entirely ineffective, however, it did not figure largely in his
thoughts until Germany's invasion of Russia and Stalin's demand that
Britain take some of the pressure off the Russians by opening a Second
Front. The demand struck Churchill as reasonable; besides which, supporting the Russians in any case served Britain's own interest. Stalin's
demand was the easier to meet for Churchill's government's having only
recently decided to put massive resources into building up a force of four
thousand heavy bombers with aircrews to match, with the express aim
of taking ruination to German industrial cities (it was assumed that all
cities were more or less industrial) and despair to their inhabitants.[13]
Churchill therefore saw Bomber Command as killing two big birds with
one big stone. Its offensive henceforth constituted Britain's best effort in
lieu of a Second Front. The casualties incurred were evidence that the
British were not, as Russians caustically intimated at military meetings
and as Stalin roughly rubbed in when Churchill went to Moscow in
October 1942, averse to taking losses. The damage it did to German

industry and communications was assumed by everybody to weaken the Germans' ability to carry on the war. (It is by now, after much historical controversy, generally agreed that this was indeed so, though not exactly in the way anticipated.) The opening at last of a Second Front in June 1944 did not lessen Churchill's feeling of obligation to assist the Russians by bombing the common enemy. He still felt it, though perhaps he need no longer have felt it so strongly, at the Yalta Summit in January 1945. The destruction of Dresden was in some measure a consequence.[14]

Churchill had more faith in the aim of the bombing offensive in supporting Russia than he had in the Air Staff's assurance that, given enough bombers and men to fly them, they could reduce Germany's military power to a point which would make an Allied landing a walkover. He would dearly have liked to believe this but he couldn't. His fundamental scepticism puzzled and irritated the air barons, because his public manner and speech were heartily supportive and enthusiastic about their work. By instinct and principle he was loyal to comrades, he respected the gallantry of the aircrews, he knew all too well what fearful losses they were suffering, and once he had recovered from the shock in 1941 when the Prof brought the bombers' inaccuracy to his notice, he never doubted that the bombing strategy was worthwhile. He saw more of Air Chief Marshal Sir Arthur Harris, from early 1942 the Commander-in-Chief of Bomber Command, than of any other field commander.[15] Although Harris cannot be counted as one of his intimates, he often visited Chequers, more often in fact than the Chief of Air Staff.[16] And yet Churchill was never an all-or-nothing believer in the Harris creed that aerial bombardment, properly done, could win the war on its own; and there is evidence that sometimes he felt queasy about it.

Whatever his inward reservations, Churchill backed the Harris side of argument about the size and the operations of Bomber Command. One such argument blew up soon after Harris became its Chief and it marks another of the Prof's many interventions. His forte being the neat statistical demonstrations that Churchill so much appreciated, he produced some figures purporting to show how effective the area bombing campaign was going to be:

> We know from experience that we can count on nearly 14 operational sorties per bomber produced. The average lift of the bombers we are going to produce over the next fifteen months will be about 3 tons. It follows that each

of the bombers will in its lifetime drop about 40 tons of bombs. If these are dropped on built-up areas they will make 4000–8000 people homeless ... [Germany had fifty-eight towns of over 100,000 inhabitants.] If even half the load of 10,000 bombers were dropped on the built-up areas of these fifty-eight German towns the great majority of their inhabitants (about one-third of the German populations) would be turned out of house and home.'[17]

Thus did the concept of 'de-housing' – one of the several euphemisms that did the Air Ministry yeoman service – enter the war glossary. For once, the Prof ran into troubled water. Other distinguished scientists, similarly engaged in assisting the war effort and persuaded that Lindemann's neat little digests were not always correct, pointed out that the basis of his calculations was faulty and his prognosis too optimistic; and they were correct. Churchill however retained faith in the Prof, as he almost always did, and his confidence in Bomber Command was to that extent fortified.

Aerial bombardment as a major strategy had its critics from early on. A constant vein of criticism, which acquired extra weight towards the end of the war when Harris's bombers were more reliably able to hit particular targets, was that his single-minded fixation on area bombing discounted the bombing of economic targets of peculiar importance such as artificial rubber and ball-bearings – what Harris dismissed as 'panacea targets' – and oil. Mapping the essential arteries of Germany's oil supply (all *ersatz*, after the Rumanian oil fields were lost) was not easy in the early years but, by the autumn of 1944, 'it was possible to identify an oil situation so catastrophic that it could be exploited with decisive military effect'.[18]

When the Chief of the Air Staff advised him in June 1944 that the decrypt evidence dictated that the first priority in the bombing of Germany should be given to oil targets, he [Churchill] replied 'Good'. But he did not throw his weight behind the unsuccessful efforts by the Air Staff to direct the attention of Bomber Command to the Intelligence which continued to justify this priority throughout the second half of the year.[19]

Harris did not wholly ignore Portal's urgings (they were never anything more positive than that), but overall he persisted in the city bombing that continued to dominate his thinking. Churchill could have intervened in this as in other arguments about strategy but is not known ever to have done so. In the several tussles between pigmy Coastal Command and giant Bomber Command, Churchill came down on the bombers' side, which was all the more strange, considering the crucial importance of what he boldly insisted on calling the Battle of the Atlantic. He gave no support to the very sensible plea that the huge concrete U-boat shelters the Germans were building at St-Nazaire should be bombed before they became perfectly bomb-proof; as in due course they became. Then it was argued that Coastal Command, playing its part in combating the U-boats at sea, deserved to be given earliest access to the very long-range aircraft just coming on stream and the new navigational and target-finding devices that the Prof and other boffins had invented. The Prof advised Churchill that they would be better employed over Germany, and so they were. It is likely that if Churchill had espoused the Admiralty's case in later 1942 rather than Bomber Command's, victory in the Battle of the Atlantic would have come six months earlier.[20]

All in all, it is difficult to understand Churchill's mind regarding the bombing strategy. It became the most controversial aspect of his warlordship. He was as immovably wedded to it as he was to his Mediterranean strategy. (The influence of the Prof was here at its most potent.) Churchill's almost blind support for Bomber Command throughout the controversies that raged about it was of a piece with the fact, which has not so far attracted the attention it perhaps deserves, that he never prodded and questioned Air Chief Marshal Harris as he did the equivalent army and navy commanders-in-chief. He left Bomber Command on its own and, by the time his intervention was badly needed, he had lost effective control of it.[21]

War Direction

Two of Churchill's favourite concepts were 'war direction' and 'war machinery'. The industrial metaphor appealed to him; in the spring of 1942 he once described Bomber Command as the sharp end of 'a great plant for bombing Germany'.[1] We have seen how naturally 'war machinery' came to his mind in the First World War. It did so again in the Second. Churchill liked to think he had a great 'war machinery' responsive to his hand, as efficient and fine-tuned as he and his engineers and inspectors could make it, and with all the material and moral power behind it that a totally mobilised economy and population could provide. That was his ideal. Considering the low base from which he began, and the economy's systemic defects, it is astonishing how nearly the ideal was achieved.[2]

It is tempting to suppose that Churchill's ideal of supreme command was formed when in the 1930s he wrote a weighty biography of his ancestor the first Duke of Marlborough, a winner of victories whose success rested on his handling the levers of politics and statecraft as well as strategy, logistics and leadership. Churchill would have been less than human if his ambition to be a glorious war leader and national hero had not been fortified by ancestral pride, but his proximate inspiration lay much closer at hand. Experience of leadership and management in 1914–18 and the ensuing post-mortem on how it might have been done better were more than sufficient to explain his conviction that the military must accept civilian partnership (to put it no more strongly) in the making of top-level decisions on strategy and major operations; that there must be a total mobilisation of the 'home front'; and that it was natural, by every law of psychology and politics, for a nation to give its best in war when it had an inspiring and authoritative leader. Britain had at last found such a leader in its third year of the First World War. By its fourth year the home front was totally mobilised and David Lloyd

George was on the way to establishing the proper participation of civilian with military judgement in the formulation of strategy. But he had not got very far and he found it an uphill battle.

It was still a battle in 1940. Although Britain had so often been engaged in fighting around the Empire, and although its navy stood permanently at the ready, the making of war ('defence', we would now say) was not the primary purpose of government and administration that it was to the military powers of the Continent. Improved means of war management were nevertheless recurrently debated. Already before 1914 the Empire had acquired a 'strategic brain' in the Committee of Imperial Defence, the army had a functioning intellectual organ in its General Staff and an embryo of the same had been implanted into the Admiralty. Debate and innovation continued through the interwar years with, for example, the establishment of the Chiefs of Staff Committee and the consolidation of the CID, but progress was limited by the pacific assumptions of the period, by Treasury constrictions and by the absence of determined political backing.

A Minister for the Co-Ordination of Defence was appointed in 1936 – not Churchill, as he had hoped and as would have appeared reasonable – but a lawyer, Sir Thomas Inskip, who, by no means entirely through his own fault, proved incapable of doing what his job title implied. When under the darkening clouds of early 1939 he went so far as to suggest a need for 'industrial mobilisation', he was moved to another office. By the spring of that year, however, the prospect of war was coming so close that even Chamberlain's government had to concede the case; though it did so in minimal terms. The Ministry of Supply that became operational in May was allowed to handle little other than War Office, that is army, business; the Admiralty and the Air Ministry were allowed to keep their own business to themselves. The nine months of the 'Phoney War' produced no improvement. The Norwegian campaign showed that the war-directing body, the Ministerial Co-Ordination Committee, needed more decisive direction than an unwarlike Neville Chamberlain could provide. Churchill's sitting as its regular chairman in its last days proved an unsatisfactory experience both for the Chiefs of Staff, who resented Churchill's commanding presence, and for Churchill himself, who knew that in the last resort he was *not* in supreme command and that the Chiefs could appeal from him to the Prime Minister. Muddle was still the rule, wrote the future Chief of Air Staff John Slessor, 'before the highly efficient centralised control by the Prime Minister and Minister of Defence in constant working contact with the Chiefs of Staff'.[3]

Some of Churchill's war machinery was thus already in place before 10 May 1940 but the rest of it was his creation and it included signal novelties. The first novelty, inconspicuous but powerful, was the transfer from the Admiralty of that secret weapon of administrative efficiency, his innocently named 'Statistical Branch', directed by his friend and scientific adviser Professor Lindemann. The second and more sensational novelty was his creation of a Ministry of Defence, with himself as the minister and General Hastings Ismay as his chief of staff. The third was the recruitment to the Cabinet of two extremely capable non-party men who were to become effectively his deputies in charge of the industrial side of the war machine: Ernest Bevin, the giant of the Trade Union movement, to be Minister of Labour and National Service, and Sir John Anderson, a distinguished administrator. As Chamberlain's successor in the office of Lord President of the Council, Anderson chaired the Cabinet's Home Affairs Committee and took overall responsibility for organising the 'Home Front'.[4] Both men were soon fixtures in the War Cabinet and it is not too much to say that together they presided over an administrative machinery that by mid-1942 had succeeded in mastering the problem that had so much bothered Churchill in 1916–18: the matching of military and industrial demands to manpower and material resources.[5]

The fourth novelty was the most effective of all, and that was simply the extraordinary drive and dynamism Churchill brought to the centre of affairs. Government offices were accustomed to work at a measured pace and by fixed procedure, a style of doing business that could be described as leisurely or painstaking, according to the point of view. Now everything changed. One of Churchill's many bright private secretaries recalled what happened:

> The effect of Churchill's zeal was felt immediately in Whitehall. Government departments which under Neville Chamberlain had continued to work at much the same speed as in peacetime awoke to the realities of war. A sense of urgency was created in the course of a very few days and respectable civil servants were actually to be seen running along the corridors. No delays were condoned; telephone switchboards quadrupled their efficiency; the Chiefs of

Staff and the Joint Planning Staff were in almost constant session; regular office hours ceased to exist and weekends disappeared with them.[6]

As Churchill began, so he went on. He never took a holiday, except when forced to do so by illness, and he admonished his staff that a change of work was just as refreshing. He worked all hours himself and expected them to do the same, with little consideration for their comfort or convenience. Queries and orders of utmost urgency left his office with the red stamp 'Action This Day' upon them; and there was trouble if this didn't happen. His passion for getting on with the war was infectious and it is significant that even those close companions who subsequently admitted to being from time to time bored, irritated or worn out by him always balanced their criticisms with the conclusion that, nevertheless, less would have been achieved without the example and stimulus of his energy and enthusiasm.

By making himself Minister of Defence Churchill acquired a constitutional status vis-à-vis the Chiefs of Staff Committee that paralleled the status he already had as Prime Minister vis-à-vis the civilian heads of the military (in the larger sense) departments. That a Chiefs of Staff Committee already existed made Churchill's task so much the easier; it only needed a strong chairman or equivalent to produce a shared view of priorities and a common purpose. It was an institution without parallel in Germany or the United States. In Germany, Hitler cemented his own supreme position by dealing with the three armed services (the Luftwaffe virtually was one) separately. In America, where there were only two (army and navy each having its own air arm), they simply *were* separate and accustomed to competing with one another for attention and resources. They liked it that way, and no President ventured to bang their heads together until Roosevelt formed the Combined Chiefs of Staff Committee, more or less on the British model and with the head of the United States Army Air Force included as an independent Chief, in February 1942. Even after that British visitors to Washington were appalled to note how much inter-service quarrelling went on. American visitors to Britain in 1940/41, on the other hand, were amazed to witness a system of war direction in which the armed services were relatively harmonious in their relations with one another, where their chiefs were accustomed to sit in council together, and where decisions once taken were swiftly acted upon.

General Ismay's important part in these arrangements was to be what Churchill not very flatteringly called his 'handling machine', in other words 'a two-way channel of communication on military matters between the Prime Minister and everyone in Whitehall who was concerned with military business'.[7] The hottest of those channels was the one joining Churchill to the Chiefs. Ismay had to explain to them what the boss wanted, which was sometimes unreasonable, and to the boss what they thought of it, which was sometimes unrepeatable. Fortunately, Ismay's patience, good humour and discretion enabled him to do this double act without forfeiting the confidence of either party, and he respected the service proprieties by refraining from adding his signature to theirs on the principal products of their committee, the submission of professional advice to ministers and the issue of 'orders and instructions to commanders in the field'.[8] But Churchill was never far away from the Chiefs of Staff. Even when they were meeting on their own, his man Ismay could be there and often was; Churchill himself would normally be in the chair of the Defence Committee (or of the smaller 'Staff Committee' that came to substitute for it) as he was also, of course, in the chair of the War Cabinet, which the Chiefs might be required to attend.

There is no better balanced a summary of this all-important relationship of Churchill with the Chiefs of Staff and the Defence Committee than that later given by his wartime deputy Clement Attlee in one of the interviews he gave to Francis Williams. Williams had asked him, whether Churchill did not have too much 'personal control over the strategic planning of the war'.

> *Attlee*: No. Winston was the driving force, a great War Minister. No one else could have done the job he did. But there was quite a lot of discussion at the Defence Committee. We surveyed the whole strategic field.
> *Williams*: Was there much disagreement?
> *Attlee*: Occasionally, yes.
> *Williams*: But Churchill had his way?
> *Attlee*: Pretty often. Very often. But there were quite a lot of occasions when he didn't. He'd get some idea he wanted to press, and after we had considered it the rest of us would have to tell him there was no value in it. But you needed someone to prod the Chiefs of Staff. Winston was sometimes an awful nuisance ... but he always accepted the verdict of the Chiefs of Staff

when it came to it, and it was a great advantage for him to be there driving them all the time ... We always accepted their professional advice. Even Winston did after a struggle. We never moved on a professional matter without them.[9]

The grounds on which Churchill justified to himself his confident insistence on sharing with the Chiefs the consideration of major strategic and operational matters seem to have been, first, his own high opinion of himself – that, as a soldier of varied experience and a man of extensive military learning, he was well qualified to share ideas with professionals; secondly, his conviction that professionals who attained the top of the tree might still not be the brightest of their kind; and, thirdly, his perception that behind them lay organisations given, like the departments of the civil service and bureaucracies everywhere, to self-interest, paper-pushing and playing safe.

Churchill herein displayed some vanity and prejudice. His military experience was in truth rather limited and he had no experience of all the things that officers learned at Staff College. Again and again, the Chiefs of Staff and other military men close to him observed that he rarely gave thought to the time-taking logistical arrangements that must support well-planned operations. He became irritable and impatient when told that things could not be done as quickly as he desired or, worse, could not be done at all. On the other hand, there is evidence that he could come up with military ideas that won the Chiefs' approval. One of Churchill's private secretaries recalled how, on some particular occasion, the Chiefs of Staff 'just did not know what was the right course to pursue ... on a purely military matter'. Churchill 'introduced some further facts into the equation that had escaped their notice and the solution became obvious'.[10]

There is an important question here that needs to be aired. Was not Churchill's impatience sometimes justified? German generals, who were well placed to judge, were of the opinion that their British opposite numbers were generally slow off the mark and that the British army was better in defence than attack, let alone in counter-attack.[11] Their further opinion, that British soldiers in general were not so good at fighting as theirs were, was reluctantly and of course privately shared by Churchill himself.[12] Was not British military caution and deliberateness part of the explanation of why the campaigns in which the British

army was heavily involved – North Africa, Italy, Normandy and then
Germany itself – always took longer to finish than expected? (Unless of
course they finished more quickly than hoped, as in Greece, Crete and
the Dodecanese islands.) There was among the senior generals a perva-
sive fear, founded on the Somme, of taking heavy losses that was
morally respectable but discouraging to bold and risky operations.
Churchill himself shared this mental torment, his relish of the bold and
risky being at odds with the fears of costly failure that still dogged him
until Operation Overlord was successfully accomplished.

Churchill may not have been misguided in thinking that his generals
and the War Office performed the better for his prodding and probing.
He actually thought the generals would appreciate the interest he
showed in them. On the whole they didn't. Wavell and Auchinleck seem
to have suffered most from his attentions, and, being men of sensitive
self-respect as well as many worries, they showed their irritation; as did
their nearest admiral in 1941/42, Andrew Cunningham. 'Jumbo' Maitland Wilson, later in the war, appears not to have been bothered by
them. The peaceable Dill tried to explain to Auchinleck that Churchill
had many worries too, some of which were beyond the military ken.[13]
This explanation of course had truth in it, but by no means all of
Churchill's proddings were prompted by high political considerations
and the burdens of office; he could simply be impatient and interfering.

His suspicions about the service departments may more often have
been justified. The War Office, the object of many other complaints
besides Churchill's, fell more often under his lash than the Admiralty or
the Air Ministry. Colville tells how he once asked Churchill which of the
two ministries he disliked most, the Foreign Office or the Treasury.
'After a moment's thought he replied: "the War Office!".'[14] How far his
generalised prejudices against bureaucratic departments were justified it
is impossible to say. He was egged on in these prejudices by Beaverbrook, who knew how to run no businesses but his own, and by the
Prof, whose brief included the identification and exposure of bad practices and wastefulness. The minutes and telegrams Churchill shot off
daily through the early months of the war were often directly founded
on information from the Statistical Branch. For example, in early July
1941, he was able to point out to the Secretary of State for Air that the
2920 tons of bombs his men dropped in May was less than half the stock

of bombs provided, and to inquire whether some of the bomb-making production lines could not be found more useful work elsewhere.[15] Inefficient use of human resources, a preoccupation from his Ministry of Munitions days, was a matter that constantly appeared in the Statistical Branch's work and in Churchill's minutes; he never ceased to worry at the (seemingly irremoveable) imbalance between the number of soldiers in the front line and the number of those behind it: the ratio of head to tail, one of the standard ways of measuring the efficiency of armies. Injustice might sometimes be done to frenzied officials, just as it might be to frustrated generals, and there was unavoidable overlap with the work of the statistical sections of some ministries, but it is impossible to doubt that Churchill's system of surveillance kept everybody on their toes and encouraged efficiency. Churchill's boundless energy and zeal could motivate the most phlegmatic or critical, an unending fireworks display that illuminated even the darkest night.

We must now consider the criticisms that were made of his system, and the individuals who owed their prominent places in it to his favour and promotion. For all his virtuous protestations to the contrary, Churchill did not like criticism. His reception of it, however, was discriminating. He distinguished between the criticisms of those who were sincerely trying to help Britain win the war and the criticisms of those who, he thought, weren't. He had a point when he reminded the House of Commons that, in its debates about the conduct of the war, public expressions of misgiving might not be helpful; the British public might understand that it was just part of the parliamentary game but foreign observers would receive a less happy impression. Such observations did not do much to rein in the critics. The quality of his government's direction of the war was formally debated several times in 1941 and 1942, votes of confidence followed and on one occasion the critics mustered as many as 25 votes against 475, with over thirty abstentions.[16] Churchill had no difficulty in surviving these attacks, of which, in truth, too much has been made. The debates accompanying them were no more than mock battles, the real purpose of which was to air criticisms at the highest public level, a higher level than was otherwise ordinarily open. It was the airing that mattered, not the votes of confidence.

Party politics being nominally in suspense, these attacks were launched by a miscellany of disparate individuals with differing motives, and what fundamentally doomed them to failure was the fact that, taking Churchill all in all, there was no alternative to him, and the attackers themselves knew it. Prestigious names such as Sir Stafford Cripps, Lord Beaverbrook, Anthony Eden and Ernest Bevin were mentioned from time to time, and publicised here and there, but hardly ever as candidates for the replacement of Churchill, simply as co-adjutors who would take some of the work off him and supposedly manage it better. Churchill's concept of leadership and his natural egotism made such proposals abhorrent. Ever the House of Commons man, he told the House that he would resign if so instructed but he would neither share ultimate responsibility with anyone else, nor make over part of his power to anyone not responsible to the House, notably to a sealed-off military supremo envisaged by one set of critics. Because the parliamentary attacks were not organised, and because the motives of some of the attackers were to say the least questionable, these parliamentary criticisms got nowhere. Churchill did make a few changes to his administration in February 1942, but that was all: there was no larger change to the war machinery or to his handling of it than the clarification of the functions of the Ministry of Supply and an endorsement of Ernest Bevin's sphere of influence as Minister of Labour and National Service.

That was a pity, because some of the criticisms were just and sensible. They were criticisms which, had they been presented constructively in a less adversarial atmosphere, might have made the war machinery better. A dispassionate observer could not believe that the Prime Minister and Minister of Defence was not taking too much on himself; his liking for doing things himself and having a finger in every pie surely meant that he was wasting time and energy on matters of secondary importance. The point was, in a managerial sense, a good one. If other people were delegated to take over some of the lesser parts of the Prime Minister's load, the prime ministerial mind ought to be fresh and freer to do justice to the major parts which he alone could fulfil: chiefly, his roles as the heroic leader of the nation in arms, the manager of Britain's relations with its allies, and the acclaimed representative of Britain's cause to the world at large. In those parts of his work, his supremacy and excellence were undoubted. No one wanted him to give them up.

It was in relation to the military part of his work, the share he took as Minister of Defence (that is, the share that he as Prime Minister had authorised himself to take) in the formation of strategy and planning of major operations, that doubts arose.

What went on between Churchill and the Chiefs of Staff did not begin to become public knowledge until after the war. It was only with the publication in the later 1950s of some of the diaries of the distinguished soldier Sir Alan Brooke, chairman of the Chiefs of Staff Committee, 1942–45, that the story began to be told.[17] From Westminster and Whitehall insiders at the time, however, no secrets were hidden; indeed, Churchill's own flamboyant style of government worked to bring things into the open. Anyone who knew how much the Chiefs of Staff endured in their relations with Churchill could reasonably believe that they should be left more on their own to get on with what they and their elaborate organisations were trained to do. It was rumoured again, as it had been earlier in his Admiralty days, that Churchill was usurping their prerogative by issuing orders that should have proceeded only from a military Chief. Churchill's critics believed that he was capable of doing this, but when Lord Hankey asked Sir John Dill in May 1941 whether it was true that Churchill was sending orders to Wavell, Dill told him either he or 'someone in his confidence' always checked them before they were despatched.[18] Churchill never overruled the Chiefs of Staff on any of their legitimate military concerns. They might have to put up with a great deal of huffing and puffing, and with hours of annoyance and waste of time, but no instance is known of his not ultimately yielding to their united opposition.

More serious was the matter of the Chiefs of Staff Committee's position vis-à-vis the War Cabinet. In the most considerable of the critical debates, that of 1 and 2 July 1942, Aneurin Bevan questioned whether the War Cabinet ever had the opportunity to learn what the Chiefs of Staff really thought, since Churchill by one means or another could always get at them in advance.[19] Churchill angrily interjected, 'That is not true'; but it possibly was true. Equally worrying to the critics was the thought that Churchill was capable of bringing the weight of the War Cabinet to bear on the Chiefs of Staff in order to compel them to agree to something against their better professional judgement. That he tried to do this at least once is evident in the case of Ernest Bevin, Minister of

Labour and National Service. The formidable Bevin told him he 'shouldn't come asking the Cabinet for its opinion on matters about which they knew nothing and which were too serious to be settled by amateur strategists'.[20]

Such were the major criticisms made of Churchill's 'war machinery' and of the way he worked it. They prompt tantalising questions. Might that machinery have produced better decisions if rationalised along the lines the critics suggested? By what criteria could it be judged that they were 'better'? Whether Churchill was breathing down their necks or not, the Chiefs of Staff were still responsible to the War Cabinet, and on strategic and military matters the War Cabinet of course tended to take Churchill's opinion seriously, even if its members were not all the docile puppets of anti-Churchillian supposition. Unless Churchill died – a contingency by no means unlikely, considering his age and illnesses and the travelling risks he insisted on taking – he could not be shifted from the heart and centre of the nation at war, not just because of the official positions he held but because he was his own inimitable, expansive and assertive self. As General Sir John Kennedy, not one of Churchill's uncritical admirers, simply put it in July 1942, there was 'no one else with the personality for the job'.[21]

Therein lay the unadmitted heart and centre of the complaints about him. It was not his war machinery as such that the critics were really aiming at, it was how he dominated and used it. He interfered in parts of it where he was not really needed. He used it in self-indulgent ways that suited him and suited no one else. His normal inconsiderateness showed itself here as much as anywhere. He had always kept unusual hours. Now he made everyone else keep them too. His short-hand typists, one of whom recalled having to work without a break until 4.30 a.m. on the 'Never in the field of human conflict' speech, regarded their ordeals as contributions to the war effort, and in any case they respected and admired him.[22] But senior officials and Cabinet colleagues found these late hours more difficult to take in their stride. To be summoned at short notice to a Sunday morning meeting to deal with an emergency, even to a midnight meeting if the emergency was very great, these were inconveniences that could be considered to go with the job; but having to carry on after dinner till two o'clock in the morning or even later for no better purpose than to watch film shows, listen to

Churchill's monologues and play along with his whims, those were afflictions that weighed heavily on overworked men who had to be up and about early next morning. It says something about their code of politeness, duty and respect that none of those who suffered under these afflictions, not even the arch-sufferer Sir Alan Brooke, is known ever to have protested to his face.

Brooke, in particular, but others too were capable of confronting him with criticism of his sometimes maddening ways in committee, but they seem to have felt obliged to put up with the exhausting *longueurs* of attendance at Chartwell, Chequers and, occasionally, Ditchley Park. There is no evidence that Clementine, who had long ago established her right to go to bed at a sensible hour, ever tried to change this side of his behaviour. She tried to change other sides – her letter of 27 June 1940 about the bad effects that stress and strain were having on his manners is justly celebrated – but she presumably gave up the late-night side as a bad job.[23] Churchill was a man of many parts, most of them estimable, some extraordinary, but some, frankly, tiresome. But if ever there had been a time when the tiresome parts might have been magicked away, it had long gone by. In his later sixties, he simply was as he was: unchangeable. If the nation wanted Churchill at all, it had to have him whole.[24]

Having Churchill whole also meant having his cronies. The quality of a head of any high office is largely measured by the appointments he makes and the persons he consults. Churchill 'consulted' – swapped opinions about the war with – an enormous number and variety of people. Lunches and dinners in his house were usually occasions for having guests to talk and to hear him talk. He tended to talk so much himself on social occasions and in official committees that it was reasonable for others to wonder whether he took in what others said, but the fact is that he usually did take it in, storing much in his elephantine memory for future reference. There were certain intimate friends to whom he talked more than others; since most of them were politically unaccountable and invisible to the public eye, it was possible to suspect that he was subject to improper and 'sinister' influences, the sort of influences suspected in earlier times of kings' favourites, mistresses and confessors. The critics need not have worried. Churchill was his own man and no one else's. In the end he always backed his own judgement.

There were three cronies-in-chief: Brendan Bracken, Lord Beaverbrook and Frederick Lindemann, 'the Prof', created Lord Cherwell in
1941. There was a fourth to begin with, Desmond Morton, an Intelligence
officer who had been extremely close to Churchill in the thirties and
who remained close throughout 1940. But for reasons that are not clear
he thereafter fell out of favour, and later wrote bitterly about his rejection.[25] Each of the three was very odd in his own way and each had his
own mode of usefulness. The Irish-born Bracken, an MP since 1929 and
a financial press lord, had made himself acceptable to Churchill as a
political aide-de-camp, loyally ready to do whatever Churchill asked
him to do and what he thought would be good for Churchill: an oper-
ator and fixer, experienced in all the ways of Westminster, he was
happier working out of sight than in it. There was not a lot he could do
so long as Churchill was in the political wilderness; but once his hero
was back in high office, the usefulness of such a friend had no limits.
His main uses to Churchill during the war, beyond his role as confidant
and gofer, were twofold. He took on a part of the Prime Minister's work
that would have been a distraction from directing the war: the patronage. What went on there was not in the public eye. Very much in the
public eye and part of the war machinery, because it was integral to
Churchill's plan of confiding in the people and maintaining an open
society, was the Ministry of Information which Bracken took over in the
middle of 1941. That ministry had so far found no popularly acceptable
midway between, on the one hand, the necessities of military censorship
(which the services departments instinctively stretched beyond reason)
and, on the other, the press's commitment to freedom of information
and comment (subject to a good deal of self-censorship). Brendan
Bracken's flair for press relations and fearlessness in face of the service
departments, together with his establishment of a *modus vivendi* with
the BBC ('turning confrontation into cooperation') enabled him to turn
the M.o.I. into the smooth functioning and relatively uncontroversial
institution it remained till the end of the war.[26]

Beaverbrook's value to Churchill and to the war effort was more
difficult to perceive. An Empire-crazy Canadian scrambling to the
heights of the English plutocracy, he had been a crony for more than
twenty years. He was a political busybody and press magnate. Like
Bracken, he could argue with Churchill and get away with it; unlike

Bracken, he intermittently differed from Churchill on matters of high policy. Clementine never liked or trusted him, and many friends shared her feelings. The senior servicemen and Labour stalwarts her husband relied on, Brooke and Bevin for example, detested him. Bevin's refusal to collaborate with him in 1942 effectively ended his ministerial career. Churchill, however, found him fascinating. Not the least of his fascinations was his buccaneering experience of business and finance; Churchill liked his talk of how to outsmart others, get things done and make money. He insisted that Beaverbrook's company bucked him up more than anyone else's – it was as if he had to have a shot of it now and then – and twice he entrusted Beaverbrook with positions of high importance in the war machine.[27]

In mid-May 1940 Churchill made him head of the new Ministry of Aircraft Production. Churchill believed, probably correctly, that the rate of aircraft production could be faster and, with questionable judgement, gave Beaverbrook *carte blanche* to increase it. For some months he did just that, by methods that caused amazement and outrage.[28] For example, he liberated German Jewish engineers from the internment camps into which all 'enemy aliens' had been promiscuously bundled, he intercepted and piratically seized materials destined for other departments, he enthused the public by calling for the surrender of aluminium kitchen vessels (to be 'turned into Spitfires'), and he used his newspapers to work up public fury against those who thwarted him. All this was done at much cost to all the other departments within his range. It meant, among other things, permanent war with the Air Ministry.[29] Churchill took him off the job in 1941 and moved him to the Ministry of Supply. There he failed to make a mark. The ministry already existed, so he could not compose one to suit himself, and he ran into trouble with Bevin, the powerful Minister of Labour and National Service whom Churchill backed when he refused to hand over any part of his empire. Although restored to ministerial office in 1943, and privately as close to Churchill as ever, his meteoric irruptions into the vitals of the war machine were over.

Frederick Lindemann was the crony who mattered most. Until late 1942, when he entered the Cabinet as Paymaster-General, he held no higher offices than being the Prime Minister's personal scientific adviser and the head of the Ministry of Defence's tiny Statistical Department

9. Churchill firing a Tommy Gun, 1944; the American officer also firing, top right, is General Eisenhower. This kind of gun was more reliable than the one with a drum magazine that he holds in the picture used by Goebbels to portray him as a gangster. (*Imperial War Museum*)

10. Broadcasting to America, with his characteristic 'psalm verses' script typed out large for him. The light suit and knotted tie only appeared on informal occasions, always bearing that mysterious slip of medal ribbon. Can it be the American Distinguished Service Medal, 1918? (*Imperial War Museum*)

11. Churchill in recently blitzed Liverpool, late 1940 or early 1941. His hat is in his hand, ready for waving. (*Imperial War Museum*)

12. Churchill addressed Congress twice during the war, on 26 December 1941 and on 19 May 1943. This appears to be on the latter occasion. (*Imperial War Museum*)

13. Churchill in Air Commodore's uniform with General Sir Alan Brooke, chairman of the Chiefs of Staff Committee, and General Dwight Eisenhower, Supreme Commander of the Allied Expeditionary Forces, 1944. (*Imperial War Museum*)

14. The Big Three at Yalta, February 1945. Roosevelt and Churchill do their best to look cheerful, although the former was mortally ill. (*Imperial War Museum*)

15. Potsdam, July 1945. A sad picture: Churchill, aware that Eastern Europe was becoming a Soviet Empire, puts a good face on his inner grief. Truman is out of his element. Only Stalin is at his ease. (*Imperial War Museum*)

16. Churchill visiting the Siegfried Line on 3 March 1945, with Brooke, Montgomery and the American General Simpson, commander of the 9th Army. (*Imperial War Museum*)

17. Churchill, Brooke, Montgomery and Simpson crossing a Bailey Bridge, 3 March 1945. (*Imperial War Museum*)

18. Churchill leading the symbolically momentous landing on the east bank of the Rhine, 25 March 1945. Behind him comes Brooke. (*Imperial War Museum*)

19. Churchill with Brooke and Montgomery. Brooke's diary records this 'excellent lunch' on the east bank of the Rhine, 26 March 1945. (*Imperial War Museum*)

20. In his study, January 1956. (*Hulton/Getty Picture Library*)

that Churchill brought with him from the Admiralty to Downing Street.[30] His influence now became vast and ubiquitous. Churchill consulted him whenever he chose and not only about matters strictly scientific; his backing of the bombing offensive, which other scientists in government service thought positively unscientific, was part of the reason why Churchill allowed it to go on so long without interference. As for the Statistical Department, hitherto the Prof and his clever young men had only rarely been able to work outside the Admiralty. Now they were made free of the whole apparatus of government, working 'on what, in a broad way, could be called the logistics and economics of the war, including particularly the use of scarce resources such as shipping and manpower'.[31] They also reduced to a common form, for Churchill's benefit, the statistics that issued from the various departments in their own departmental styles. Lindemann's Statistical Department was central to Churchill's ambition that he should be able to keep an eye on the workings of every part of the war machine: he needed an overview of its week-by-week functioning, all the way from the blunt base where men and women and raw materials were poured into it to the sharp end where the fighting went on.

This was an astonishingly bold and powerful idea. Most heads of government in wartime are content to leave their appointees to manage their respective ministries and departments on their own and, until given striking evidence to the contrary, to accept their reports of what they are doing. Self-respecting heads of departments in any case won't normally accept the responsibility unless they are left to do it their own way. The critics of Churchill's insistence on supervising things *his* way ('dictatorial!') alleged that he only got away with it because his appointees were 'yes men'. The charge was absurd. Some were easier-going than others – A. V. Alexander, the First Lord of the Admiralty, for example, and to some extent Churchill's long-time friend and admirer Archie Sinclair at the Air Ministry – but most certainly were not. Sinclair, in fact, stood up to him within a few weeks of his appointment, refusing to make a senior RAF officer apologise to Beaverbrook for what Beaverbrook thought an 'unfounded charge'.[32]

The contrast with Churchill's 1951 Cabinet is striking. Free of wartime pressures and sitting loose to his party, he filled his Cabinet with congenial souls, including his wartime companions Ismay and Alexander, giving them jobs for which they were in fact ill suited. In the early 1940s, however, he made up his all-party national government and from time to time refreshed it with the most suitable men (women were not in the picture) from whatever source, and he did so with such decisive bold-ness that it even included from the start the Trade Union boss, Ernest Bevin. Labour men indeed were so prominent in the administration that Conservatives were given to complaining that Churchill had leaned too far in their direction. On the other hand, there were men who were virtually non-party like Sir John Anderson and Lord Woolton, whose varied background in retailing and distribution made him an excellent Minister of Food. Almost everyone in the administration (and out of it) complained about the favour shown to Beaverbrook.

Military appointments (and disappointments) caused him more trouble and destined him to more criticism than civil ones. Having made himself Minister of Defence and acquired the close relation with the Chiefs of Staff that has already been described, he could legitimately claim an interest in them, just as he could also claim the right to cor-respond directly with the Commanders-in-Chief in the various theatres of war, an unprecedented exercise of authority that the military pro-fessionals on the whole disapproved of. How far his will could be asserted in any particular case depended on the Chief concerned or, perhaps, the departmental minister. It is undeniable that he had favourites and unfavourites. He had, for example, a soft spot for Gen-eral Sir Harold Alexander, treating him with unfailing consideration and giving him or keeping him in commanding positions for which some at the time and many since have judged him inadequate. He retained the services of the ageing naval chief inherited from Cham-berlain, Admiral Sir Dudley Pound, for many months beyond the evident decline of his powers, partly because Pound was loyal and untroublesome, partly because Churchill did not look forward to hav-ing to deal with the most obvious successor, the tough Sir Andrew Cunningham, whom in the end he nevertheless had to accept. Yet he appointed the even tougher General Sir Alan Brooke to succeed Sir John Dill (whom he nicknamed 'Dilly-Dally') as army Chief in November 1941 and, what gives the ultimate lie to the allegation that he could not stand contradiction, kept him there until the end of the war, despite the ferocious arguments that marked their relationship: 'When I thump the table and push my face towards him, what does he do? Thumps the table harder and glares back at me.'[33]

Churchill early in the war showed a penchant for comrades-in-arms from the Great War and would have used them more often if they had been willing or if their appointments had not been blocked. We have already seen how he brought some of them back when he was First Lord of the Admiralty. He would have liked the sixty-seven-year-old Marshal of the Royal Air Force Lord Trenchard to become an all-Services supremo in case of invasion in mid-1940; he placed the new-born Directorate of Combined Operations in the care of the sixty-eight-year-old Admiral Sir Roger Keyes. He also cherished the dashing, the eccentric and the unfashionable, generally with good results. His most dramatic and controversial appointment was that of the forty-two-year-old Captain Louis Mountbatten to be Director of Combined Operations and a vice-admiral with a seat on the Chiefs of Staff Committee (which the Chiefs resented); a year later, Mountbatten was further promoted to admiral and, with the Americans' approval, Supreme Commander, South-East Asia. Against all orthodox opinion Churchill backed the oddball General Orde Wingate's Chindit project to harass the Japanese behind their lines in Burma by air-supplied guerrilla operations. He insisted on the recall to usefulness of the pensioned-off tank genius Percy Hobart, he placed the inventive and eccentric Engineer officer Millis Jefferis under the Prof's protection, and he objected when he heard that keen and worthy applicants for commissions were being rejected on social grounds.

Churchill could also get rid of commanders whom he judged to be sluggish or ineffective, though it has to be noted that on these occasions he was not acting alone. On the two occasions when he removed holders of high office in the RAF, the men he replaced them by were undoubtedly of superior ability: Sir Cyril Newall, replaced as Chief of Air Staff by Sir Charles Portal, and Sir Richard Peirse, replaced as Commander-in-Chief Bomber Command by Sir Arthur Harris. His replacement of Ironside by Dill as CIGS in May 1940 was also a step in the right direction.[34]

His two removals of Commanders-in-Chief of the British and imperial army in the Middle East excited and have continued to excite more criticism, some of it as much from admiration of their resistance to

Churchill's chivvying as from reasoned rejection of Churchill's judgement. General Sir Archibald Wavell had long borne with an unusually complex command, painful shortages of military materials and excessive Churchillian prodding before a series of operational failures drove Churchill to replace him in July 1941. Increasingly desperate for some military success in the desert war, Churchill pinned his hopes on General Sir Claude Auchinleck, but by August 1942 the latter's record in battle with the formidable Rommel had been insufficiently successful to retain either Churchill's confidence, or for that matter Brooke's, or – what mattered above all – that of the troops. Both Wavell and Auchinleck (like Cunningham) had affronted Churchill by their response to his proddings – Wavell had memorably instructed Churchill that 'a big butcher's bill is not necessarily evidence of good tactics' – but that seems not to have been a significant factor in his decision to sack them. The vindictiveness of which the Prime Minister was occasionally accused, especially in those nerve-racking early months of his leadership, is generally considered to have determined the dismissal of Admiral Sir Dudley North in September 1940; nominally for having failed to stop a few Vichy French warships passing through the Straits of Gibraltar, but essentially because he had gone out of his way to make London aware of how badly everyone at Gibraltar and in Admiral Somerville's fleet had felt about the action against the French fleet at Tel-el-Kebir.[35]

No account of Churchill's war machinery can be complete without specifying the parts of it he invented and installed. Some have already been mentioned. Of these the Ministry of Defence was the most important: a ministry with a minuscule staff but enormous leverage. In Churchill's hands it became a device for assimilating military with civilian authority: 'Thus for the first time the Chiefs of Staff Committee assumed its due and proper place in direct daily contact with the executive head of the Government, and in accord with him had full control over the conduct of the war and the armed forces.'[36] Loosely connected with it was the Prof's Statistical Department or Branch, whose work of universal surveillance and evaluation has already been emphasised. Churchill created new ministries to meet new needs at home (including those of Aircraft Production, Production, Fuel and Power, and Reconstruction) while, to handle on the spot the multiple problems arising in particular regions overseas, he delegated powers to variously-titled

Ministers for the Far East (soon brought to an end), the Middle East (under R. G. Casey, a concession to Australian feeling), Washington (for matters of supply), the Mediterranean Command (held from December 1942 by Harold Macmillan) and West Africa.

Churchill's innovations on the military side were numerous and all in one way or another successful, even if they did not always turn out as he had envisaged. His original vision of the Commandos, conceived just after Dunkirk, was of a force much larger and more effective than could ever in practice be realised; which is not to depreciate the usefulness of what the Commandos were actually able to do. Likewise the Special Operations Executive found for itself a field of usefulness different from the over-ambitious goal – to 'set the Continent on fire' – proposed by its progenitor. Like all other citizens of democracies, Churchill at first failed to comprehend both the ruthlessness with which Germany would maintain itself as an occupying power and the added control it derived from 'collaborators'. As the months went by, however, he came to value SOE's necessarily secret work of promoting and arming resistance movements in every theatre of the war, and it was his support that saved it from its persistent enemy, the rival secret service MI6.[37] The Directorate of Combined Operations, another of the institutional births in June 1940, was from the very start an inter-service body, setting the example and finding the way for what would have to become familiar if ever Britain was to land forces on what had become Hitler's Continent. 'MD1' (Ministry of Defence One, popularly known as Churchill's Toyshop) was the little specialised engineering outfit at Whitchurch, on the Thames by Pangbourne, where Millis Jefferis invented the 'sticky bomb', the PIAT anti-tank projector and other useful novelties.

Bletchley Park, 'Station X', in officialese the Government Code and Cypher School, was not one of Churchill's creations, having been located at Bletchley for two years before he became Prime Minister, and by May 1940 it was beginning to decypher German naval and military codes to good effect. Churchill instantly adopted it and sheltered it under his wing. He had always been excited by Intelligence work, he relished his daily dose of Bletchley's decrypts, and he was enthusiastic about its military uses – more enthusiastic, indeed, than some of the distrustful admirals and generals to whom Bletchley's secrets were mysteriously fed. He did not restlessly fuss about it as he did about some

other of his treasures, apparently confident that such an unusual establishment of such unusual people was best left to get on by itself; he only
visited the place once, and humorously remarked to the head of the
Secret Intelligence Services as he left: 'I know I told you to leave no stone
unturned to find the necessary staff, but I didn't mean you to take me
so literally!'[38] What Churchill saw and sensed on that occasion obviously impressed him. When, not long after, one of the cryptanalysts
took to him a letter from four of them telling how their work was
impeded by various shortages (the visitor to Bletchley now is told they
were even short of pencils), Churchill's response was: 'ACTION THIS
DAY. Make sure they have all they want on extreme priority and report
to me that this has been done.'[39]

The Family at War

Churchill, the oldest of the Big Three and fifteen years older than Hitler, was approaching his seventy-first birthday when the war finally finished. It was a wonder that he was still alive. He had repeatedly risked death with the same insouciance as when he was a young cavalry lieutenant and a middle-aged colonel, and he would have come really close to it on several occasions if strong-minded companions had not restrained him. He had lived through air raids, steamed through U-boat infested seas and flown through the Luftwaffe's skies; it has been reckoned that as Prime Minister he travelled 105,728 miles by land, sea and air outside the UK.[1] He had often been unwell and at least once been close to death from pneumonia. He had driven himself unsparingly, he had remained in charge after the European war ground to a halt, and by the time the results of the general election of 1945 were announced, just before the end of the Pacific war, he was not only very tired but also, understandably, cast down. Clementine, whose own occasional low spirits and tiredness never kept her from giving priority to his comfort and happiness, had even worried lest the war would so much wear him out that he would die when it was over.[2]

Something that she did not say, but which is obvious enough, is that he had been helped to survive the war as well as he did because he had in some sense enjoyed it. The reader will recall his admission to Clementine on the eve of the First World War: 'Everything tends towards catastrophe and collapse. I am interested, geared-up and happy.' He remained interested, geared-up and happy through most of the Second. Not long after the European part of it was over, he turned from his work to say to his physician and confidant, 'I feel very lonely without a war. Do you feel like that?'[3] Astonishingly, he managed in the war publicly to appear confident and calm even when in private he was gloomy. Of course he was made unhappy – much more than that, absolutely cast down – by the disasters and disappointments that showered upon him in his first two years as Prime Minister, and he went through some very bad days indeed in the early months, the months of French collapse, of Dunkirk and of threatened invasion. He never liked hearing of human losses and sufferings, and he did what he could – more, sometimes, than his commanders liked – to minimise them. Losses and sufferings, however, were the very stuff of war and no clear-headed warlord would let them divert him from the over-arching purpose, 'victory whatever the cost'. Directing the war towards victory was his engrossing task, and he found it fascinating, frustrations and setbacks included. Even in the final weeks, when his joy at the approaching defeat of Germany had long been overshadowed by the approaching power of the Soviet Union, his spirits remained high and infectious, dampened only by the fatigue that increasingly weakened his performance.

He did not allow the war to derange, to any greater degree than was unavoidable, the long-established comfortable priorities of his life: the services of his valet, morning in bed, his after-lunch siesta, daily hot baths (twice daily, if possible), secretaries to take dictation at any time, films after dinner, late night working – and, of course, cigars, alcohol and good food. These good things could usually be guaranteed at his two official residences, Number Ten Downing Street in Westminster and Chequers, near Wendover, under the lee of the Chiltern Hills in Buckinghamshire. Chequers was where he preferred to be, and almost always was, at weekends; the only occasions when he was not able to stay there were clear moonlit nights during the Blitz, when it was thought that the house might be too visible to bombers. In the manner of monarchs of earlier times, he invited himself and his entourage to pass fifteen such weekends at Ditchley Park in leafy Oxfordshire, close to Blenheim, the property of a rich Conservative MP Ronald Tree, who was, on the whole, happy to have him.

Number Ten on the other hand could no longer be thought a safe place to live and work during the Blitz (which went on intermittently into 1942) and the months of the V1s and V2s in 1944–45. The British government was not caught unprepared. Aerial bombardment had been expected, and two crucial decisions had been taken: the heart of government would *not* move out of London into some rural refuge, and comprehensive underground premises would be prepared to enable the

Cabinet and its attendant officials to continue to function even during bombing. By the time Churchill became Prime Minister, those premises, known then and open to visitors today as the Cabinet War Rooms, were ready and working beneath the St James's Park end of the New Public Offices between King Charles Street and Great George Street. The warren of corridors and rooms included a bedroom and study for the Prime Minister. It was necessarily pokey and primitive, and he only slept there three times, preferring – as soon as the Ministry of Works and Clementine had made it ready – the windowed suite of rooms constructed and reinforced directly above the basement, known as the Downing Street Annexe or simply the Annexe. Life there could approximate to the comfortable domesticity he enjoyed and give him the luxuries he had come to accept as normal.[4]

When he was travelling (which was, as we shall see, often) these priorities of course were likely to be relaxed, but he refused to be discouraged by privations and inconveniences. It must be remembered that aeroplanes in those days were noisy and vibrating (because of piston-driven engines) and flights were bumpy (because they could not usually fly above the weather). Churchill's worst discomforts were probably when he twice had to fly in a roughly converted and, of course, unpressurised Liberator, the longest-distance bomber of them all, the first time to Moscow in the summer of 1942 for his first encounter with Stalin and, soon after that, to Casablanca for the big Anglo-American conference in January 1943. He took a liking to its experienced pilot, Captain Vanderkloot, and spent a good many hours in the co-pilot's seat beside him, especially when he could have the thrill of seeing the sun come up.

> The bomber was [on the first occasion] unheated, and razor-edged draughts cut in through many chinks. There were no beds, but two shelves in the after cabin enabled me and Sir Charles Wilson, my doctor, to lie down. There were plenty of blankets for all.[5]

They flew from Lyneham to Gibraltar, from Gibraltar to Cairo (stopping there long enough to replace Auchinleck with Montgomery), from Cairo to Teheran, and thence to Moscow; then a few days later, back to Britain by the same route. General MacArthur later commented, 'A flight of 20,000 miles through hostile and foreign skies may be the duty of young pilots, but for a Statesman burdened with the world's cares it is an act of inspiring gallantry and valour.'[6] The conditions must, however, have been made a bit more bearable for him by being allowed to smoke. No evidence appears that anyone ever dared stop him smoking his cigars, and his granddaughter, in her book about his travels, relates the extraordinary fact that 'his oxygen mask [was] adapted so that he could enjoy both oxygen and a cigar'.[7]

The flight to Casablanca in January 1943 was enlivened by an episode so alarming that he described it in some detail.

> In order to heat the 'Commando' [the plane's name] they had established a petrol engine inside which generated fumes and raised various heating points to very high temperatures. I was woken up at two in the morning ... by one of these heating points burning my toes, and it looked as if it might soon get red-hot and light the blanket. I therefore climbed out of my bunk and woke up Peter Portal [Chief of Air Staff] who was sitting in the well beneath, asleep in his chair, and drew his attention to the very hot point. We looked around the cabin and found two others ... We then went down into the bomb alley ... and found two men industriously keeping alive the petrol heater. From every point of view I thought this was most dangerous ... Portal took the same view. I decided that it was better to freeze than to burn, and I ordered all heating to be turned off, and we went back to rest shivering in the ice-cold winter air about eight thousand feet up, at which we had to fly to be above the clouds.[8]

None of his other wartime journeys was quite as alarming as that. The five increasingly desperate flights he made to France in an RAF De Havilland Flamingo in May and June 1940, seeking to take the measure of the impending disaster and then to save something from it, were hazardous but relatively short. He made many short flights in the course of visiting the fighting fronts, like the flight from Naples (or close by) to Corsica in a Dakota with General 'Jumbo' Maitland Wilson in 1944.[9] The Boeing flying-boats on which he went three times between Britain and America in 1942 were slow but luxurious – 'I had a good broad bed in the bridal suite at the stern with large windows on either side [and] nothing was lacking in food or drink ... We passed an agreeable afternoon and had a merry dinner' – and there would have been no special risk, had they not got lost on the way home from the first trip and found themselves almost over German-occupied and heavily-defended Brest.[10] Later in the war he flew on different occasions in the British

Overseas Air Corporation's flying-boats 'Berwick' and 'Bristol' (very similar to Short Sunderlands), an Avro York (a comfortably converted RAF transport plane) and, in the last months of the war, a spacious and comfortable American Skymaster placed at his disposal by the American General 'Hap' Arnold.

Most of his journeys to and from North America were made by sea, in battleships – the *Prince of Wales* (a few months before the Japanese sank it), the *Duke of York* and the *Renown* – and, towards the end, the giant passenger liner the *Queen Mary*, adapted to carry thousands of troops. In the battleships he could choose his own accommodation – the 'guest quarters' at the stern proving 'almost uninhabitable through vibration in heavy weather at sea', he took over 'the Admiral's sea-cabin on the bridge' on his way to Placentia Bay – and he got his exercise by 'making my way three or four times a day through all the compartments and up and down all the ladders to the bridge'.[11] He was usually out of luck with the weather. The crossing in December 1941 was particularly stormy and risky. To minimise the danger from U-boats the *Duke of York* went as fast it could, which meant leaving its attendant destroyers behind. 'We were battened down and great seas beat upon the decks. Lord Beaverbrook complained that he might as well have travelled in a submarine.'[12] Churchill described it to Clementine as 'the longest week I have had since the war began'. In haven at last in the White House, he told her: 'I am very well and have not suffered from seasickness at all, though I took two doses of Mothersill the first day.' He had spent most of the crossing time in bed, but not resting. The Chiefs of Staff and other officials were repeatedly with him as grand strategy was thrashed out, 'official telegrams and secret news' (Ultra, no doubt) were brought in as they arrived, and secretaries were on call to take dictation. It is pleasant to note that all the great affairs of state on his mind did not prevent him asking Clemmie to let him know 'the length of your stockings, so that I can bring you a few pairs to take the edge off Oliver Lyttelton's coupons'.[13]

It was only to be expected that the nearest thing to luxury was found in the *Queen Mary*, first honoured by Churchill's patronage in August 1943: 'the utmost comfort, with a diet of pre-war times'. How many of his two-hundred-plus party that went by special train from Addison Road in London to join the ship on the Clyde enjoyed the same amenities is unclear; the many thousands of service men whom the huge ship carried back to Europe certainly didn't. For the Chiefs of Staff and all the officials in attendance this voyage was no more of a holiday than were any of his overseas trips; there was a Chiefs' Committee meeting daily, and most careful consideration was given to the strategy and tactics of dealing with the American counterparts waiting at the other end. Things must have been easier for Clementine (who was of the party this time) and their daughter Mary, who was there in consequence of the parents' decision in late 1942 that she and Sarah, both of them by now uniformed officers, should take it in turns to accompany their father on his foreign travels as family aides-de-camp and, so far as their wilful papa permitted, minders.[14]

The whole Churchill family, like most families in Britain then, was engaged in war work. Clementine wore herself out, keeping her demanding husband happy when he was at home and accompanying him whenever he wanted her to be with him. Theirs was a close and affectionate relationship but also an unusual and complicated one. He loved her with all the love he did not devote to his primary commitment, public duty. She loved him with a love that accepted that proviso and was generous enough to include the consciousness – a consciousness shared by their children – of being entrusted with the care of a national hero. That sense steeled her to bear his demands for instant attention, his occasional lack of consideration for others, his talent for not hearing what he didn't want to hear, the odd hours he kept, the odd people he liked – and his frequent absences.

Those absences in fact may have been their salvation. Close friends had observed from early on in their marriage that Clementine must find it a relief to get away from him sometimes. Yet their affection for one another remained constant and unmistakable. When they were apart, and could find the time, they wrote loving and often thoughtful letters to one another which are delightful to read.[15] They discussed people and events, they shared news and gossip, she kept him up to date with family news and political gossip, and he told her how he was getting on with the plans he had obviously discussed with her before he left home. She never hesitated to tell him when she thought he was wrong. A letter of February 1942 suggests that she had, in her daughter's terms, 'blown up' on discovering that his Cabinet reshuffle was going to include office for

Lord Beaverbrook, whom she had thought a bad influence on her husband for more than twenty years.[16]

Clementine had plenty to do besides keeping Winston happy. There was all the entertaining, both official and private – though the two would overlap when cronies like Bracken and the Prof or comrades-in-arms like Portal came for a meal or to stay overnight. Clementine had a good housekeeper at Chequers 'and a permanent staff of cheerful Service-women' to support her, but she was ultimately the person in charge and, given her husband's tendency to show boredom with guests he found uninteresting, the vigilant hostess. Her daughter cites, as an example, what went on there between mid-January and early September 1944: twenty-four out of thirty-three weekends wholly or partly taken up with official entertaining, the guests sometimes coming in 'shifts' so that there might be no gaps between one lot and another. Back in London, lunch almost always had a business aspect, and the evenings might do so too, as for example when, six times in 1944 alone, the King dined with them informally.[17]

Although she gave much time to supporting Winston (and to visiting his constituency on his behalf), Clementine also managed to take a leading part in three valuable activities. The two closest to her heart were the Wartime Fund of the YMCA (Young Women's Christian Association), providing hostels, canteens and clubs for servicewomen and women workers away from home, and the Fulmer Chase Maternity Home. Her daughter's delicate description of the rationale for the latter recalls an aspect of life then that may be difficult to realise now, several social revolutions later:

> Many officers in all three services made unusually early marriages, many of them were of small means, and few of them had established homes. Their wives for the most part lived with their own families or 'followed the drum', living in lodgings or rented accommodation; many of them were serving themselves in one of the Women's Services. When the time came for them to have their babies, their husbands might be abroad or at sea, and some of them were already widows.

At Fulmer Chase in Buckinghamshire, and at the post-natal establishment soon established nearby, these young women could be well and kindly cared for, which was good also for their husbands' peace of mind.[18]

More demanding and public than either of those good works was the Aid to Russia Fund started in October 1941, known also as the months went by as the Red Cross Aid to Russia Fund and, because she broadcast and appeared in public on its behalf, Mrs Churchill's Fund. It was of course convenient for the government that the cause of Russia should become popular in Britain, but in fact it needed no official promptings to do so; the whole of the political Left was enthusiastic about it, and the hardships and endeavours of the Russian people, well publicised by Soviet propaganda, elicited generous sympathy in all classes. The fund that Clementine headed raised over six million pounds by the time the war ended and spent it on such medical supplies as the Soviet Red Cross requested. It was an unhappy irony that her six weeks' visit to Russia and the 'Order of the Red Banner of Labour' which rewarded her labours in the late spring of 1945, coincided with her husband's ever-growing anxieties about the shape of things to come in the huge areas of Europe that Stalin's armies had liberated.

Randolph, twenty-eight when the war began, had a more fulfilling and certainly a more useful time in the war than in any of the rest of his tumultuous life. His relations with his parents were never easy. Although he and his father were in some way truly fond of each other and shared many interests (not least brandy), and although as a practising journalist and aspirant politician he enthusiastically supported his father's policies, the two of them could rarely be long together before they were having a row, making it up and then having a row again. Adjectives often used in description of him were 'quarrelsome' and 'explosive'. Randolph was in the war from the start, an officer in his father's old regiment, the 4th Hussars. It was not surprising that a man of his temperament and parentage should have sought adventure and excitement. He got into one of the early commandos and in 1940 went with it to the Middle East but was kept on the Staff when he got there and made a press liaison officer.[19] He then found a place in the earliest version of the Special Air Service and, along with Fitzroy Maclean, took part in a very dashing raid on Benghazi before suffering a back injury when the SAS's founder David Stirling crashed their car.[20]

Fit for service again by October 1942, his next fifteen months were divided between military service with the Commandos in North Africa, Sicily and Italy, and family service with his father on his trips to

Casablanca and Turkey in early 1943 and to Teheran for the first Big Three summit meeting at the end of the year. Then began a series of adventures quite as dashing in their very different ways as any his father had experienced in India and Africa. Fitzroy Maclean, who had taken a liking to him in the desert and cleverly reckoned that his explosive and emotional style would go down well with Serbs and Croats, engaged him for service in liaison with Tito's partisans. Maclean judged aright. Randolph was there through most of 1944, enduring much hardship, including an aeroplane crash; his service with Tito, of whom he became an extravagant admirer, only ended when he went to Athens in February 1945 to be with his father on the circuitous way home from Yalta.

Mary was still only seventeen when the war began. For the first nine months of it she therefore lived with her parents in Admiralty House, Whitehall, filling some of her time with voluntary work for the British Red Cross. With the onset of the Blitz she was sent to live at Chequers, from which base (her parents only appearing at weekends) she became a full-time worker with the Women's Voluntary Service of Aylesbury. In September 1941, without any parental pushing and indeed hoping against hope to remain incognito, she joined the ATS, the army's Auxiliary Territorial Service. After basic training at Aldermaston and technical training at Park Hall Camp near Oswestry, she served in anti-aircraft batteries. This work was as controversial as it was exciting. General Frederick Pile, the commander of Britain's anti-aircraft defences, had persuaded Churchill that much of the technical work, the management of the searchlights, the radar and the rest of the targeting instrumentation, could be done by women – everything, in fact, except the actual firing of the guns, which it was not thought proper for anyone but a man. Mary duly became actively engaged in the defence of London, mostly with a battery in Hyde Park, rose through the ranks to become a captain – and in 1945 went with her battery in the wake of the Allied armies first to Brussels and then on to Hamburg, only being 'demobbed' (demobilised) in the spring of 1946. She must have been one of the first Allied servicewomen to see Belsen.

Of the three daughters, Diana, the eldest, was the least able to devote herself entirely to the war. She was married (to the young Conservative politician Duncan Sandys) and already had a child. None of that stopped her signing on as an air raid warden or doing office work in the

Admiralty. The latter service, however, had to end when another baby was on the way; the remainder of her war was entirely domestic, caring for her children and for her husband during his long recovery from a serious accident.

Sarah continued her stage career through the first two years of the war. The entertainment business was valued for its effect on morale both civilian and military and she could have stayed in it for the rest of the war, had she chosen to do so. In 1941 she chose otherwise. Impelled to some degree by the unhappiness of her situation in a failing marriage, she decided to go into the WAAF, the Women's Auxiliary Air Force. The rapid acceptance of Mrs Oliver (her name until the divorce was finalised in 1945) was facilitated by her loving father, but she quickly proved her worth by becoming skilled in the eye-straining, patience-testing work of photographic interpretation: wringing meaning out of the aerial photographs taken whenever weather permitted all over Europe, sources of invaluable information about what was happening 'on the other side of the hill'. They would work twelve-hour shifts, then have thirty-six hours to recover – with eye-tests every eight weeks. Medmenham, near Henley-on-Thames, was the work's headquarters. She was able sometimes to be with the parents at weekends, sometimes making the trip by motorbike.[21] From this routine her only major reliefs were when, like Mary, she served as a sort of aide-de-camp to her father on his more extensive overseas trips.

Sarah was the daughter with Churchill on the longest of his overseas excursions, the one that began under his usual cover of 'Colonel Warden' in mid-November 1943, went as far as Teheran, ended with his return to London on 18 January 1944, and included his worst illness of the war. He had been more or less unwell since, slightly feverish after the usual inoculations, he had left London in mid-November; and as usual he had taken no care of himself. His physician had hoped that the few days on HMS *Renown* would serve as a rest cure, but he played cards with Randolph when he wasn't working and on the first night stayed up till five a.m. At Malta, Moran recorded, Churchill was 'still mouldy ... he will not take any precautions but expects me, when summoned, to appear with a magic cure'. He arrived at Teheran with laryngitis – the result, Sarah told her mother, of talking too much and too late the night before leaving Cairo and then missing his afternoon nap. Stalin was already there and her father wanted to start work straightaway. 'However, Moran and I went into action, got our heads bitten off; but finally, luckily, no meeting and he had dinner in bed like a sulky little boy and was really very good.'[22]

Churchill managed to keep going (not without a good deal of private bad temper and gloom) through the Teheran conference but, as they voyaged home via Cairo, Moran was convinced that his feisty charge was sickening for something. Churchill himself sensed it, and allowed Moran to cancel the planned visit to Alexander's Italian HQ, substituting a visit to Eisenhower's quieter and warmer HQ at Carthage, not far south of Tunis. On arrival there, the doctor's fears were proved correct; it looked like pneumonia. Moran's responsibilities were fearsome: 'we have nothing here in this God-forsaken spot – no nurses, no milk, not even a chemist'. He sent to Cairo for a pathologist and nurses. On 14 December the diagnosis of pneumonia was confirmed, Clementine (under the pseudonym of 'Mrs Warden') and chest specialists were summoned from London, and the Deputy Prime Minister was sent a draft bulletin to make public the news that could not have been kept secret much longer (though Churchill's location of course remained a mystery). While he was really ill, with fibrillations of the heart as well as pneumonia, he was a good patient, 'consenting not to smoke and to drink only weak whisky and soda'. Sarah helped to keep him quiet by reading him *Pride and Prejudice*. As he emerged from the crisis, his normal wilfulness and impatience reasserted themselves; the doctors, backed of course by wife and daughter, had much difficulty in persuading him that he was still at risk.[23] Minimal bulletins were issued daily. For instance, on 21 December, 'The Prime Minister continues to improve. The condition of the circulation is more satisfactory. The PM sat by his bed for an hour today.' That gave absolutely no idea of the activity he was generating and how he was behaving. A truthful bulletin for 25 December would have read strangely. Harold Macmillan, Minister Resident at Allied Headquarters in North-West Africa, was present for most of the day. Churchill began his Christmas with a two-hour conference with General Eisenhower and other military chieftains in his bedroom. He then emerged for lunch 'in a padded silk Chinese dressing-gown decorated with blue and gold dragons – a most extraordinary sight ... rather like a figure in a Russian ballet'. Lunch ended nearer four than three. Churchill dictated minutes and telegrams until retiring for a sleep at about half-past five. He woke to have dinner in bed, then reappeared to join the Guardsmen's party going on below and only finally retired about eleven. Macmillan's thoughts at the end of the day echoed those of most of Churchill's close companions: 'He really is a remarkable man. Although he can be so tiresome and pig-headed, there is no one like him. His devotion to work and duty is quite extraordinary.'[24]

Within a week his minders had persuaded him not to try to return to Britain but to convalesce for a while at the villa in Marrakesh where he had stayed after the Casablanca conference a year before. Diverted by the arrival of Beaverbrook and the Duff Coopers, he gradually recovered strength, did some sightseeing and even took up his brushes and paints again – the only painting he did during the entire war. He also took advantage of the unusual circumstances to 'grip' (one of his favourite verbs) the planning of the risky amphibious operation to land a force at Anzio, just south of Rome, hoping thereby to expedite the capture of the Italian capital: Operation Shingle, 'the equivocal offspring of an insistent Churchill, a compliant Alexander and an ambitious Clark, with Eisenhower playing midwife'.[25] Moran had only once before had to call in any other doctor, and that was in February 1943 when Churchill, soon after returning from North Africa, developed 'a patch on the lung' that slowed him down for a week but required no issue of medical bulletins.

Nor was anything publicly admitted about Churchill's first minor heart attack, when he was in the White House just after Christmas 1941. That was a tricky moment for his doctor. Moran describes how, while his stethoscope was telling him of the great man's 'coronary insufficiency', he did 'some quick thinking ... The textbook treatment for this is at least six weeks in bed. That would mean publicising to the world – and the American newspapers would see to this – that the PM was an invalid with a crippled heart and a doubtful future.' If he kept quiet about it and Churchill died, he would be drummed out of his profession. If he went public, the effect on Britain and the American alliance would be disastrous. He took a brave decision. 'Right or wrong, it seemed plain that I must sit tight on what had happened, whatever the consequences.'[26] After this, it was no wonder that the doctor devoted the rest of the war, not to mention much of the period of un-expected Churchillian activity that followed, to keeping a close eye on his precious charge and, incidentally, recording in intimate close-up the great man's conversation and behaviour with very much the same admiration and honesty as James Boswell recorded Dr Johnson's.[27]

Moran illuminates better than anyone else in the entourage the strains and annoyances Churchill was actually under, and how he coped with them. If he suffered at all from depression as clinically identifiable, as distinct from the depressions brought on by wartime disasters and disappointments, they certainly never prevented him from doing whatever he wanted to do.[28] Sleep was no problem because he usually took barbiturate sleeping pills, casually referred to as 'reds'. Apart from weak whisky and sodas at breakfast and after, he didn't drink much in private, perhaps because he drank all he needed at the main meals and during the long post-prandial sessions that always followed dinner. If Moran ever put anything in his diary about Churchill's consumption of alcohol, which one might have expected, he didn't print it.[29]

Churchill's defensive crack about his drinking, that he had 'taken more out of alcohol than alcohol had taken out of him', seems to sum it up. It amused him to make jokes about abstainers and to claim that drink was good for him; which, indeed, it might have been. Drink never interfered with his conduct of really weighty business, but it could make him more rambling than usual in committees and it could lead him to say things in late night company that he would not have said earlier in daytime; that was perhaps one of the causes of Eleanor Roosevelt's reservations about him.

His head for drink was actually an advantage in dealing with the Russians. Any meals with them included ritual toasts in vodka. The abstemious Brooke was hard put to it on such occasions. With his boss in Moscow on 10 October 1944, he recorded that lunch was

> a complete banquet, starting with masses of hors-d'oeuvres which included caviar; we passed on to sucking pig, then small scallops of mushrooms, followed by fish, then chicken and partridges, and finishing up with ices. We had as usual a series of speeches proposing everybody's health ... and we all had to reply in turn. Finally Stalin himself got up and began a long speech ... Finally Molotov proposed the health of the three great leaders [in champagne] and we had to drain our glasses. Luckily till then I had got off lightly and had only one vodka and one glass of white wine.[30]

They had been at table for three hours but the party was not yet over;

'coffee, brandy, smoke and fruit' awaited them in the next room. To Brooke, all this was tiresome and offensive, 'listening to half-inebriated politicians and diplomats informing each other of their devotion and affection, and expressing sentiments very far from veracity'.[31] For Churchill, such occasions presented no great difficulty. He had been making speeches and keeping at least half-sober through big dinners for more than forty years. These Russian ones were just a bit more demanding than the usual, and did him no harm. The senior official at the Foreign Office, Sir Alexander Cadogan, glad to escape a similar giant feast at Yalta in February 1945, noted with astonishment that 'the PM seems well, though drinking buckets of Caucasian champagne which would undermine the health of any ordinary man'.[32]

Churchill's theory and practice regarding food and drink (and also his attitude towards 'lesser breeds without the law') is neatly summarised in his account of the dinner he hosted on the way home from Yalta for King Ibn Saud of Saudi Arabia. That monarch had travelled 'with an entourage of some fifty persons, including two sons, his Prime Minister, his Astrologer, and flocks of sheep to be killed according to Moslem rites'; amongst those fifty Moran noted His Majesty's Food-Taster and the Chief and Second Servers of Ceremonial Coffee.[33]

> His reception was organised at the Hotel du Lac at Fayoum oasis, from which we had temporarily removed all the residents. A number of social problems arose. I had been told that neither smoking nor alcoholic beverages were allowed in the Royal Presence. As I was the host at luncheon I raised the matter at once, and said to the interpreter that if it was the religion of His Majesty to deprive himself of smoking and alcohol I must point out that my rule of life prescribed as an absolutely sacred rite the smoking cigars and also the drinking of alcohol before, after, and if need be during all meals and in the intervals between them. The king graciously accepted the position. His own cup-bearer from Mecca offered me a glass of water from its sacred well, the most delicious that I had ever tasted.[34]

Did it really happen like that? Yes – though Churchill might have mentioned that the outcome of his diplomatic *démarche* was that each party ate the foods and drank the drinks to which it was accustomed and tolerated the other's practices; which, for the British, meant putting up with sheep being slaughtered nearby and, in one instance, roasted at a fire built on the floor of a bedroom in the hotel. Churchill's companions watched with some anxiety to see what he would do when given the holy water; his personal assistant Commander Thompson observed with relief that 'he managed to give the impression that he really enjoyed it'.[35] Churchill was not embroidering the story to amuse his readers; this was the event and the encounter as it actually happened. He liked to make things happen his way and usually succeeded in doing so. It was in his nature to dominate people who were less than his equal, and his occasional lack of consideration for them was legendary, but he interested, impressed and amused them as well. President Roosevelt being emphatically an equal, Churchill flattered and blandished, but the President was not just responding in kind when he 'cheerfully scrawled' at the end of a lengthy business message at the end of January 1942, 'It is fun to be in the same decade with you'.[36]

Churchill's share of the fun disappeared abruptly when the results of the general election became known on 26 July 1945. Free, until the very last hours, of doubt that his party would be triumphant, and unwilling to believe the few who told him not to be so confident, he had looked forward to returning to Potsdam where the last of the wartime Summit conferences still had work to do. Now it was all over: 393 Labour members returned to Parliament, and only 213 Conservatives. Churchill at once did the proper constitutional thing, tendered his resignation to the King and recommended him to send for Clement Attlee. Stalin, who was amazed that a governing party could lose an election, could scarcely believe his eyes when he saw Attlee and Bevin in the chairs where Churchill and Eden had recently been sitting.

The war was not quite yet over but it very soon would be. Churchill issued a farewell message to the people which included the dark saying that the end 'might come quicker than we have hitherto been entitled to expect'. That was cheering news, and of course it turned out to be true; the war would be over within three weeks. For Winston and Clementine, however, the immediate situation had no cheer at all. For more than five years they had lived in official establishments, with staff and food and transport provided in quantity and quality proportionate to the requirements of a head of government. Suddenly and unexpectedly he was out of a job and they were homeless. What was to become of them?

Chartwell was shuttered and under wraps, as it had been since 1940;

only the little cottage in the grounds was fit to live in. They were in the process of purchasing a house in Kensington, but had been so busy with greater matters that its completion was still weeks away. The considerate Attlees did not wish to hurry them out of Number Ten, but Churchill was too steeped in constitutional proprieties to consider lingering there; besides, writes their daughter with unusual passion, the place had suddenly become 'hateful' to them. They would have had to move into a hotel, had not their eldest daughter Diana and her husband Duncan Sandys offered to let the homeless couple have their flat in Westminster Gardens. While the Sandyses were finding somewhere else to live, Winston divided his time between a penthouse flat at Claridge's Hotel and the Chartwell cottage, and Clementine superintended the removal of all their possessions from Chequers and Number Ten into storage. Her heroic efforts succeeded in bringing order and comfort back to their lives by the beginning of October. Both Chartwell and No. 28 Hyde Park Gate were ready to receive him when he returned to England, a giant refreshed, after a few restorative weeks by Lake Como and on the French Riviera.[37]

To everyone's amazement (and to the disappointment of reformers in his own party), Churchill re-entered public life with as much energy as ever. In the House of Commons he was now Leader of His Majesty's Opposition. To the world at large, he was its most admired and listened to spokesman for democracy and representative government. Invited to receive honours all over Western Europe, he gave much time to promoting the cause of European solidarity (emphatically including Franco-German reconciliation) and became the benevolent godfather of the Council of Europe. Honoured in the United States too, it was there that he gave in March 1946 the 'iron curtain' speech that is a prominent landmark in the onset of the Cold War. He was a world figure in a way he had not been before; and it was of some importance to the world that, in the early 1950s and just as his energies were at last fading, he devoted them to humanity's huge new war problem: the prospect of nuclear war.

12

Atoms for War

What Churchill had in mind when he told the British people that the war might be over sooner than they expected was, of course, the atomic bomb. He had known of its possibility for many years but only very recently had it materialised into reality. It was on 17 July 1945, while he was at Potsdam waiting for the conference to begin, that the American Secretary for Defense Henry Stimson had told him at lunchtime that the previous day's experiment with an atomic bomb in the New Mexico desert had been successful. A first use of the new weapon against Japan was therefore imminent, and Churchill believed it might be decisive.

'The bomb' as everyone was soon calling it, was dropped on Hiroshima on 6 August. Of course Churchill understood that it was a major world-historical event. He had prepared a statement to be released on the occasion of the bomb's first use (a statement his successor was happy to issue on 6 August), giving the British public its first news of what had been secretly brewing over the past four years and concluding with these powerful and apposite words: 'This revelation of the secrets of nature, long mercifully withheld from man, should arouse the most solemn reflections in the mind and conscience of every human being capable of comprehension.'[1] It was an exemplary statement but we have to wonder whether he himself did much solemn reflecting about it until several years later. When at last he did so, the effects would be momentous.

Churchill had given little thought to the bomb through the three years preceding those summer days at Potsdam; so little, indeed, that British interests in its development and prospects were less protected than they might have been. His inattention, however, is understandable. We know with hindsight that the bomb was going to change the world, but only a handful of top-level physicists, mathematicians and engineers understood that possibility, and they had no means of communicating their knowledge to society at large, sealed off as most of them were beneath the anonymity and camouflage of 'Tube Alloys' in Britain and the 'Manhattan Project' in the United States. In any case, Churchill's urgent concern was simply to get the war over as quickly as possible with such weapons as were already to hand or might come to hand; in respect of Germany these weapons proved to be sufficient, and in respect to Japan they very nearly proved to be so. Churchill was not misguided in concentrating on the many mundane matters that daily pressed upon him while the search for the ultimate weapon went on in its own secret way and at its own pace. If such a weapon were to be discovered, and if it were to become available before the war was finished, well and good. But until he had positive knowledge of its birth, he pinned no great hopes on it. He took an interest in the early British work on it but, once the core of its development had moved to the United States, months went by without him having to think about it at all. He intervened in its transatlantic development when the men in charge of its British share sought his backing, but he does not appear to have originated any interventions of his own. It was one of the matters he was content to leave to trusted and capable lieutenants: in this case, his scientific adviser Professor Lindemann and the most trusted administrator in his government (and the only other adviser with any serious scientific knowledge), Sir John Anderson.

Churchill had long been as well aware as other followers of popular science, not to mention science fiction, that in the nuclei of atoms of certain minerals might lie huge explosive forces if only the means of corralling and releasing them could be discovered – a potential which in the opinion of serious scientists lay beyond the limits of reasonable imagination. The Prof had talked with Churchill about this as long ago as the mid 1920s. From those conversations Churchill had drawn material for his sombre 1924 essay 'Shall We All Commit Suicide?', with its rhetorical questions: 'May there not be methods of using explosive energy incomparably more intense than anything heretofore discovered? Might not a bomb no bigger than an orange be found to possess a secret power ... to concentrate the force of a thousand tons of cordite and blast a township at a stroke?'[2] He was nearer the mark than he can then have imagined; the first tentative blueprint for the atomic bomb envisaged at its heart 'a sphere with a radius of less than about three centimetres'.[3]

Atomic science continued to attract his attention and his intelligence. Churchill wrote a long letter to Lindemann early in 1926 about the relations of music and mathematics, enclosing a note on atomic theory and asking his scientific guru if he had got it right.[4] The atomic theme recurred in an article, 'Fifty Years Hence', in the *Strand Magazine* of December 1931; 'nuclear energy', wrote Churchill, could bring huge benefits to mankind but it could also bring calamity: 'explosive forces, energy, materials, machinery will be available upon a scale which can annihilate whole nations'. 'There is no question among scientists that this gigantic source of energy exists. What is lacking is the detonator. The Scientists are looking for this.'[5]

Lindemann, who was slower than some top-line scientists to believe that such a bomb could actually be made, talked with Churchill again at the end of the 1930s, when those limits were beginning significantly to shift. Tantalising possibilities were coming into view in the laboratories of the United States and Britain, of Germany, Denmark and France – in fact, wherever the highest levels of mathematics and physics were cultivated. Nuclear fission had been discovered, and uranium was identified as the material from which, sooner or later and somehow or other, nuclear explosions might be generated. This was the phase when Albert Einstein, the most acclaimed scientist in America but not himself engaged in this line of work, was sufficiently agitated by what his professional friends were telling him to write a letter of warning to President Roosevelt.[6] German scientists who had remained in Germany – all the Jewish ones had left and were currently toiling in the front lines of British and American research – had to be expected to go full-steam ahead with atomic research and development; it was crucially important that the democracies should do no less. Roosevelt listened and took what for the time being seemed sufficient executive action, which in the event did not amount to much. In Britain, however, what Churchill was hearing from the Prof was that although, according to the best current calculations, it indeed appeared that nuclear explosions could probably be produced, the quantities of uranium required, the size and weight of the supporting machinery, and the chances of its being a damp squib rather than a real explosion were all so great that nothing of conceivable military value was to be expected for many years. Churchill's first wartime mention of anything nuclear was, not surprisingly, a note

to the Air Minister explaining that we must not be fooled by German
claims to have invented some new, mysterious and terrible weapon. (In
fact Germany did enter the war with a mysterious and temporarily terrible secret weapon, but its menace came from magnetism: the magnetic
mine that caused Churchill and the Admiralty to wonder for a few anxious weeks in the autumn of 1939 whether the war would be over before
it began.)

Early in 1940 the situation and outlook suddenly changed; a change
which here has to be reported in the simplest terms. Only a tiny proportion of uranium was of promising fissionable nature. The refugee
physicists Rudolf Peierls and Otto Frisch considered what might happen
if that livelier bit, U235, could somehow be winnowed out from the
stolid mass, U238. They hypothesised how that might be done, and came
up with the disturbing conclusion that only a small quantity of uranium
235, processed and detonated in an effective way, would be needed to
produce the gigantic explosion everyone was thinking of.[7] The general
conclusion was that Peierls and Frisch had probably got it right. The scientists already connected with the government had no difficulty in
persuading their Whitehall contacts that this was serious. So far, the
only involvement of any government department had been an attempt
to secure the stock of uranium known to be held in Belgium; a half-
hearted attempt that failed. (The Germans got it instead.) Now in the
spring of 1940 a small subcommittee of the Ministry of Aircraft Production's Committee for the Scientific Survey of Air Warfare was
established, the 'Uranium Committee', known (for reasons too strange
to require explanation here) as the MAUD Committee. Britain's pursuit
of a nuclear weapon had begun.

At this time, and through the following eighteen months, research in
Britain went ahead faster than in the United States, with increasing confidence that in due course – no one thought it could be in less than two
years and some thought it would take five – a nuclear weapon could be
developed. The greater intensity of the British effort at this stage was not
surprising, given that there was not in the United States the same
urgency there was in Britain to crack the problems before Germany did,
as there was every reason to suppose it would. Scientists in British and
American universities and science-based industries continued freely to
exchange information in the internationalist spirit of pre-war days, an

exchange which Churchill expressly encouraged and from which he anticipated great benefits.[8]

By the early summer of 1940 the scientists on the MAUD Committee felt the time was ripe for engaging the interest, and tapping the superior resources, of the government. That meant engaging the support of the Prof, who had so far been among the sceptics. Lindemann being notoriously tricky to approach, the way was cleared by Professor Francis Simon, another of the fine German scientists who had sought safety in Britain in the 1930s and who was one of the 'nuclear community'. Lindemann had made a place for Simon at the Clarendon Laboratory in Oxford, of which, Lindemann being for most of the time absent on Churchill's service, Simon was the acting head. He knew all about the work of the MAUD Committee and arranged for Lindemann to hear the story straight from Rudi Peierls himself. Lindemann listened to the younger man, asked acutely pertinent questions, grunted in his usual noncommittal way – and was converted. The researchers, confident now that they had a friend at court, pressed on devotedly with their work.

The British nuclear bomb project was officially launched in the middle months of 1941. The Cabinet's Scientific Advisory Committee (which had so far known nothing of the MAUD Committee) received and accepted that committee's reports; at the same time, the Prof (who had just become Lord Cherwell), armed with the same reports, judged the time ripe for bringing Churchill behind the project. Churchill at once sought the Chiefs of Staff's opinion, putting before them what his Scientific Adviser had put before him. The minimal terms in which he did so do not suggest great enthusiasm. 'Although personally I am quite content with the existing explosives, I feel we must not stand in the path of improvement, and I therefore think that action should be taken in the sense proposed by Lord Cherwell, and that the Cabinet Minister responsible should be Sir John Anderson.'[9] It is possible that Churchill, anxiously preoccupied with day-to-day events, many of them dispiriting, did not really understand the weight of what was involved. The Chiefs having given their approval, and the War Cabinet having been bypassed (Churchill was determined to keep the whole business very secret), the way was clear for serious investment in trying to manufacture the thing. ICI's bid to undertake it was rejected but ICI's director of research was appointed chief executive and Sir John Anderson became chairman of the elusively-titled 'Directorate of Tube Alloys', vaguely seen to be under the wing of the Department of Scientific and Industrial Research.

British research and preparations were still at this stage in the lead, but the United States was catching up fast and would soon overtake it. President Roosevelt was as keen as Churchill said he was that the two countries, by this time co-belligerents in all but practice and about to become allies in reality, should join forces as equal partners in what by now was recognised to be a project capable of winning or of losing the war. For a variety of reasons, the partnership did not work out quite like that. Churchill himself appears to have done nothing to promote it; and the eager enthusiasm with which he normally replied to Roosevelt's letters was entirely lacking when the President took the initiative in proposing a combined effort.[10]

The patriotic sentiment that moved Churchill may move others to regret that Britain lost its early lead and became more of a junior than an equal partner in the work that culminated at Hiroshima; but those developments were in some ways inevitable. Sir John Anderson saw them coming. In late July 1942 he put it plainly to Churchill that, although the British would like to go it alone (not least because 'a pool of atomic experience' would be useful to have in the country when the war ended), the size of the undertaking was evidently beyond British means. It would be prudent to make terms with the Americans while we still had something to offer.[11] Production of the necessary materials and manufacture of appropriate plant required the investment of very large sums of money and the construction of industrial plant well beyond the means of the British wartime economy, stretched as it was to produce enough conventional weapons to keep the armed forces going. In due course 'Tube Alloys' itself was brought to face this fact; by which time the 'Manhattan Project' was well under way and it was possible for the American scientists and administrators (and the many European refugee scientists working with them) to believe that they could dispense with outside help.

British attempts to collaborate through 1942 and early 1943 met with disappointment. Partly responsible was endemic American neurosis about British hidden agendas and ulterior motives; the employment of ICI's top man as chief executive of the British project, for example, made the American business community suspicious, and in the end he had to go. From the British standpoint, it could look as if a British invention was being turned to uniquely American advantage. There were awkward discussions about the future uses of the many patents that had been registered, most of the early ones British and French. There were security considerations, the American military in the formidable person of General Groves, overall director of the Manhattan Project from September 1942, being properly security-conscious and predictably wary of aliens. For such reasons, and for others less easy to identify, Anglo-American collaboration – which might have been expected to burgeon after the United States's entry into the war – went into the doldrums in 1942. By the beginning of 1943, the latest communication from Washington made it look as if it was dead: killed off by the American partner, and (though neither Churchill nor any other Briton knew this or could have believed it) with the President's assent. Sir John Anderson immediately minuted the Prime Minister: 'This development has come as a bombshell and is quite intolerable. I think you may wish to ask President Roosevelt to go into the matter without delay.'[12]

Churchill, taken aback by this flaw in the Special Relationship, said he would raise it with the President at the Casablanca Summit meeting that was imminent. He is not known to have done so, but he certainly did raise it with the President's right-hand man, Harry Hopkins. Hopkins promised to look into it, but nothing happened. Churchill spoke to Roosevelt about it in Washington in May 1943, and told Anderson that things were looking up, but still nothing happened on the ground. The British continued to find themselves shut out. Churchill by now was considerably worked up and ready to do battle. The opportunity came when Henry Stimson, the Secretary for Defense, and Vannevar Bush, the President's closest scientific adviser, visited London in July. A series of meetings cleared up the misunderstandings that had clouded the partnership through the past eighteen months. In particular, the British had not understood the Americans' apprehension regarding the financial disclosures that would have to be made to Congress when the war was over. The Americans for their part were relieved to discover that the British were not so focused on post-war exploitation of the industrial processes that they were unwilling to disclaim interest in them. Sir John Anderson promptly went to Washington to engage Sir John Dill's help

in 'squaring the American army' (notably General Marshall) and other
possibly hostile figures, while Churchill completed the circle by joining
the President in signing the Quebec Agreement on 19 August 1943.[13]

Upon the terms of this agreement, much was to hang. The principal
terms and the preamble demand quotation in full:

> Whereas it is vital to our common safety in the present War to bring the
> Tube Alloys project to fruition at the earliest moment; and whereas this may
> be more speedily achieved if all available British and American brains and
> resources are pooled; and whereas owing to war conditions it would be an
> improvident use of war resources to duplicate plants on a large scale on both
> sides of the Atlantic and therefore a far greater expense has fallen upon the
> United States: It is agreed between us, *First*, that we will never use this agency
> against each other. *Secondly*, that we will not use it against third parties with-
> out each other's consent. *Thirdly*, that we will not either of us communicate
> any information about Tube Alloys to third parties except by mutual con-
> sent. *Fourthly*, that in view of the heavy burden of production falling upon
> the United States as the result of a wise division of war effort, the British
> Government recognize that any post-war advantages of an industrial or com-
> mercial character shall be dealt with as between the United States and Great
> Britain on terms to be specified by the President of the United States to the
> Prime Minister of Great Britain. The Prime Minister expressly disclaims any
> interest in these industrial and commercial aspects beyond what may be con-
> sidered by the President of the United States to be fair and just and in
> harmony with the economic welfare of the world.[14]

The Quebec Agreement succeeded in banishing the clouds that had
come over the earlier good relations between the two parties. The partnership was re-established, but Britain was from now on the junior
partner, a partner whom Americans of the more nationalistic kind
would later want to get rid of. British and Allied scientists and engineers
who had long been waiting for their chance to participate in the great
work at last got it; and the gigantic Manhattan Project, by far the biggest
industrial enterprise the world had so far seen, majestically, and with a
remarkable degree of secrecy, followed its guiding star, with no certainty
until very near the end that it would actually get anywhere. Meanwhile,
the war went on, no one having any realistic idea as to when it might be
ended until some sadly false hopes were raised in its European theatre
in September 1944. Thought was nevertheless being given by many good

minds to the organisation of the post-war world. What would the
United States and Great Britain respectively do with their nuclear know-
how after the war had ended? To some in Britain it seemed hard that
fear of arousing American suspicions should prevent even modest
preparation for an independent post-war administrative body to take
over and carry forward the British share of the wartime collaborative
work; and no serious American objections were in fact made to the
conception of the experimental establishment at Harwell.

A question of altogether greater moment was whether the United
States's and Britain's plans for the post-war world – plans much more
enthusiastically worked on in Washington than in Westminster – should
include disclosure of the secret of the bomb and sharing it with the
Soviet Union and the rest of the international community. Already in
the spring of 1944 Churchill was being invited, even pressed, to consider
the merits of such a policy by some of the advisers he most respected –
Smuts, Anderson, Cherwell – but his response was disappointing. In this
international field, as in the field of domestic social policy, he simply
would not give much of his mind to what came after victory. More even
than earlier in the war, he found such mental effort a distraction from
the main and very demanding business of the hour, to bring Germany
to surrender. His imagination, which played so fruitfully over many
aspects of international relations, in this respect was sterile. The more
he heard talk of internationalising control of nuclear energy, the more
he insisted that the partners who had, he supposed, unique access to its
secrets should keep those secrets to themselves.

He was very concerned about its secrecy, at home and abroad: an
exact parallel with his relish for the 'Ultra' secret. The Chiefs of Staff
heard no more of the project for four years after giving their general
assent to its preliminary stage in 1940. When Sir Henry Tizard, their
chief adviser on scientific developments, asked to be let into the secret
in mid-1945 he was sent away with a flea in his ear, Churchill unnecessarily observing, 'He surely has lots of things to get on with without
plunging into this exceptionally secret matter'.[15] The Deputy Prime
Minister confessed to having been kept in the dark until he got to
Potsdam. Admiral Lord Mountbatten was only told about it two weeks
before Hiroshima. The point needs no further emphasis. Churchill fan-
tasised that the British and Americans could keep the secret to

themselves, that the Americans would be happy to do so, and that the
Russians would trail years behind. When at Potsdam, with carefully
planned casualness, Truman mentioned the bomb's existence to Stalin,
Churchill took Stalin's casual response to signify ignorance and surprise.

The best hopes of the men who were conscientiously pondering the
control of atomic power after the war lay in the effect that might be
made on Churchill by an encounter with the godfather of the nuclear
community, Niels Bohr. This good and gallant man was smuggled out
of his native Denmark into neutral Sweden from whence he was brought
in an unarmed Mosquito (unconscious from lack of oxygen for most of
the way) to England in October 1943. Two months later he was in America and Los Alamos, learning from his friends and disciples how hopeful
they were of achieving what he had not believed possible. He was equally
fascinated and disturbed: not by the prospect of an atomic weapon in
itself but by the possibility that what could be a source of blessings for
humankind might become a source of curses, intensifying international
suspicions and fanning an arms race to hitherto undreamt of heat.
Better, he argued, to allay suspicions by opening up the secret and
sharing it, under control of an international organisation, with the rest
of the world.

He was found sensible and impressive by every dignitary he talked to
on both sides of the Atlantic – until he came to Churchill. Anderson and
the Prof paved the way for an interview, and the Prof accompanied Bohr
to meet Churchill on 16 May 1944.[16] The Prime Minister was preoccupied with the approach of D-Day and much else besides, and Bohr's
English was slow and discursive, but Churchill's refusal to try to understand the seriousness of what his visitor was saying, and the incivility of
his manner towards his distinguished visitor, was inexcusable. Bohr had
much better luck with Roosevelt, with whom he had a long and encouraging meeting on 26 August. Within three weeks, his hopes were dashed.
Churchill had rebuffed him; Roosevelt now double-crossed him. When
the two leaders met privately at Roosevelt's mansion a few weeks later,
they signed this casually drafted memorandum, known to history as the
Hyde Park Agreement on 19 September 1944.

1. The suggestion that the world should be informed regarding Tube
    Alloys, with a view to an international agreement regarding its

control and use, is not accepted. The matter should continue to be regarded as of the utmost secrecy; but when a 'bomb' is finally available, it might perhaps, after mature consideration, be used against the Japanese, who should be warned that the bombardment will be repeated until they surrender.

2. Full collaboration between the United States and the British Governments in developing Tube Alloys for military and commercial purposes should continue after the defeat of Japan unless and until terminated by joint agreement.

3. Inquiries should be made regarding the activities of Professor Bohr and steps taken to ensure that he is responsible for no leakage of information particularly to the Russians.[17]

The meaning and subsequent history of this memorandum invite comment. Drawn up and initialled on the spot, as a piece of instant diplomacy it anticipated Churchill's 'percentages memorandum' with Stalin, a few weeks later. Its prime purpose was to block Niels Bohr, about whom Churchill had become unreasonably obsessed. (How Roosevelt was persuaded to come round to his view of Bohr is not known.) Its other, better purpose was to cement Britain's long-term interest in the partnership, the precarious tenure of which was apparent to anyone who understood American politics and constitutional procedures. Anderson and Cherwell had both been urging Churchill to try to get a guarantee that Britain would not be sold down the river after the war was over. Churchill presumably supposed that he had succeeded in doing this; whether the President gave the matter much thought is doubtful. Churchill had no means of determining what a successor President might do, and in any case it hardly bore thinking about what Congress would determine when at last it knew of all the things that had been done without telling it, and the purposes to which so much American taxpayers' money had been applied. America's giant Manhattan Project is not mentioned in the agreement, Roosevelt consulted none of his intimates about what he was signing and told none of them what he had signed, and he cared so little about the suitable lodging of the document that it was tucked away by one of his aides in the files concerning naval supplies and even became temporarily lost.[18] That

212 CHURCHILL AND WAR

Germany was not mentioned is easily explained. September 1944 was a month of much optimism that Germany would be defeated before the year was out, and the best estimate for the Manhattan Project's completion was not before the middle of 1945.

What should be done about nuclear power after the war was one question. Whether to use it to bring the war to an end – which everyone who understood its capabilities assumed it had the power to do – was another, about which there was little point in talking until the chances became odds on of the bomb becoming an actuality. That momentous point was reached in April 1945. General Groves told his country's strategic planners of his confidence that the all-important test would take place in July, and they accordingly slotted a first use of the bomb into their schedules for August. Covert debate about the best way to use it and about the propriety of using it at all began within the several American communities that were privy to the secret, but nothing of the kind could happen in Britain because Churchill persisted in keeping the atomic card so close to his chest. The Chiefs of Staff got nowhere when they sought to be brought into the secret in the winter of 1944–45. The Quebec Agreement entitled Britain to consultation about its use. For 'Britain' it might as well have read 'Churchill'. In June 1945, without consulting either the Chiefs or the War Cabinet, he gave to the United States – in effect President Truman, whom he had not yet met – Britain's *carte blanche* to go ahead on its own, simply by initialling a minute instructing the British representatives on the Combined Policy Committee to concur with whatever the Americans decided.[19]

That might have been the end of Churchill's involvement in the matter but, as history turned out, it wasn't. He had an opportunity to intervene at Potsdam, and took it. Anyone who today wishes that the bomb had not been used that summer (and who is not worried by the probability that, if not used then, bigger versions of it would probably have been used with worse consequences not many years later) must note how the Japanese government's wavering endeavours to negotiate a surrender proceeded *pari passu* with the final stages of the Americans' production of the weapon intended to concentrate the Japanese mind. If only the Japanese government had been a bit more decisive, if only there had been last-minute hitches at Los Alamos – and if only the Allies had not been demanding unconditional surrender. That formula was presumed by the Japanese to require the dethronement and possible trial of their Emperor, a dignitary whose sanctity and authority for the Japanese was equivalent to, or greater than, that of the Pope for Roman Catholics. By the time the Potsdam Summit conference began, Tokyo's attempts to negotiate via Moscow were well known to the Allies (through the excellence of their code-breakers) and the question of the Emperor was identified as the principal obstacle in the path of negotiations. Might not the formula of unconditional surrender be relaxed to accommodate this peculiar Japanese sensibility? Churchill, who had experienced the ambivalence of that formula when Italy sought to withdraw from the war in September 1943, was willing to relax it now. In fact he had already thought of it before President Roosevelt's death in April 1945.[20] Roosevelt's successor, Harry Truman, and his delegation came to Potsdam with a draft 'surrender demand' that included it. Urged on now by the British Chiefs of Staff, Churchill put the point to Truman on 18 July and reported his conversation thus to the Cabinet back home:

> I dwelt upon the tremendous cost in American life and, to a smaller extent, in British life which would be involved in forcing 'unconditional surrender' upon the Japanese. It was for him to consider whether this might not be expressed in some other way, so that we got all the essentials for future peace and security, and yet left the Japanese some show of saving their military honour and some assurance of their national existence, after they had complied with all safeguards necessary for the conqueror.[21]

Henry Stimson, the Secretary of Defense, at the same time was putting the same point to the President, but James Byrnes, the Secretary of State, was putting a different one. The American delegation in fact was divided on the issue, and in the end the Potsdam Proclamation issued on 26 July included neither any explicit reference to the question of the Emperor nor any reference to the bomb explicit enough to enable the Japanese to understand what was coming.[22] Having already experienced the total destruction of most of their cities by American bombing, it was impossible for them to understand that 'the utter devastation of the Japanese homeland' and 'complete and utter destruction' signified anything worse. References to 'the unintelligent calculations ... of self-willed militaristic advisers' and to 'war criminals' might as well have been thought threatening to the Emperor as not.[23] Tokyo took no notice, preparations for dropping the only two bombs available went steadily ahead, and the first of them was exploded over Hiroshima on 6 August. Whether there were equally valid arguments for dropping the second one on Nagasaki as soon after the first as the 9th has been much debated. (Churchill is not known to have commented on it.) A defensible opinion is that the use of the first one at any rate was lawful and justified, and that its delayed shock (which took several days to sink in), compounded by dismay at the Soviet Union's entry into the war on the 8th, was what brought the Emperor to require his government and armed forces to accept the Allied terms. Even that took several days. It was the 14th before Clement Attlee was able to tell the British people that the war in the Pacific was at last over.

Churchill was not more excited about the surrender of Japan and the tremendous event that accompanied it – his paragraphs about it in *The Second World War* may fairly be described as perfunctory – only because by this time he was more interested in what effect the bomb would have on Anglo-American relations with Russia. He, of course, was by no means the only person on the Western side to have this in mind; it was only natural that some of those who approved the use of the new weapon against Japan should think also of what impression it would make on the Soviet Union. No one who was hostile to Communism before June 1941 was likely thereafter to do more than sink that hostility for the duration of the war beneath admiration for the Russians' war effort and gratitude at the unexpected acquisition of so mighty an ally. Churchill sank his hostility with heroic determination, but he had more reason than most to remain aware of the awkward and menacing aspects of the giant he had embraced. His relations with Stalin and Molotov, like British relations with Soviet officialdom in general (not that they amounted to much), were rich in disappointing experiences of rudeness, ingratitude and distrust.

Churchill, who never entirely resolved the ambivalence of his feelings about Stalin, swallowed his pride and for long put up with those rebuffs in the interests of the common cause. By the summer of 1944, however, Stalin was giving him and the Western allies weightier things to worry about. It was becoming obvious that Stalin's plans for the nations of Eastern Europe, which his armies were well on the way to liberating, would not be like those that Britain and the United States had in mind for the West. This was going to happen whether Britain and America liked it or not, and the 'percentages' agreement Churchill made with Stalin in November 1944 about post-war spheres of influence in Eastern and South-Eastern Europe was a sensible attempt to salvage something from the inevitable.[24] Poland, however, was not on that list, because it was already the subject of insoluble differences. As autumn passed into winter and winter into spring, and the Russian armies continued to press forward, Central as well as Eastern Europe, including Prague, Budapest, Vienna and, above all, Berlin, seemed likely to fall into Soviet hands. Churchill suffered the pain of seeing his war of liberation turning, for all but Western Europeans, into no more than a transfer from one tyranny to another. Hence the title and theme, and relative lacklustre, of the closing volume of his memoir-history of the war: *Triumph and Tragedy*.

Churchill's main interest in the bomb (which he always referred to, and presumably conceptualised, as 'the new explosive') therefore was that it might 'make the Russians more humble'. Sir Alan Brooke reported with distaste Churchill's excitement about it.[25] The Chiefs of Staff joined him for lunch at Potsdam on 23 July and found him, in Brooke's words, 'completely carried away ... We now had something in our hands which would redress the balance with the Russians! The secret of this explosive, and the power to use it, would completely alter the diplomatic equilibrium which was adrift since the defeat of Germany. Now we had a new value which redressed our position (pushing his chin out and scowling), now we could say if you insist on doing this or that, well we can just blot out Moscow, then Stalingrad, then Kiev, [etc etc] And now where are the Russians!!!'[26]

There being no cause to doubt the truthfulness of Brooke's account, we have to admit that this was rash and dangerous talk, disclosing the negative side of that ambivalence towards Stalin which surprised and bothered Churchill's close companions. But it turned out to be mere sound and fury. Three days later, Churchill was out of office and the question of the post-war use of the bomb was in other hands. We cannot tell whether this initial mood of intoxication would have lasted or what might have come of it had he remained in office. We can be sure that the Chiefs of Staff would have enforced prudence (as Brooke says he himself did on that occasion). If Churchill *had* been returned to office, would he have had any more influence on President Truman than latterly he had had on President Roosevelt? Truman was as astonished as everyone else – or appeared to be – by what Churchill said after he, Truman, introduced him to the awestruck throng at Westminster College at Fulton, Missouri, on 5 March 1946.[27]

'From Stettin in the Baltic to Trieste in the Adriatic, an iron curtain has descended across the Continent.' That 'iron curtain' has since then figured in every book, speech and essay about the world after the war; the heart of Churchill's oration was to warn the non-Communist world about the danger it was facing and to suggest the need for a steadfast response. Stalin and the world-wide Communist movement denounced Churchill for fomenting distrust between the wartime allies; in fact, for causing or at any rate making more likely the Cold War that had unmistakably begun by the second half of 1948. Once that had happened, it was obvious to every non-Communist that Churchill had done no more than foretold the future; but in March 1946, his message did not go down so well. It was a message about the fragility of peace and a call to shed optimistic illusions that not many wished to hear.

> From what I have seen of our Russian friends and Allies during the war, I am convinced that there is nothing they admire so much as strength, and there is nothing for which they have less respect than for weakness, especially military weakness ... If the Western Democracies stand together in strict adherence to the principles of the United Nations Charter, their influence for furthering those principles will be immense and no one is likely to molest them. If, however, ...

He spoke with cautious optimism about the United Nations and urged the formation of the 'international armed force' (anticipated in articles 46–48 of its charter) as a first step towards its empowerment. But when he came to the bomb, he was not so trusting. The secret of it, he argued, was best left with the three states that (so he thought) had it: the USA, Britain and Canada, and not confided to the UN until it 'truly embodied and expressed the essential brotherhood of man'.[28]

Churchill thought much more about the bomb after the war, when it had become a reality, than he had done during the war itself, when it was still only a dream. He continued intermittently to harp on the use that could be made of the bomb in dealings with the Soviet Union. His general supposition was that the Russians would in the last resort back down when credibly threatened with its use, but it is impossible not to believe that if they had not done so and the Americans *had* used it to enforce their will – as for example when affronted by the blockade of Berlin in 1948 – Churchill would have approved.[29]

Churchill had kept almost everyone else in the dark about the bomb while he was in charge. Now he was kept in the dark while Clement Attlee was in charge. Party politics had resumed, Churchill's job as Leader of the Opposition was to attack the government, and there was no state of national emergency to make it desirable for the party leaders to sink differences and exchange confidences. Churchill seems to have assumed that Britain would in any event acquire the bomb, either making it itself or being provided with it (or with the means to make it) by its big brother across the Atlantic.[30]

This picture, of an equal atomic partnership between Britain and America and a shared responsibility to use the atomic power for the general good, remained in Churchill's head throughout the next five years, and was totally fictitious. He rejoiced to believe that Britain lay safe under the protection of American atomic power and assumed that, if Britain had not yet made a bomb but urgently needed to possess one, the Americans would provide it. Through no fault of his own (other than his self-delusion about the working of the Special Relationship), he became detached from the realities of the relationship as it developed through those years. He seems not to have known what decisions (if any) the Labour government took in respect of atomic energy and presumably thought it right that the matter remained top secret. There is no published evidence that he showed any detective curiosity about the matter, such as he had shown in respect of rearmament in the later 1930s. He knew, at least from the Minister of Defence's minimal admission to the Commons on 12 May 1948, that 'adequate progress' was being made towards the acquisition of atomic weapons. He would have supposed that Britain was being given all the help to which it was entitled under his agreements with President Roosevelt. The subjective causes of his insouciance were his naive trust in American good faith and his surprising ignorance of American political processes.[31] If he had known what was happening to the Anglo-American atomic partnership created (as Churchill supposed) at the Quebec Summit in August 1943, and sealed by himself and the President at Hyde Park a year later, he would have been very troubled indeed. For the truth is that by 1949 the Americans had unilaterally dismantled it.

In most other departments of Anglo-American diplomatic and military relations the spirit of the wartime alliance gradually revived, but not in the atomic one. No longer even a junior partner, Britain was left to go it alone.[32] The essence of what happened is that some Americans, including Truman's first Secretary of State, James F. Byrnes, the administration's chief scientific adviser, Vannevar Bush, and dominant senators such as Vandenberg and Hickenlooper, plainly sought to remove Britain from the partnership. Other Americans, including President Truman and his Secretary of State from 1947, Dean Acheson, who would have liked to have been more friendly, found that circumstances forbade them from being so. In the international field, the United States could not conveniently exploit its dominant position in atomic statesmanship so long as it had its war-wasted poor relation Britain in tow. Domestically, the privy agreements initialled by the wartime leaders on their happy pinnacles would merely infuriate hard-nosed members of Congress, should they find out about them. It needed no knowledge of them to encourage Congress, concerned at first with the *industrial* uses of atomic power, as early as the summer of 1946 to pass the McMahon Act forbidding the exchange of atomic information between the United States and any other nation (which of course involved *military* uses as well, and included Britain too). And as the chill of the Cold War fell upon the policy-makers, security and suspicion became again the order of the day.

It was not until the end of November 1950 that Churchill was brought to realise that the partnership agreements he had made with President Roosevelt, plus the agreements Clement Attlee had made with President Truman in November 1945, before Truman himself had become aware of all the complications and been got hold of by the America First men, had crumbled into dust.[33] The occasion of Churchill's enlightenment was Attlee's rushed visit to Washington following Truman's announcement on 30 November 1950, just after the war in Korea had taken a very alarming turn, that he would if necessary authorise the use of the bomb. Alarm, for different reasons, was felt just as much in London. If it were to be used against the Chinese, and if the Russians (presumed to be backing China's intervention) were to take action on China's behalf, what would be the situation of Britain as the ally of the United States and as the base since 1948 of several squadrons of American B–29 bombers (nuclear-armed, for all that the British government knew) and a target ready-made for Russian counter-attack? On 3 December, just before he left, Attlee sent 'My dear Churchill' a 'Top Secret' letter explaining what had happened to the wartime agreements. He expressed his belief – it could be no more – that the United States, now formally free to do with its nuclear weapons what it willed, would nevertheless show some regard for its ally's feelings.[34]

Churchill was so put out by this news, which the Prof confirmed to him, that a couple of months later he took the extraordinary step of writing directly and personally to President Truman, emphasising the point about the American bases and requesting the publication of the 1944 agreement as a right and proper way to assure the British public that their national interests had not been disregarded.[35] Truman's hand-written response put an end to that idea: 'I hope you won't press me in this matter. It will cause unfortunate repercussions both here and in your country, as well as embarrassment to me and to your government.'[36] Churchill and Britain were learning, the hard way, that being one President's very good friend could turn into becoming another President's poodle.

13

Atoms for Peace

Churchill became Prime Minister again at the beginning of November 1951. He had hoped to return to Number Ten after the close-fought General Election in February the previous year, but the Labour Party had squeezed back to power with an overall majority of eight. Now, nearly two years later, the Conservatives' overall majority was not much larger: only seventeen, with the embarrassing knowledge (embarrassing, anyway, to democrats who pondered upon it) that more voters had voted for their opponents than had voted for them – a quirk of the British 'first past the post' electoral system. Churchill of course was not in the least embarrassed, nor did he pay any attention to those who said that at seventy-seven he was too old for the job. He proceeded to compose a Cabinet mainly of moderate Conservatives and wartime trusties, among them two of his favourite generals: Harold (now Lord) Alexander and Hastings (now Lord) Ismay, neither of them used to politics and the former ill-suited to it.

The election had been enlivened and embittered in its later stages by his opponents' charge that Churchill was a 'warmonger'; a charge all the more upsetting to him inasmuch as he had for some months been in process of becoming, in his Cold War utterances, something of a 'peacemonger'.[1] The proximate ground for this charge – in itself, of course, something the Left had tended to believe for more than forty years – was not anything he had said about the bomb but his indignant criticism of Labour's failure to meet the Persian government's nationalisation of the Anglo-Iranian Oil Company's installations at Ibadan more forcefully. The *Daily Mirror* angered him with its headline: 'Whose finger do you want upon the trigger, Attlee's or Churchill's?' 'I am sure we do not want any fingers upon any trigger', he retorted. 'Least of all do we want a fumbling finger.' Then he turned to the larger issue: 'I do not believe that a Third World War is inevitable. I even think that the danger of it is less than it was before the immense rearmament of the United States. But I must now tell you that in any case it will not be a British finger that will pull the trigger of a Third World War. It may be a Russian finger or an American finger or a United Nations Organization finger, but it cannot be a British finger.'[2]

It was clear from what came next that it could not be a British finger because, at present, 'Our influence in the world is not what it was in bygone days'; but, even if British influence were again to be mighty, 'I am sure it would be used as it always has been used to the utmost to prevent a life-and-death struggle between the great powers'. The historical truth of that judgement was questionable but the important thing was that Churchill's mind had for some months been taking two significant turns: away from the bomb as a usable weapon to the bomb as a non-usable deterrent, and away from Cold War rhetoric towards co-existent summitry.

A tantalising obscurity hangs over both the timing of his mental shift and what meanings he attached to the words that mapped it. What is clear, at least, is that by the end of the 1940s words like 'showdown' had disappeared from the vocabulary he had been using about the Soviet Union since 1944, to be replaced by the words 'deterrent' and 'co-existence'. No longer considering the use of the bomb desirable, indeed now considering it unthinkable, his mind had turned instead to the avoidance of war. Here he was enmeshed in the same conundrum as everyone in the atomic era who similarly sought to escape from the logic of war by embracing the paradoxes of deterrence. How could the threat of the bomb be relied on to deter a prospective attacker unless its possessor was really prepared to use it if the attacker refused to be deterred? We cannot tell whether Churchill, as the earliest prominent political apostle of deterrence, would at such a terrible juncture have allowed the use of the bomb or not. We can only say that, if his mind never resolved the dilemma, he was in good company.[3] Plenty of others who followed him in preaching deterrence as the likeliest way to prevent the Cold War becoming a hot one were just as unable to be confident that it would succeed. They could only believe that it would and, if they were in positions of power, pursue policies calculated to move along the road towards that desired end. (The Cold War having ended without a nuclear conflict, the reasonable presumption is that those who did believe so were justified.)

Churchill's last contribution to world history and last major act of statesmanship was to raise his standard at the start of that road. Old men generally are supposed to become more conservative and rigid in their thinking. Churchill in his old age became less conservative and more flexible. He was less furiously imperialistic than he had been, accepting the facts of an independent India and an Egypt outside British control; he managed civilly to socialise with Pandit Nehru and even, once, with Eamon De Valera. He admitted to his physician and confidant Charles Wilson, Lord Moran, that he had been wrong – at least, not wholly right – about India, and that in the course of his long life he had 'made many mistakes'. He now preferred moderate Conservatives to hard-liners and he would have liked, when he formed his Cabinet, to leaven it with a few Liberals. He could not shed his emotional attachments to the United States and the Commonwealth (as what was left of the Empire was now known), but his forceful promotion in the later 1940s of the Council of Europe and the ideal of European Community – in both cases including the reconciliation of France with Germany – were astonishing intellectual ventures for so veteran a statesman. And although with regard to the United States he was wedded to the wartime vision of Special Relationship, his ideas about policy to be adopted towards Moscow came to differ markedly from those prevailing in Washington. In the later 1940s, he had sometimes sounded like a hawk compared with the President. In the early 1950s, he more often sounded like a dove.

Although we cannot determine the timing of his change of mind concerning the bomb, we can identify the external events that caused it to move. The first of these was the establishment of several American B–29 bomber bases in Britain in 1948–49. The occasion of their first arrival in East Anglia was the 'Berlin blockade', and its politico-military significance was obvious: eastern Europe and western Russia were brought within range of America's heaviest bombers which, for all that the Russians knew, could carry atomic cargoes.[4] Their presence, welcomed by the British government (no more than a ministerial sub-committee and the Chiefs of Staff seem to have been involved) as a signal strengthening of the Anglo-American military capability, was at first thought of as temporary; an unusual measure to meet an unusual challenge. In 1949, however, when the United States requested the use of bases in Oxfordshire and was given them, the arrangement looked as if it were becoming permanent. Britain was on the way to becoming America's aircraft-carrier, conveniently anchored off the European coast.

It began to occur to the government – and no doubt also to Churchill, observing from without – that this situation had negative as well as positive aspects. From the high diplomatic point of view, it invited reference to Churchill's wartime agreement with Roosevelt and their joint undertaking that the bomb would not be used without the concurrence of both parties. But what did the Special Relationship amount to now that the war was over? The fact that America had welshed on that agreement might not have mattered so much if it were a case of America's using the bomb in a cause that did not involve British interests or in a place of no British concern; a case that was just imaginable. It would, however, matter very much indeed if it were a case of American use of the bomb from British bases in a cause *not* agreed by Britain – a case not unimaginable, especially while the British Chiefs of Staff remained uninformed about American war plans. Confidential negotiations and private talks over many months in London and Washington found no way round the American insistence that United States armed forces anywhere in the world were bound to obey their Commander-in-Chief the President's orders to do whatever he judged necessary for his country's defence, whenever he so judged it. London could get no more from Washington about this matter than that, as allies, the Americans would try to consult. Britain would have to rely on American good faith.[5] The only points that were clear and acknowledged on both sides were that the American bombers were in Britain by British invitation, and that if ever Britain asked for them to be removed, removed they would have to be.[6]

The other negative aspect of the American bases was more practical and, from later 1949, disturbing. In the event of armed conflict between the West and the Soviet Empire, those bases made Britain an inviting and obvious target for Russian attack. It did not escape the notice of minds already sensitive to imbalances in the Anglo-American partnership that, while Britain could probably be bombed from Russian bases with conventional bombs and ballistic missiles, the United States could not. An aircraft carrier in the front line could expect no less. As of early 1949, the Soviet Union in fact had no great bomber force and atomic-armed rockets were still unthinkable.[7] But what if – or rather, what *when* – the Soviet Union should acquire a bomb of its own, and match the Americans in the development of ballistic missiles with atomic warheads?

Churchill understood after Hiroshima, as did every other intelligent Briton and American, that the Russians would set about acquiring an atomic bomb of their own. Estimates of how long they would take to do so varied in proportion with appraisals of Russian scientific expertise and guesses as to how many 'Western' secrets had been given away by spies. The four years that actually intervened between America's first test explosion in July 1945 and Russia's in August 1949 fell between the more pessimistic and the more optimistic estimates; the Joint Intelligence Committee's estimate had been for early 1951. Now that it had happened, Western strategy had to be reconsidered. Tough talk about using the bomb before the Russians got it was still just possible, for it would take time for them to build up stocks and means of delivery; but now, in all strategic essentials, the landscape was radically altered. So far as Britain was concerned – Britain, still without a bomb of its own and host to all those bomb-carrying B–29s – the prospect was not of being bombed in the way it had been during the Second World War (though no doubt worse) but in the entirely new way prefigured at Hiroshima and Nagasaki (and quite certainly worse).

It seems to have been in the course of the year 1950 that Churchill's mind made the decisive turn from assuming the inevitability of war to attempting to avoid it and, more than that, believing that it could be avoided. National self-interest was not the whole of his motivation but it was certainly one of the factors. Britain could not for much longer consider itself safely sheltered behind American atomic supremacy. The American air bases were much on his mind; so was the Russian bomb; and so also was his own country's failure – so far as he and everyone else outside the atomic research establishments' tight security could tell – to acquire a bomb of its own. Ignorant of the way that the wartime atomic agreements had been ditched by the United States (even after Attlee's careful explanation, it never suited him to take that in), and supposing that collaboration had continued between the two governments and their atomic establishments, he repeatedly expressed surprise and regret at Britain's apparent backwardness.

This became so notable a theme of his speeches in 1950 that it gave his political opponents another pretext for calling him a 'warmonger'. So little was warmongering in his mind that he felt obliged to issue a formal denial: 'Mr Churchill wishes to make it clear that he has never urged, nor does he now advise, the large scale manufacture of the atomic bomb in this country, which our danger from air attack renders specially unsuitable.'[8] Taking it for granted that the United States would make up the deficit, he opined that production of a 'prototype' would do, presumably for the same reason that had decided the Labour government (meaning the Prime Minister, the Foreign Secretary and the Chiefs of Staff) to go for a British bomb in the first place: to assert Britain's title to be regarded still, in the face of all appearances, as a 'Great Power'. Churchill's own government, when it took office at the end of October 1951, unhesitatingly took over the project, as he told the House in its first Defence debate on 6 December. He included a grudging acknowledgement that his suspicion of Labour's lack of zeal in this respect had been unjustified. 'We found that a great deal of work had been done, not only in making the crucial materials required for making atomic bombs, but in preparing to manufacture these weapons. I think the House ought to know about that. Considerable if slow progress has been made.' Progress continued to be made. The first British test of an atomic device was successfully conducted on 3 October 1952 and the Atomic Weapons Research Establishment at Aldermaston delivered the first production model atomic bomb to the RAF just over a year later. (The RAF, however, had as yet no bomber able to deliver it.)[9]

As to the purpose of possessing atomic bombs and the capacity to deliver them, Churchill was now repeatedly using the work 'deterrent'. He sought to prevent war, not to make it practicable. The same principle underlay his approval of the formation in 1949 of NATO and the attempt in the early 1950s to construct a West European defence force. Conventional forces remained indispensable to a credible defensive posture, familiar forces for use in the familiar style; fear of massive drops of Russian paratroops even caused him to resurrect, not very successfully, the Home Guard. But the advent of atomic weaponry had introduced an unfamiliar factor into the military equation Here were weapons which, he was coming to think, were better not used at all. But, paradoxically, they could not be dispensed with, as the early nuclear disarmers were beginning to assert, because of the very nature of international relations. Power, of whatever sort, would assert itself as surely as water finds its own level. No system of supranational organisation had yet been found to alter these facts: the League of Nations had not succeeded in altering them; the United Nations so far was not succeeding. A great preponderance of power in any one state, unless it was to impose itself on all other states, had to be met by an equivalent presence of power among those others. Churchill still held the time-honoured doctrine of the balance of power, but now, instead of accepting that the pressures it was designed to contain must now and then explode into that ultimate 'appeal to arms' which had for centuries been sanctified in European political thought, he believed that the prospect of an exchange of atomic weapons was so terrible, so totally unthinkable, that even the most ideologically opposed of national leaders must hesitate to appeal to it. With 'deterrence' therefore soon was bracketed that other word and concept new in his vocabulary, 'co-existence'.

To the ideological Left, and to everyone whose mind was beginning to turn in the early 1950s in the direction of Nuclear Disarmament (the movement proper is usually dated from 1954), Churchill's position was difficult to understand. Co-existence suggested amity; deterrence implied menace. How could a statesman speak of his desire for improved relations with a foreign country at the same time as he was improving his own country's means of doing damage to that country? For Churchill, the matter was simple. His policy was analogous to that of the homely maxim, 'Strong fences make good neighbours'. It was in the nature of international relations that a powerful state won more respect than an impotent one. It was in the nature of a Communist Great Power to take advantage of its neighbours' weaknesses, but it would be natural for any realistic Great Power to respect its neighbours' strengths. The Soviet Union was a Great Power as well as a Communist one. He had to admit, after his return to office, that his policy towards Russia was to some extent one of appeasement, but, he insisted, it was the good kind of appeasement, appeasement from strength (which might have earlier succeeded against Hitler if Britain had chosen it) and not appeasement from weakness (which had merely encouraged Hitler to carry on). In the realm of realistic politics – a very different thing from the realm of peace propaganda, wherein the Soviet Union and its allies and agents were unmatched – rearmament was not merely compatible with the pursuit of peace, it was inseparable from it. Churchill was in fact pursuing what, when the United States did the same thirty years later, was called 'the twin-track approach' to détente and arms control. That approach was applauded by its admirers as an invention of President Reagan, but it was not. It had been attempted between 1951 and 1955 by Winston Churchill.

It was in the course of the 1950 election battle, at the end of a speech in Edinburgh's Usher Hall on 14 February, that this new direction of his thoughts was revealed. It was a speech in his grandest manner, making plenty of party points but carrying his audience above the party battle to loftier considerations about the state of the world and the prospects for humankind. The bomb, he frankly acknowledged, was a 'frightful weapon'. He was glad it was in responsible American hands, but: 'It is my earnest hope that we may find our way to some more exalted and august foundations for our safety than this grim and sombre balancing power of the bomb.' He recalled the long letter he had sent to Stalin in April 1945, pleading for action to check the looming division of the world into two mutually hostile and suspicious groups of states, and he quoted one of its paragraphs.[10] He did not doubt that Labour's Foreign Secretary Ernest Bevin had done his best to maintain communications with Moscow: 'Still, I cannot help coming back to the idea of another talk with Soviet Russia upon the highest level. The idea appeals to me of a supreme effort to bridge the gulf between the two worlds, so that each can live their life [sic], if not in friendship at least without the hatreds of the cold war ... It is not easy to see how things could get worsened by a parley at the summit if such a thing were possible.'[11]

For so long as Churchill and the Conservatives were in Opposition, 'talks on the highest level' was not something he could himself hope to arrange. He could only continue to say that he thought a Summit meeting might do something to defuse the existing tensions, and hope that someone would take him seriously. But neither Clement Attlee nor Harry Truman was interested; which is to say, that neither the Foreign Office nor the State Department recommended so radical a departure from their established ways of conducting business. The Foreign Secretary denounced Churchill's Edinburgh ideas as 'stunt proposals'; and Churchill was impatient with the Foreign Office's fussiness and complications.[12] Even when he was back in Number Ten, he had to wait until Harry Truman gave way to a President who would, he supposed, be more amenable to his persuasions. His wartime companion Dwight Eisenhower's acceptance of the Republican nomination delighted him, and through the second half of 1952 he looked forward to the coming year as the time when his hopes might be realised.

But 1953, although it brought the death of Stalin (in early March) as well as a new President, turned out to be year of disappointments. President Eisenhower was always considerate towards an old friend of whom he was genuinely fond, but he proved to be even more hostile towards Communism and more unimaginatively suspicious of Russia than his predecessor had been. Churchill found to his bewilderment that he was unable to influence Ike as he had, in the early months of their connection, influenced Roosevelt. Unwilling to believe that his comrade-in-arms had become so rigid and bomb-minded, Churchill at first put it down to the sinister influence of Eisenhower's Secretary of State, John Foster Dulles, but he soon realised that the serious-minded President needed no coaching in wariness of the men in the Kremlin, whether the old gang or the new one.[13] It didn't help Churchill that his Foreign Secretary, Anthony Eden, shared the Americans' reservations. The Foreign Office ethos was hostile in principle to independent ventures and to the isolation of a single issue from the whole cluster of issues that were involved at any one time in the relations of one state with another; Foreign Office and State Department together were just then promoting throughout Western Europe the idea that its states needed to rearm because the Soviet Union was implacably hostile.

Churchill did not, however, allow himself to be discouraged. He was becoming obsessed with the thought that if only he could set up a man-to-man meeting with Malenkov (who for the first months after Stalin's death was most prominent figure in the Kremlin), and if they together could transcend politics to face the global hazards of a continued atomic arms race, their shared human concern *might* (he was not foolishly optimistic) put their countries on the way to a diplomatic breakthrough. It is true but irrelevant that egotism and the seizing of an excuse for not

retiring was one of the mainsprings of this, his 'last hurrah'. He wanted
to go down to history as a man who cared as much about peace as war
– indeed, cared *more* about peace than war, because he had never waged
war for its own sake but always for the sake of a better world to follow
the peace. He would rather have been awarded a Nobel Prize for Peace
than the one for Literature that came his way in 1953. He was absolutely
right about the hazards of the arms race, and he was intelligently
pragmatic about the Soviet Union, reckoning that its people would
covet the same amenities of life as were normal in the West, and that
the enlargement of trade between the two camps would facilitate
co-existence – until the time when the Communist regime would collapse under the weight of its own delusions and debilities. (He gave it
forty years, which was just about correct.)

He gave peace his best shot in a House of Commons speech on 11 May
1953, a speech that enthused the Opposition and the general public as
much as it annoyed the Americans, the Foreign Office and his Cabinet
colleagues, whom he had not taken into his confidence. It was the easier for him to do this because at this very time he was filling in at the
Foreign Office for Eden, who was undergoing extensive surgery. At the
end of a masterly *tour d'horizon*, he turned to the Soviet Union, remarking that there were signs – admittedly, faint ones – of a more biddable
atmosphere in Moscow; 'amicable gestures' which had 'so far taken the
form of leaving off doing things [to us] which we have not been doing
to them'. Then came an astonishing passage:

> It would, I think, be a mistake to assume that nothing can be settled with
> Soviet Russia unless or until everything is settled ... Therefore, I think it
> would be a mistake to try to map things out too much in detail and expect
> that the grave, fundamental issues which divide the Communist and non-
> Communist parts of the world could be settled at a stroke by a single,
> comprehensive agreement ... It would certainly do no harm if, for a while,
> each side looked about for things to do which would be agreeable instead of
> being disagreeable to each other.

He repeated, what he had said so often to Stalin during the war, that
he fully understood Russia's need to feel secure on its western borders;
but, he insisted, such security could be assured without dividing the
world into two hostile camps.

I must make it plain that, in spite of all the uncertainties and confusion in which world affairs are plunged, I believe that a conference at the highest level should take place between the leading Powers without long delay ... confined to the smallest number of Powers and persons possible. It should meet with a measure of informality and a still greater measure of privacy and seclusion. It might be that no hard-faced agreements would be reached, for there might be a general feeling among those gathered together that they might do something better than tear the human race, including themselves, into bits.

I only say that this might happen, and I do not see why anyone should be frightened at having a try for it. If there is not at the summit of the nations the will to win the greatest prize and the greatest honour ever offered to mankind, doom-laden responsibility will fall upon those who now possess the power to decide. At the worst the participants in the meeting would have established more intimate contacts. At the best we might have a generation of peace.

He concluded by reminding the Members on the Opposition benches, who had been listening to these startling passages with the closest attention, that no one was to read into them any intention to run down Britain's defence programme or to loosen the bonds of alliance with 'the free nations'. He had simply sought to 'contribute a few thoughts which may make for peace and help a gentler breeze to blow upon this weary earth'.[14]

The fact was that Churchill had lost his taste for war. He had studied war for sixty years and lived it for fifteen of them, and it had been getting worse all the time. He had never cherished illusions about it. We have repeatedly seen how his excitement about it had never been wholly uncritical. Heartily though he threw himself into those early campaigns when he was, so to speak, seeking his fortune, it hadn't needed much exposure to the grim realities of frontier warfare against warrior tribesmen to make him admit that his profession had a dark side to it. On the other hand, there was a brighter side, to which he readily attached himself. Principles of chivalry and professional self-respect did much to moderate the nastiness of conflicts between civilised belligerents, as did those laws and customs of war which more or less guided the conduct of wars between states that subscribed to them. Gallantry of course he admired wherever he saw it; but he was quick also to applaud displays of chivalry and generosity by enemy fighters, acknowledging such displays not merely as proofs of military virtue but also as testimonies to the common humanity to which belligerents subscribed. Churchill respected the institutions embodying that common humanity, the International Committee of the Red Cross and its Geneva Conventions. He also willingly accepted the restraints on combat imposed by the several Hague Conventions, with the not unreasonable caveat that he didn't see why one side should stick to those rules if its opponents didn't.

The First World War had given him a shock. He had entered it with an enthusiasm that had impressed, even amazed his Cabinet colleagues, and his zeal for its successful prosecution had remained constant throughout its unexpected four and a half years and the disappointments it brought him. He never doubted that it was a war that had to be fought and had to be won. But he could not believe that it was followed by a good peacemaking. The cost to Britain and the other belligerents had been awful and he considered the methods by which it had been fought were more costly than they needed to have been. Worse than that, he observed that it had been made more frightful by two historic developments on neither of which there appeared to be any natural restraint. The first of these was popular involvement. In sharpest distinction from the wars of the eighteenth century about which he knew a great deal, wars conducted by political elites for limited ends, the First World War (like the French Revolutionary Wars and the American Civil War before it) was a people's war, a democratic war, fuelled by the commitment of entire national populations and inflamed by the simplicities and xenophobia of a popular press; good for social mobilisation and self-sacrifice but bad for judicious decision-making and calm diplomacy. We have seen how Churchill was well aware of the handicaps this placed on a wartime Cabinet faced with making 'unpopular' decisions; he partly blamed the same populist frenzy for the failure, after the war was over, to make a reasonable and non-vindictive peace treaty with the vanquished.[15]

The other historic development which made the conduct of war less restrained than it had been and operated by a logic of its own was the 'technological imperative': the applications of science and technology to military purposes and the obligation felt by even the most virtuous military men to avail themselves of the most efficient and effective new weaponry on the market. Again and again throughout history the appearance of such weapons had been met by cries of outrage from military elites and attempts to ban them; again and again such attempts had proved fruitless. What killed quickest, at the longest distance, with the least risk to the killer, would willy-nilly find its way into someone's service; and once someone had it, everyone else would need to have it too. Sometimes these innovations were compatible with the requirements of the laws and customs of war, sometimes not; when they were not, as in the cases of submarine warfare and aerial bombardment, the laws and customs usually made way.

Reviewing the First World War soon after its conclusion, Churchill sagely noted that it 'differed from all ancient wars in the immense power of the combatants and their fearful agencies of destruction, and from all modern wars in the utter ruthlessness with which it was fought'.[16] 'When all was over', he concluded, 'Torture and Cannibalism were the only two expedients that the civilised scientific Christian States had been able to deny themselves; and these were of doubtful utility.'[17]

The Second World War did not produce much obvious cannibalism (some understandably went on in the German camps where Russian prisoners of war were allowed to starve to death), but it did produce torture, carried over from the pre-war practice of all the one-party dictatorships. In most other respects, the Second World War reproduced the horrors of the First in greater quantity and force. The major belligerents now had much greater capabilities of doing damage to their enemies. To this was added the Nazi beliefs, which determined Gemany's conduct on its Eastern Front, that Slavs were inferior people whose lives didn't matter much, and that Jews and Communists were dangerous peoples whose lives mattered not at all.

It was different in the West, where initially neither side wanted to *begin* city bombing and where Hitler hoped to attract nearby neutrals to his cause. Those early and partial aerial restraints (there was little evidence of them in the war at sea) soon yielded to the pressures and temptations of events. The Luftwaffe's bombers turned from terror attacks (Warsaw, Rotterdam and, later, Belgrade) to city bombing ('the Blitz' on London, Coventry, Plymouth and other cities). The RAF girded itself up to respond in the same coin but with compound interest. For Hitler, city bombing was only one and never the most important of his means of damaging Britain. For Churchill, 'the bombing offensive' was the most important of his means of damaging Germany; and immensely damaging it became. By the second half of 1944, when Bomber Command and the USAAF together were dropping enormous weights of bombs on German targets, and Hitler's 'reprisal weapons' were raining explosives on London (and Antwerp), all sense of restraint had vanished from the air war. Churchill never felt entirely at ease about being involved in such a slaughterous exchange, but felt that he had no choice; which, at least until the success of the Normandy landings and the return of Allied armies to the Continent, was understandable.[18]

He wrote no precise reckoning of the awfulnesses of the Second World War as he had of the First, but there was no mistaking his opinion of it, that it marked a new low in the record of humankind and a further proof, as if any was needed, of his melancholy conviction that man's capacity for self-harm was limitless. Where were those 'broad, sunlit uplands' of improved civilisation which he used hopefully to hail in the distance? Not for some years in war-torn Europe and not at all, by his lights, wherever Communism reigned. It is essential not to forget that the theme of the closing volume of his Second World War epic was 'How the Great Democracies Triumphed and so were Able to Resume the Follies which had so Nearly Cost them their Life'.

It took several years for Churchill fully to understand that the bomb might be their ultimate folly. Although he sounded an appropriately solemn warning in the statement released directly after Hiroshima, he seems to have come thereafter – as did many others – to think of it as just another step in the age-old pursuit of more powerful explosives and as a weapon that was, in a no doubt regrettable last resort, usable. What had happened to Hiroshima and Nagasaki was not, after all, so different from what had happened to Hamburg and Berlin, Osaka and Tokyo. He must have heard of 'radiation', but, like most other people, he understood little about it until, like everyone else, he was made aware of the sinister atmospheric fall-out from the American H-bomb tests in the Marshall Islands in the spring of 1954. What he had already come to recognise as a terrible danger to potential belligerents – not least to Britain – was now revealed as a terrible danger to non-belligerents as well; to the whole world, in fact. Churchill felt the urge to devote all his energies to bringing about a Summit meeting at which he would make sure his Soviet counterpart understood the situation. It was unfortunate that this call upon his energies came just when those energies were fast fading.

The year 1953, when Churchill's health really began to fail, was a disappointing year for him. He had hoped for much from a 'Western' Summit in Bermuda in June, but that had to be postponed to suit the French (whose presence Washington insisted upon, to Churchill's annoyance). Then, on 23 June, Churchill suffered a stroke that kept him out of action for nearly three months. When at last he did meet the Americans in Bermuda in early December, it was only to find them as intransigent as before; indeed even more so, banging on about 'Red China' and trying unsuccessfully to persuade the British to join them in admiring their anti-Communist idols Chiang Kai-shek, now under American protection on the island of Taiwan, and Syngman Rhee, the unsavoury boss of South Korea.

Churchill's fears that the United States would do something dangerous with its bombs were heightened during 1953 by the knowledge that it had transcended *atomic* science by moving into the *nuclear* era. On 1 November 1952, just four weeks after the British A-bomb test, the United States successfully tested an H-bomb on Eniwetok atoll in its usual South Pacific testing area.[19] The fact that this test was of something new was public knowledge – 'one of the worst-kept secrets of recent years', commented the *Daily Herald* – but the American authorities had been careful to make nothing of it and it aroused curiously little public attention after an initial flurry of newspaper articles, perhaps because no radiation or fall-out effects were reported.[20] Churchill knew enough about it, however, and about the Soviet Union's test of something similar nine months later, to refer in the last of his 1953 House of Commons speeches to 'the rapid and ceaseless developments of atomic warfare and the hydrogen bomb'.[21] What came next was startlingly original, and set the tone for what was to come in the following year.

These fearful scientific discoveries cast their shadow on every thoughtful mind, but nevertheless I believe that we are justified in feeling that there has been a diminution of tension and that the probabilities of another world war have diminished, or at least become more remote ... Indeed, I have sometimes the odd thought that the annihilating character of these agencies may bring an utterly unforeseeable security to mankind ... When I was a schoolboy I was not good at arithmetic, but I have since heard it said that certain mathematical quantities when they pass through infinity change their signs from plus to minus – or the other way round ... It may be that this rule may have a novel application and that when the advance of destructive weapons enables everyone to kill everybody else nobody will want to kill anyone at all. At any rate, it seems pretty safe to say that a war which begins by both sides suffering what they dread most – and that is undoubtedly the case at present – is less likely to occur than one which dangles the lurid prizes of former ages before ambitious eyes.

His faithful physician thought the speech, delivered on 3 November, so remarkable – not least, as being delivered by a seventy-nine year old who was still recovering from a severe stroke – that he printed much of it in his book. His description of its immediate aftermath offers a vivid vignette of the irrepressible veteran.

I found the PM in his room, tired but in good heart. 'That's the last bloody hurdle. Now, Charles, we can think of Moscow.' He gave a great yawn, opening his mouth very wide. 'Your pill cleared my head. Now I can turn my mind to other things. You do not realise, Charles, how much depends on the Russians. I must see Malenkov. Then I can depart in peace.' His face was grey. I wanted him to go back to No. 10 to rest. But he was worked up and was all agog to hear what they were saying in the lobbies about his speech. 'The House liked it, I think. That mathematical bit was my own; it will go round the world.' He emptied his glass and, rising with an effort from his chair, tottered out into the Lobby.[22]

The need to 'think of Moscow' – and hardly less of Washington, given that the point of a British nuclear capability was also that it would put Britain in a better position to restrain the American hawks – became only more acute in 1954. Nuclear shocks came thick, fast and early. Crucial for their transmission were the Chairman of the Joint Congressional Committee on Atomic Energy, the publicity-minded Stirling Cole, and the *Manchester Guardian*, which maintained the highest vigilance on atomic developments and reported Cole's speeches in full. In mid-February it reported his revelations about the November 1952 test at

Eniwetok. Churchill, who began every day with a pile of the day's news-papers on his bed, read them and was appalled to discover that the destructive power of this new bomb was larger than he had so far under-stood.[23] Twice at least subsequently, on major public occasions, he recalled his reaction: 'the entire foundation of human affairs was revo-lutionised, and mankind placed in a situation both measureless and laden with doom'.[24] Eniwetok was bad; but worse was hot on its heels. On 1 March on Bikini atoll there was exploded a modest-sized thermo-nuclear device which was expected to yield five to six megatons but which actually yielded about fifteen megatons. (A megaton was equiva-lent to a million tons of TNT. The Hiroshima Bomb had been merely 20 kilotons, equivalent to 20,000 tons of TNT.) The scale of this explosion was awesome but, what was more frightening to those who reflected upon it, it had turned out very much larger than expected. The spectre was raised of a destructive force that might escape human control.

The United States authorities did not seek to publicise what had happened but the news soon got out, because of the widespread fall-out and the fury in Japan about its effect on the crew of a trawler, the *Lucky Dragon*, that had been in the wrong place at the wrong time. It now appeared that one such bomb could wipe out a whole city, that the atmospheric fall-out would infect whole regions, and that an exchange of such weapons might destroy the planet. Not merely did the weapons themselves present a fearful prospect for the future. These nuclear tests, to which American citizens had patriotically, and South Sea Islanders unhappily, resigned themselves, were now seen to present fearful possibilities in the present. Churchill was as disturbed as anyone else by these developments. Twice in later March he had to speak about them at Prime Minister's Questions in the House of Commons.[25] The *Manchester Guardian*'s man heard him on the first occasion:

> Sir Winston shook the House by the emotional force with which he pro-claimed more than once that nothing in the whole world of affairs dominates his and the government's thoughts like the stupendous problems and perils belonging to the spheres of atomic and hydrogen development. Here was no play-acting or pretence. These remarks were the expression of a man deeply moved and, by consequence, deeply moving everybody else. There can rarely have been a statesman whose mental and emotional processes were so transparent. They are an open book for anyone to read.[26]

Churchill was disturbed but not panicked. He stuck to his twin-track strategy. On every suitable occasion he spoke of his wish to set up that peace-seeking summit meeting from which he continued to *hope* – he wouldn't go so far as to say *believe* – that good would result. At the same time he made sure than Britain did not fall behind the front-runners in the atomic arms race. The H-bomb was an abhorrent weapon but, if possession of it was the only way to keep the peace in the weird circumstances of the Cold War world, a peace-loving nation that could afford it and could acquire it had to have it. How to acquire it and how quickly it might be acquired were questions that now came into discussion simultaneously at Aldermaston, in the Cabinet and in the Ministry of Defence.[27] Churchill first opened the matter to a select group of ministers on 13 April. The Chiefs of Staff, having found out all they could from Aldermaston's Sir William Penney, readjusted their defence policy in light of the new situation, and concluded that Britain must have the H-bomb in order to wield enough influence in the world to prevent a nuclear war happening. They reported in those terms to the Defence Policy Committee (Churchill plus the most senior Cabinet ministers), which took it upon itself to order the preparation of the production process to begin.

The Defence Policy Committee's decision was not revealed to the full Cabinet until Churchill was back from another of his North America trips, in the course of which he told the Prime Minister of Canada and the President of the United States what had been decided and had 'obtained the latter's approval'. (What, one wonders, if the President had disapproved?)[28] The Cabinet's approval did not come until 26 July, after a lot more discussion and awkwardness than Churchill had expected; several of its members expressing themselves concerned on religious grounds and everyone wondering how the general public would react when it too was finally told. That did not happen until, nine months later, Churchill introduced the Defence White Paper to Parliament in March 1955.

By that time, Churchill's project for a Summit meeting with the Kremlin had come to an end in a spectacular pyre of Churchillian determination and wilfulness. While in Washington he had strenuously sought to persuade the President that a meeting with Malenkov (or any of the other Soviet leaders) could lead to an improvement in the international situation and was worth trying. While returning to Britain on the *Queen Elizabeth* he insisted on sending a telegram to the Russian Foreign Secretary Molotov, and wrung from Anthony Eden his approval of it, although Eden was as sure as the head of Churchill's Private Office that such a gesture should not have been made without Cabinet approval and that there would be trouble when they got home.[29]

Their fears were justified. There was indignation and disapproval in the Cabinet. Some of its members expressed strong objections to his unauthorised initiative, one or two talked of resignation, and Churchill was obliged to make something of an apology: 'in his anxiety to lose no opportunity of furthering the cause of peace, he might have taken an exaggerated view of the urgency of the matter'. Cabinet meetings continued to be unhappy through the month of July, neither side willing to give way to the other until, on the 26th, Churchill found an opportunity to give way gracefully. Moscow had just issued a proposal for a pan-European security conference of Foreign Ministers. That, he said, changed the situation. They could all agree that a two-man Summit would be pointless while so much larger an event was in view. So ended Churchill's last great foreign policy initiative.[30]

What was by no means ended was his ambition to prevent the outbreak of nuclear war. The Americans worried him hardly less than the Russians. His ideas about the United States were, as always, an extraordinary bundle of likes and dislikes, dancing on top of an unquestioned conviction that Britain and America were destined by their shared origins, language and ideals to work together. From that he never wavered. But just as he could be sentimental and ignorant about Americans and their country, not least about their President, so also he could be realistically worried about them and the dangers they presented.[31] Throughout the early 1950s he was worried that the hawks in America and in Washington (whose complicated politics he seems never to have understood) would precipitate the very show-down he had himself earlier contemplated. He did not believe that the Russians wanted to start a nuclear conflict; but he did believe that some Americans were capable of doing so. The President was not one of them, but Churchill was privately disappointed that his friend showed himself so unhelpfully suspicious of Moscow and all its works. Churchill, for his part, was not so inflexible. He continued to make that distinction between the Soviet

regime and the Russian people that had justified his momentous decision of 22 June 1941, believing that the people could not be as
ideologically hidebound as their rulers and that, given some experience
of co-existence, they would find that non-Communist neighbours could
be regarded with something other than hostility.

It was significant that he inserted a glancing rebuke to the American
hawks into the speech he made on 12 July 1954, regaling the Commons
with an account of his visits to Washington and Ottawa as 'thirty vibrant
hours'. Some of the speech was familiar stuff about the value of the
Special Relationship and how well he got on with Eisenhower ('many
hours of conversation with the President alone'), and some was about
the great issues then shaking the diplomatic world (West Germany and
NATO, China and the UN, the pacification of Indo-China), but at the
last he turned to the nuclear question and did so in striking terms,
expressing the hope that his words would carry far beyond Westminster.
The Foreign Secretary, he recalled, in a speech just before they went to
America, had 'used the remarkable phrase "peaceful co-existence". This
fundamental and far-reaching conception certainly had its part in some
of our conversations', and he was glad that the President had endorsed
it. Continuing, he slid in his rebuke to the warmongers:

> The House must not underrate the importance of this broad measure of
> concurrence of what in this case I may call the English-speaking world. What
> a vast ideological gulf there is between the idea of peaceful co-existence
> vigilantly safeguarded, and *the mood of forcibly extirpating the Communist
> fallacy and heresy* [my italics]. It is, indeed, a gulf. This statement is a recog-
> nition of the appalling character which war has now assumed and that its
> fearful consequences go even beyond the difficulties and dangers of dwelling
> side by side with Communist States. Indeed, I believe that the widespread
> acceptance of this policy may in the passage of years lead to the problems
> which divide the world being solved or solving themselves, as so many prob-
> lems do, in a manner which will avert the mass destruction of the human
> race and give time, human nature and the mercy of God their chance to win
> salvation for us.[32]

After that, there was not much for him to say. Nor, as a matter of
physical fact, was there much more that he could do. He turned eighty
at the end of November and he knew that everyone was wondering (as
many had wondered for several years already) when on earth he was

going to retire. Political historians have made good mileage out of the question of when exactly he should he have retired. Not later than his stroke in the summer of 1953 seems to be their consensus answer. Thereafter he lacked the will, the energy and sometimes the health to do all the things that an active Prime Minister should have done; it was only when the occasion demanded it, as for example on the occasion just referred to, that he could still put on a good show. It was clear to his family and intimates that inwardly he knew that it was time for him to go but that he was finding excuses for hanging on.

At least one of those reasons was unattractive: ambivalence towards his successor designate, Anthony Eden, a loyal lieutenant who deserved better and whose prospective task became more difficult as each passing month brought nearer the next General Election. But the principal reason Churchill gave himself (and others) for staying on was the keeping of the peace. This had been his dominant concern for the past five years. He had tried to set up a Summit meeting with the Soviet leader, and failed; it remained for his successors to follow in his footsteps and perhaps succeed. He had clarified the principle on which the security of the West might best be assured: co-existence based on a non-aggressive deterrent capability. And now, in what had to be the last months of his half-century of service in the House of Commons, he was presiding over the equipment of his country with the most potent deterrent available: to make peace, not war. The opportunity to explain this paradox came, at last, just before his retirement, in the Defence debate on 1 March 1955. It is one of the finest orations he ever delivered and he took enormous pains over it.[33]

'Deterrence' was its main theme; put slightly differently, 'defence through deterrence'. He recapitulated the terrors of the H-bomb, enlarging on the factor of fall-out, as it is called, of wind-borne radio-active particles.

> There is both an immediate direct effect on human beings who are in the path of such a cloud and an indirect effect through animals, grass and vegetables, which pass on these contagions to human beings through food. This would confront many who escaped the direct effect of the explosion with poisoning or starvation, or both. Imagination stands appalled.

All-round disarmament and concentration on the peaceable uses of nuclear power was, of course, the ideal exorcism of these prospects, but the way to that was tortuous and tangled. Pending its satisfactory navigation, there was no way to deter attack other than to promise instant and massive counter-attack; a promise only madmen could refuse – and he did not think that the men in the Kremlin, whatever else they were, were mad. Preparing to secure peace by perfecting the power to eliminate Soviet airfields and submarine bases, and industrial and administrative targets, with nuclear weapons was, by all previous historical standards, an extraordinary and crazy-looking strategy, but the point of it was that the more perfect it was made, the less likely was it ever to be implemented. This brought him to the part of the speech that attracted most notice.

> A curious paradox has emerged. Let me put it simply. After a certain point has been passed it may be said, 'The worse things get, the better' ... It may well be that we shall by a process of sublime irony have reached a stage in this story where safety will be the sturdy child of terror, and survival the twin brother of annihilation.

He ended his swan song – for that is in effect what it was and what he meant it to be, although in fact he did speak again, twice, later in the month – with a look to the future and a final sentence that has often been repeated by admirers who probably have not known its sombre original context.

> To conclude, mercifully, there is time and hope if we combine patience and courage. All deterrents will improve and gain authority during the next ten years. In that time, the deterrent may well reach its acme and reap its final reward. The day may dawn when fair play, love for one's fellow men, respect for justice and freedom, will enable tormented generations to march forth serene and triumphant from the hideous epoch in which we have to live. Meanwhile, never flinch, never weary, never despair.

The press gave this speech the attention and respect that it deserved. So did the House of Commons. There were no interruptions, not even from Aneurin Bevan, who must already have been planning the political explosion he was to unleash, to the confusion of his own party, the following day. Only the *Daily Worker* and the *Daily Mirror* refused to be impressed: the former because it was tied to Moscow's line; the latter because it took delight in puncturing the hero-worship that was developing around the great man.[34] The *Daily Express* of the same date reported that the speech was accompanied by 'murmurs of horror or agreement', and headed its coverage with two of Churchill most pregnant phrases: the one about survival being the twin brother of annihilation and his agonised question, 'What are we to do if God becomes weary of mankind?' That was strikingly to paraphrase what he actually said, early in the speech: 'What ought we to do? Which way shall we turn to save our lives and the future of the world? It does not matter much to old people', but it upset him to look at children 'and wonder what would lie before them if God wearied of mankind'. The *News Chronicle* picked out 'Never Despair' for its headline; the *Daily Sketch* ventured a modest play on the letter H: 'Churchill names it H for Hope'.[35]

To sum up Churchill in his final role as peacemaker: his was a noble endeavour that did much good, though not wholly in the way he expected. He was not wrong to sense the beginnings of a change in the atmosphere in Moscow, and perhaps he was right to associate it with Malenkov, but no one who was close to him in his last two years in office believed that he was capable of successfully managing a man-to-man meeting with a Soviet counterpart, even if the Soviets had consented to such an extraordinary event.[36] He was too old, too emotional, too easily tired and notoriously too reluctant to undergo the preliminary briefings the Foreign Office and the Cabinet thought advisable. On the other hand, he played a conspicuous part in bringing before the British public the horrible hazards of thermonuclear warfare. He spoke out about those hazards and he affirmed the necessity of averting them with a public eloquence and force not yet within the range of a President of the United States (America being still gripped by anti-Communist fever) or a leader of the Soviet Union (orthodox ideology forbidding the thought that Soviet possession of H-bombs could be as hazardous as American). British men and women thus alerted to the onset of perils quite unlike any previously imagined might not understand Churchill's argument that the best way to make sure the worst never happened was actually to prepare for it; but there is a good case for placing Churchill among the earliest promoters of the campaign that culminated in the first of the nuclear arms control treaties, the Atmospheric Test Ban Treaty of 1963.

A Mind for War

The early formation of the war side of Churchill's mind remains obscure. We have seen how there was nothing remarkable about his school days; Winston the boy took to fantasies and games of war as naturally and instinctively as boys generally do in the years of childhood and adolescence. There was the difference that he had the blood of a famous warrior duke in his veins. It is possible that some of John Churchill's genes emerged from two centuries of dormancy to the later Churchill's advantage. It is indisputable that by the time he came to write about his ancestor, and to reflect upon his nation's history, he found inspiration and satisfaction in the first Duke's achievements; but by then, the early 1930s, his ideas about war and war's place in world history were already well formed. Although the boy Winston knew his own worth, there is no evidence that he was given to boasting about his ancestry, and if he had done so his peers would probably have sat on him. His year and a half at Sandhurst displayed a growing seriousness of attitude – the careless schoolboy could hardly otherwise have turned into an efficient officer cadet – but it was not until he had joined his regiment that his great transformation began, and his regiment had no more to do with it than to threaten him with so much boredom and waste of time that he took to serious company and books instead.

Churchill's early life invites one to recall the quatrain:

> The Halls of Life are bright and fair,
> The Waiting-Room is full;
> And some get in through the door marked *Push*,
> And some through the door marked *Pull*.

The young Winston got in through *both* doors, and great changes happened to him once he had done so. First, he rapidly managed to become a military pundit and celebrity (or notoriety, according to the way you viewed him). We have seen how his early military adventures were possible only because, first, he and his mother between them were able to persuade powerful men to take him under their wing or to make exceptions in his case; and, secondly, because he pressed into the places where he wanted to be without embarrassment. Such behaviour would not have been surprising in any well-connected, thick-skinned, bumptious young aristocrat, a type then by no means uncommon, and in most would have been taken simply as a form of self-assertion and showing off. For Churchill, however, it was also the means of seriously enlarging his professional military expertise and of writing excellent campaign reports that subsequently became good books.

Then there was the social dimension of his busy life. This was educational too. He did not go in for parties, balls and whoring, and although he did not entirely ignore the demands of the London Season, he tended to be gauche and unforthcoming in the presence of pretty young women. What he liked were lunches and dinners and week-end parties where mandarins and generals and parliamentarians talked about politics and world affairs, and where the atmosphere was heady with the consciousness of riches and power. His birth and connections opened the way to meeting persons of distinction, his singular chutzpah making sure he met them. When he was not quite yet twenty-one, he recalled,

> I had the privilege, as a young officer, of being invited to lunch with Sir William Harcourt. In the course of a conversation in which I took, I fear, none too modest a share, I asked the question, 'What will happen next?' 'My dear Winston', replied the old Victorian statesman, 'the experiences of a long life have convinced me that nothing ever happens.' Since that moment, as it seems to me, nothing has ever ceased happening.[1]

In the book he wrote about himself when young, *My Early Life* (1930), there are many such stories, recording with complacent amusement how he brashly put himself forward on social occasions, incidentally revealing how comfortable he felt in those inner circles. He may have been bumptious, but he was evidently a valued guest; someone with lively and original talk to contribute. His first book, about the North-West Frontier, so much interested the Prime Minister Lord Salisbury that he asked the young man to come to see him. Churchill made a particular point of turning up on time (something he was not good at) and reckoned that he ought to make an excuse to go after twenty minutes:

> But he kept me for over half an hour, and when he finally conducted me to the door, he dismissed me in the following terms: 'I hope you will allow me to say how much you remind me of your father, with whom such important days of my political life were lived. If there is anything at any time that I can do which would be of assistance to you, pray do not fail to let me know.'[2]

And so he immediately did. It was absolutely in character for Churchill to ask Sailsbury to persuade Sir Herbert Kitchener to drop his objections to Churchill's joining the Sudan expedition: leading to the astonishing spectacle of a Prime Minister leaning on the nation's senior soldier to suit the purposes of a controversial young cavalry lieutenant.

My Early Life is by universal consensus the most enjoyable and easiest to read of Churchill's books. It has its sober passages – the deaths of Mrs Everest his beloved nurse and the father whom he hardly knew, the bloodshed of battle and its harrowing aftermath, a thoughtful passage about religion – but the general tone is light-hearted, ironic, affectionate and amusing, not least at his own expense. Understandably, it gives simplified and sanitised accounts of episodes and experiences which we know to have actually been distressing or unpleasant: his and his mother's constant money troubles, for example, and aspects of colonial warfare he had written about more frankly at the time. Finishing as it does with the start of his political career in early 1901, and passing quickly over his childhood and school years, *My Early Life* is mostly about his six years in the army, without too much about his having been a newspaper correspondent for most of the time as well.

Many illustrations have already been given of his clear and compelling accounts of campaigns and battles. What *My Early Life* inimitably adds to them is its sketches of characters and, better still, of situations. There are not many pages about Aldershot, for example, but no one can understand the officer corps that used to gather there without reading them. They centre on Colonel Brabazon, colonel of the 4th Hussars when the young Churchill joined it. A gallant and experienced officer with a colourful past (and a colourful present implied in one economical allusion), Brabazon was also a dandy 'in the style of the previous generation', with 'an inability real or affected to pronounce the letter "R"'. The upsets of his earlier career had caused him once to be appointed to a regiment less stylish than he liked. 'To the question, "What do you belong to now, Brab?", he replied, "I never can wemember, but they have gween facings and you get at 'em fwom Waterloo."'[3]

A fine example of Churchill's talent for sketching a historical situation (with evident input from the social sciences and with lashings of irony) comes at the start of chapter 11, 'The Mahmund Valley'. After briefly describing how the valleys wind like fertile corridors between the mighty cliffs, he turned to the inhabitants.

> Except at harvest-time, when self-preservation enjoins a temporary truce, the Pathan tribes are always engaged in private or public war. Every man is a warrior, a politician and a theologian. Every large house is a real feudal fortress ... Every family cultivates its vendetta, every clan, its feud ... The life of the Pathan is thus full of interest; and his valleys, nourished alike by endless sunshine and abundant water, are fertile enough to yield with little labour the modest material requirements of a sparse population.
>
> Into this happy world the nineteenth century brought two new facts: the breech-loading rifle and the British Government. The first was an enormous luxury and blessing; the second, an unmitigated nuisance. The convenience of the [rifle] was nowhere more appreciated than in the Indian highlands ... One could actually remain in one's own house and fire at one's neighbour nearly a mile away ... Fabulous prices were therefore offered for these glorious products of science. Rifle-thieves scoured all India to reinforce the efforts of the honest smuggler. A steady flow of the coveted weapons spread its genial influence throughout the frontier, and the respect which the Pathan tribesmen entertained for Christian civilisation was vastly enhanced.
>
> The action of the British Government on the other hand was entirely unsatisfactory ...

No need to reproduce any more. The paragraph that follows, summarising British policy on the frontier, leads straight into his recollection of the march into the country of the 'pestilential' Mahmunds and his first experience of frontier fighting. Three chapters on his Indian adventures are followed by three on the Sudan and ten on South Africa, no less than four of them telling the story of the armoured train, his capture by the Boers and his escape from them. He was obviously very fond and proud of this story; the question of whether he was quite entitled to be so has already been examined.

He devotes several pages to the self-education that continued through these early years of soldiering, but gives a wrong impression of when it began. He had actually begun that stiff course of reading not in India but while he was still at Aldershot in the summer of 1895, when he confessed to his mother that he was 'getting into a state of mental stagnation' and that he felt the need of someone to guide him.[4] What this self-improving young man was looking for was in fact a tutor such as he would have had at Oxford or Cambridge. Whether such an adviser was ever found does not appear, but within a week of writing that letter he had got his teeth into Henry Fawcett's *Manual of Political Economy* ('a capital book') and was planning to read Edward Gibbon's *Decline and Fall* and W. E. H. Lecky's *History of European Morals from Augustus to Charlemagne*.[5] All three books were of a pronouncedly rationalist character; Churchill was already on the road to the scientific atheism that became fixed in him by Winwood Reade's *Martyrdom of Man* and another of Lecky's classics, *The Rise and Influence of Rationalism*.

His service in India brought with it his first experience of war. He grew up in an age when Britain's military detachment from the European Continent was absolute. India was the only part of the Empire other than South Africa where military action against a foreign power was possible, and the enemy in view here was Russia. British troops were regularly stationed in India, to the number of some 80,000.[6] One cause of their being in India was to discourage Russian ventures in the region of Afghanistan and its northern neighbours, where diplomats, agents and spies had been playing the 'Great Game' in Asia for many decades. The more obvious cause of India's having so large a British military force in it was, however, to stiffen the locally raised, British-officered Indian army in the event that the civil authorities needed help in suppressing disorder, and to fight beside those Indian soldiers in the recurrent campaigns against the frontier tribesmen who were forever disturbing the security of the anarchic North-West Frontier; a theatre of action which most film-makers and writers (including Churchill) made more glamorous than it actually was.

Nowhere else than in Africa and India can the young British hussar and war-correspondent have expected to find himself in action. Churchill took it for granted that, just as the British Empire had largely been built by fighting, so readiness to fight was the necessary means of preserving it. Every schoolboy in those years of patriotic history books and imperial pride knew about the heroes who had made or maintained the Empire: James Wolfe at Quebec, Robert Clive at Plassey, Arthur Wellesley at Assaye and Waterloo, Horatio Nelson at Aboukir Bay and Trafalgar; and, more recently, Henry Havelock's liberation of Cawnpore, Colin Campbell's relief of Lucknow and Garnet Wolseley's mission to relieve Khartoum. Churchill had these and all such empire-building feats of arms in his head from school onwards, and later wrote admiringly of them in *The History of the English-Speaking Peoples.*

Until the later 1940s he never budged in his conviction that what had been won by force could legitimately be kept by force. Although events compelled him thereafter to witness the first steps of the Empire's dissolution, he had grave misgivings about its consequences. He was concerned not only for his beloved country's standing in the world, but also for the wellbeing of its colonial populations. British imperial rule, he believed, took order, justice and the elements of modern science to backward peoples. Churchill rejoiced that Britain had been expansively powerful enough to achieve this. He said so again and again in his books and in his speeches from these early years until the sunset of his life. If his early reading included the Sandhurst and Staff College pundit G. F. R. Henderson's 1891 article, 'Military Criticism and Modern Tactics', he would have found nothing strange in this passage: 'That a capacity for conquest is inherent in the English-speaking race, it would be useless to deny. Whether this attribute is the gift of Providence, whether it is the outcome of climate, of freedom or of blood, is a question with which we have no concern; it is enough that it exists.'

By the early twentieth century, the capacity for conquest of territories overseas had ceased to be as important to Britain as the capacity to defend its past conquests. In particular, it needed to maintain its present security against a Great Power unexpectedly displaying an equal capacity for conquest, and an even great hunger for it, Germany. In 1914 and again in 1939 it was to thwart Germany's ambition to dominate the Continent that Britain went to war. The dramatic core of Churchill's two multi-volume books about the First and Second World Wars is the story of Britain's battle to save itself and the other free nations of Europe from inclusion in the German Empire or, hardly less humiliating, domination by its overshadowing closeness. It was not his fault that readers were easily led by their amplitude and magisterial tone to respect them as 'histories' of the wars; he never claimed for them more than that they were 'contributions to history'. He correctly judged that they were valuable contributions to history. He had himself been at centre-stage for the whole of the second war and much of the first, and knew things that no one else knew; he understood the value of documentary evidence and printed a great deal of it (too much, in fact, for the liking of his American publishers on the second occasion); and he was able to construct books on so grand a scale by employing bands of helpers who dug up materials and often drafted whole passages for him, the master story-teller, to turn into 'his own'.

'Memoir-histories' is the best description of them, as frankly signalling the element of the personal that went into their making. That element adds to their overt charms but also to their hidden hazards. His vivid memories of particular moments and incidents, recounted in colourful and moving prose, are wonderful; many examples have already been given. But besides recalling what he had seen, he was more concerned to describe what he had done, and this is where the hazards lie for the unsuspecting reader. In both books he was concerned not just to describe but positively to justify his actions. His helpers sometimes ran into squalls when questioning the accuracy of his memory or the fairness of his interpretation.[7] He never took easily to the idea that he was wrong, and these books were meant to show that he had almost always been right. They were weapons in the battle for his reputation and his place in history.

Clement Attlee, who knew him as an antagonist across the floor of the Commons for thirty years and as his loyal deputy close up for five, summed up this side of Churchill very well. 'He was always, in effect, asking himself. "How will I look if I do this or that?" and "What must Britain do now so that the verdict of history will be favourable?" ... He was always looking around for "finest hours", and if one was not immediately available, his impulse was to manufacture one.'[8] Churchill was a tremendous patriot, of an age gone by and a kind long gone out of fashion. He was not so unreflective or dull-witted a patriot as to have believed in 'My country right or wrong', but he found it difficult to believe that there was much wrong with the history of his own country, and he found it easy and pleasant to believe that there was much that was right in it; and not merely right, but of benefit and good example to the world at large: parliamentary government, the rule of law, toleration of differences, freedom of individuals and so on. The achievement of those blessings was the moral main theme of *The History of the English-Speaking Peoples* he had complete, in draft, by 1939. With little sense of the economic and social undercurrents of history, he liked to highlight the roles of exceptional individuals, ready to work, fight and if necessary die for their beliefs – which, if they were in the mainstream of liberal progress, were *ipso facto* beneficent ones. The exceptional individuals he most liked to celebrate were the men and women who had saved England (after 1707, of course, Britain; but he went on calling it England) in perilous times: King Alfred, King Canute, Queen Elizabeth, John Churchill, William Pitt the Elder, William Pitt the Younger, Horatio Nelson.[9]

Churchill's *History of the English-Speaking Peoples* petered out around 1900. When in the later 1950s he exhumed the 1939 draft and set the usual band of helpers to work on its revision, he declined to bring it up to date apparently on the ground that, the twentieth century having so far been such a terrible one, he couldn't bear to contemplate it. He may, however, have thought that he had already written enough about the twentieth century, and that what he had written was in its essentials the continuation of that history: the story of Britain facing up to the need to defend itself *and* the independent states of Europe against the latest in the series of continental would-be hegemonists: Kaiser Wilhelm II's German Empire and Adolf Hitler's Third Reich.

Churchill's monumental books *The World Crisis* and *The Second World War* were both designed to fit within this world-historical context. They told the latest chapters in the nation's story as a Great Power and as a power for good in the world; and one cannot doubt that Churchill's serenity on becoming Prime Minister sprang from the vision of himself as the latest in the series of leaders with whom Providence (he was not a religious man, but he did use religious language when it expressed his beliefs) had blessed Britain in its hours of need. Britain was again making history, and history was Churchill's natural element. Sir Isaiah Berlin put it very well:

> Mr Churchill's dominant category, the single, central, organising principle of his moral and intellectual universe, is an historical imagination so

strong, so comprehensive, as to encase the whole of the present and the whole of the future in a framework of a rich and multi-coloured past ... [He] sees history – and life – as a great Renaissance pageant: when he thinks of France or Italy, Germany or the Low Countries, Russia, India, Africa, the Arab lands, he sees vivid historical images – something between Victorian illustrations in a child's book of history and the great procession painted by Benozzo Gozzoli in the Riccardi Palace. The eye is never that of the neatly classifying sociologist, the careful psychological analyst, the plodding antiquary ... The units out of which his world is constructed are simpler and larger than life, the patterns vivid and repetitive like those of an epic poet, or at times like those of a dramatist who sees persons and situations as timeless symbols and embodiments of eternal, shining principles.[10]

Churchill thus had a serious emotional investment in these books that were both histories on the grand scale and memoirs of his own share in that history-making. It is not surprising that he did not want that share to be undervalued. Both books contain a strong apologetic element. *The World Crisis* was concerned to show in particular that his judgement had not been at fault about the Dardanelles and that he had been justified in his criticisms of the pointlessness of infantry offensives like those at the Somme and Passchendaele. Historians continue to find room for disagreement about the Dardanelles and Gallipoli, but Churchill's mastery of the casualty statistics made him difficult to controvert about the Western Front. Coming out as it did, volume by volume through the 1920s, there were plenty of reviewers who had lived through the same episodes as he had done and who were well placed,[11] as well as perhaps polemically driven, to comment on his more factual or judgemental passages.* The very fact that it invited a first-class historian's professional scrutiny of course testifies in its own way to Churchill's book's continuing value.[12] So compelling is the drive of the narrative, so constant the sense of great issues being determined, so well suited to those issues the author's high style and so lively his

* Their comments and those of later scholars have all been superseded by the Australian historian Robin Prior's 1983 book *Churchill's 'World Crisis' as History* (1983), required reading for anyone who wishes to know what are the book's factual, and to some extent judgemental, strengths and weaknesses.

companionship along the way, that it continues to be a good book to
recommend to anyone beginning a study of the First World War –
besides being for the most part a delight to read.

More still was at stake for him when he got to writing his book about
The Second World War. Even with the usual team of helpers, this was a
formidable enterprise for a man of his age who had, in any case, other
important things to do, including being Leader of Her Majesty's Opposition. The two great aims that braced him to his task were (in no order
of priority) the presentation of *his* version of the war and the making of
a lot of money. In both aims, he succeeded brilliantly. The money side
of it is copiously dealt with elsewhere.[13] What matters here is his version
of the story. He told it so grandly that, for the many years that passed
before critical treatment of it became possible, only readers with inside
knowledge, personal experience or a developed historical sensitivity
could tell that it was in some respects unbalanced, partial and even in a
few places untrue.

In those respects it was no different from (and in fact better than)
most of the other books about the war that began to appear soon after
the war's conclusion and have gone on appearing ever since. Commanders who had had to make controversial decisions wanted to present
their case to the world; a case pressed also by loyalist biographers.
Understrappers and hangers-on who had been close to the great men of
the war were eager to sell their (usually embroidered) stories. The
appearance of two books of the latter kind in the USA, both tending to
Churchill's discredit, goaded him to get going in 1946 without further
loss of time. It was clear that, if he didn't look after his place in history,
nobody else might; he also no doubt took it as given that no one else
would do it so well.

He was not, however, going to be writing an autobiography such as
anyone else might have written. This was to be a contribution not just
to the history of Britain and the British Empire, it was to commemorate
his nation's share in the struggle to save Europe from imminent German domination and the world from the possible consequences of that.
It was a contribution to world history, by the man who had been at the
heart of that struggle and who had fruitlessly tried to avert it. To the first
volume, he wanted to give the title 'The Unnecessary War'. In his preface to it he claimed, 'There never was a war more easy to stop than that

which has just wrecked what was left of the world from the previous struggle.' His publishers did not consider that title striking enough and preferred *The Gathering Storm*; a title truthful enough in its own way but missing the personal point that its author intended. There was, however, no misunderstanding the thrilling substance of the volume: Churchill's story of his campaign against the feeble appeasement policies of the MacDonald, Baldwin and Chamberlain governments became the received and orthodox version for the next generation. Only after his death and a decent interval following it did historians begin to cast quizzical eyes on his version, to discover that things were not quite as black and white as he had painted them.[14]

The short titles of the six volumes – such as *The Gathering Storm* and *The Grand Alliance* – are not nearly so expressive of the dramatic purpose and unity of the whole as the less often noted (and, because of where they are actually printed, less noticeable) 'Themes'. 'How the English-Speaking Peoples through their Unwisdom, Carelessness and Good Nature Allowed the Wicked to Rearm' despite Churchill's warnings is the Theme of *The Gathering Storm*. He then takes charge and what follows is *Their Finest Hour*: 'How the British People Held the Fort Alone till Those who hitherto had been Half Blind were Half Ready' (that is, the Americans). The United States being slow to join in, the next instalment told 'How the British Fought on with Hardship their Garment until Soviet Russia and the United States Were Drawn into the Great Conflict', thus forming *The Grand Alliance*. 'How the Power of the Grand Alliance became Preponderant', the Theme of the curiously titled fourth volume, *The Hinge of Fate*, covered the months from Japan's onslaught and the bad months in Russia and the Western Desert to the better times of Russia's recovery and the clearance of North Africa. The war now began to go more prosperously. *Closing the Ring* was an appropriate title for the volume about 'How Nazi Germany was Isolated and Assailed on All Sides'. The hopes engendered in that part of the drama were, however, delusory. Human folly and wickedness – constants in Churchill's philosophy of history – reasserted themselves. Russian Communism and *Realpolitik* on the one hand, American refusal to heed Churchill's warnings on the other, made the last months of the war a tale of *Triumph and Tragedy*: 'How the Great Democracies Triumphed, and so were Able to Resume the Follies which had so nearly

Cost them their Life'. As the one phase of world history closed, another opened. His final volume was in effect an introduction to the Cold War: heralded by his famous speech at Fulton, Missouri, in March 1946, and well under way by the time he finished writing.

The conception of such a work was heroic and its execution was admirable. The initial readership was measured in millions, and it has gone on being read ever since. The personal note that sounded through every part of the story the author had been personally involved in was no obstacle to its readability. It reads so well, in fact, that the contented reader can be lulled into taking it for the standard history of *The Second World War* that its straightforward title leads him or her to expect. That is in fact how its official sponsors (as one might describe them), Sir Edward Bridges and Sir Norman Brook, successive Secretaries to the Cabinet with responsibility for all the departmental war histories, hoped it might be taken.[15] This was of course flattering to Churchill and by no means unacceptable to him, but, to do him justice, it was to credit him with an even more ambitious work than the one he had actually undertaken. In the preface to the fourth volume Churchill wrote, as he wrote in similar terms in the other volumes:

> The tale is told from the standpoint of the British Prime Minister, with special responsibility, as Minister of Defence, for military affairs. Again I rely upon the series of my directives, telegrams and minutes, which owe their importance and interest to the moment in which they were written, and which I could not write in better words now ... As they are my own composition, set forth at the time, it is by these that I prefer to be judged. It would be easier to produce a series of after-thoughts, when the answers to all the riddles were known, but I must leave this to the historians, who will in due course be able to pronounce their considered judgments.

By now, half a century later, plenty of 'considered judgments' have been pronounced, some by wartime colleagues and comrades who had their own memories of events, and some by historians reviewing the story from outside. The former were quick to restore to their proper place individuals whose roles Churchill had, they thought, undervalued, and to correct the impression, so easily received from Churchill's self-based narrative, that he was more wise and perceptive than everyone else. Of course, in some ways he *was* just that: he was a polymathic warlord with more energy than most and an abundance of bright ideas; but he could also be unwise and pig-headed, erratic and combative. It was, for instance, galling to the Chiefs of Staff to realise that Churchill's readers would gain no glimpse of the silliness of some of the ideas he made them waste time on, and of the turbulence of many of their debates with him. The chairman of their committee through the latter half of the war, Field-Marshal Sir Alan Brooke (later Lord Alanbrooke), was unsurprisingly the first to break the spell cast by Churchill's literary wizardry, showing how much more argument there had been than appeared in the Churchill's account, and how maddening Churchill's behaviour had sometimes been.[16] Brooke's lead has been followed over the years by many others.*

It was a blessing that, as usual, Churchill enlisted a team of expert helpers (indeed he could not otherwise have undertaken such a work) who were strong-minded enough to call his attention to forgotten, unwelcome or undervalued facts; it was a measure of his residual historical professionalism that, notwithstanding the discomforts they caused him, he retained their services to the end. 'The Syndicate' (as the core of helpers were known) produced much of the material and many of the first drafts of text; Churchill dictated the passages about

---

* No historian has done for *The Second World War* what Robin Prior did for *The World Crisis*; and, so much larger than the latter is the later work, no one historian could venture to do it. It has, however, been made the subject of an equally illuminating work of a different kind by David Reynolds. His original and striking book, *In Command of History: Churchill Fighting and Writing the Second World War* (2004), shows that Churchill had not been wholly joking when he told people that he was not afraid of the verdict of History because he would have written the History.[17]

One of Reynolds's more striking revelations is the extent to which Churchill's decisions about what to include and how much to tell were influenced, not only by his prejudices and preferences (which was only to be expected), but equally by the political events of the years in which those decisions were being taken. The book would, for example, have revealed much more wartime irritation and displeasure regarding President Roosevelt and United States policy in general had Churchill not felt bound by Cold War necessities to maintain the 'Special Relationship', and had not his wartime friend and occasional sparring partner Dwight Eisenhower become a candidate for the Presidency.

matters that most interested or excited him, decided what should go in and what shouldn't, and put the finishing stylistic touches to the whole. The outcome of their combined operation was, as one of the Syndicate put it, like a great banquet: the work of many hands, all toiling under the direction of the master chef who put on the finishing touches and could justly claim credit for the result.

The Second World War, the final volume of which was published in 1954, was the last and largest of his writings about war. War was not the only thing he wrote about for publication. It is important to remember that, besides everything else, he was a professional writer, financially dependent throughout his life on his literary earnings: journalism in newspapers and periodicals, collections of essays and speeches, books and multiple reprints of books.[18] He would write about anything that paid enough. One of his most charming pieces is 'Painting as a Pastime', which began in the *Strand Magazine* in 1921–22 and was included, along with other good essays by no means all military, in the collection *Thoughts and Adventures* (1932), *en route* to becoming a little book on its own. Only a quarter of the men who figured in his collection of essays *Great Contemporaries* (1937) were distinctly military. In 1940 the *Sunday Dispatch*, whose editor Charles Eade was a Churchill loyalist, astonishingly carried such ephemera from his past as 'My Plane Caught Fire – Dive to Earth at 120 Miles per Hour' and 'Rowdy Meetings were a Relief'. There can be no doubt, however, that his writings about war were what he valued most, and he was prepared to give them the most serious attention. War was the most exciting activity a man could be engaged in, and war was what settled the destinies of nations.

'The story of the human race is War', he wrote in 1925.[19] From the time he first began to think about it, Churchill accepted war as a natural phenomenon, and not necessarily a bad one. This was the common assumption on the Conservative and Imperialist side of British political life. Imperial wars for him were no more than a particular case of the general truth, that war was an unsurprising feature of international relations, just as historically it had been the principal maker and breaker of nations. States could not help competing with one another, as the Great Powers on the Continent were always doing. Those that had it in them to become big and powerful did so; those that hadn't such capability and couldn't defend themselves would go under unless they could get protection or happily find themselves in a position where it suited all parties to leave them alone. It was natural to his mind that Great Powers should dominate or absorb small ones that got in their way, and in war planning he never gave much thought to small states' rights and entitlements under the international law of peace, war and (what mattered most to them) neutrality. One doubts whether he could imagine what it was like to live in a small state.

But was war also in itself 'a good thing', a matter for positively moral and religious satisfaction, as some nationalist ideologues before 1914 liked to proclaim? The noisiest of them, the German Heinrich von Treitschke, declared that 'The hope of expunging war from the world is not only senseless, it is also deeply immoral'. Neither in his early days nor later in life did Churchill say anything closer to that than that war brought out the best, as it brought out also the worst, in man. There were other respects in which his acceptance of war and excitement about it fell short of the extremer views canvassed around the beginning of the twentieth century. There was at that time something of a vogue for rephrasing these received truths in Darwinian terms, which was easy enough to do. Although he occasionally slipped into that sort of language, he evidently felt no serious interest in doing so or need to do so. History and observation were enough for him.

Nor did he go in for the interpretation of the histories of nations in racial terms, as did the Slavophiles in Russia and the Balkans, the self-styled 'Anglo-Saxons' in Britain and the eastern United States, and, wherever German was spoken, the 'Teutons'. When thirty years later Churchill met the concept of 'racial purity' in its Nazi formulation, he thought it obscene and absurd. His use of the words 'race', 'nation' and 'people' was loose and insignificant, like his indifferent references to 'England' and 'Britain'; what mattered to him was whether a people, whatever its racial make-up, had become a viable unit of power on the world's stage. He never showed any surprise that the supreme racial and linguistic mixture of all time, the United States, quickly acquired such cohesion and collective spirit as to become a Great Power. When in the later 1930s he inscribed his understanding of British history into his *History of the English-Speaking Peoples*, it bothered him not a jot that England's early centuries witnessed a series of invasions and conquests by foreigners and that the developing English state displayed through more than a millennium a capacity to absorb all sorts of peoples. Unlike cranks who try to find a racial basis for Englishness in the Anglo-Saxons, Churchill expressed reservations about them and wrote with more admiration of the Danes and the Normans. He hailed the early Archbishop of Canterbury Theodore of Tarsus (a city in today's Turkey) as 'the earliest of the statesmen of England'. He recorded with gratitude the contributions to British life of Jewish and other immigrant peoples; Battenbergs, Rothschilds and Lindemanns could be just as patriotic as Smiths, Joneses and Robinsons. He rejoiced to mark the growth of a political culture that knitted all comers into a shared Englishness that constituted a lesson for others and included a talent for rule – and a talent for war.[20]

On the international plane, it was his simple and reasonable understanding that power simply abhors a vacuum. Not without cause did statesmen, diplomats and international lawyers refer to states as powers, and the major ones as the Great Powers. Britain had made itself a Great Power by its successful wars of the eighteenth century, in the first of which Churchill's famous ancestor had played the leading role. How much the story of the first Duke of Marlborough already inspired and instructed the mind of his descendant before the 1930s is unclear. There is, however, no mistaking the extent to which John Churchill's descendant was inspired when in the early 1930s he set about researching and writing perhaps the best of all his books, his four-volume biography *Marlborough: His Life and Times.* Conceived and composed in the grandest manner, it embodies also the history of Great Britain through Marlborough's years, and its apologetic (indeed, panegyric) purpose, the rescue of Marlborough's reputation from Macaulay's mauling, did not prevent it from being hailed as a masterpiece of historical writing. Its shortcomings and biases on the biographical and political-historical sides, which were no more than successor generations may discover in any earlier work, are of no concern here.[21] What matters is that the book enabled Churchill to display with impressive amplitude his grasp of war in the context of international relations, his appreciation of its political and social sources and constraints, his fascination with 'the art of war' and expertise in military matters, his soldierly excitement about battle, and his admiration for the kind of national war leader he would himself like to be – and, though he could not foresee it, actually would be only a couple of years after completing the work. It is, of all his books, the one that tells us most about Churchill and war.

The war Churchill was writing about, known to history as the War of the Spanish Succession, was one of the series of wars recorded with relish in his *History of the English-Speaking Peoples* in which Britain joined with other states to 'defend the liberties of Europe' against the threatened hegemony of one great state in particular; wars fought of course for national self-interest but also justified by the principle of the balance of power. In Churchill's own lifetime, the balance was threatened, first, by Germany and then (as he perhaps too hastily concluded) by the Soviet Union. In Marlborough's day, and for the century following, the threat came from France. French power was threatening enough on its own; it became intolerable when Louis XIV virtually united his country with Spain by proclaiming, as successor to the childless Charles II of Spain, his grandson, the Duke of Anjou, as Spain's King Philip V. Against this superpower, which Churchill once described as a 'totalitarian monarchy', the threatened states, Britain, the United Provinces (the modern Netherlands) and Austria (the Habsburg Empire), assembled a coalition embracing Portugal, Savoy, Denmark, Prussia and various German princes.[22]

Marlborough's burdens went well beyond the military ones of assembling and leading the coalition's army (largely British and Dutch) facing the French in the region that is now Belgium, and of forming a grand strategy with his counterpart the Austrian Prince Eugene, commander of the army facing the French across the Rhine. As his monarch's chief continental representative, he also had to manage the diplomacy and politics essential to the formation and maintenance of what his descendant called 'The Grand Alliance'. Marlborough was a 'warrior-statesman', just what his descendant aspired to be. Managing his own Grand Alliance only a few years later, Churchill may well have reflected that the difficulties intermittently experienced with his allies were no worse than those Marlborough had to put up with from the Dutch. At the same time he could have found consolation in enjoying, with President Roosevelt, almost as harmonious a relationship as Marlborough had with Prince Eugene.

Wars determined the course of history, and battles determined the outcomes of wars. Churchill wrote exceedingly well about battles, and

not just because they absorbed and thrilled him. They settled the fates
of nations. Taking war as seriously as he did, Churchill had the same
views about it as conscientious meat-eaters may have about slaughter-
houses; those who enjoy their products ought to know what goes on
in them. Correctly reckoning that his readers would have no idea of
what battles were actually like in the early eighteenth century, and that
they might draw wrong conclusions from his descriptions of the usually
slow movements of armies and their baggage trains, Churchill found it
necessary to point out that Marlborough's battles were in fact

> far more sudden and intense than those of the Great War. Instead of
> struggles lasting for several weeks along fronts of seventy or eighty miles,
> all was brought into a small compass and a single day. Sometimes two hun-
> dred thousand men fought for an afternoon in a space no larger than the
> London parks put together, and left the ground literally carpeted with a
> quarter of their number, and in places heaped with maimed or slaughtered
> men. The destiny of nations flowed with the blood from their brief colli-
> sion ... and another fearful but glorious name was inscribed in the annals
> of war.[23]

Blenheim was his prime example of how the destinies of nations had
been changed by one great battle. 'It changed the political axis of the
world.' It put an end to the grandiose ambitions of Louis XIV.
'Although long years of bloodshed lay before him, his object hence-
forward was only to find a convenient and dignified exit from the arena
in which he had so long stalked triumphant.' As the star of France was
halted in its rise, so had England's star risen to rival it, and whatever
may have been the economic and demographic bases of the country's
growing power (these were not things that Churchill cared to dwell on),
it was simply 'the island troops' that determined the issue. Churchill
went to town in his description of them:

> Their discipline, their fighting energy, their readiness to endure extraordi-
> nary losses, the competence and team-play of their officers, the handiness of
> their cavalry and field artillery, their costly equipment and lavish feeding,
> their self-assured, unaffected disdain of foreigners, became the talk of
> Europe.[24]

Within a year, another nation's destinies had been settled by battle; not
in consequence of fighting a battle but by failing to do so. Marlborough

with the Anglo-Dutch army, campaigning in 1705 in the region south of Brussels and in the proximity of the village of Waterloo, believed that he and the Dutch colleague with whom he got on very well, General Overkirk, had manoeuvred Marshal Villeroy's army into a position from which it could not escape without severe loss. His bread supplies were running low (Churchill admired Marlborough's care about such logistical matters) and it was now or never. But Marlborough and Overkirk could not begin a battle without the consent of the Dutch 'field deputies', through whom the cautious republic kept an ultimately controlling eye on their commanders. The deputies, sustained by knowledge that the other Dutch generals were more cautious than Overkirk, hummed and hawed and delayed their decision until the opportunity had passed. 'Thus', judged Churchill, 'set the star of the Dutch Republic.' If they had fought then, the French would have been driven out of the Low Countries and Marlborough would have had the prestige and authority to carry the coalition to final victory in 1706. The opportunity, once passed, never returned. The war went on. The Dutch

> were to exhaust their wealth in series of seemingly interminable campaigns. Their sea-power and their share in the New World were to pass insensibly, but irresistibly and soon, to England. In the end England ... would leave them to their fate. But if the valiant Republic, to whom Protestant civilisation owes an inestimable debt, was to be deprived of its fruition in modern times, condemned to be a minor Power while rivals grew so great, this was the fatal scene. Here by the cross-roads of bodeful Waterloo ... the destinies of Holland turned.[25]

Churchill's admiration of his noble ancestor was no doubt extravagant, but his close study of how Marlborough and the other notable commanders of the time went about their business produced two of the most interesting elements of the book: a description of what commanding an army in battle then involved, and a disclosure of the intensity of Churchill's interest in generalship, the very heart of his fascination with war. Commanding campaigns and battles in Marlborough's days was, he pointed out at some length, not at all like what it was for a general in the war of 1914–18, whose 'life was not different, except in glory, from that of a painstaking, punctual public official, and far less agitating than that of a Cabinet Minister'. The eighteenth-century general had to carry a multitude of considerations in his head and, when the day of battle

came, the decisions upon which all would turn evolved 'from the eye and
brain and soul of a single man which from hour to hour was making
subconsciously all the unweighable adjustments, no doubt with many
errors, but with an ultimate practical accuracy'. It was the quality of
these mental processes that determined the greatness of the commander,
and they were in the last resort mysterious.

> That is why the campaigns of the greatest commanders often seem so sim-
> ple that one wonders why the other fellow did not do as well ... The great
> captains of history, as has been said, seem to move their armies about 'as eas-
> ily as they ride their horses from place to place'. Nothing but genius, the
> daemon in man, can answer the riddle of war, and genius, though it maybe
> armed, cannot be acquired, either by reading or experience.

What made the great commander more remarkable still was that he
had to evolve his orders, not in the calm of a Western Front HQ, but
amidst the noise, confusion and hazards of battle. Churchill gave very
good detailed descriptions of campaigns and battles, and he understood
exactly what it was like for Marlborough and his kind.

> In the midst of the scene of carnage, with its drifting smoke-clouds, scurry-
> ing fugitives, and brightly coloured lines, squares and oblongs of men, he sat
> on his horse, often in the hottest fire, holding in his mind the position and
> fortunes of every unit in his army from minute to minute, and giving his
> orders aloud ... His appearance, his serenity, his piercing eye, the tones of
> his voice – nay, the beat of his heart – diffused a harmony upon all around
> him.[26]

Churchill's admiration for these skills knew no bounds. We may conclude that he could imagine no more glorious and fulfilling role in life
than to have commanded an army in the age before war was, from his
Romantic point of view, spoiled by modern science and technology.
'That age', he concluded, 'has vanished for ever ... But let us not pretend that modern achievements can be compared, except by
million-tongued propaganda, with the personal feats which the very few
great captains of the world performed.'[27]

There was another difference between the old world and the new that
he liked to emphasise, and that was the extent to which the conduct of
war was marked by customary civilities and courtesies and, he would
give the reader to understand, a greater humanity in general. Citing the

clause in the English declaration of war that guaranteed the safety in England of French and Spanish 'persons and estates', he ironically continued:

> This passage will jar the modern mind ... Of course, nowadays, with the many improvements that have been made in international morals and behaviour, all enemy subjects ... and the English women who had married them would, as in every other state based on an educated democracy, be treated within twenty-four hours as malignant foes, flung into internment camps, and their private property stolen to assist the expenses of the war. In the twentieth century mankind has shaken itself free from all those illogical, old-world prejudices ...[28]

Like most other military historians of his time, Churchill was led by such contrasts and by his appreciation of 'the age of chivalry' to overdo the 'civilised', the more humane side of eighteenth-century warfare. In studying Marlborough's wars, he was viewing that warfare at its best; he knew little or nothing of how savage war tended to be in other theatres, for example where the Habsburgs bordered on the Ottoman Empire, or where Marlborough's nominal ally Charles XII of Sweden fought the Russians. Marlborough's campaigns were in a prosperous part of Europe so used to war that its civilian populations must have had as good an understanding of how to turn the laws and customs of war to their advantage as the military men. The rules regarding sieges of fortified towns, operations that could turn very nasty indeed for civilians, were particularly elaborate, and Marlborough was punctilious in observing them (although he did not often have to do so, preferring the shorter and sharper method of battles). He was naturally a humane man, his armies were disciplined professionals and, more important, they were well provisioned; they did not often need to wring food from peasant households.

Marlborough, however, enforced the law rigorously when it suited him, as it did in Bavaria in July 1704, before Blenheim. Max Emmanuel, the Electoral Prince of Bavaria, had broken his allegiance to the Emperor to become an ally of Louis XIV. Unable to defend his borders and unwilling to surrender, he gave Marlborough an excuse for putting pressure on him by (the technical term) 'devastating' his territories: sending the cavalry to burn villages, seize movable stores and destroy such militarily serviceable places as were undefended. In another place, his *History of the English-Speaking Peoples*, Churchill's strikingly described this policy as 'delivering the country to military execution'. Although not as extensive as the French devastation of the Palatinate in 1689, it was, like that, considered controversial and excessive. Marlborough himself professed distaste for it, pleading – as commanders always do at such times, and as Churchill might in due course have pleaded in respect of area bombing – that 'nothing but absolute necessity could have obliged me to consent to it'.[29] Churchill did not think much of that, commenting 'Men in power must be judged not by what they feel, but by what they do. To lament miseries which the will has caused is a cheap salve to a wounded conscience.' He was happier to record all the times his hero made humane arrangements (or arrangements as humane as the very primitive circumstances permitted) for the care of the wounded after battle, the exchange of prisoners and the liberal grantings of parole, which in those days was scrupulously observed by men of honour.

'Honour' mattered to officers and gentlemen in Marlborough's times to an extent which is now very difficult to realise. It mattered scarcely less in the years when Churchill was writing about them, and it had positively come to matter more in international relations. The rise of nationalism, together with the larger involvement of populations in politics, encouraged politicians to raise the temperature of debate by evoking the concept of a nation's honour, taking it for granted that states were entitled to fight for what they regarded as their 'honour' as well, of course, as for their 'vital interests'. The prevailing late nineteenth-century view that Churchill followed held well-knit nations to be communities of spirit as well as matter; statesmen commonly attributed to their countries a 'conscience', and consequently a compulsion to act in accordance with it. Oxford's Professor of Military History, Spencer Wilkinson, in 1910 published a long essay which concluded: 'The true responsibility of a nation is not for the preservation of peace, but for abstention from wrong, and the penalty of wrongdoing, whether it takes the shape of peace preserved by cowardice or of a war in an unjust cause, is for nations, as for individuals, their own corruption and degradation.'[30] The honourable obligation to stand by 'gallant little Belgium' worked powerfully on British public opinion in August 1914.

A quarter of a century later, Churchill was telling the British people that the Munich Agreement was not just a defeat, it was a degradation.

But self-interest and a decent respect for the opinion of mankind might incline nations, whatever the state of their collective moral feelings, to seek peaceful rather than warlike solutions to their differences with other members of the society of states, and to conclude wars, when they happened, in a conciliatory rather than vindictive spirit. Peacemaking mattered greatly to Churchill. War was war, and had to be fought with might and main; but the combatants were equally human beings and should respect each other as such. Once war was over, human feeling and good internationalist sense required the healing of wounds and the making of a non-vindictive, even (in the famous words of his *Second World War* motto) a 'magnanimous' peace. The treaties of Vienna and Paris in 1814 and 1815, settling the Napoleonic Wars, were models of statesmanlike wisdom.

Looking back on the eighteenth and nineteenth centuries, Churchill numbered among their other achievements the maintenance of the peace of Europe, through much of the time, by acceptance of the principle of the Balance of Power and by means of the Concert of Europe: the concurrence of the Great Powers to sort out their differences peacefully and to impose settlements upon smaller states' quarrels before they spread. 'Harmony between [the Great Powers] was too much to expect. But at least it might be arranged that the jars of international life should not lead inevitably to war.'[31]

The 1890s and early 1900s were years of much constructive activity in the fields of international law and organisation. Liberals and internationalists everywhere entertained high hopes that the unprecedented Peace and Disarmament Conference that convened in 1899 in The Hague would have among its wholesome results legal obligations upon states to take disputes to arbitration. Neither then nor at the follow-up conference in 1907 would the Great Powers agree to be obliged to go to arbitration, but there was a general consensus that it could settle interstate disputes of the lesser, non-threatening kind. Indeed, since the 1850s it had increasingly done so. Arbitration was a new field for the practice of diplomacy, a high-class skill that Churchill much admired: 'polite, discreet, pacific, and on the whole sincere'.[32] Churchill valued it as an effective instrument in preventing war and maintaining the front of

civilisation. He met diplomats and senior Foreign Office officials as well
as experienced statesmen in the salons, house parties and holiday resorts
where he liked to spend his time, and he wrote with admiring warmth
of their work in *The World Crisis*. 'Many quarrels that might have led to
war have been adjusted by the old diplomacy of Europe and have, in
Lord Melbourne's phrase, "blown over".'[33]

He found an opportunity for an engaging portrayal of the old diplomacy at work in his description of the Agadir Crisis that threatened the
peace of Europe through the summer of 1911 – which, he said, first
turned his mind seriously to the coming European crisis. 'The Great
Powers [in this case, Germany and France] marshalled on either side,
preceded and protected by an elaborate cushion of diplomatic courtesies and formalities, would display to each other their respective arrays',
with their allies and neighbours half-hidden and secretly consulted
behind them. 'At the proper moment these seconds or supporters would
utter certain cryptic words indicative of their state of mind' and the
leading protagonists would move – move perhaps only slightly, but significantly enough for those who understood the code – 'and the whole
formidable assembly would withdraw to their own apartments with cer-
emony and salutations and congratulate or condole with each other in
whispers on the result. We had seen it several times before.'[34] His record
of the weeks immediately preceding the outbreak of war in the summer
of 1914 shows how he continued until the last days to hope that they
would see it again.

Of the considerable body of international law produced at The Hague
Conferences of 1899 and 1907, two elements particularly interested
Churchill. One concerned maritime commerce in wartime: the rights of
neutrals and the definition of contraband of war. Would it stick to munitions and other primary military necessities or would it spread to include
foodstuffs? Even if the latter were legally declared 'free goods', Churchill
felt sure that such legal title would not survive the challenge of war. He
spoke in the debate on the Navy Estimates in May 1904 and warned
against over reliance on 'international assurance'. The 'pretty ribbons' of
internationalist idealism would not for long restrain belligerents from
doing what military necessity demanded. 'Notwithstanding many Hague
Conferences to the contrary,' he insisted, 'corn would be declared contraband of war', whether it was Britain or its supposititious enemies doing

the blockading. He had difficulty in conceiving that war could remain limited, even if it began so, and when he was in charge of blockade in both world wars he proved impenetrable to humanitarian pleas for its relaxation.

The other element of those conferences that attracted him was their attempt to set in order and to universalise the moderating rules of combat and practices regarding occupation of enemy territory. These rules were already familiar as *customary* international law to the officer corps of all civilised armies, about which Churchill had learnedly written in *Marlborough*. These Land Warfare Regulations had not long been agreed before Churchill himself was the thankful beneficiary of two of them, concerning respectively the immunity of civilians and the humane treatment of prisoners of war. His books about wars in India and Africa frequently touched on the subject. The contrast between civilised and uncivilised warfare (as the standard distinction then ran) impressed itself painfully upon him. The restraints that instinctively operated when Briton met Boer were simply not there when Briton met frontier tribesman. It was a matter that remained important to him for life, not least because of the chivalric elements surviving in these laws and customs from their ancient origins in the code of knighthood. He liked chivalry and took to people who seemed to represent it. Political realist and tough fighter that he was, he was prepared to go far in pursuit of victory in war – how far, will be seen – but there was a limit beyond which even he would not go. This limit was not one prescribed by international law, it was a principle from the codes of the knight and the gentleman: 'I have no scruple', he once said, 'except not to do anything dishonourable.'[35] The same principle appeared in his noble memorial tribute to Neville Chamberlain: 'The sole guide to a man is his conscience; the only shield to his memory is the rectitude and sincerity of his actions ... With this shield, however the fates may play, we march always in the ranks of honour.'[36]

15

The Conduct of War

Near the close of *Marlborough*, Churchill philosophised about the individual's nescience concerning the future; the only 'rule of conduct' that could surely sustain the soldier and the statesman was, he believed, 'fidelity to covenants, the honour of soldiers, and the hatred of causing human woe'.[1] The question has now to be considered, how far Churchill's style of war-making conformed to this ideal. Did it stay within the limits of the honourable and – not the same thing – the lawful? In civil society, morality and good feeling may forbid what law allows; in wartime, law may forbid what military necessity demands. Some Britons raised their voices on certain occasions during the Second World War to suggest that Churchill allowed military necessity too wide a scope. Their criticisms annoyed him, but it was to his credit and to the credit of the free democratic state he headed that they were allowed to make them publicly and to get away with it.[2] Criticism of a more wholesale kind came from the enemy side. The German propaganda machine in the Second World War made Churchill out to be a gangster and a terrorist. German writers since then, joined from time to time by writers in other lands, have alleged that the bombing of German cities which Churchill authorised went beyond the limits of legality. He has even been called a 'war criminal'. The charge is misguided but it usefully prompts consideration of how such an idea can have arisen; which itself involves an inquiry, so far as evidence allows, into just what Churchill believed about the laws and ethics of war.

Assessment of Churchill's mentality in this respect has to rely on observation, not just of what he said and did but equally of what he did *not* say or do. As so often happens in historical inquiry, what is not said may be what matters most, because it was not thought necessary to say it. People do not talk about what is taken for granted. Churchill's soldierly mind was formed at a time when war was a normal condition of

life, when states were free to go to war when and as they chose, when
the direction of war was a gentlemanly profession, and when 'officers
and gentlemen' – a familiar coupling, pregnant with meaning – imbibed
from history, family, school, colleagues and colonels an imperative
understanding of what you might do, and what you might not do, in
war.

These conventional rules of conduct were called the 'laws and
customs of war', even before the Geneva and Hague regulations had
filtered into national military manuals; they embodied customs of
warfare between civilised states which were so firmly accepted as to
acquire the force of law. Where they were clearly beyond dispute, as for
example in not breaking parole and in not killing prisoners, it was a
matter of gentleman's honour to observe them. Where they were less
clear and subject to interpretation, as for example in the conduct of
sieges and assaults, the management of occupied territory and the legit-
imacy of 'devastation', experienced officers and the pioneers of
international law debated about particular cases, weighed military and
moral imperatives against one another, and tried, with little success, to
come to agreed conclusions. The laws and customs of war, so far as
there was clarity about them, were shaped by men of war and were
stated in easily intelligible language. Their observance rested on the
moral and religious principles of the officers in charge, and the means
of dealing with unforeseen eventualities was left to the good sense and
principles of the men on the spot. This was the mental world Churchill
was brought up in, and in these respects it was not much changed from
the earlier world he described in such detail in his great *Marlborough*
biography.

By the time he died, the world was very different. The charter of the
United Nations and its juridical offshoots determined what should be
the proper peaceful behaviour of states towards each other; most of the
old violent forms of state action were ruled out, and international
law even intruded into how states should organise their own internal
affairs (in particular, human rights). The laws of war had swollen
hugely in quantity and detail, being the outcomes of international
conferences peopled largely by non-military delegates: diplomats, politicians, 'experts', even lobbyists. Themselves produced by political
processes, their product was comfortingly camouflaged as 'international

humanitarian law'.[3] Political pressure in the General Assembly grew through the 1960s, demanding yet more 'humanitarian law' to cover areas of warfare that had so far only been regulated, very patchily, by the post-1945 war crimes trials: wars of national liberation, guerrilla warfare, armed conflicts that might not be inter-state wars at all, and – a weighty left-over from the Second World War – aerial bombardment.[4]

All of this must have seemed to Churchill misguided and counter-productive, if he ever knew anything about it, which he probably didn't. He left the launching of the United Nations to the Foreign Secretary and observed its early years with sceptical detachment. He had little interest in the setting up of the international criminal court that established itself at Nuremberg, leaving it entirely to the Foreign Office and the government's law officers. 'Nuremberg' was an American project, heartily seconded (with totally different ends in view) by the Soviet Union; Britain went along with it reluctantly because it had no choice. But there was no doubt as to Churchill's determination that the 'atrocities, massacres and cold-blooded mass-executions' committed in German-occupied countries should in due course be avenged. It was he who drafted the Three-Power Declaration published in October 1943, informing the perpetrators of those deeds that 'they will be brought back, regardless of expense, to the scene of their crimes and judged on the spot by the peoples whom they have outraged'.[5]

This intention found what appears to be its first expression as early as February 1941. On the 2nd of that month his private secretary recorded the news of 'sadistic atrocities, unsurpassed in horror' being committed against Jews in Romania; 'The PM has sent a minute to the Foreign Secretary: "Would it not be well to tell General Antonescu that we will hold him and his immediate circle personally responsible"' if these atrocities go on?[6] Within eighteen months this personal revulsion had hardened into public commitment. He assured New York's Jewish community on 21 July 1942 that 'Our resolve is to place retribution for Nazi butcheries and terrorism among the major purposes of this war'.[7] That covered the mass of the miscreants. What was to be done with 'the major criminals whose offences have no particular geographical location' was still to be decided. His own preference was that the fifty or hundred most evil and dangerous of them, if taken alive, should be executed by summary political or military process. His mind being made up about those matters, he put them along with so many others to that area at the back of his mind labelled 'Pending the end of the war'.

The war crimes trials that he had not done much to promote duly took place, to his satisfaction and astonishment: 'I would never have believed in the atrocities committed by them [some of the Nuremberg defendants] if I had not seen the evidence which revealed their terrible crimes.'[8] One aspect of the post-war vogue for criminal prosecutions of the losers, however, came to bother him. Possessed as he was by old-fashioned principles about the honour of the military profession and the responsibilities of high command, he became unhappy about the long imprisonment pending prosecution of senior German officers, generals and field-marshals. He thought this a humiliation for distinguished prisoners, he rightly doubted whether it was consistent with the 1929 Geneva Convention, and he suspected they were guilty of no more than having done their duty in difficult circumstances. It is true that he did not look closely enough at their cases to inquire whether or not they had actively facilitated or participated in atrocities perpetrated by the German security services – but neither did anyone else in those early post-war years. (If they had done so, Manstein for one would not have got off as easily as he did.) Churchill's friend Field-Marshal Montgomery did not conceal his conviction that, if Britain had lost the war instead of winning it, he and other leading British generals would have been in the dock instead of Keitel, Jodl and Manstein. When the Nuremberg verdict was published, Churchill remarked to Ismay that, if things had gone differently, 'you and I would be in a pretty pickle'.[9]

Montgomery's comment brings us to the heart of the matter concerning Churchill and the laws of war. Churchill was a humane, indeed in some respects an unusually sentimental and soft-hearted man, given to tears when moved. Evidences of his humanity and human sympathies, often strangely juxtaposed with evidence of other and tougher attributes, appear all through his life. For instance, he hated the atrocities that marked the frontier wars of his youth; his heart bled for the Mahdist wounded left dying in the desert after Omdurman; he was enthusiastic about the Geneva Conventions for the protection of the wounded and prisoners of war (and he paid tribute to the German military authorities when they observed them); he was incredulous when his hero 'Jackie' Fisher predicted unrestricted submarine warfare, and appalled when in 1914 the admiral proposed holding German civilians as hostages and killing one each time a Zeppelin dropped a bomb; he wept over the sufferings of British and Allied civilians under bombardment and regretted the necessity of having to bomb German civilians; he stigmatised undeclared minefields as 'the lowest form of warfare', and it was not he but Asquith, the Prime Minister, who ordered the neutral areas of the North Sea to be mined in October 1914.[10] His record regarding policy towards the vanquished was one of consistent magnanimity. There is no more striking or beautifully expressed an example of it than what he said in the Commons on 12 November 1946:

> There must be an end to vengeance and retribution. I am told that Germany must be punished. I ask: When did punishment begin? It certainly seems to have been going on for a long time. It began in 1943, and continued during 1944 and 1945 when the most frightful air bombardments were cast upon German cities, and when the general exhaustion of their life under the cruel Nazi regime had drained the last ounces of strength from the German race and nation. [The Nazi leaders having been brought to justice, root-and-branch de-nazification now was all the rage. He thought it was going too far.] After all, in a country which is handled as Germany was, the ordinary people have very little choice about what to do ... Everyone is not a Pastor Niemöller or a martyr, and when ordinary people are hurled this way and that, when the cruel hands of tyrants are laid upon them and vile systems of regimentation are imposed and enforced by espionage and other forms of cruelty, there are great numbers of people who will succumb. I thank God that in this island home of ours we have never been put to the test which many of the peoples of Europe have had to undergo.

Notwithstanding the genuine humanity that showed in these and countless other instances, he also knew that war could be a dreadfully demanding affair that overturned the norms of peacetime and hardened, unless first it broke, the softest of hearts. It opened up a condition of existence which only men of war themselves could understand, and it drove men to decisions and deeds of whose moral merits only their military peers could judge. Another of Churchill's wartime companions, Air Marshal Sir Arthur Harris, in his memoirs wrote something that matched Churchill's thinking. Justifying the work of Bomber Command, he said: 'there was nothing to be ashamed of, except in the sense that everybody might be ashamed of the sort of thing that has to be done in every war'.[11] Unless you were a pacifist and decided to keep out of it altogether, that was the fact you had to live with and be ready to die with.

What then was Churchill's philosophy of war? It was largely home grown. There is no trace of his having read Clausewitz, who was available in a not very good English translation from 1908, but on one major and basic point his ideas coincided with those of the great Prussian writer. This was that war is by its very nature chaotic, unpredictable and chancy. Often and again he affirmed this maxim.[12] For example: 'The longer one lives, the more one realizes that everything depends upon Chance ... In war, which is an intense form of life, Chance presents herself nakedly from moment to moment as the direct arbiter over all persons and events.'[13] An eloquently comprehensive statement came in *My Early Life*, as he recalled Britain's approach to the war against the Boers:

> Let us learn our lessons. Never, never, never believe any war will be smooth and easy, or that anyone who embarks on that strange voyage can measure the tides and hurricanes he will encounter. The Statesman who yields to war fever must realize that once the signal is given, he is no longer the master of policy but the slave of unforeseen and uncontrollable events. Antiquated War Offices, weak, incompetent or arrogant Commanders, untrustworthy allies, hostile neutrals, malignant fortune, ugly surprises, awful miscalculations – all take their seat at the Council Board on the morrow of a declaration of war.[14]

This inherent unpredictability of war, the certainty only of uncertainty and therefore the predestined hollowness of the warmaker's predictions and promises, can actually constitute a sound plank in the pacifist's platform. For Churchill of course it meant only that war, unavoidable from time to time as it seemed to be in the imperfect society of states, was an admittedly imperfect means of settling their squabbles. It was therefore one of the sources of his lifelong interest in preventing the gathering of squabbles and suspicions to the point where war was the only way out. It was also one of the explanations he gave himself, perhaps too readily, when things went wrong. It made him more fatalistic than he need have been. Aneurin Bevan put his finger on this in one of those parliamentary confrontations that Churchill so much disliked. At a time when the war was going embarrassingly badly, in the course of seconding the 'No Confidence' motion on 2 July 1942, Bevan remarked that 'The Prime Minister wins debate after debate and loses battle after battle'. He was making a legitimate point. Churchill could always talk himself out of any disastrous hole by grandiose rhetoric about the hazards and disappointments inseparable from any belligerent enterprise and the imperative to carry on regardless.

A second and less obvious Clausewitzian conclusion was a dramatic extension of the principle of unpredictability. Besides being a realm of Chance, war was also a realm of Necessity. Not only did this mean that in war you would find yourself doing what you had not expected to do, it also meant that you might find yourself having to do what you could never have wished to do. This was because of the common tendency of modern wars to escalate towards total levels of violence. Not for nothing have the worst of them been characterised as 'total'. It happened in both of Churchill's world wars that restraints observed in the early phases yielded willy-nilly to two escalating tendencies, both of them irresistible so long as neither party acknowledged defeat. The first of these was the practice of reprisals. The laws and customs of war have always had to allow reprisals, sometimes the only way to stop an enemy gaining military advantage by doing unlawful things, but being of their nature escalatory they have never found a place in the legal instruments of war, being subject merely to the general principle of proportionality and the specific rule that 'the right of belligerents to adopt means of injuring the enemy is not unlimited'.[15] The other tendency towards escalation came from science and technology with their unceasing and, in both world wars, successful search for ever bigger and more effective weapons.

About these tendencies, and how to deal with them, the international law of war as it was before 1945 had little to say.* As the custodian of its Geneva parts, the International Committee of the Red Cross likes to remind subscribers (and as the textbooks affirm with regard to the parts made at The Hague), the laws of war are and always have been strictly

---

* I do not imply that it necessarily has found more to say in its post-1945 forms.

neutral regarding the merits of the case and as between belligerents. But since the law's avowed purposes included minimising the horrors and damages of war and preserving the civilised values common to all belligerents, it is natural to suppose that somewhere within it lay the presumption that wars would not be carried on to the bitterest and most destructive end, and that evident losers would have the sense to give up before that stage was reached. Such a supposition might have been understood to be the spirit of these laws. But it was certainly not in their letter, which contained no more about the ending of a war than a mass of humanitarian detail about what should happen once a war was ended, including how the victor should treat the population of an occupied country and how prisoners should be returned to their homelands.

The First World War was brought to an end by Germany's recognition in the autumn of 1918 that, as its allies were succumbing, its army was exhausted and war-weary, and further fighting promised diminishing returns, it had better seek an armistice while the fighting was still being conducted on foreign fields. Germany's foremost soldier, Ludendorff, after something like a nervous breakdown, recovered his nerve and wanted to go on fighting to the bitter end, like the Japanese militarists in 1945, but he was denied that opportunity. The guns duly fell silent at 11 a.m. on 11 November 1918, and the German armies marched home in good order into a Germany hardly damaged at all by enemy action.

The Second World War did not come to an end so rationally, either in Europe or Asia, and very extreme things happened in consequence. Consider first the case of Japan. To the rest of the world's eyes, it was clear by 1945 that Japan was doomed to defeat. Whether the Japanese government and armed forces could see this as clearly, and what if anything it would do about it, was however unclear. Their armed forces were notoriously not of a surrendering disposition, they were doing unexpectedly great damage to American ships by kamikaze attacks, and the government had long been under the thumb of the hypernationalist military. Very secretly, non-fanatical men in government had been engaging in secret talks with Moscow (then still neutral) about the possibility of a negotiated peace. America and Britain learned of those talks but could not judge whether the military would go along with such peace terms as might be arranged. During the fateful days when the atomic

bombs were being prepared, they received from Tokyo no overt encour-
agements to hold their hand – perhaps because they had not made clear
enough how revolutionary a hand they actually held. That they should
wait indefinitely while fighting continued and Allied servicemen (and
their brothers and sisters in Japanese hands) went on dying every day,
and while they could only guess how the Japanese military would react,
was unthinkable. (That uncertainty is worth emphasising, because critics of the Hiroshima decision often slide from the fact of secret talks with
Moscow to the assertion that Japan was on the verge of surrendering.)
We have already seen what happened. It was correctly reckoned, with
Churchill's concurrence, that a sudden and awful shock, such as the
bomb promised to be, would prompt the Emperor and his ministers to
make up their collective mind. In the event, the Hiroshima shock of 6
August was seconded by another shock, the Russian declaration of war
on 8 August, which is generally thought to have shared in producing the
desired effect. But, had Russia not moved on that date and had the second bomb not been dropped on the 9th or (as was originally planned)
shortly thereafter, the effect would doubtless have been the same.

No such confident reckoning is possible about the ending of the war
in Europe. Had the bomb been available six months earlier, it might
presumably have been considered for use against Germany, although
what form that use might have taken and whether it would have succeeded is impossible to know and pointless to think about. The concept
of a sudden and awful shock, aptly code-named 'Thunderclap', was current in British strategic planning from August 1944 and, after some
delay, was administered by the combined American and British bomber
forces to Dresden on the 13/14 February 1945; but it was not the one huge
shock initially conceived, it was not obviously successful in bringing
about the end of the war, and it became the principal grounds for
charging Churchill with war crime.[16]

Criticism of this Dresden raid and of Churchill's encouragement of
it has rested on two propositions: that Dresden was not a legitimate
military target; and that Germany was nearly defeated anyway. Let the
latter proposition be considered first. The defeat of Germany had looked
to be within reach in early September 1944, when the Allies had broken
out of their Normandy bridgehead and for some weeks moved fast
across France (Paris being liberated on 25 August) towards the German

frontier and the Rhine (most of Belgium being liberated in early September, Luxembourg by the middle). Operation Market Garden to seize the bridge across the lower Rhine at Arnhem began on 17 September, with the promise of opening the way to the Ruhr. It proved to be, in the tragic phrase, a bridge too far. The great port of Antwerp, logistically indispensable, remained unusable until the end of November. The Allied land campaign became bogged down, hopes of an end to the war by Christmas were abandoned, and there were several indications that Germany was by no means yet defeated. V1 flying-bombs and V2 ballistic missiles, which Churchill correctly defined as 'literally and essentially indiscriminate in nature, purpose and effect', were causing death, damage, fear and depression in London.[17] Jet fighters were restoring some edge to German air defence, and it was known that huge resources had been put into producing a fearsome new generation of U-boats.[18] What was worse, in mid-December the Wehrmacht showed what it could still do in the Ardennes offensive that knocked the Allied armies off-balance for several weeks. In January 1945, when the Dresden operation was planned, the end of the European war was not yet within sight.

Though offensive action on the ground was temporarily halted, it was still possible in the air. The British and American air chiefs in mid-January 1945 were already debating what to do, and whether to revive the 'Thunderclap' plan, when their attention was drawn to the desirability of supporting the gigantic Russian offensive just then beginning on the Eastern Front. If anything seemed likely to hasten the end of the war, that was it. Some thought that the Red Army could best be helped by targeting oil production, others that support could better be given by smashing communications centres in the German rear. Dithering was brought to an end by Churchill who, as ever, was anxious to show willing to Stalin and was going to be meeting him at Yalta within a week. In one of his very rare interferences with RAF self-rule, he gave orders that Berlin, Chemnitz, Leipzig and Dresden, the great cities astride communications behind Germany's *Ostfront*, were to be attacked as soon as weather conditions permitted.[19] When Churchill told them what was about to happen, the Russians were delighted.

The bombings, when they were executed on the night of 13/14 February by the RAF and on the following day by the USAAF, were uncommonly successful in their destructive and disruptive purposes. Dresden and the other eastern cities (bombed soon after, with inferior results) had long been on the RAF's hit list as places of industrial and administrative importance. Dresden, far from being the non-industrial city of pacifist and humanitarian belief (following Goebbels's propaganda), was in fact of even more industrial importance than British Intelligence knew; its information was out of date and omitted the Zeiss-Ikon works, which, along with most others in the city area, were put out of action for weeks or for ever. The bridges and railways were damaged enough to achieve the raid's other purpose, the stoppage for a while of traffic through the city, although a minimal service was restored within a few days; the *Reichsbahndirektion* had over 100,000 workers permanently available in that area for reconstruction work and profound experience had made them good at the job.[20]

There therefore appears to be no cause for specially stigmatising either the bombing of Dresden or Churchill's share in it. Dresden was as much of a military objective as many of the cities already attacked as such. It was subjected to a city area bombing of the kind that had been going on for three years. The raid had the additional and particular purpose of assisting the Russian offensive which, at the time the action was planned, appeared to be the likeliest means of bringing the war to a long-desired end (incidentally, shortening the sufferings of the vanquished as well as those of the victors). That military objective was achieved, a massive quantity of collateral destruction was done, and between 35,000 and 40,000 people were killed. That the raid had been, in Bomber Command's terms, unusually successful was partly due to the unusual failure of German air defence and the local administration's neglect and mismanagement of the shelters and civil defence preparations.[21] Dresden being a cultural jewel as well as a legitimate target, the German propaganda machine succeeded in selling it (with much exaggeration of the casualties) to a war-weary world as the worst example yet of what Goebbels's machine had long denounced as 'terror-bombing'. Since Goebbels did Churchill the honour of singling him out as the arch-terrorist, the whole history of Britain's strategic bombing offensive must now be considered. If Dresden itself was nothing out of the ordinary by the standards prevailing in early 1945, what was there in its prehistory that bred an 'ordinary' so awful?

Churchill was among the earliest proponents of aerial bombardment. His Royal Naval Air Service had bombed German military objectives, with some success, soon after the beginning of war in 1914. At that time, he could conceive of no other targets proper to be bombed. His ideas had developed by the time when, four years later, he was helping to plan the air war to be unleashed on Germany in 1919. With whatever character it began, the war had turned into, and been experienced and vaunted as, an all-out struggle between whole populations, each totally mobilised to maximise its national war effort. The theoretical gap between non-combatants and combatants shrank to nothing: why should not factory, railway and government workers be regarded as contributing essentially to the war? Both nations' navies sought in their own ways to inflict suffering on the other's population, and so did their developing air forces. German Zeppelins indiscriminately bombed London and other accessible places from the earliest months of the war and German multi-engined bombers continued the work; by 1918 Britain too had acquired heavy bombers, which raided the cities of the Ruhr from airfields in France and were intended to do much more in the 1919 grand offensive that never happened. The aim was not primarily to kill enemy civilians. It was to terrify them and to discourage them from working in the factories, railway junctions and other industrial places that were the primary targets; but some civilians were inevitably be killed nevertheless. Bombing inaccuracy could be relied on to have that expected double effect. The theory of city bombing as it was practised in the Second World War was already fully formed by the end of the First; Churchill, who knew from his extensive knowledge of war history that non-combatants had always suffered in such staple military practices as blockades, sieges and naval bombardments, accepted it as an inevitable and necessary modern development.

The years between the wars heard much talk about the frightfulness of city bombing and witnessed several attempts at the international level to limit and even to ban it, but all failed; not least because, following the regular pattern of international humanitarian legislation, all parties were willing to say they would not do a bad thing, but they were not willing to forego possession of the means of reprisal in the event that a bad thing was done to them. The Second World War began with protestations on all sides that the basic legal principle of civilian immunity would be observed, and so it scrupulously was for the duration of the 'Phoney War' in the west and into the summer of 1940, neither Germany nor Britain finding it necessary to go further. Such restraint was doomed to crack, however, when the stakes got higher. They got higher for Hitler when Britain declined to make peace as expected (and as military reason dictated) after the fall of France, and higher for Churchill when Britain (defying military reason) determined to hold on in trust of future salvation, meanwhile hitting back against Germany with the only means available. So Hitler launched the 'Blitz' and Churchill launched Bomber Command.

As Churchill sometimes remarked, when reporting Bomber Command's effective city bombings and the German propaganda machine's complaints about them, 'they began it'.[22] This was perfectly true as a reflection of British and German experience in 1940 and 1941; the 'Blitz' did very much more damage to British cities and war production than Britain's bombers, inadequate and ill-navigated as they were at that time, did in those years to German cities and factories. Bomber Command's poor early record, however, was not for lack of will. The Royal Air Force had for many years been gearing up for city bombing – its bombing doctrinaires even proclaiming that they could win the war on their own – and was only not doing it better because of poor planning and out-of-date equipment. About the middle of 1941 the Butt Report, instigated by the Prof, placed Bomber Command's failure beyond question. What, then, was to be done? The new Chief of Air Staff, Charles Portal, produced the answer. The existing practice must be inverted. Instead of aiming to hit a military objective and mostly bombing the area all around it, Bomber Command must bomb the area and expect to hit the military objective within it. From early 1942, with Air Vice-Marshal Arthur Harris enthusiastically in command, four-engined heavy bombers beginning to enter service, and with the Prime Minister's backing Bomber Command began to do precisely this.

The legal and ethical pros and cons of area bombing and the way it was done continue to excite controversy, although the space for sensible disagreement has considerably shrunk since serious study began forty years ago.[23] Several red herrings have polluted the debate from the start. First, the one that began in the United States and was cultivated by its airmen to the effect that area bombing (bad) was the British practice and 'precision bombing' (good) the American. It is true that the USAAF set out to specialise in the latter; but what actually happened, as the war went on, was that the British got better at precision bombing and the Americans discovered that in European weather conditions they often had to resort to area bombing.[24] It is usually forgotten that the bombing of Dresden was a combined operation, and that, had weather conditions been different, the USAAF would have done its bombing first.

The second red herring is the 'terror' one, never wholly separable from its tainted origin in German propaganda, which was rich in self-righteousness and double standards as well as lies. By labelling the British bomber crews as *Terrorflieger* and calling the 1944 V1 and V2 'reprisal weapons' (V standing not for Victory, as Londoners ingenuously supposed, but for *Vergeltung*, reprisal), Goebbels and his propagandists spread the implication that Bomber Command was doing much worse things to civilians than the Luftwaffe had done. In the limited material sense, and as between Britain and Germany through the last three years of the war, that was indeed the case. The weight of bombs dropped on Britain between the end of the Blitz and the time of the V-weapons was negligible compared to the ever increasing weights being dropped on Germany. Churchill was quite frank about it, publicly relishing the fact that what the Germans had started, they were getting back in spades. German civilian life was part of the target, as British civilian life had been earlier on and, in the London area, still was in the winter of 1944/45.

In any case, the comparison merely of numbers of civilians killed in those two countries, though it was convenient for the German controversialist to limit the comparison to that, was only part of the story for his British counterpart, who might not wish to leave out of account the millions of civilians killed by various means in Germany's invasion, occupation and exploitation of its eastern neighbours. To bring them also into the balance, to view also the razed cities and desolated landscapes of Poland, the Ukraine and Russia, not to mention the Holocaust, once the facts about it were known, was to go way beyond the purview of the laws of war; it also suggested that those laws themselves were not entirely adequate to the demands of a war against such an enemy.

Churchill on several occasions showed uneasiness about Harris's offensive: most notably when, watching an Air Ministry film that showed German cities on fire beneath the assault, he burst out 'Are we beasts? Are we taking this too far?'[25] Of course he knew that some parts of the British public had doubts about it, and he might well have known that some of Harris's RAF peers had doubts about to too.[26] He must also have known that the Air Ministry gave disingenuous answers to questions as to what Bomber Command was actually doing. Harris himself was not ashamed of what he was doing and would have liked the ministry to be more open about it: his view was that this was total war and the British public had better not be fooled that it was engaged in anything less.[27]

Churchill himself might not have become directly involved in the question of the ethics of Harris's conduct of operations, were it not for the minute he addressed to the Chief of Air Staff, Harris's only superior – his only superior, that is, other than the Minister of Defence himself or the Allied Combined Chiefs of Staff – on 28 March 1945:

> It seems to me that the moment has come when the question of bombing of German cities simply for the sake of increasing the terror, though under other pretexts, should be reviewed. Otherwise we shall come into control of an utterly ruined land ... The destruction of Dresden remains a serious query against the conduct of Allied bombing ... the Foreign Secretary has spoken to me on this subject, and I feel the need for more precise concentration upon military objectives, such as oil and communications behind the immediate battle zone, rather than on mere acts of terror and wanton destruction, however impressive.[28]

No documentary context for this minute has been discovered, nor has anyone yet come up with a comprehensive explanation of it. Its date should be noted: six weeks after Dresden, but in the midst of other post-Dresden raids, the justifications for which were more questionable – especially considering that by this date the war really was at last approaching its end. Churchill himself was moved to minute the Air Ministry a few weeks later again, 'What was the point of going and blowing down Potsdam?'[29] It has been surmised that his minute to Portal was a calculated attempt to distance himself from the uproar about Dresden, but if it was that, he put strangely little punch behind it.[30] An alternative explanation might be that the substance of the minute, contrasting so strangely with what Churchill himself had said through the past four years, actually came from the Foreign Secretary or some other concerned source, and that Churchill was content to forward it to Portal without feeling personally committed. A certain lack of commitment is indeed suggested by the tameness with which Churchill took Portal's subsequent rebuke and substituted a minute that amounted to a withdrawal of the earlier one. If he had felt strongly about the matter, he could have made sure that his original minute to Portal was less open to the obvious riposte that he was abruptly changing his mind and pulling the rug out from under loyal servants.

In theory he could even have forced the issue by sacking Harris, as he had sacked top commanders earlier in the war, but there are several reasons why he could not have taken such a dramatic step. For one thing, Portal might have threatened to resign too, in sympathy. For another, Harris was a popular chief of Bomber Command, and Bomber Command itself was popular with the greater part of the British public; its leader's dismissal would not only have rocked RAF morale, it would have stirred up a formidable political row, exactly the sort of thing a tired old man with bigger worries wouldn't wish to face or, at that stage of the war, consider worth facing. Gentler or earlier Churchillian persuasions might have succeeded in moderating Harris's obsessive zeal, but, as was observed already,[31] they were not forthcoming. Churchill did nothing to support those, including Portal himself in 1944–45, who believed that Harris should be brought back under control, and by the time his minute of 28 March seemed to show, however momentarily, that he shared Portal's belief, it was too late. The war ended with Churchill still ultimately responsible for a city-destroying policy that had outlived, though by how much is arguable, its usefulness and its justification.

It is clear that Churchill had no great interest in the codified international law of war, peace and neutrality (to give the laws and customs of war their official title and context). We have already seen how he found the law's stance of neutrality regarding belligerents particularly irksome. Its permissions and its bans were impartially directed towards each and every side in war. Uninterested in whether belligerents' causes were 'good' or 'bad', the law's universe was peopled simply with those who observed the law, those who broke the law, and those who needed the law's protection. This clinical attitude, which Foreign Offices perforce adopted until it was in their pressing national interest to drop it, annoyed Churchill because on occasion it made 'good' Britain seem the bad belligerent and 'bad' Germany the good one.

A notable instance of this galling reversal of roles came in February 1940 when the German merchant ship *Altmark,* known to be conveying several hundred British prisoners taken by the *Graf Spee* during its brief commerce-raiding career, was reported to have entered Norwegian territorial waters, within which it could remain all the way back to Germany. Churchill, then still at the Admiralty, ordered that the ship be stopped and searched. This was promptly done, in the face of solemn Norwegian protests and shrill German cries of outrage. The prisoners were found and released after a short scuffle, and the *Altmark* was left to continue its voyage without them. What international law actually required in this instance was, as so often, indeterminate; and, again as usual, each side produced 'experts' to justify its own position.[32]

Churchill was no different from other war leaders of his own age (and perhaps of ours) in his attitude towards neutrals. Neutrals were viewed simply as pieces on the chequerboard of power; the law regarding them was respected only insofar as it was politically and militarily necessary or advantageous to respect it. How to handle Norway perplexed both British and German governments through the period of the Phoney War. Norway's neutrality was of advantage to Germany so long as Britain respected it. For so long as Germany took advantage of it, Britain was at a disadvantage. Chamberlain's government for many months could not make up its mind what to do. Churchill's mind was made up by December 1939. He put the case for mining the waters through which German vessels passed to and fro and at the same time eased his own mind in a long memorandum to the Cabinet that concluded thus:

> The final tribunal is our own conscience. We are fighting to re-establish the reign of law and to protect the liberties of small countries. Our defeat would mean an age of violence, and would be fatal not only to ourselves but to the independent life of every small country in Europe. Acting in the name of the Covenant, and as virtual mandatories of the League and all it stands for, we have a right, and indeed are bound in duty, to abrogate for a space some of the conventions of the very laws we seek to consolidate and reaffirm. Small nations must not tie our hands when we are fighting for their rights

and freedom. The letter of the law must not in supreme emergency obstruct those who are charged with its protection and enforcement. It would not be right or rational that the Aggressor Power should gain one set of advantages by tearing up all laws, and another set by sheltering behind the innate respect for law of its opponents. Humanity, rather than legality, must be our guide.[33]

Who dares say that he was wrong? But what he was proposing was, technically, law-breaking. So too were or would have been several of the other breaches of the rights of neutral states he authorised or desired in the course of the war. It cannot be denied that his strong-mindedness in this respect came not solely from conviction of the rightness of the British cause. As already noted, small states were only small places in his world view. Big states, states capable of playing the parts of Great Powers on the world stage, were the only political entities that mattered; in the event of trouble between them, small states had either to keep out of the way (if they could) or sign up under one Great Power banner or another. The naval strategies and amphibious operations Churchill loved to pore over at the Admiralty paid no attention at all to the political complications with regard to the Baltic States. In January 1916 he wrote casually to Fisher about 'bringing in Denmark' on the way to 'domination of the Baltic'.[34]

The ideas of 'bringing in' Norway, and even, if it could be managed, Sweden, came naturally to Churchill in the winter of 1939/40. He would have brought in Turkey if he could. Ireland's neutrality throughout the war infuriated him, and his Cabinet colleagues repeatedly had to press the argument that an Ireland that was neutral but not unfriendly was better than a partially occupied Ireland seething with indignation.[35] The Foreign Secretary had difficulty in persuading him that Allied air bases in the Portuguese-owned Azores were better obtained by diplomacy than by force, even if that took somewhat longer. The behaviour of Spain, a strategically significant and ideologically hostile neutral, was under strict surveillance, and its neutrality was only respected in consequence of calculations that it was more useful to the Allies that way; and besides, Britain and the United States soon found out how they could maintain an economic squeeze on it. The only neutral state that was secure from the Allies' pressures was of course Switzerland, whose neutrality was of value to them; they were thankful that the outcome of

Hitler's calculations as to whether to leave it alone or invade it was that its neutrality was of value to him too.

Hitler and the Nazified elements of German opinion did not, as a matter of fact, value international law as the British and Americans and their Allies did. Its long history from Roman origins through the centuries of Christian Europe made it part of the history of a civilisation that the Thousand Year Reich was out to destroy. Its foundation in the equal rights of states, whatever the nature of their peoples, was incompatible with the Nazi-German dogmas of Aryan racial superiority and the subordination to it of peoples of other races. That is why there was an irreducible element of humbug in Nazi propaganda's appeals to the laws of war. German observance of them was selective. The Wehrmacht generally dispensed with them on the *Ostfront*, which was the easier to justify in view of Moscow's dogma (similarly seeking a break from the past) that the existing international law was a bourgeois construction, waiting to be put into history's dustbin. As against the British and other 'Westerners', however, Germany found good grounds, both racial and practical, for observing the laws of war, and – with the grim exception of the SS and with serious qualifications in respect of the Waffen SS – the Wehrmacht was at least as good at observing them as the Allied armies.

That is why, if they had taken possession of England after overcoming the initial resistance on the beaches, the German military would certainly have wanted to put Churchill on trial for a serious breach of that part of the laws of war contained in the Geneva Gas Protocol of 1925. In the summer of 1940 he was determined to 'drench the beaches in mustard gas', a drastic measure that was unlikely to have delayed a massive German invasion for long, there being only enough mustard gas in stock for one day's drenching.[36] In retrospect this looks like a risky and rash thing to have done, since Germany would have been given an excuse to use gas in reprisal and the British military and civilians would have come off worse. That at least one senior general, the normally sober-minded CIGS General Sir John Dill, also wanted to use it is a measure of the state of stress they were all in directly after Dunkirk. Other senior soldiers thought differently, but Churchill, in a high state of excitement, insisted on it and got his way. On twelve airfields the RAF prepared accordingly. Fortunately its motley collection

of aircraft was never needed. Churchill did not, however, let the matter drop. Vexed that stocks of gas were found to be so low, he harried
every gas-connected department and official through the next twelve
months with such success that the less than 500 tons of the stuff that
had been available in July 1940 had risen to 13,000 tons, some of it
bought from the United States.

About gas and its uses Churchill was somewhat obsessive and in some
ways unreasonable. It was certainly not unreasonable to be prepared for
defence against it and to be ready to use it in reprisal. Churchill's belief
that Germany would surely use it was shared by everyone else in high
command. Wherever the British and American armies went, they always
had gas in reserve. He did not know that, although Germany indeed had
plenty of gas in stock and was inventing varieties much nastier than any
that Britain possessed, Hitler had no intention of being its first user;
partly, perhaps, because he himself had been gassed in the First World
War. Nor was it unreasonable of Churchill, despite the universal prejudice against it and the 1925 Protocol, to side with those who maintained
that gas was no more awful or reprehensible a weapon than many others
against which there was not the same outcry. When the urge to use it was
strong upon him he further alleged, with what truth is debatable, that
'nearly everyone recovers' from gas attacks.[37]

What was less reasonable was the passion with which he pushed the
case when he felt that Britain was in mortal danger. One such occasion
was, as has been seen, at the time of imminently threatened invasion in
1940. Others came in 1943 and 1944, when rumours of giant rockets
abounded and flying bombs actually began to come over. These gave
him a real fright, which persisted even after it was realised that their load
was only high explosive, not the gas that had been feared. On 6 July 1944
he demanded from the Chiefs of Staff 'a cold-blooded calculation'
whether 'drenching' (that word again) specified German cities with gas
would dramatically shorten the war and whether gas would make it possible to 'stop all work at the flying bomb starting points'. Recurring to
a familiar theme, he wrote, 'I do not see why we should always have all
the disadvantages of being the gentleman while they have all the advantages of being the cad'. It is fortunate for his reputation that on this
issue, as on so many others that we have noticed, the warlord's freedom
of command was subject to so many constitutional constraints.

The Chiefs of Staff, who had been thwarting his wish to use gas against the V-weapon sites since October 1943, now set the Joint Planning Staff to work on these uncomfortable questions, out-Churchilling Churchill by inquiring also about the quest for biological weapons that had been going on since 1940. Their very comprehensive report was in Churchill's hands on 27 July 1944 and in the Chiefs' hands a day later. The Porton Down establishment had succeeded in designing a promising anthrax bomb, but its production (in America) was so far behind schedule that there was no point in considering it until some time in 1945. Gas bombs were available in vast quantity but, following the wide-ranging reasonings of the Joint Planning Staff, the Chiefs did not recommend their deployment, not least because of a domestic factor that Churchill might well have thought of for himself: Germany would retaliate in like mode and, for long-suffering Londoners, that might prove to be the last straw.

Churchill yielded to their argument ungraciously: 'I am not at all convinced by this negative report. But clearly I cannot make head against the parsons and the warriors at the same time.' That was silly. No 'parsons' (or 'ununiformed psalm-singing defeatists', as earlier denounced) had been involved in the consideration of this terrible question. The sums had been worked out and a result reached by experienced military men; men tough-minded enough not to rule out the use of biological weapons when they were ready. Eisenhower may have added his voice to those opposing the first use of CBW (as we now call them). These exchanges in July 1944 may be thought not to show Churchill at his best; but to his credit it should be noticed that, although he had known about the biological weapons research at Porton Down since 1940, he seems to have been so appalled when the Prof told him the anthrax bomb was ready to go into production that he kept the secret as closely as he had kept the secret of the atomic bomb project – and when he asked the Chiefs of Staff whether the time had not come for Britain to pull out its last stops, he did *not* think of the anthrax bomb as one of them. It was the Chiefs and their planning staffs who thought of it. Churchill had not asked for it to be thought of and he had himself only ever thought of using it in reprisal against the German first use that he never ceased to fear.[38]

16

Bladon

Tennyson wrote in his 'Ode on the Death of the Duke of Wellington' in 1852:

> Lead out the pageant: sad and slow,
> As fits an universal woe,
> Let the long procession go,
> And let the sorrowing crowds about it grow,
> And let the martial music blow;
> The last great Englishman is low.

It might have been designed also for Churchill's funeral in 1965. The similarities between the two events are many and significant, but more significant still is the contrast between the final resting-places of the two great men. Both of them were men of war, celebrated at their passing by processions and rituals of unparalleled martial splendour, but their funeral monuments were as different as could be: for the one, 'the most famous work of sculpture of the Victorian Age' in St Paul's Cathedral; for the other, an ordinary grave in the churchyard of an inconspicuous village in Oxfordshire.[1] For all his military prowess and his fame as a leader in war, Churchill chose that his monument should be of the simplest, with no military suggestions at all.

This decision was of a piece with the general tenor of his public life after 1945. The modest military uniforms he had so often worn during the war were soon set aside, but that did not mean he lost his love of dressing up. From the summer of 1946, when he was appointed to the ancient and by now honorary and peaceable office of Lord Warden of the Cinque Ports, he had at his disposal a stagey outfit suggestive of the First Lord of the Admiralty in a good production of *HMS Pinafore*. Eight years later, the Queen conferred on him the distinction of the Garter; henceforth, its great sash and star shone on the broad black-and-white front of his dress clothes on all formal occasions, and he had become *Sir* Winston Churchill, the most distinguished of knights. He could have become a peer on retirement in 1955 – a duke if he had so chosen, with robes of course to match – but he declined such an elevation; he preferred to stay in the Commons, and with diminishing frequency continued mutely to attend the House, even after it had to be in a wheel chair.

As Leader of the Opposition from 1945 to later 1951 (leaving most of the work to Anthony Eden) and then as an easy-going Prime Minister for four-and-a-half years, Churchill now and then took notice of the wars continuing in the world (the Cold War and its eruption in Korea, the post-colonial conflicts involving Britain in Palestine, Malaya and East Africa, and France in North Africa and South-East Asia) and was very seriously concerned, as we have seen, about the nuclear future, but the war that interested him most was the war that was over, the war he had helped to win. He liked writing history, he had long laid plans for writing this particular history, and he was determined that his place in history should be properly appreciated. From the spring of 1946 until 1953, completion of his six-volumes on *The Second World War* was his consuming private interest, and the Nobel Prize for Peace his dearest private hope. In public life, he stood before the world no longer as a warlord but as the pre-eminent international statesman, godfathering the cause of European community in the later 1940s and that of European security in the early 1950s. Western European defence was always in his mental map but it was now the responsibility of others, not least his wartime friends Montgomery and Eisenhower. Churchill, in his last official years, stood increasingly *au dessus de la mêlée*.

His retirement in April 1955 was universally thought to be overdue. Given plenty of time to prepare for it, and reinforced by Lord Moran's mysterious pills, he could still manage a formal public occasion. Through the next two years he did some revision on his *History of the English-Speaking Peoples,* but most of its preparation for publication was done by secretaries and hired hands. So was most of the writing of a very well remunerated 'Epilogue' to the 1959 abridgement of his *Second World War.* It was evident to all who came close to him that his mind was inexorably declining. The unwillingness to concentrate that had already vexed his colleagues before the war ended became an inability to do so. He read a lot and could play his favourite game, bezique, for hours on end, but conversation was increasingly difficult. Sometimes he failed to finish sentences, sometimes he could find nothing to say; none of which was helped by his becoming considerably deaf and, like many old people, averse to using his hearing-aid. His physical state declined too: a succession of minor strokes, a broken hip, the heart ever suspect; there was no let up in the struggle for survival persistently chronicled by his faithful physician. Of this decline, the public was scarcely if at all aware. Self-respect and vanity joined to maintain his dapper appearance in public. Most of the press loyally maintained a conspiracy of silence about his condition. The crowds that cheered his appearances and wavings at the window in the Hyde Park Gate window in the early 1960s could not see the two men supporting him on either side.

During his last years, there was being prepared for him the most elaborate martial funeral since 1852 – indeed, the only such funeral since 1852, because Mr Gladstone's in 1898, although unusually protracted and magnificent, had nothing martial about it; and Earl Haig's in 1928, though it included lying-in-state in both Westminster Abbey and St Giles, Edinburgh, had no such royal commitment. Queen Elizabeth II had authorised his being paid the highest of all honours: a lying-in-state followed by a state funeral; honours normally reserved for a monarch. Whatever government was in office – in the event, it was the Labour government of Harold Wilson – would not wish any expense to be spared. Churchill himself knew that he was to have a state funeral and he had expressed an emphatic wish that there should be 'plenty of bands'; what other wishes he may have expressed, apart from that respecting his place of burial, remains obscure.[2]

Churchill died on Sunday 24 January 1965. The wheels of the Earl Marshal's well-oiled machinery began to turn. The coffin was moved on Tuesday evening from Hyde Park Gate to Westminster Hall, where, from Wednesday through Friday, covered simply by a Union Jack and the Knight of the Garter's insignia, it stood high on a catafalque guarded at each corner by officers of the armed services, and visited for twenty-three hours out of the twenty-four in awed silence by an almost unbroken line of mourners stretching back along the Thames embankment at times as far as Lambeth Bridge. Meanwhile the Dean and Canons of St Paul's were preparing for the biggest service the cathedral had ever had to cope with, and the streets between Westminster and the City resounded at night to the tramp of rehearsals for the great event on the coming Saturday.

Churchill could not have wished for more bands than he got: eight in all, according to *The Times*, suitably spaced out along the huge procession; four from the Guards regiments, two each from the Royal Air Force and the Royal Marines. The Royal Navy sent no band but provided the close-order phalanxes of sailors drawing the guncarriage with the draped coffin on it and bearing up its rear, flanked by men from the RAF Regiment with rifles reversed (as were all others in the procession). Big Ben had been silenced from a quarter to ten; no sounds broke the stillness other than the bands' funeral music, the rhythmical beat of men's boots on the asphalt, the subdued clip-clopping of the cavalry, and the guns in St James's Park firing ninety blanks at one minute intervals. There were no mishaps like those that had held up the funerals of Nelson and Wellington: the Prince of Wales and his brother the Duke of Clarence being thirty-five minutes late for Nelson, and Wellington's funeral car being so huge and heavy that it subsided into the mud by the Duke of York's Steps. Churchill's gun-carriage, by contrast, reached the Valhalla of Britain's heroes precisely on time, and the Herculean guardsmen who had borne it from the catafalque to the carriage bent themselves to their next nerve-racking task of carrying it up the steps and along the nave to the central point under the dome.

The martial note was sustained in the cathedral, where the uniqueness of the occasion was signalised by the Queen's arrival unprecedentedly in advance of the coffin, and the presence of representatives from every government in the world that could afford to send them. (Only the People's Republic of China positively declined to send anyone at all. Ireland, where Churchill was on the list of oppressors headed by Cromwell, sent only its Minister for External Affairs.) The hymns were his favourite ones, all of the stirring sort: 'Fight the good fight', 'He who would valiant be', 'O God our help in ages past' and 'Mine eyes have seen the glory of the coming of the Lord'. Trumpeters sounded the traditional salutes to the military dead: the Last Post, followed by the Reveille. And then the guardsmen took up their burden again and carried the coffin to the gun-carriage at the foot of the steps, followed by the pall-bearers, among them three field-marshals, a marshal of the Royal Air Force and an admiral of the Fleet.

The procession, considerably attenuated by now and accompanied by bagpipes instead of bands, proceeded to the Tower of London, from whose pier the coffin was to go by water to Waterloo. For radio listeners there were personal tributes from Australia's Prime Minister Sir Robert Menzies and America's former President Eisenhower. The latter's simply expressed affection and admiration for the 'soldier, statesman and citizen that two countries were proud to claim as their own' and his closing line, 'And now to you, Sir Winston – my old friend – farewell', touched all who heard it.[3]

Now began a poignant transformation. The martial grandeurs were over. At each stage of Churchill's last journey the atmosphere perceptibly changed; the warrior was left behind and the civilian reappeared. No warship but a modest official launch, the Port of London Authority's *Havengore*, took him along the grey and choppy Thames; no military salutes here but the astonishing spectacle of the workaday cranes of Hays Wharf dipping their heads as the boat passed by, with its sparse police escort. An ordinary black hearse took him from Festival Pier to Waterloo Station. He left Waterloo in an ordinary train, pulled by the superannuated locomotive bearing his name, for the rustic station of Hanborough in Oxfordshire, watched in silence along the way by fellow-civilians (some in their old service uniforms) gathered at stations opened for the occasion. From Hanborough, another plain hearse, with no press or publicity and none but the family in attendance, carried him to his unpretentious resting-place in the quiet country churchyard of Bladon, just outside the walls of the palace where he had been born.[4]

Notes

Notes to Chapter 1: Blenheim

1. This I heard from the family's archivist when he addressed a party of visitors, myself among them, on 10 September 2003. How to equate it with Randolph Churchill's assertion (i, pp. 228–29), that Winston had hardly been to Blenheim at all before 1892, I do not know.

2. Randolph Churchill, i, pp. 172–73. Winston got himself 'a box of cannon' also.

3. Clare Sheridan, *Nuda Veritas* (1927), p. 14. Her account tallies in most essentials with that given by Winston's son (and may, indeed, be his principal source).

4. Randolph Churchill, i, pp. 133–35, 193–34.

5. Readers unfamiliar with athletics may like to know that 'the 220' was shorthand for a race over 220 yards. Harold Threlfall was great-uncle to Frances Walsh, the wife of my friend since Cambridge days, Dr John Walsh. Mr Threlfall in due course became responsible for the construction of the naval base at Rosyth. He recalled Churchill visiting the place and being instructed by him to get on with it fast, regardless of the trammels of Admiralty bureaucracy.

6. 3 June 1888, quotations from Randolph Churchill, i, *CV*, i, pt 1 p. 166.

7. Ibid., pp. 180–81. I have conflated the two letters.

8. Colonel Brabazon to Lady Randolph, in Randolph Churchill, i, *CV*, i, pt 1, p. 553.

9. Randolph Churchill, i, *CV*, i, pt 1, p. 409. He was wrong about being 'physically better'. Illnesses continued to dog him. Only when he was in India do we hear less of them.

10. Randolph Churchill, i, p. 548.

11. There is, alas, no illumination about this period in David Scott Daniell, *4th Hussars: The Story of the 4th Queen's Own Hussars, 1685–1958* (1959) p. 223.

12. Letter of mid-1895; I regret having lost the reference. Captain James ran the 'crammer' where Churchill had been prepared for the Sandhurst entrance exams.

13. Randolph Churchill, i, p. 352.

14. A letter to his mother dated 21 April 1897 casually notes that backing might be sought from Sir Edgar Vincent, the Ambassador in Constantinople, the King of Greece and Lord Rothschild. Randolph Churchill, i, pp. 341–42.

15. That friend was the Irish-American politician Bourke Cockran, with whom he sporadically corresponded until the older man's death.

16. Randolph Churchill, i, *CV*, i, pt 1, p. 603.

17. His newspaper articles are printed in Randolph Churchill, *CV*, i, pt 1, pp. 604–18.

18. Footnote in *The Story of the Malakand Field Force*, pp. 240–41. Because their name later became used for a much more sinister purpose, these Spanish *campamentos de reconcentración*, and the British versions of them in South Africa a few years later (both very badly managed), have come to figure in popular parlance about human rights and the laws of war as progenitors of the Nazis' concentration camps, to which in purpose and actuality they bore no likeness whatever.

19. For Howard, an early and extreme version of the Richard Hannay type, see *Henry Howard: A Recollection by a Friend* (1899). The friend was fellow Balliol man Hilaire Belloc.

20. Randolph Churchill, i, *CV*, i, pt 1, pp. 619–22. It tends to confirm my belief that the American side of his ancestry was of such little interest to him in these early years that the reports of these meetings make no mention of his Brooklyn-born mother.

21. The 'Company' was Cecil Rhodes's British South Africa Company. Letter of 4 August 1896 in Randolph Churchill, i, *CV*, i, pt 1, p. 676.

22. *My Early Life*, chapter 10. By 'alone', he meant alone in that luxurious compartment. His 'dressing-boy', presumably a batman, would of course have travelled in lesser style.

23. General Blood's letter in Randolph Churchill, i, *CV*, i, pt 2, p. 830.

24. See his very revealing letter to his mother, 25 October 1897, in Randolph Churchill, *CV*, i, pt 2, pp. 811–13. Most of the *Telegraph* pieces, together with some of the later *Morning Post* ones, may conveniently be read in their original form in Frederick Woods, *Young Winston's Wars* (1972). I have sought without much success to find out what exactly he sent to the *Pioneer*. No copies of the paper itself are available in this country. The British Library has a copy of the book made out of his reports, *The Risings on the North-West Frontier … Compiled from the Special War*

Correspondent of the Pioneer (Allahabad, 1898). The doings of the Malakand Field Force are only part of its story. The substance is similar to what Churchill was sending to London, but much of it is about actions he can only have known at second hand, and it is obviously intended for Indian as well as British readers. Its style and appendices are altogether more official and gazette-like.

25. Randolph Churchill, i, p. 358.
26. Woods, *Young Winston's Wars*, p. 51, letter dated 8 October.
27. Readers of Kipling will recall the similar experience of Privates Ortheris, Mulvaney and Learoyd in the story 'On Greenhow Hill', in *Life's Handicap* (1892).
28. *Malakand Field Force* pp. 4–5. There is more of this in Chapter 14, below.
29. Woods, *Young Winston's Wars*, p. 38. That atrocity was the digging up of dead Muslim Indian soldiers in order to do the mutilation.
30. *Malakand Field Force*, pp. 4–5.
31. Letter of 21 October 1897, in Randolph Churchill, i, *CV*, i, pt 2, p. 807.
32. Woods, *Young Winston's Wars*, p. 14; Randolph Churchill, i, p. 358, and *CV*, i, pt 2, pp. 792, 799, 800, 861.
33. Randolph Churchill, i, p. 362.
34. Randolph Churchill, i, *CV*, i, pt 2, pp. 797, 793.
35. *Malakand Field Force* p. 288.
36. Letter of 25 October 1897, in Randolph Churchill, i, *CV*, i, pt 2, p. 810. Expanding bullets caused such a stir that they were banned two years later by one of the declarations signed at the Hague Peace and Disarmament Conference.
37. Woods, *Young Winston's Wars*, p. 47.
38. Woods, *Young Winston's Wars*, p. 50.

Notes to Chapter 2: The Sudan and South Africa

1. See Randolph Churchill, i, *CV*, i, pt 2, p. 949 and her letter to him dated 29 November 1898.
2. Randolph Churchill, i, p. 394.
3. The only other one of note was fellow officer Lord Fincastle, who had some experience already, had won a Victoria Cross, was writing for *The Times* and, like Churchill, turned his reports into a book. Churchill envied him his VC but professed to be satisfied with a mention in despatches.
4. I follow the appraisals of Frederick Woods and Hugh Cecil, the latter in his chapter, 'British Correspondents and the Sudan Campaign of 1896–98', in Edward M. Spiers (ed.) *Sudan: The Reconquest Reappraised* (1998). Cecil,

having read them all, opines that Churchill had 'the courage, the chutzpah and the fluency of the true professional as well as front-line experience'.

5. Howard, *Recollection* (1899), pp. 267 and 275. I have conflated bits of two letters.

6. Quotations all from *The River War*, ii, chapters 17–19.

7. See Ian Beckett, *The Victorians at War* (2003), pp. 236–37.

8. Shrewdly cited by Roy Jenkins, *Churchill* (2001), p. 40, from the seventh Marquess of Anglesey's definitive *History of the British Cavalry*, v (1982). That book appears in library catalogues as the work of George C. H. V. Paget.

9. *River War*, ii, pp. 135–36.

10. Frederick Woods, *Young Winston's Wars* (1972), p. 110.

11. All from Woods, *Young Winston's Wars*.

12. It seems obligatory to quote, when referring to it, Hilaire Belloc's couplet 'Whatever happens, we have got / The Maxim Gun, and they have not', from his verses 'The Modern Traveller', canto 6.

13. Churchill's figures, in *River War*, ii, pp. 198–200, are: Kitchener's army, twenty officers and 462 men killed or wounded; Dervish army, 9700 killed and between 10,000 and 16,000 wounded.

14. *Second World War*, vi, p. 545.

15. Woods, *Young Winston's Wars*, p. 126.

16. *River War*, ii, p. 162.

17. For the former, see *River War*, i, p. 55, and ii, pp. 212–13. For the latter, Woods, *Young Winston's Wars*, pp. 138, 151.

18. *River War*, ii, pp. 212–15. This matter was only hinted at in his newspaper letters.

19. *River War*, ii, pp. 195–97.

20. The subtitle was: *An Historical Account of the Reconquest of the Sudan*. Churchill didn't like his friend's sketches but I can't see why.

21. Randolph Churchill, i, p. 452.

22. It was not surprising that the austere Maurice Ashley simply ignored the two South Africa books in his study of *Churchill as Historian* (1968).

23. *London to Ladysmith*, pp. 321–22.

24. *London to Ladysmith*, p. 498. At p. 313, after Spion Kop, the generals are represented as 'brave, capable, noble English gentlemen, trying their best at what may be impossible'.

25. *My Early Life*, last page of chapter 26.

26. *My Early Life*, chapter 24.

27. *Ian Hamilton's March*, p. 58. That is not the only indication that he knew some Surtees.

28. There was a minor stir in 1971 when, Churchill's reputation at that time being almost beyond reproach, the aged Sir Hubert Gough's criticisms of parts of the Indian and South African passages of *My Early Life* came to light. See John Ramsden, *Man of the Century* (2002), p. 205.

29. *Anglo-Saxon Review*, 8 (March 1901), pp. 240–47. For more on this, see the next chapter.

30. *London to Ladysmith*, p. 323. See also p. 319, and *Ian Hamilton's March*, p. 76.

31. *London to Ladysmith*, pp. 456–57.

32. See Randolph Churchill, i, pp. 462–65. All accounts of the episode have been examined by Churchill's granddaughter, Celia Sandys, who has been over this ground with critical care and has clarified hitherto obscure matters in her attractive book *Churchill: Wanted Dead or Alive* (1999), to which I gratefully acknowledge my debt.

33. Randolph Churchill, i, *CV*, i, pt 2, p. 1085.

34. Best, *Churchill*, p. 13.

35. Randolph Churchill, i, *CV*, i, pt 2, p. 1115.

36. Andrew Roberts, reviewing Celia Sandys, *Churchill: Wanted Dead or Alive*.

Notes to Chapter 3: Amateur Admiral

1. Speech on 23 October 1901.

2. The 'Theme' of volume ii, covering the years 1900–14. 'Themes' were a device borrowed from his father's *Second World War*.

3. Churchill would not have been surprised that, just over a century later, as I check the text of these paragraphs, the headline in *The Times* (12 October 2004), reads: 'Services rebel against MoD for wasting taxpayers' cash'.

4. *My Early Life*, chapter 18.

5. *Anglo-Saxon Review*, 8, March 1901.

6. David Eddershaw, *The Story of the Oxfordshire Yeomanry: The Queen's Own Oxfordshire Hussars* (1998), p. 46.

7. Mary Soames, *Speaking for Themselves* (1998), p. 46. Note the expression, 'I made the General …'

8. Mary Soames, *Speaking for Themselves*, p. 23.

9. Randolph Churchill, ii, *CV*, ii, p. 912.

10. Ibid., p. 911. See also Randolph Churchill, ii, p. 196. He recalled those German visits at some length in a 1924 article, 'The German Splendour', reproduced in *Thoughts and Adventures*.

11. Speech of 15 February 1907. Note that the word 'military' as then used referred to the army only, in antithesis to 'naval'.

12. A remarkably similar contrast showed at the White House forty-one years later when Churchill and Truman, and their respective Chiefs of Staff, met to discuss NATO's naval command. Admiral Sir Roderick McGregor, reported John Colville, 'was too overawed to do more than stutter a few disjointed words. General Slim stepped into the breach and presented the case coolly and calmly.' *Fringes of Power*, ii, p. 291.

13. Stephen Roskill, *Churchill and the Admirals* (1977), pp. 28–29.

14. Stewart Ross, *Admiral Sir Francis Bridgeman* (1998), p. 152.

15. *World Crisis*, pt 1, chapter 3.

16. *World Crisis*, pt 1, chapter 10.

17. *Speaking for Themselves*, p. 99. 'Cats' is nicely ambiguous here; in their private language, Clemmie played 'Kat' or 'Cat' to Winston's 'Pug'.

18. The historian who is virtually rewriting the history of the pre-1914 navy reminds us that new War Staff was but the old Naval Intelligence Division writ large: renamed, given three extra clerks and one of Churchill's favourite admirals to be its chairman. Nicholas Lambert in Murfett, *The First Sea Lords* (1995).

19. *World Crisis*, pt 1, chapter 4, and Strachan, *First World War*, i (2001), p. 381.

20. Nicholas Lambert, 'British Naval Policy, 1913–1914: Financial Limitation and Strategic Revolution', *Journal of Modern History*, 67 (September 1995), pp. 596–626.

21. James Goldrick, *The King's Ships Were at Sea* (1984), p. 62.

22. Lord Hankey, Secretary of the Committee for Imperial Defence during Churchill's First Lordship, pays particular tribute to this in *Supreme Command*, i, p. 147.

23. *World Crisis*, part 1, near end of chapter 9.

24. *World Crisis*, pt 1, chapter 9. It is odd that as good a military historian as John B. Hattendorf seems unaware of Churchill's telephonic share in the decision of the 26th. See his chapter on Battenberg in Murfett, *The First Sea Lords*, p. 83. Roy Jenkins on the other hand seems to have been unaware of Battenberg's share – see his *Churchill*, p. 239.

25. Fisher in December 1914, cited by David French in Paul Smith (ed.), *Government and the Armed Forces, 1856–1990* (1996), p. 93; *World Crisis*, pt 1, chapter 11.

26. That sharp officer was Herbert Richmond, subject of Arthur J. Marder's *Portrait of an Admiral* (1952), p. 125. Signalling, it may be mentioned, was not the Royal Navy's forte at this time. Apart from the mixed quality

of signals radioed from Whitehall, the arrangements for ship-to-ship signalling were so often defective as to find mention in every naval battle narrative.

27. Gilbert, iii, p. 620, citing Spears's diary.

28. Figures from Robin Prior, *Churchill's 'World Crisis' as History* (1983), p. 250. The Germans' view of Q-ships is portrayed in the 1932/33 film *Morgenrot* (director, Gustav Ucicky), which features a suggestively Churchillian civilian in a dark suit and a bowler hat as the villain of the piece. Any German filmgoer who knew of Churchill's part in evolving the Q-ships cannot later have been surprised by Goebbels's portrayal of him as a gangster.

Notes to Chapter 4: Antwerp and Gallipoli

1. Mary Soames, *Speaking for Themselves* (1998), p. 96.

2. *World Crisis*, pt 1, chapter 15.

3. Gilbert, iii, p. 131, and Robin Prior, *Churchill's 'World Crisis' as History* (1983), p. 32. I here acknowledge my debt to Prior's invaluable book and my admiration of him as one of Australia's many fine war historians.

4. Marder, *Portrait of an Admiral* (1952), pp. 111–12. 936 were taken prisoner and 1500 interned. Figures from Gilbert, iii, p. 125.

5. Gilbert, iii, *CV*, i, p. 163.

6. Gilbert, iii, p. 121.

7. From a retrospective article in the *Sunday Pictorial*, 26 November 1916, in the Churchill Archives at Churchill College, Cambridge. Gilbert, iii, p. 817, says it was Churchill's first public act of self-defence against all the mud being slung at him.

8. See his report to Grey and Kitchener in Gilbert, iii, *CV*, iii, pt 1, pp. 160–61, printed almost whole in *World Crisis*, pt 1, chapter 15.

9. The 'bracing' bit, calling to mind the conclusion of his 'Finest Hour' speech on 18 June 1940, comes in a telegram to Kitchener in Gilbert, iii, p. 167. For the question of his share in the Belgians' counsels, see Emile Joseph Galet, *Albert King of the Belgians in the Great War* (1931). In some ways it was the 'Escape from Pretoria' all over again.

10. C. R. M. F. Cruttwell, *History of the Great War, 1914–1918* (1934), pp. 97 and 109.

11. *World Crisis*, pt 2, chapter 5.

12. But if they also thought that Fisher's judgement was unbalanced, they would have discounted it. As Churchill himself noted, this episode peculiarly invited the multiplication of 'ifs'.

13. 'I did not do it, and from that moment I became accountable for an operation the vital control of which had passed to other hands.' Article in *Strand Magazine*, March 1931, reproduced in *Thoughts and Adventures*.

14. This is not only my surmise, it is also Robin Prior's.

15. *World Crisis*, pt 2, ch. 11.

16. *World Crisis*, pt 2, near end of chapter 11.

17. Churchill later cited evidence to the effect that they were nearly out of it, but 'the modern Turkish official histories', if they are to be relied on, say otherwise. See Edward J. Erickson, 'One More Push: Forcing the Dardanelles in March 1915', *Journal of Strategic Studies*, 24 (2001), pp. 158–75.

18. Minutes of 14 May, addressed to 'Secretary, First Sea Lord, Chief of Staff', in *World Crisis*, pt 2, chapter 18.

19. Violet Bonham Carter, *Winston Churchill as I Knew Him* (1966), p. 344.

20. 1930 magazine article, 'The Truth about the Dardanelles', in the Churchill Archives, Chartwell Papers, 8/279A.

21. Churchill printed them in *World Crisis*, pt 2, chapter 18. Fisher's opening line, 'If the following conditions are agreed to, I can guarantee the successful termination of the war ...', is interestingly anticipatory of what the 'bomber barons' would claim twenty-five years later.

Notes to Chapter 5: Mud and Munitions

1. *World Crisis*, pt 3, chapter 3.

2. The whole of it is powerfully summarised at the close of chapter 24 of part 2 of *The World Crisis*.

3. Gilbert, iv, *CV*, i, pp. 311–12.

4. Letter of 29 May 1915, in *World Crisis*, pt 1, chapter 18. Haig reminded him that such luxuries had to be paid for.

5. The expression first appears in his letter of 5 July 1915 to Archibald Sinclair, in Gilbert, iv, p. 1.

6. His two letters of resignation are in Gilbert, iii, pp. 561–65.

7. Illustration 47 in Gilbert, iii.

8. Gilbert, iii, p. 635, and iv, p. 150.

9. Gilbert, iii, p. 654.

10. Gilbert, iii, pp. 658, 672.

11. Gilbert, iii, p. 625.

12. Letter to Clementine, 8 February 1916, in Gilbert, iii, p. 662.

13. *World Crisis*, pt 3, chapter 20.

14. That claim was stoutly maintained also by the official historian Sir James

Edmonds, the Oxford historian Sir Charles Oman and the post-1945 military writer John Terraine.

15. *World Crisis*, pt 3, chapter 2. Robin Prior joins Trevor Wilson and Ian Beckett in concluding that Churchill won the argument, 'handling his material with the greatest perspicacity and being scrupulous in his attempts to check its validity. The need to prove a case eventually led Edmonds, Oman and Terraine into error. Churchill too may have been seeking to prove a case, but in this instance it is the amateur historian who has demonstrated the superior analytical ability.' Robin Prior, *Churchill's 'World Crisis' as History* (1983), pp. 229–30; I have altered the tenses of two verbs to make the quotation fit.

16. *World Crisis*, pt 3, chapter 24.

17. Gilbert, iv, p. 5.

18. *World Crisis*, pt 3, chapter 14.

19. C. R. M. F. Cruttwell, *History of the Great War, 1914–1918* (1934), p. 611.

20. *World Crisis*, conclusion of pt 3, chapter 6. Admiral Sir Reginald Bacon published a sixty-page rebuttal of Churchill's version in 1925 in his book *The Jutland Scandal*, pp. 171–234. I have no competence to judge where the merits of the argument lay; it is obvious, however, that Bacon was just as capable of reconstructing situations to suit his cause as was Churchill. I also notice that Stephen Roskill does not take sides in *Earl Beatty: The Last Naval Hero* (1980).

21. The brief biography of him, by Keith Grieves, *Sir Eric Geddes* (1989), views Churchill's criticisms entirely and simply from Geddes's side.

22. That striking expression first appears in *World Crisis*, pt 3, chapter 12. Its fuller version, in his memorandum of 9 November 1916, is 'the greater application of mechanical power to the prosecution of an offensive on land', in appendix N.

23. To do Churchill justice, it must be observed that in his 'Blood Test' chapter he does take those obligations to the French fully into account.

24. *World Crisis*, pt 2, chapter 22; Churchill citing from the committee's minutes.

25. For those campaigns and a scholarly counterblast see Brian Bond's admirable *The Unquiet Western Front* (2000).

26. It is interesting and pleasant that Prior, having scraped the colour off many places where it was overdone, concludes by acknowledging that Churchill's *World Crisis* will continue to be read because of its humanity, its lucidity, 'the power and stately nature of the writing' and its convincing seriousness.

27. *World Crisis*, pt 3, chapter 14. There is a reassuring correspondence between those last three sentences and the judgement of two great experts.

'Sensible choices were on offer. They were not taken, and far more questionable choices were made instead.' Robin Prior and Trevor Wilson, *Passchendaele: The Untold Story* (2nd edn, 2002) p. 107.

28. *World Crisis*, pt 3, chapter 7. Already by September 1918 Churchill was interested enough in Sassoon to wish to meet him; see Gilbert, iv, pp. 150–51, which includes a passage about their meeting from *Siegfried's Journey* (1945).

29. J. P. Harris, *Men, Ideas and Tanks: British Military Thought and Armoured Forces, 1903–39* (1995), early pages. The Director was to chair the 'Admiralty Landships Committee', which became a joint Admiralty–War Office concern in June. Harris acknowledges that Swinton had much to do with the later development of the tank, but insists that, although he claimed to be its inventor, he wasn't.

30. Harris, *Men, Ideas and Tanks*, pp. 29–31, and in Bond and Cave (eds), *Haig: A Reappraisal* (1999), pp. 146–47; *World Crisis*, pt 3, chapter 14; Gilbert, iii, pp. 591–92.

31. The more important parts of this memorandum are reproduced in *World Crisis*, pt 3, chapter 14, and in Gilbert, iii, pp. 591–92.

32. Memorandum of 21 October 1917, largely reproduced in *World Crisis*, pt 3, chapter 12.

33. Memorandum of 16 March 1918, in Gilbert, iv, p. 74.

34. Gilbert, iv, pp. 62–63, exactly reproduced.

35. Edward M. Spiers, *Chemical Warfare* (1986), p. 14.

36. I mean the first serious bombing attacks. Italy's dropping of bombs on Libyan tribesmen in 1911 is the 'first' for international lawyers.

37. This very long memo is to be found in *World Crisis*, pt 3, chapter 12, and appendix N. The quotations that follow are from the latter pages. It is worth noting that this switch towards 'mechanical power' that Churchill was advocating in 1917 was soon after adopted by the British army as it absorbed the war's lessons. See David French, *Raising Churchill's Army* (2000), pp. 275–76, citing the Adjutant-General in 1927: 'We must not forget that the object is to replace muscle power by mechanical power and so reduce the wastage in war of human loss.'

38. Hilaire Belloc, *Cautionary Verses*, many editions. 'Aunt Jane' first appeared in the collection *New Cautionary Tales*.

39. See *World Crisis*, pt 3, chapter 13, near the beginning.

40. Walter Layton's unpublished draft memoirs, p. 170, in the archives of Trinity College Cambridge, Layton Papers, box 147. The memoranda referred to were of course internal ones, not the weighty set-pieces Churchill put before the War Cabinet.

41. Layton's draft memoir, p. 173. Was this Churchill's name for it? Remembering that he called his 1940 stapling device his 'clomper', one presumes so.

42. This and the following quotations all from *World Crisis*, pt 3, chapter 12.

43. Layton went on to become an important figure on the liberal side of British public life, including editorship of the *Economist* and chairmanship of the *News Chronicle*. There is a short biography of him that cites occasionally from his unpublished memoir: David Hubback, *No Ordinary Press Baron* (1985). In these activities of Walter Layton in the First World War it is not difficult to see a foreshadowing of Professor Lindemann's usefulness to Churchill in the Second.

44. Schwab's shipbuilding feats invite one to view him as a First World War precursor of the Second's Henry Kaiser. The subsequent importance to Churchill was in facilitating his visits to the United States in 1929 and 1931–32.

45. The same, incidentally, was said of Dwight Eisenhower.

46. Gilbert, iv, p. 38.

47. 'Shameful' does not seem to me too strong a word for what they did. Conservative Party spirit had its vicious aspect.

48. Gilbert, iv, pp. 41–42. Gilbert does not comment on the immense significance of these passages.

49. See, e.g., his letter to the Prime Minister on 11 July 1918, in Gilbert, iv, *CV*, i, p. 342.

50. *World Crisis*, pt 3, chapter 13.

51. Gilbert, iv, *CV*, i, pp. 343–47.

52. W. R. Hancock, *Smuts* (1952), i, p. 442, gives the impression that once that committee was set up, the priorities problem was solved. He seems not to have known about the Admiralty's prerogatives. Nor does anyone else. Having sought in vain for good scholarly writing on this area of the war, I hope some appropriately learned reviewer will improve my version.

53. Speech of 4 April 1917, in *Complete Speeches*, pp. 2545ff. It was his ability to make speeches like this, damaging to the government and in this case to the Prime Minister personally, that led Lloyd George soon afterwards to find a place for him in the government.

54. *World Crisis*, pt 3, chapter 20.

55. All quotes, except 'Half our mistakes ...', are from the 4 April speech cited immediately above. I have reversed the order of two sentences.

56. *World Crisis*, pt 3, chapter 10.

57. Letter of 24 March 1918 in Gilbert, iv, pp. 81–82.

58. Hankey's diary for 24 March, cited by Gilbert, iv, *CV*, i, p. 277.

Notes to Chapter 6: From Peace to War

1. *The Aftermath*, chapter 2, 'Demos'.
2. *Second World War*, i, pp. 7 and 13.
3. I follow the account of this odd episode in Robert Rhodes James, *Churchill: A Study in Failure* (1990), pp. 102–24, which give a fine summary of Churchill's anti-Bolshevik frenzy.
4. Gilbert, iv, p. 814.
5. He and Trenchard had conceived this plan, which gave the air force something to do, while he was still at the Ministry for War and Air. See Gilbert, iv, pp. 216–18.
6. Epping became Woodford in 1945 and retained him to the end. This complicated interlude is charted at some length in Geoffrey Best, *Churchill: A Study in Greatness* (2001), pp. 111–17.
7. *World Crisis*, i, chapter 5.
8. *Second World War*, iv, pp. 43, 81. He was, however, not the only one who should have known better; see Raymond Callahan, 'Churchill and Singapore', in Brian Farrell and Sandy Hunter (eds), *Sixty Years On: The Fall of Singapore Revisited* (2002).
9. I here follow Roy Jenkins, *Churchill* (2001), pp. 425–27. Jenkins always pays close attention to what Churchill wrote and how much he earned.
10. 23 November 1932.
11. Cited by Rhodes James, *Churchill: A Study in Failure*, p. 245. The bit about the supreme nobility of death in battle was rather rich, coinciding as it did with Churchill's own often expressed opinion!
12. Baldwin stopped short, however, of appointing Churchill to the new office of Minister for the Coordination of Defence in June 1936.
13. See Williamson Murray, MacGregor Knox and Alvin Bernstein (eds), *The Making of Strategy: Rulers, States and War* (1994), pp. 408–9.
14. This speech of 5 October 1938 is reproduced in full in Cannadine's selection, pp. 129–43. It also appears of course in *Into Battle*.
15. *Second World War*, i, p. 320.
16. See *Into Battle* pp. 160–61, 181–82.
17. This was an obsession inherited from 1914. *Second World War*, i, p. 458.
18. I am indebted to Corrrelli Barnett for this interpretation of Pound, which I find credible.
19. Stephen Roskill, able to let himself go after completing the official history, is emphatic that the prime responsibility for their despatch was Churchill's. See *Churchill and the Admirals* (1977), p. 200.
20. Readers of his *Second World War* wondering how it was that Churchill

could have cognisance of all the multifarious matters figuring in the selection of minutes appended to each volume, will find the explanation in the work of the Statistical Branch.

21. The official historian, a naval professional himself who knew exactly what had been going on, wrote at the end of his Norway chapter that Churchill 'used, during critical periods of naval operations, to spend long hours in the Admiralty Operational Intelligence Centre and the tendency for him to assume direct control therefrom is easily to be understood'. Stephen Roskill, *The War at Sea, 1939–45* (1954), i, p. 202.

22. *Second World War*, i, p. 511.

23. The events of these crucial forty-eight hours have invited much exegesis – not least because Churchill's own account of them, *Second World War*, i, pp. 522–24, is inaccurate. Jenkins's detailed account, *Churchill*, pp. 582–87, follows Andrew Roberts, *The Holy Fox* (1991), ch. 21.

Notes to Chapter 7: Democratic Warlord

1. *Second World War*, i, p. 526.

2. Did any of the other national leaders in that war do as much? I doubt it. I should like to read a systematic comparison of Churchill's performance with those of Hitler, Stalin and Roosevelt in Churchill's own time; and, most tempting of all, with a great civilian democratic leader in an earlier age, Abraham Lincoln. Such a comparison is glimpsed in two valuable books, Eliot A. Cohen, *Supreme Command: Soldiers, Satesmen and Leadership in Wartime* (2002), and, on a more sharply focused scale, Andrew Roberts, *Hitler and Churchill: Secrets of Leadership* (2003).

3. Montgomery, cited in the *Oxford Companion to the Second World War* (1995).

4. Churchill devotes a whole page to that unfortunate speech in *Second World War*, i, p. 461.

5. Roy Jenkins, *Churchill* (2001), p. 610. Churchill's denial comes at the start of *Second World War*, ii, pt 1, chapter 9. The drama of those days is skilfully conveyed by John Lukacs, *Five Days in London: May 1940* (1999).

6. The virtue of this decision has been disputed by several historians, the most professional being John Charmley in *Churchill: The End of Glory. A Political Biography* (1993). He summed up his well-told story, which only goes to 1945, by implying that, if Chamberlain and Halifax had won the argument in the War Cabinet and a peace deal with Hitler had been arranged, Britain might have preserved more of its empire, its continuing independence would not have become dependent on the United States,

and the Labour Party would not have won the post-war general election. These provocative and flimsy hypotheses fell on stony ground. Each of them is disputable in itself but behind all three is the incredible assumption that an independent and free Britain could have survived in close proximity to a Europe entirely dominated by the Third Reich.

7. Roy Jenkins, *Churchill* (2001), p. 619, justly describes it as 'one of the most extraordinary and, it might be said, benevolently half-baked plans ever to go through the British government decision-making machinery'. It is a measure of the near hysteria of the moment that its proponents included Lord Halifax, Jean Monnet and Charles de Gaulle.

8. This is admitted even in a learned and useful book about the elements of disunity, where it is noted that 1940–45 was nevertheless 'a historical period in which the people of Britain were, in fact, unified [recognising] that because Britain was at war, they were all "in it together"'. Sonya O. Rose, *Which People's War?* (2003), p. 286.

9. *Second World War*, ii, p. 136.

10. David Cannadine, *The Speeches of Winston Churchill* (1990), p. 5. This useful selection with Cannadine's excellent introduction was first published under the title *Blood, Toil, Tears and Sweat* (1989).

11. Broadcast address of 30 March 1940, in *Into Battle* p. 183.

12. A. P. Herbert in *Winston Spencer Churchill: Servant of Crown and Commonwealth*, ed. James Marchant (1954), p. 106.

13. It is worth recalling that the actor Paul Eddington, playing the part of Minister of Administrative Affairs in the BBC's 1983 series *Yes Minister*, used to glide into Churchillese when practising stirring passages.

14. Isaiah Berlin several years later published a splendid study of the intellectual content and psychological power of these speeches under the title *Mr Churchill in 1940*. This little book, published undated by John Murray, began as a long essay in the *Atlantic Monthly* (1949) and the *Cornhill Magazine* (same year). Some passages are cited in Geoffrey Best, *Churchill: A Study in Greatness* (2001), pp. 187–88 and 333–34.

15. Cannadine, *The Speeches of Winston Churchill*, p. 11.

16. The citation is from Aneurin Bevan's speech of 2 July 1942, of which more is said below.

17. This famous turn of phrase comes near the beginning of his speech in the Mansion House, 10 November 1942; the same upbeat speech in which he thumbed his nose at the Americans by declaring that he had not become His Majesty's First Minister in order to preside over the liquidation of the British Empire.

18. That was not quite how his translator had thought it should be begun, nor

is it how the version in *Into Battle* begins, but Churchill insisted on his idiosyncratic version, and French listeners loved it. See Ismay's *Memoirs* (1960), pp. 175–76, and Gilbert, vi, p. 856.

19. Speeches of 6 July and 10 November 1944. The first V1 fell on 13 June and the first V2 on 8 September. A fine description of their impact and effect on the population of London and South-East England may be read in Maureen Waller, *London 1945. Life in the Debris of War* (2004).

20. For all this and what follows, see Paul Addison's books, *The Road to 1945: British Politics and the Second World War* (1975) and *Churchill on the Home Front, 1900–1955* (1992), chapters 10 and 11.

21. That very long broadcast speech was on 21 March 1943; see *Onwards to Victory*, pp. 33–45.

22. Reproduced in Peter Lewis, *A People's War* (1986), p. 244.

23. For a brief summary see Best, *Churchill*, chapter 4.

24. Whether those populations were in fact as wholly war-minded as he and most other Britons supposed is a matter for debate, but that is irrelevant here.

25. *Into Battle*, pp. 166–67.

26. Debates of 25 June 1941 and 10 December 1942 respectively in the slim volume *Secret Session Speeches*, ed. Charles Eade.

27. Near the end of his speech at the close of the big critical debate, 2 July 1942, *The End of the Beginning*, pp. 146–47.

28. *Second World War*, iv, pp. 814–15.

Notes to Chapter 8: The Grand Alliance

1. Respectively by Marc Bloch (1946) and Ernest May (2000).

2. Jon Meacham, *Franklin and Winston: Portrait of a Friendship* (2003), is good on the personal aspects of their relationship. Warren Kimball, *Forged in War: Churchill, Roosevelt and the Second World War* (1997), and John Charmley, *Churchill's Grand Alliance: The Anglo-American Special Relationship, 1940–1957* (1995), remain basic for its politics.

3. *Second World War*, i, p. 345.

4. There was also the political string, that Britain was expected to abandon its pre-war dreams of continued Imperial Preference in trade and finance.

5. *The Unrelenting Struggle*, pp. 229–37.

6. For that reckoning I am indebted to Paul Addison's long entry in the new *Oxford Dictionary of National Biography*, which he kindly let me see in draft.

7. I have not come across any historian of the war who does not consider

them to have been helpful to the Grand Alliance, as Churchill liked to call it, rather than otherwise.

8. *Second World War*, iii, p. 583, in the chapter devoted to the plans, chapter 34. To be precise, it was two Chiefs plus an ex-Chief, Dill, on his way to an important post in Washington.

9. *Second World War*, iii, p. 579.

10. Some writers like to describe him as pro-American rather than anti-British, but to me he seems distinctly the latter.

11. Alex Danchev, 'Being Friends: The Combined Chiefs of Staff and the Making of Allied Strategy in the Second World War', in Freedman, Hayes and O'Neill, *War Strategy and International Politics* (1992), p. 208.

12. Churchill, whose impatience with Dill has already been mentioned, cannot take any other credit for this most happy appointment than that he allowed it to continue. See Danchev, *Very Special Relationship* (1986).

13. A small precedent was the Allies' rushed response to the Western Front crisis of April 1918, when Marshal Foch was named supreme commander of all Allied armies; but his office was the whole of it. There was no subordinate integration. Multinational service under a unified command has of course become familiar since, notably in NATO.

14. See Keegan, *Churchill's Generals* (1992), p. 177.

15. Elizabeth Barker, *Churchill and Eden at War* (1978), pp. 226–27. On p. 223 she sagely reckons that he was 'hankering for a sort of personal comradeship-in-arms with Stalin'.

16. See the second volume of his 'Sword of Honour' trilogy, *Officers and Gentlemen* (Penguin edn), p. 240.

17. 'Stalin hates the guts of all your top people. He thinks he likes me better', and so on; conveniently cited by Kimball, *Forged in War* (1998), p. 145. On the triangular relationship generally, see Robin Edmonds, *The Big Three* (1991), and Reynolds, Kimball and Chubarian (eds), *Allies at War* (1994).

18. Churchill gives a fair account of the latter episode in *Second World War*, iv, pp. 678–81. It is clear that he never believed the Soviet story.

19. Writers with Poland written on their hearts call all this 'the betrayal of Poland'. I cannot imagine what feasible course of action they think Britain (not to mention France) could have pursued that would have improved Poland's situation.

20. *Second World War*, vi, p. 198. Cold Warriors were to look back on this with horror, as 'giving away the Balkans', but considered in its context it was realistic and practical.

21. *Second World War*, iv, p. 428.

22. *Second World War*, iv, p. 433. 'The snout' presumably was Germany's

industry and cities. Note that Churchill did not say, 'soft underbelly of the Axis'. What he did say was ill-judged. The Italian government proved soft enough but the Italian terrain not at all so.

23. See Chapter 14, below, for much more about the writing of those six volumes.

24. For a succinct account of their relations, see Goeffrey Best, *Churchill: A Study in Greatness* (2001), chapter 19; for a full one, François Kersaudy, *Churchill and de Gaulle* (1990).

Notes to Chapter 9: Strategy

1. Whether he was as successful on the military-strategic side is, however, the subject of much writing and the matter for continuing debate. At the very time of writing this chapter, another relevant and good book has appeared: Douglas Porch, *The Path to Victory: The Mediterranean Theater in World War Two* (2004).

2. See Reynolds, *In Command of History: Churchill Fighting and Writing the Second World War* (2004), pp. 169–74 and 323.

3. See *Second World War*, ii, chapter 12, 'The Apparatus of Counter-Attack'.

4. I here acknowledge some debt to the Israeli scholar Tuvia Ben-Moshe's valuable book *Churchill: Strategy and History* (1992).

5. This was early made clear by Sir Michael Howard in his 1966 Lees-Knowles Lectures, published as *The Mediterranean Strategy in the Second World War*.

6. See Ben-Moshe and Sheila Lawlor, *Churchill and the Politics of Power, 1940–41* (1994), and Charles Cruickshank, *Greece, 1940–41* (1996).

7. *Second World War*, iii, p. 269.

8. Porch, *The Path to Victory*, in his summing-up chapter, at pp. 664–65, reminds us how successful and useful 'Anvil' actually turned out to be; something you don't learn from Churchill's volumes. On p. 660, Porch calls the Ljubljana Gap idea 'pure pie in the sky'.

9. *Alanbrooke's War Diaries* (2001), pp. 667–68.

10. For the details, in context of the whole complicated story magnificently told, see Norman Davies, *Rising '44: The Battle for Warsaw* (2003).

11. See his summing up of the affair in *Second World War*, vi, p. 409. He removed from his draft several more critical and indeed bitter paragraphs because, by the time of writing, his friend Ike was standing for President, and he was not willing to embarrass him. See Reynolds, *In Command of History*, pp. 471–72.

12. *The Strategic Air Offensive against Germany* is the precisely descriptive

title of the excellent official history by C. K. Webster and Noble Frankland, 4 vols (1961). Readers interested to know the eventful story of its composition will enjoy Frankland's autobiographical *History at War* (1998).

13. That figure of 4000 was soon found to be impossibly optimistic. If it had been seriously attempted, British industry could hardly have produced anything else.

14. For much more about his, see below, Chapter 15.

15. Webster and Frankland, *The Strategic Air Offensive against Germany*, iii, pp. 79–80.

16. I am indebted to Lady Soames for kindly allowing me to study the Chequers lists of visitors who stayed for lunch or dinner. If my counting is correct, Harris was at Chequers twelve times in 1942, nine in 1943, five in 1944 (plus once to tea along with the USAAF General Eaker) and three before the war ended in 1945. Portal's score was lower, but he often stayed the night as Harris did only once. Professor M. R. D. Foot has reminded me that too much should not be read into this, since Harris's HQ was only a few miles away.

17. Extract in Thomas Wilson, *Churchill and the Prof* (1995), p. 74, which is informative about the controversy that followed.

18. Hinsley, *British Intelligence in Second World War* (1979–84), ii, appendix 12.

19. Hinsley, in Blake and Louis (eds), *Churchill*, p. 426.

20. Stephen Roskill, *Churchill and the Admirals* (1977), p. 139.

21. Reynolds, *In Command of History*, p. 481. See below, Chapter 15, for an extended treatment of the ethical and legal aspects of the bombing offensive.

Notes to Chapter 10: War Direction

1. *Second World War*, iv, p. 165.

2. His critics have really done no more than point out that his agenda goes beyond the simply historical and that there's more to the wartime story than is in his book. What *is* in his book remains part of that story, and is a significant one. As to the economy, I continue to respect Correlli Barnett's *Audit of War* (1986).

3. Slessor, *The Central Blue* (1956), p. 278.

4. For Bevin, a safe Labour seat was quickly found. Anderson was already an Independent MP for the Scottish Universities and had been Chamberlain's Home Secretary. Churchill kept him on in that office until Chamberlain's resignation in September.

5. In that sentence is condensed the matter of many books. Good summaries may be found in Margaret Gowing, 'The Organisation of Manpower in Britain during the Second World War', *Journal of Contemporary History*, 7, pts 1 and 2 (1972), pp. 147–67, Peter Howlett, 'New Light through Old Windows: A New Perspective on the British Economy in the Second World War', *Journal of Contemporary History*, 28 (1993), pp. 361–79, and the invaluable Thomas Wilson, *Churchill and the Prof* (1995), especially chapter 6, 'Manpower and Strategy'.

6. John Colville in John Wheeler-Bennett (ed.), *Action This Day: Working with Churchill* (1968), pp. 50–51.

7. Ismay's official title was Military Secretary to the War Cabinet, but he was also in some less defined way the senior official in Churchill's hand-made Ministry of Defence.

8. *Memoirs*, pp. 168, 170.

9. Francis Williams, *A Prime Minister Remembers* (1961), pp. 45–46.

10. John Keegan, *Churchill's Generals* (1992), p. 7.

11. These German opinions and their British equivalents are comprehensively reviewed in David French, *Raising Churchill's Army* (2000); also in Dominick Graham and Shelford Bidwell, *Coalitions, Politicians and Generals* (1993); and, just published, Max Hastings, *Armageddon* (2004).

12. See in particular his reactions to the surrenders at Tobruk and Singapore. But he was already noting it in the Norwegian campaign; see *Second World War*, i, pp. 510–11.

13. See Danchev 'Waltzing with Winston', in Paul Smith (ed.), *Government and the Armed Services* (1996), p. 204.

14. John Colville in John Wheeler-Bennett (ed.), *Action This Day* (1968), p. 78.

15. *Second World War*, iii, p. 710.

16. Debate of 1 and 2 July 1942.

17. See Alex Danchev's introduction to the complete *Alanbrooke's War Diaries*, ed. Alex Danchev and Dan Todman (2001).

18. Stephen Roskill, *Hankey: Man of Secrets* (1974), iii, pp. 503, 505.

19. 2 July 1942, *Hansard*, column 536.

20. Alan Bullock, *Ernest Bevin* (2002), edited by Brivati, p. 300. That is Bullock's version of Bevin's words. My understanding of their significance differs from that of Danchev in 'Waltzing with Winston', p. 199.

21. Kennedy, *The Business of War* (1957), p. 249.

22. Elizabeth Nel (née Layton) on television, 15 January 2004. One presumes she was given time to recuperate.

23. That letter, which might have mentioned his late hours but doesn't, is in

Mary Soames, *Speaking for Themselves* (1998), p. 454; also most of it is in Geoffrey Best, *Churchill: A Study in Greatness* (2001), p. 180.

24. Ismay goes to some lengths to excuse his beloved master's wilfulness – see, for instance, p. 174 of his *Memoirs* – but I have not noticed anyone else doing so.

25. See R. W. Thompson, *Churchill and Morton* (1976). A case may be made for considering the South African Field-Marshal Smuts as a crony too. They had been friends for many years, were dedicated imperialists, and were both given to taking large views of the international situation. Churchill often corresponded with Smuts, telling him what was going on or under consideration and seeking his approval – which Smuts usually gave. It seems likely that Smuts's calm appraisals of inflammatory situations sometimes had the good effect of calming Churchill down.

26. Quotations from the excellent biography by Charles Edward Lysaght, *Brendan Bracken* (1979). These judgements are confirmed by Jason Tomes in the recent *Oxford Dictionary of National Biography*.

27. Conscious of the criticisms made of his closeness to Beaverbrook, Churchill went to some trouble to explain it in *Second World War*, iv, pp. 66–67.

28. I have sought in vain for any scientific evaluation of this episode, which seems to invite it. The nearest approach is in Anthony Furse, *Wilfrid Freeman: The Genius behind Allied Survival and Air Supremacy, 1939–1945* (1999). Chapter 8's heading speaks for itself: '"Magic is Nine-Tenths Illusion": The Beaverbrook Myth'. The quotation is Bevin's response to Churchill's saying that Beaverbrook was working magic at the MAP.

29. His biographers admit that here, as elsewhere, 'he proceeded by rows'. Maurice Dean is the historian cited by Anne Chisholm and Michael Davie, *Beaverbrook: A Life* (1992), pp. 396, 386.

30. Thomas Wilson, *Churchill and the Prof* (1995), p. 213, says it never numbered more than six or seven at any one time. Along with Fort's recent biography, Wilson is my main source. At the time it was more often known as the Statistical Branch.

31. Bryan Hopkin, *A Short Account of My Life* (privately printed), p. 18; Sir Bryan, to whose kindness I am indebted for the gift of his book, was the Prof's private secretary from November 1941 to mid-1944.

32. Churchill's *War Papers*, ii, p. 933n.

33. Danchev relates this in his enjoyable essay 'Waltzing with Winston', p. 208. That glare was all the more formidable for coming through round-lensed horn-rimmed spectacles.

34. I accept Alex Danchev's conclusion that Ironside did not resign, as

Churchill wrote in his memoir-history, but was pushed. See 'Waltzing with Winston', p. 197.

35. It can however be persuasively argued that it was no business of even a senior serving officer to offer opinions on matters of high politics. Stephen Roskill gives two seemingly more convincing instances of vindictiveness in *Churchill and the Admirals* (1977), p. 94.

36. *Second World War*, ii, pp. 15–16.

37. SOE's work is still not yet well enough understood. A good brief overview of it all is provided in *The Oxford Companion to the Second World War* by its principal historian (and former member) M. R. D. Foot; to whom I am grateful for good advice and several kindnesses.

38. David Stafford, *Churchill and Secret Service* (2000), p. 2. Is that story authentic or is it one of the apocryphal ones? General Groves is reported as having said about the comparable establishment at Los Alamos: 'At great expense we have assembled here the largest collection of crackpots ever seen'. Martin Green, *Children of the Sun* (1977), p. 387.

39. Christopher Andrew, in Malcolm Smith and Ralph Erskine (ed.), *Action This Day* (2001), p. 14, as good a book as any for an *entrée* to the Bletchley story. That letter, bearing the signatures of Turing, Welchman, Alexander and Milner-Barry, is reproduced in F. H. Hinsley, *British Intelligence during the Second World War*, ii, appendix 3.

Notes to Chapter 11: The Family at War

1. That calculation is from the magnificent new Churchill Museum attached to the Cabinet War Rooms.

2. Mary Soames, *Clementine* (1979), end of chapter 22.

3. Moran, *The Struggle for Survival* (1996), 22 June 1945.

4. The complex history of the Cabinet War Rooms is admirably unravelled in an Imperial War Museum booklet, *Cabinet War Rooms*, by Peter Simkins (1983).

5. *Second World War*, iv, p. 411.

6. Cited from Martin Gilbert by Mary Soames in *Speaking for Themselves: The Personal Letters of Winston and Clementine Churchill* (1998), p. 469.

7. Celia Sandys, *Chasing Churchill* (2003), p. 152. The prefatory matter to her book includes a handy chronological list of all his travels out of the UK.

8. *Second World War*, iv, pp. 604–5.

9. Moran, *The Struggle for Survival*, 14 August 1944.

10. *Second World War*, iv, pp. 628–29.

11. *Second World War*, iii, 381–82.

12. *Second World War*, iii, p. 556.

13. Soames, *Speaking for Themselves*, pp. 459–61. Mothersill was a patent medicine. Lyttelton was the minister whom Churchill perhaps mistakenly believed to be in charge of clothes rationing, which allowed individuals fixed quantities of coupons (e.g. one coupon for a pair of stockings, five for a dress) to be spent *à choix*.

14. Sarah Churchill, *Keep On Dancing* (1981), p. 66. 'Papa' is how they addressed him.

15. Their youngest daughter Mary (Soames) edited and published a large number of them in *Speaking for Themselves*. His wartime absences in fact were usually so packed with business that he did not write as often as before the war and again after it.

16. Soames, *Speaking for Themselves*, pp. 463–64. It was par for the course that he appointed his old friend all the same.

17. Soames, *Clementine Churchill*, chapter 23.

18. Soames, *Clementine Churchill*, chapter 21.

19. His journalistic experience and family connection obviously qualified him for such a post. On the other hand, it is impossible not to suspect that commanding officers were not keen to have him with them.

20. Most of this is cautiously based on Anthony Kemp, *The SAS at War* (1991), and Randolph's son Winston's biography, *His Father's Son: The Life of Randolph Churchill* (1997). Their stories do not always match.

21. See Sarah Churchill, *Keep On Dancing* (1981), chapter 5.

22. Sarah Churchill, *Keep on Dancing*, p. 70.

23. The information and the quotations here come from Lord Moran's book at the dates indicated.

24. Harold Macmillan, *War Diaries, 1943–45* (1984), pp. 337–39.

25. Douglas Porch, *The Path to Victory* (2004), p. 528 (apparently quoting Blumenson). Churchill's part in its planning is thoroughly examined and perhaps overly emphasised by Carlo d'Este, *Fatal Decision: Anzio and the Battle for Rome* (1991).

26. Moran, 27 December 1941.

27. The decision, whether or not to publish his diaries and reflections about his many years with Churchill, was as difficult as the one he had to make in the White House, although not under such pressure to decide quickly. Publication meant – in a technical sense, at least – breaking his Hippocratic Oath not to disclose what went on between him and his patient. Non-publication meant thwarting mankind's legitimate wish to know things that no one else could tell it about the greatest Englishman of the century. Moran conscientiously took much advice and found that

as many judicious persons urged publication as deprecated it. To the family's annoyance, but humanity's benefit, he published.

28. Far too much has been made of Churchill's 'Black Dog', as he called the depression that darkened patches of his earlier years and returned in later life. (The puzzling expression came from the folk expression for a bad mood, 'to have a black dog on your shoulder'.) The 'Struggle for Survival' that Moran oversaw was about Churchill's heart and lungs, not his mind.

29. No critical historian has yet worked, or been encouraged to work, on Moran's original papers. Moran's son, the second Lord Moran, has published the wartime sections with a few additions and an interesting introduction but no analytical commentary: second Lord Moran, *Churchill at War, 1940–45* (2002).

30. I have cut some of the description of Molotov's speech.

31. Three days later Brooke was happy to dine by himself on tea and two boiled eggs before going to the Bolshoi: see entry for 13 October.

32. *Diaries*, 9 February 1945.

33. Moran, 17 February 1945.

34. *Second World War*, vi, pp. 348–49.

35. Gerald Pawle, *The War and Colonel Warden* (1974), p. 361. Churchill omitted to mention that he was later given something else to drink. 'Did not know what it was. It seemed a very nasty cocktail. Found out afterwards that it was an aphrodisiac', Gilbert, vii, p. 1225, citing a note dictated by Churchill during the writing of the volume.

36. Warren Kimball, *Forged in War* (1997), p. 140.

37. In these, as in all passages about the Churchills' home life, I rely entirely on Mary Soames's biography of her mother and on the interviews she has kindly given me.

Notes to Chapter 12: Atoms for War

1. *War Speeches*, vi, 'Victory' (1946), p. 224. Gilbert, viii, p. 119n., says he drafted it himself at Chequers over the previous weekend. Parliament was not sitting at the time.

2. Essay originally in the *Pall Mall Magazine*, September 1924. Reprinted as one of the chapters in his *Thoughts and Adventures* (1932).

3. The Peierls–Frisch Memorandum, February 1940, reproduced by Lorna Arnold in *Cold War History*, 3 (2003), p. 124.

4. This was unearthed from the Lindemann archives by Mr Michael Gottesman, to whom I am indebted for a copy of his excellent Cambridge

M.Phil. 2003 dissertation 'Winston Churchill and Nuclear Weapons, 1945–1955'. It is gratifying that, totally independent of one another, we have come to similar conclusions.

5. Also reprinted in *Thoughts and Adventures*. I have abbreviated the middle sentence.

6. The letter was really the product of a concerned group of scientists. Its story, and how it was brought to the President's attention, may be read in Richard Rhodes, *The Making of the Atomic Bomb* (1988), pp. 304–14.

7. Had they done their sums right? Gowing describes how 'Peierls and Frisch showed their memorandum to Professor Oliphant, who sent it in March 1940 to Sir Henry Tizard, who sent it in turn to G. P. Thomson', who showed it to Professor Cockcroft, and so on. There are readable descriptions of their momentous calculation in Rhodes, *The Making of the Atomic Bomb*, pp. 321–25, and in Margaret Gowing's excellent book, *Britain and Atomic Energy, 1939–45* (1964), pp. 40–43. Gowing is my principal source in these paragraphs.

8. Information about British nuclear research was one of the many British 'secrets' that Henry Tizard and John Cockcroft took to Washington for exchange purposes in the autumn of 1940.

9. Cited in Gowing, *Britain and Atomic Energy*, p. 106; also (without adequate explanation) in *Second World War*, iii, p. 730.

10. Gowing, *Britain and Atomic Energy*, p. 123. One can only presume that Churchill wanted Britain to go it alone, and was advised that it could do so.

11. Cited from official papers by Ian Clark and Nicholas Wheeler, *The British Origins of Nuclear Strategy* (1989), pp. 36–37.

12. The bombshell was the 'Conant Memorandum', in Gowing, *Britain and Atomic Energy*, pp. 156–57.

13. Gowing, *Britain and Atomic Energy*, pp. 165–71.

14. The fifth clause concerned the establishment of a Combined Policy Committee (in Washington: three Americans, two British and a Canadian) to oversee the collaboration and to bring the joint project to fruition.

15. Gowing, *Independence and Deterrence: Britain and Atomic Energy, 1945–52*, 2 vols (1974), i, p. 163n.

16. Gowing, *Britain and Atomic Energy*, p. 355, mildly remarks that 'this was one of the Prime Minister's less happy days'. She might have said that it was a very bad one. The event is unmentioned by Gilbert.

17. Gowing, *Britain and Atomic Energy*, p. 447.

18. Gowing, *Britain and Atomic Energy*, pp. 341–42. Gilbert, vii, p. 970n., tells us that Churchill's copy was safely stored in the Cabinet War Rooms.

19. Gowing, *Britain and Atomic Energy*, p. 372.

20. Ronald Spector, *Eagle against the Sun* (Penguin edn, 1986), p. 546.

21. John Ehrman, *Grand Strategy*, v, pp. 302–3; cited also in Gar Alperovitz, *The Decision to Use the Atomic Bomb* (1995), p. 243. Churchill worked these phrases into the Potsdam part of *Second World War*, vi, p. 555.

22. In other respects 'the assurances given to Japan ... were generous in the extreme', as Churchill told the Commons on 16 August 1945. As for that lack of explicitness, there were good reasons for it. If the bomb in the event were to prove less terrible than predicted – and although the test had been a success, a second success could not be relied on – Tokyo's will to go on fighting might not have been weakened.

23. The proclamation may be read in *Second World War*, vi, pp. 556–57. Also in Gowing, *Britain and Atomic Energy*, appendix 9.

24. *Second World War*, vi, p. 198.

25. Very soon after the conclusion of hostilities, Brooke, like all the military Chiefs except Harris, was ennobled, becoming Lord Alanbrooke. For convenience he will here continue to be Sir Alan Brooke.

26. *War Diaries*, p. 709.

27. The immediate and almost universal reaction to that speech was so shocked and disapproving that the President felt obliged to insist that he had not known what Churchill was going to say. Nobody now believes that. Truman and several others in Canada and Washington were in the know and were glad, believing that Churchill could get away with saying what no other public man yet dared to say. See Ramsden, *Man of the Century* (2002), chapter 4.

28. I have reversed the order of words (while, of course, maintaining the sense) in that last quotation; see Cannadine's Penguin edition of the *Speeches*, p. 299.

29. As might be expected from its title, this phase is usefully reviewed by David Carlton in his *Churchill and the Soviet Union* (2000), chapter 6. There being very little direct evidence of any sort, Carlton has to speculate, as do all who write about him, about what might have been in Churchill's mind from time to time. Michael Gottesman in his dissertation, 'Winston Churchill and Nuclear Weapons', p. 35, finds that Churchill only once *publicly* spoke in favour of its use, and that was in the less than wholly public situation of a New York dinner given by Henry Luce.

30. I do not know how otherwise to interpret his various references to the matter in his Commons speech of 7 November 1945.

31. He was also of course very busy, having again to earn his living by writing, planning the memoir-history of the war he wanted to write, and

performing as the world's undisputed senior statesman and prime founder of the Council of Europe.

32. The painful and complicated story is admirably unravelled and displayed in Margaret Gowing's *Independence and Deterrence*, the sequel to her *Britain and Atomic Energy*. She was indispensably assisted in this larger sequel, itself published in two parts, by Lorna Arnold, to whose wisdom, learning and friendship I am much indebted.

33. Those agreements, 'The Washington Declaration' of 15 November 1945 and the 'Groves-Anderson Memorandum' of 16 November 1945, are reproduced in Gowing *Independence and Deterrence*, i, pp. 78–86.

34. Gilbert, viii, pp. 572–73.

35. Letter of 12 February 1951, in Gilbert, viii, p. 595. This must be the letter mentioned, without a date, by Gowing, *Britain and Atomic Energy*, p. 313. The timing is curious. Why, if he was going write such a letter at all, had he not written it earlier? Perhaps because by 12 February he was gearing up for the motion of no confidence in the government he was scheduled to move on the 15th, accusing the Prime Minister of feebleness; which indeed he proceeded to do. Considering the pains that Attlee had taken confidentially to inform Churchill of the actual situation, this was somewhat of a dirty trick. See *Hansard*, 15 February 1951, column 630.

36. Dated 16 February 1951, in Gilbert, viii, p. 596.

Notes to Chapter 13: Atoms for Peace

1. It must be hoped that Sir Marrack Goulding's book *Peacemonger* (2002) about his UN peacemaking experiences will help to correct the definition given in *Chambers's English Dictionary* (1988): 'a peacemaker from the point of view of those who think him a sentimental busybody'.

2. Speech in his constituency, 6 October 1951.

3. For a brisk discussion of this matter see the closing pages of chapter 6 of Peter Hennessy's *The Secret State: Whitehall and the Cold War* (2003).

4. In fact the B–29s that arrived in the summer of 1948 were not yet equipped for atomic delivery. From mid-1950, all were. Margaret Gowing, *Independence and Deterrence: Britain and Atomic Energy, 1945–52*, 2 vols (1974), i, p. 311n.

5. See Gowing, *Independence and Deterrence*, i, pp. 314–15.

6. The process of removal of course might take a long time. Readers may recall the *contretemps* between the British Prime Minister and the American Secretary of State in the excellent 1988 TV political drama *A Very British Coup*.

7. Churchill enjoyed secret intelligence about the bombers; see David Stafford, *Churchill and Secret Service* (2000), pp. 376, 378–79.

8. Gilbert, viii, p. 538.

9. Gowing, *Independence and Deterrence*, i, pp. 234–35.

10. The whole of this passionately thoughtful letter may be found in *Second World War*, vi, pp. 431–34.

11. *Collected Speeches*, vii, pp. 7043–44.

12. Ernest Bevin cited by Henry Pelling, *Winston Churchill* (1974), p. 582; Moran, 15 June 1954.

13. This awkward relationship may conveniently be viewed in John Charmley, *Churchill's Grand Alliance: The Anglo-American Special Relationship, 1940–1957* (1995), and Peter G. Boyle (ed.), *The Churchill–Eisenhower Correspondence, 1953–55* (1990). For a convenient summary, Geoffrey Best, *Churchill: A Study in Greatness* (2001), pp. 292–98.

14. This great speech, besides resting under the date 11 May 1953 in *Hansard*, may also be read in *Complete Speeches*, viii, pp. 8475–85. Martin Gilbert quotes bits of it and sketches the context of American and Foreign Office disapproval in Gilbert, viii, pp. 828–32.

15. See the semi-detached fourth volume of his *World Crisis* series, *The Aftermath* (1929), chapter 2 of which is actually titled 'Demos'.

16. The passage continued: 'Germany having let Hell loose kept well in the van of terror; but she was followed step by step by the desperate and ultimately avenging nations she had assailed. Every outrage against humanity or international law was repaid by reprisals.' That was not quite correct. No direct reprisals were possible, for instance, for the atrocities visited on the civilians of Belgium and the territory of north-east France; revenge was understandably demanded after the war was over.

17. Gilbert, iv, pp. 913–14. These sentences are used almost word for word on the second page of *The World Crisis*.

18. There is much more about Britain's bombing offensive in Chapter 9, above, and Chapter 15, below.

19. I use the familiar terms A-bomb and H-bomb merely for convenience. Both of these experimental attempts, like the Adam and Eve of them all at Alamagordo in July 1945, were properly described as 'devices', in no way capable of being delivered. Tom Lehrer misunderstood these matters when, introducing his song 'Who's Next?', he set America's criticism of the Russian 'bomb' against its own self-righteousness at only having a 'device'.

20. *Daily Herald*, 17 November. The *Daily Mail* of the same date was quite sensational: 'US Explodes the H-Bomb' ... '1000 times worse than the A-Bomb', etc.

21. For the argument about whether the Russian device was 'a true hydrogen bomb' or not, see Lorna Arnold, *Britain and the H-Bomb* (2001), pp. 27–29. She points out that, whatever its proper description, it promised more military utility than the Eniwetok device.

22. Moran, *The Struggle for Survival*, 3 November 1953.

23. Gilbert, viii, p. 952.

24. House of Commons, 1 March 1955. The other occasion was also parliamentary, 12 July 1954.

25. 23 and 30 March 1954, *Hansard*, columns 1050–54 and 1840–46 respectively.

26. *Manchester Guardian*, 23 March 1954, p. 1.

27. In this paragraph I rely largely on Arnold, *Britain and the H-Bomb*, pp. 49–57.

28. Arnold, *Britain and the H-Bomb*, p. 54, and Gilbert, viii, pp. 999–1000 and 1029.

29. John Colville recorded in his diary, 2 July 1954, that the old man had been both 'ruthless and unscrupulous' in this business.

30. Gilbert, viii, pp. 1025 and 1036. He continued, however, to talk in private about its prospective virtues. See Moran, *The Struggle for Survival*, for August 1954.

31. For instances of such sentimentality, see Moran, 10 January 1952 and 24 June 1954.

32. 12 July 1954, *Hansard*, cols 46–47; my italics.

33. *The Speeches of Winston Churchill*, ed. Cannadine (1990). Its hardback title (1989) was *Blood, Toil, Tears and Sweat*. I note that his text has a few tiny differences from the one in *Hansard*. Moran, *The Struggle for Survival*, 1 March 1955, reports Churchill as saying that its preparation took twenty hours, with eight hours more for checking the facts.

34. 'Churchill: Another "Farewell Performance"' was its headline on 2 March; not politically inaccurate but nevertheless mean-minded.

35. For all the newspaper references in the above paragraphs I am indebted to a private source.

36. For Malenkov's speech of 12 March 1954, cited by Y. Smirnov and V. Zubok in the Woodrow Wilson Center's *Cold War International History Project Bulletin*, 4 (Fall, 1994), p. 15.

Notes to Chapter 14: A Mind for War

1. *World Crisis*, beginning of vol. i, chapter 2.

2. *My Early Life*, chapter 13.

3. *My Early Life*, chapter 5.

4. Letter cited in Chapter 1, above.

5. Randolph Churchill, i, *CV*, i, pt 1, p. 585.

6. T. A. Heathcote gives the figure of 73,000 in 1887. Twenty years later, there were more like 100,000. These approximations figures appear in his contribution to Chandler and Beckett (eds), *The Oxford History of the British Army* (1994).

7. Examples abound in David Reynolds, *In Command of History: Churchill Fighting and Writing the Second World War* (2004).

8. Attlee's contribution to the *Observer's* little book of memorial essays, *Churchill: By his Contemporaries* (1965). The other named contributors were Dean Acheson, Aneurin Bevan, Sir Ian Jacob and Earl Winterton.

9. He was so struck by the nation-saving valour of Joan of Arc that he gave her a lot a space too, as if to hold her out as an example from his favourite foreign country.

10. Isaiah Berlin, *Mr Churchill in 1940*, pp. 12–13.

11. The weightiest work of that generation was *The World Crisis by Winston Churchill: A Criticism*, by Lord Sydenham of Combe and others (1930).

12. Prior is only concerned with the best-known volumes, those on the 1914–18 war. He does not cover the two follow-up volumes, *The Eastern Front* and *The Aftermath*.

13. See Roy Jenkins, *Churchill* (2001), and Reynolds, *In Command of History*.

14. The most convenient guide to the revisionism regarding the 1930s is Donald Cameron Watt, 'Churchill and Appeasement', in Blake and Louis (ed.), *Churchill* (1993).

15. Thus Reynolds, *In Command of History*, pp. 57–58.

16. He placed his diaries at the disposal of Arthur Bryant, who used them to construct *The Turn of the Tide* (1957) and *Triumph in the West* (1959). Churchill being still alive, Bryant pulled the angriest of Brooke's punches. The whole unbowdlerised text of the *Diaries* was made available in an edition by Alex Danchev and Daniel Todman (2001).

17. Two documented expressions of this loaded pleasantry are cited by John Ramsden in his 1996 Inaugural Lecture at Queen Mary and Westfield College, *'That Will Depend on Who Writes the History': Winston Churchill as His Own Historian*, p. 3.

18. See Reynolds, *In Command of History*, chapters 1 and 2, and the index headings 'Journalism' and 'Writings' in Jenkins, *Churchill*.

19. The essay 'Shall We All Commit Suicide?', later reproduced in *Thoughts and Adventures*. Its prognostications of the horrors of future warfare (including, as we have seen, atomic weapons) and its closing exhortation to support the League of Nations – 'alone the path to safety and salvation'

– were so striking and unexpected, that it caused something of a sensation. See Gilbert, v, p. 50.

20. It must be said that his openness to incomers did not extend to black people; who, however, were not at all numerous in Britain until after 1945. His government from 1951 was worried about the social reaction to the West Indian immigration but did nothing helpful to manage it.

21. Nor is it of any consequence that Churchill, like others who work on a grand scale, employed research assistants. One of them was the scholarly Maurice Ashley, who tells what it was like in his *Churchill as Historian* (1968). J. H. Plumb expertly sums up the book's strengths and weaknesses in his contribution to *Churchill: Four Faces and the Man* (1968).

22. Both quotations from the end of *Marlborough*, iii, chapter 10.

23. From neighbouring pages in *Marlborough*, ii, chapter 5, 'The Structure of the War'.

24. *Marlborough*, ii, chapter 21. Considering the evident hyperbole here, we should remember that, in his detailed descriptions of the battles themselves, Churchill never failed to give credit where credit was due, regardless of nationality.

25. *Marlborough*, ii, chapter 26.

26. This may sound too good to be true but it was confirmed by the acknowledged expert, David Chandler, in *Marlborough as Military Commander* (1973).

27. This and the previous two passages both come from vol. ii, chapter 5.

28. Beginning of *Marlborough*, ii, chapter 5.

29. Letter to his wife, at the end of *Marlborough*, ii, chapter 18.

30. Spencer Wilkinson, *War and Policy* (1910). Note that it was immoral to be cowardly.

31. *History of the English-Speaking Peoples*, iii, p. 275.

32. *World Crisis*, pt 1, chapter 8.

33. *World Crisis*, pt 1, chapter 3.

34. *World Crisis*, pt 1, chapter 3.

35. Gilbert, vi, p. 618.

36. Speech of 12 November 1940, in *The Unrelenting Struggle* (1942), p. 2.

Notes to Chapter 15: The Conduct of War

1. *Marlborough*, iv, p. 600.

2. The most significant critic was the Bishop of Chichester, George Bell, with his well-conceived questions about the activities of Bomber Command. It is worth recalling that pacifistic and fault-finding pamphleteering, letters

to the press, public meetings and other forms of campaigning went on throughout the war.

3. The 1864 Geneva Convention could be printed on one page; the four Geneva Conventions of 1949 command 220 pages in Schindler and Toman's *Laws of Armed Conflict* (2nd edn, 1981).

4. Driven by an irresistible alliance of the 'Third World', new states, the Soviet bloc and humanitarian public opinion in the non-Soviet-world, these demands would very soon be met in the 1977 Protocols Additional to the Geneva Conventions. See Best, *War and Law since 1945* (1994).

5. *Second World War*, v, pp. 264–65.

6. Colville, *Fringes of Power* (1986), i, p. 417.

7. See *The End of the Beginning* (1943), p. 156. I have amalgamated two sentences.

8. To the press in New York, 1 February 1946, in Gilbert, viii, p. 190.

9. Gilbert, viii, p. 285. One can only guess as to which counts of the indictment he was looking at.

10. For the Fisher incident, see Best, *Churchill*, p. 61; for the mines, *Second World War*, i, p. 447, and Gilbert, iii, pp. 93–94.

11. Harris, *Bomber Offensive* (1947), p. 178.

12. His avowed admirers in Washington might have taken the maxim more seriously before attacking Iraq.

13. In an article of April 1926, reproduced in *Thoughts and Adventures*.

14. *My Early Life*, chapter 18.

15. 1907 Hague Regulations, article 22. Instructive definitions of reprisals were offered, however, in two of the pioneer texts, the Union Army's 'Instructions' of 1863, articles 27 and 28, and the 'Oxford Manual' of 1880, articles 85 and 86. See them in Schindler and Toman, *Laws of Armed Conflict*.

16. Here and in what immediately follows I am greatly indebted to Sebastian Cox, who has let me read the text of his excellent long essay on the Dresden affair that will appear in due course in a publication of Edinburgh University's Centre for Second World War Studies. Of course he bears no responsibility whatever for how I have used his fifty pages for the improvement of my few paragraphs.

17. Churchill in the Commons, 6 July 1944; he was in fact describing V1s but the description was equally valid for V2s. V1s were switched towards Belgium by mid-January but V2s went on falling until 27 March 1945.

18. In the event, 'not one of the new submarines sank an Allied ship', but this part-consequence of British and American bombing was not known till later. See Gerhard L. Weinberg, *A World At Arms* (1994), pp. 771–74.

19. 'Heavy attack will cause great confusion in civilian evacuation from the east and hamper movement of reinforcements from other fronts' was the precise expectation agreed on by the end of January. See Webster and Frankland, *The Strategic Air Offensive against Germany*, iii, p. 105, also cited by Cox (see n. 16 above).

20. Marshalling yards – often used in Air Ministry *communiqués* as euphemisms for urban areas – were not difficult to hit. Mere railway lines were very difficult to hit, and when they were hit were easy to repair, especially when unlimited slave labour was to hand. That was one reason why bombing the line to Auschwitz was unlikely to have achieved anything.

21. Cox's words, following plentiful evidence in the latest book about it, Frederick Taylor, *Dresden* (2004).

22. The German counter-claim, that 'Britain began it', rested on the fact that the RAF bombed oil and railway targets in the Ruhr on the night of 15 May 1940; well before the Luftwaffe began equivalent raids on British targets, but well after the Luftwaffe had made similar raids and purely terror attacks on Britain's allies Poland, France and the Netherlands.

23. The bibliography by now is huge, and very varied in quality. Of excellent quality is Tami Davis Biddle, 'British and American Approaches to Strategic Bombing', in John Gooch (ed.) *Air Power: Theory and Practice* (1995), and her *Rhetoric and Reality in Air Warfare* (2002). Any book with Noble Frankland's name on the title page may be relied on. Max Hastings, *Bomber Command* (1979) has aged well. Richard Overy's *The Air War, 1939–45* (1981) is good on this and all other aspects. The most up-to-date scholarly works on Harris himself are Sebastian Cox's edition of Harris's *Despatch on War Operations* (1995) and Henry Probert, *Bomber Harris* (2001).

24. See W. Hays Parks's magisterial essay '"Precision" and "Area" Bombing: Who Did Which, and When?', in John Gooch (ed.), *Air Power*, pp. 145–74. In the Pacific war, of course, American area bombing surpassed anything done in Europe.

25. As reported by the Australian Robert Casey, cited by Martin Gilbert, *In Search of Churchill* (1995), p. 185.

26. In various ways and at various times such big guns as Slessor, Freeman and, the head of them all, Portal himself. Whether there were many others, I do not know.

27. The law on aerial bombardment, prudently left aside in the post-war war-crimes trials, had to wait thirty years before it was at last tightened up and clarified in Additional (Geneva) Protocol Number One, 1977.

28. Webster and Frankland, *The Strategic Air Offensive against Germany*, iii, p. 112; also in Gilbert, vii, p. 1257.

29. Cited by Reynolds, *In Command of History: Churchill Fighting and Writing History* (2004), p. 491.

30. Hastings, *Bomber Command*, p. 344.

31. See Chapter 9, above.

32. Churchill gives a good account of this event in *Second World War*, i, pp. 443–47. The ambivalence of his attitude to the law is illustrated by his anger when he learned that hostile propaganda was being made out of the unlawful looting of the German captain's private property. See *Second World War*, i, p. 609.

33. *Second World War*, i, pp. 432–33. The Cabinet slowly came round to his position. Mines were duly laid on 8 April, and preparations made to land soldiers which, if the soldiers had got there before the Germans, would have been illegal too.

34. Gilbert, iv, p. 5. In mid-1917 he approved the 'bringing in' of Greece.

35. His fury was so persistent that it found a (somewhat ungracious) vent in his Victory Speech on 15 May 1945. See its fourth paragraph.

36. In this closing section I rely considerably on Edward M. Spiers, *Chemical Warfare* (1986), and Robert Harris and Jeremy Paxman, *A Higher Form of Killing* (1982). I have used the 2002 edition of the latter. Gilbert appears to err, at vii, p. 762, in saying that Churchill never proposed the first use of gas.

37. Quotations in this and the following paragraphs are all from Harris and Paxman, *A Higher Form of Killing*, esp. pp. 128–29.

38. These points are worth labouring because slipshod presentation in a television programme more than twenty years ago led to sensational press allegations that Churchill had been ready to use biological as well as chemical weapons. See Julian Lewis, 'Churchill and the "Anthrax Bomb": A BBC Myth', *Encounter*, February 1982.

Notes to Chapter 16: Bladon

1. Nikolaus Pevsner, The Buildings of England, *London*, i, 3rd edition by Bridget Cherry (1973), p. 117. The monument is by Alfred Stevens.

2. In my biography of four years ago I followed his daughter and his personal secretary Anthony Montague Browne's (one of them perhaps following the other) in asserting that 'plenty of bands' was Churchill's *only* request. Several well-placed persons have assured me he had more to do with it than that.

3. Both men went straight down from the service into the crypt, where the BBC had installed a microphone. I am indebted to Professor John Ramsden for the details about this occasion. His opening chapter in *Man of the Century* (2002) is indispensable for understanding the funeral. A singularly interesting personal account of the funeral and the atmosphere surrounding it can be found in John Lukacs, *Chuchill: Visionary, Statesman, Historian* (2002).

4. At this point, his funeral was most like that of Earl Haig, whose coffin was carried from St Boswells station to Dryburgh Abbey on a simple farm cart.

Bibliography

Books by Churchill

The Story of the Malakand Field Force (1898).

The River War: An Historical Account of the Reconquest of the Sudan, 2 vols (1899).

London to Ladysmith via Pretoria (1900).

Ian Hamilton's March (1900).

The World Crisis, 6 vols (1923–31). Strictly speaking, this is the title only of the first four volumes, covering the 1914–18 war, subsequently often published on their own. The last two (and much rarer) volumes, respectively entitled *The Aftermath* and *The Eastern Front*, are usually considered separately.

My Early Life: A Roving Commission (1930).

Marlborough: His Life and Times, 4 vols (1933–38).

The Second World War, 6 vols (1948–54). The titles of its individual volumes are 'The Gathering Storm', 'Their Finest Hour', 'The Grand Alliance', 'The Hinge of Fate', 'Closing the Ring' and 'Triumph and Tragedy'.

Churchill's Wartime Speeches, 1939–45, were published year by year in compilations by Charles Eade, under the titles: *Into Battle* (1941); *The Unrelenting Struggle* (1942); *The End of the Beginning* (1943); *Onwards to Victory* (1944); *The Dawn of Liberation* (1945); and *Victory* (1946). Those speeches and speeches made at other times may be found in *Winston S. Churchill: His Complete Speeches, 1897–1963* (1974) edited by Robert Rhodes James. Some of the best appear in *The Speeches of Winston Churchill* (Penguin edition, 1990), edited by David Cannadine.

Churchill's journalism, especially in the 1920s and 1930s, was so various and voluminous that its full extent will probably never be known. Some of its most serious pieces, many of them war-related, are reproduced in his collections *Thoughts and Adventures* (1932; American title, *Amid These Storms*) and *Great Contemporaries* (1937).

Churchill bibliographies. Much paper has passed through the presses since the pioneer in this genre, Frederick Woods, *A Bibliography of the Works of Sir Winston Churchill* (2nd edn, 1975). It has been joined within the past few years by Richard M. Langworth, *A Connoisseur's Guide to the Books of Sir Winston Churchill* (1998) – strictly for connoisseurs, and rich ones too; Buckley Barry Barrett, *Churchill: A Concise Bibliography* (2000), of which section G, pp. 127–65, is on 'Foreign and Military Affairs'; Eugene L. Rasor, *Winston S. Churchill, 1874–1965: A Comprehensive Historiography and Annotated Bibliography* (2000); and, most useful if you can get hold of it, Curt J. Zoller, *Annotated Bibliography of Works about Sir Winston S. Churchill* (2004), which includes periodical articles, dissertations and theses, and book reviews.

Further Reading

This does not pretend to be more than a guide to some of the more obvious books relevant to the matters that have appeared chapter by chapter. Readers who wish to go further should refer to the bibliographies listed above or scan the lists provided in the recent biographies by Geoffrey Best, *Churchill: A Study in Greatness* (2001), Roy Jenkins, *Churchill* (2001), Paul Addison, *Churchill: The Unexpected Hero* (2005) and Richard Holmes, *In the Footsteps of Churchill* (2005). By far the longest and most exhaustive account of Churchill's life as a whole is the magisterial *Winston S. Churchill* by Randolph Churchill (first two volumes) and Martin Gilberts (volumes 3–8). For a description of it, see Best, *Churchill*, pp. 353.

A few books illuminate more than one phase or aspect of Churchill's long career: Robert Rhodes James, *Churchill: A Study in Failure, 1900–1939* (1970); Robert Blake and William Roger Louis (eds) *Churchill* (1993), twenty-nine good essays all by experts; Stephen Roskill, *Churchill and the Admirals* (1977); Malcolm H. Murfett, *The First Sea Lords: From Fisher to Mountbatten* (1995); David Stafford, *Churchill and the Secret Service* (1997); Richard Holmes, *In the Footsteps of Churchill* (2005); and David Reynolds, *In Command of History: Churchill Fighting and Writing the Second World War* (2004).

Chapters 1 and 2: Blenheim and The Sudan and South Africa

Churchill's *My Early Life* (1930) is indispensable. As the books Churchill wrote at the time are difficult to get hold of, it is a blessing that a selection of his journalism about the North-West Frontier and Sudan – the material from which his first two books were largely made – is available in Frederick Woods, *Young*

Winston's Wars (1972). Holmes, *In the Footsteps of Churchill* (2005), chapter 2, is excellent here. These campaigns receive lavish coverage in Randolph Churchill, volume 1, and its two-part *Companion Volume*. Celia Sandys, *Churchill: Wanted Dead or Alive* (1999), about South Africa. For the Sudan, Edward M. Spiers (ed.), *Sudan: The Reconquest Reappraised* (1998).

Chapter 3: Amateur Admiral

Stephen Roskill, *Churchill and the Admirals* (1977); Peter Gretton, *Former Naval Person* (1968); James Goldrick, *The King's Ships Were at Sea* (1984); John H. Maurer, in Maurer (ed.), *Churchill and Strategic Dilemmas before the World Wars* (1998); Jon T. Sumida, *In Defence of Naval Supremacy: Finance, Technology and British Naval Policy, 1889–1914* (1989).

Chapter 4: Antwerp and Gallipoli

Richard Holmes, *In the Footsteps of Churchill* (2005); Robert Rhodes James, *Gallipoli* (1965); Geoffrey Miller, *Straits: British Policies towards the Ottoman Empire and the Origins of the Dardanelles Campaign* (1997); Robin Prior, *Churchill's 'World Crisis' as History* (1983); Paul G. Halpern, *The Naval War in the Mediterranean, 1914–18* (1987).

Chapter 5: Mud and Munitions

Robin Prior, *Churchill's 'World Crisis' as History* (1983); Robin Prior and Trevor Wilson, *Passchendaele: The Untold Story* (2002); J. P. Harris, *Men, Ideas and Tanks: British Military Thought and Armed Forces, 1903–39* (1995); Keith Grieves, *The Politics of Manpower, 1914–18* (1988); Kathleen Burk (ed.), *War and the State: The Transformation of British Government, 1914–1919* (1982).

Chapter 6: From Peace to War

Churchill's *Aftermath* (1929). Robert Rhodes James, *Churchill: A Study in Failure, 1900–1939* (1970) is good here; also Martin Gilbert, *Winston Churchill: The Wilderness Years* (1981). Adrian Fort, *Prof: The Life of Frederick Lindemann* (2003); Anne Chisholm and Michael Davie, *Beaverbrook: A Life* (1992); R. A. C. Parker, *Churchill and Appeasement* (2000); Stephen Roskill, *The War at Sea, 1939–45* (1954), vol. 1; Andrew Roberts, *Hitler and Churchill: Secrets of Leadership* (2003).

Chapter 7: Democratic Warlord

Andrew Roberts, *Hitler and Churchill: Secrets of Leadership* (2003), also chapter 3 of his *Eminent Churchillians* (1994). John Lukacs, *The Duel: Hitler vs Churchill, 10 May–31 July 1940* (1990) and *Five Days in London, May 1940* (1999). Philip Bell, *A Certain Eventuality: Britain and the Fall of France* (1974); Paul Addison, *Churchill on the Home Front, 1900–1955* (new edition, 1993); Arthur Marwick, *The Home Front: The British and the Second World War* (1976); Clive Ponting, *1940: Myth and Reality* (1990); Angus Calder, *The People's War: Britain, 1939–1945* (1969).

Chapter 8: The Grand Alliance

Warren F. Kimball, *Forged in War: Churchill, Roosevelt and the Second World War* (1997); David Stafford, *Roosevelt and Churchill: Men of Secrets* (1999); John Charmley, *Churchill's Grand Alliance: The Anglo-American Special Relationship, 1940–1957* (1995); Elizabeth Barker, *Churchill and Eden at War* (1978); David Carlton, *Churchill and the Soviet Union* (2000); Robin Edmonds, *The Big Three* (1991); David Reynolds, Warren Kimball and A. O. Chubarian (eds), *Allies at War: The Soviet, American and British Experience, 1939–1945* (1994).

Chapter 9: Strategy

Eliot A. Cohen, *Supreme Command: Soldiers, Statesmen and Leadership in Wartime* (2002), ch. 3; Ronald Lewin, *Churchill as Warlord* (1973); Richard Lamb, *Churchill as War Leader: Right or Wrong?* (1991); Tuvia Ben-Moshe, *Churchill: Strategy and History* (1992); Michael Howard, *The Mediterranean Strategy in the Second World War* (1968); Correlli Barnett, *Engage the Enemy More Closely: The Royal Navy in the Second World War* (1991); John Keegan, *Churchill's Generals* (1991); David French, *Raising Churchill's Army* (2000); Lord Alanbrooke, *War Diaries, 1939–1945*, ed. Alex Danchev and Daniel Todman (2001); Douglas Porch, *The Path to Victory: The Mediterranean Theater in World War Two* (2004); Max Hastings, *Armageddon. The Battle for Germany, 1944–45* (2004).

Chapter 10: War Direction

Thomas Wilson, *Churchill and the Prof* (1995); John Colville, *The Fringes of Power: Downing Street Diaries, 1939–1955* (1985); John Wheeler-Bennett (ed.),

Action This Day: Working With Churchill (1968); David Stafford, *Churchill and Secret Service* (2000).

Chapter 11: *The Family at War*

Mary Soames, *Clementine* (1979); Mary Soames (ed.) *Speaking for Themselves: The Personal Letters of Winston and Clementine Churchill* (1988); Lord Moran, *The Struggle for Survival* (1966) – the relevant part is also in his son's *Churchill at War, 1940–45* (2002); Gerald Pawle, *The War and Colonel Warden* (1974).

Chapters 12 and 13: *Atoms for War* and *Atoms for Peace*

Richard Rhodes, *The Making of the Atomic Bomb* (1986); Margaret Gowing, *Britain and Atomic Energy, 1939–45* (1964); also her *Independence and Deterrence: Britain and Atomic Energy, 1945–52*, 2 vols (1974); Lorna Arnold, *Britain and the H-Bomb* (2001); John Charmley, *Churchill's Grand Alliance: The Anglo-American Special Relationship, 1940–1957* (1995); Peter G. Boyle (ed.), *The Churchill–Eisenhower Correspondence 1953–55* (1990); John W. Young, 'Churchill and East–West Détente', *Transactions of the Royal Historical Society*, sixth series, 2 (2001), pp. 373–92.

Chapter 14: *A Mind for War*

This chapter is based almost wholly on Churchill's own writings. I can do little more than urge readers to go to those writings themselves. *The World Crisis* contains the highest concentration of his thoughts about war and history. Paul Addison's essay 'The Political Beliefs of Winston Churchill', *Transactions of the Royal Historical Society*, fifth series, 30 (1980), pp. 23–47, is very good; of all the biographers, he is the most sensitive to this side of the man.

Chapter 15: *The Conduct of War*

Geoffrey Best, *Humanity in Warfare* (1980), ch. 4, pp. 216–85; Adam Roberts (chapter 8) and Tami Davis Biddle (chapter 9) in Michael Howard, G. J. Andreopoulos and Mark R. Shulman (eds), *The Laws of War: Constraints on Warfare in the Western World* (1994); Ann and John Tusa, *The Nuremberg Trials* (1983). Max Hastings, *Bomber Command* (1979), remains the most readable introduction to the matter of aerial bombardment, an intricate and touchy subject. Frederick Taylor, *Dresden* (2004) is scholarly and sensible.

Index

No attempt has been made to rationalise individuals' offices and titles